J. N. Hook has long been associated with the University of Illinois, where he received his doctorate and served for a number of years as Professor of English and Counselor in the Teaching of English. Dr. Hook has also played a significant role in the improvement and advancement of English teaching throughout the nation, having served as Executive Secretary of the National Council of Teachers of English, Coordinator of Project English for the U. S. Office of Education, and director of a number of federal projects aimed at improving the preparation of teachers of secondary school English and stating its performance objectives. He is author of *The Teaching of High School English* and co-author of *Modern English Grammar for Teachers* and of *Handbook of Representative Performance Objectives in English: Grades 9–12*, all published by The Ronald Press Company, as well as a number of high school textbooks.

History of the English Language

J. N. HOOK
UNIVERSITY OF ILLINOIS

THE RONALD PRESS COMPANY · NEW YORK

Preface

Language is a reflection of human beings. People's words show what the people are or what they think they are or what they would like to be. Their words show their loves, their hates, their dreams, their successes, their blunders, their strength, their weaknesses. And just as people change constantly—at least on the surface—so the people's language changes. If nothing happened to people, language too would stay put.

Too few students, either in colleges or in the schools, ever become aware of the fascination inherent in the study of language change. The reason why elementary and secondary school teachers seldom pay much attention to the subject is likely to be either their own lack of knowledge of it or the fact that college courses too seldom illustrate for them its practical applications.

Of the several available histories of the English language, none is addressed specifically to teachers and prospective teachers. This book is an attempt to meet such a need. Few secondary and college English teachers and almost no elementary school teachers have ever taken a course in English language history; I hope that they will find here an introduction to the subject that they can put to use in their classrooms. Prospective teachers who are exposed to the book in college courses will, I trust, find it a source of information not only about the English language but also about ways that the riches of language history can be brought into their future classes.

Because of its intended readership, this book differs in several ways from other histories of the language. It has less material on phonological developments and less on the intricacies of sentence structure, such as the detailed generative-transformational analyses now provided by some books. It has more, however, on words: where they come from, what may happen to them once they become accepted, how their spellings and meanings sometimes change, how Americans use them somewhat differently from the British. The reason for emphasizing words is that the best way to interest your students in language is to build upon their already existent interest in vocabulary; they may be bored by grammatical analysis, but the vagaries of words often fascinate them. In most of the chapters of this book there is a fairly long section accounting for some of the words in Modern English. *In toto,* there is some sort of information concerning over three thousand words (listed in the Index of Words). Many of these are common words like *hand, run,* and *that,* but some are interesting rarities like *triskaidekaphobia,* "fear of the number 13."

All the chapters also have sections suggesting specific class activities. Most of these activities are intended to apply and enrich substantively the remainder of the chapter. Some represent activities that I myself have tried, some that I've read or been told about. Others are subject-based activities that I have invented in the belief that they will be profitable and interesting for both the teacher and the students.

For college classes, the book offers a fairly conventional chronological account of world language families, the ancestors of English, Old English, Middle English, Renaissance English, English from 1650 to 1800, and English from 1800 to the present, with greater than usual attention to the past three centuries. One long chapter deals with the English language in America. Three of the chapters concern what happens to words, a summary of trends in the language, and the teaching of language history in the schools. Phonology, syntax, morphology, and graphemics are all treated at moderate length, and special attention is given to vocabulary growth. The interrelationships of language and literature are illustrated repeatedly.

My indebtedness to previous scholars is acknowledged throughout the book. Albert C. Baugh's *A History of the English Language* and Thomas Pyles' *The Origins and Development of the English Language* (which I long used in my own university classes) have been especially valuable. H. L. Mencken's three fat volumes of *The American Language* contributed much to my chapter on developments in America. And, of course, the *Oxford English Dictionary* is a source to which anyone writing on this subject owes a boundless debt. A recent short book by Joseph E. Milosh, Jr., *Teaching the*

History of the English Language in the Secondary Classroom, published by NCTE-ERIC, has provided part of the rationale for the sections devoted to teaching.

I am especially indebted to Professor Jackson Campbell of the University of Illinois at Urbana for his critical reading of the manuscript and his numerous helpful suggestions. Whatever errors there may be, however, are my own.

J. N. HOOK

Waveland, Indiana
March, 1975

Abbreviations

E Mod E	Early Modern English
I-E	Indo-European
ME	Middle English
Mod E	Modern English
OE	Old English
OED	Oxford English Dictionary
W3	Webster's Third New International Dictionary

Contents

History of the

English Language

1

The Role of Language History in the Classroom

SOME TEACHERS IN ACTION

Esther Cloudman Dunn was for many years a teacher of English at Smith College. In her autobiographical *Pursuit of Understanding*, published in 1945, she recalled her own high school teacher of Greek early in the century. "Some of his brightest flashes came back over his shoulder as he looked across the roofs to the clanging trolley cars on the main street."

The day we found the Greek word for 'red' in the vocabulary, the teacher seemed to take it up in his hand. He turned it over, like the faceted jewel it was, and showed us its hidden brilliance. The word, he said, showed in its origin how the Greeks made their red-purple dye from a shell fish. It was precious, used for the garments and carpets of kings. When Clytemnestra, conscious of her guilty love affair with Aegisthus, waited for her husband, Agamemnon, to come home from the Trojan War, she decked the palace stairs with carpets of this red dye to welcome him. It was a royal purple compliment beneath which lurked a bloody warning of his coming murder.

We heard how the Greek dramatist, Aeschylus, had used this word, making it flash out again and again through the metrical lines of his great tragedy. The teacher did not tell us that Aeschylus was a classic which we should admire. Instead, he re-created, through that word for *red*, a fearful and violent moment in a great love story. He let us hear a few unintelligible but rolling lines through which the familiar word recurred. He paused when he came to it and pronounced it meticulously. We had by this delicate legerdemain already entered into Aeschylus' *Agamemnon*. It was not a classic but a heightened moment of life.[1]

[1] From *Pursuit of Understanding*, copyright, 1945, by Esther Cloudman Dunn; reprinted by permission of The Macmillan Company.

"I couldn't do that," a teacher says. "I don't know enough, and besides, modern kids would get impatient with that sort of thing." Perhaps, but let's listen to Herbert Kohl, teacher of a sixth grade in Harlem, who hadn't been able to get through to his class. Then one day a boy shouted to another, "What's the matter, psyches, going to pieces again?" Kohl says, "The class broke up and I jumped on that word 'psyches.'" The class thought it was spelled s-i-k-e-s. Kohl told the story of Psyche and Cupid, writing the words on the board.

"Then what happened? What about the history of the word?"

"I don't know too much, but look at the words in English that come from *Cupid* and *Psyche*."

I cited *psychological, psychic, psychotic, psychodrama, psychosomatic, cupidity* —the children copied them unasked, demanded the meanings. They were obviously excited.

Leaping ahead, Alvin shouted: "You mean words change? People didn't always speak this way? Then how come the reader says there's a right way to talk and a wrong way?"

"There's a right way now, and that only means that's how most people would like to talk now, and how people write now."

Charles jumped out of his desk and spoke for the first time during the year.

"You mean one day the way we talk—you know, with words like *cool* and *dig* and *sound*—may be all right?"

"Uh huh. Language is alive, it's always changing, only sometimes it changes so slowly that we can't tell." . . .

"Mr. Kohl, can't we study the language we're talking about instead of spelling and grammar? They won't be any good when language changes anyway."

We could and did. That day we began what had to be called for my conservative plan book "vocabulary," and "an enrichment activity." Actually it was the study of language and myth, of the origins and histories of words, of their changing uses and functions in human life. We began simply with the words *language* and *alphabet,* the former from the Latin for *tongue* and the latter from the first two letters of the Greek alphabet. Seeing the origin of *alphabet* and the relationship of *cupidity* to *Cupid* and *psychological* to *Psyche* had a particularly magical effect upon the children. They found it easy to master and acquire words that would have seemed senseless and tedious to memorize. . . .

"Vocabulary" became a fixed point in each week's work as we went from Cupid and Psyche to Tantalus, the Sirens, and the Odyssey and the linguistic riches that it contains. We talked of Venus and Adonis and spent a week on first *Pan* and *panic, pan-American,* then *pandemonium,* and finally on *demonic* and *demons* and *devils*. We studied *logos, philos, anthropos, pathos,* and their derivatives. I spun the web of *mythos* about language and its origins. I went to German (*kindergarten*), Polynesian (*taboo*), or Arabic (*assassin*), showing what a motley fabric English (and for that matter any living language) is. The range of times and peoples that contributed to the growth of today's American English impressed me no less than it did the class. It drove me to research language and its origins; to reexplore myth and the dim origins of man's culture; and to invent ways of sharing my discoveries with the children.[2]

The class, Kohl said, became "word-hungry and concept-hungry," and much that he tells later in the book demonstrates the truth of his statement. Words and concepts do go together. Word-hungry children become concept-hungry, and vice-versa.

The D.M.

I once spent several days visiting high school classes in an industrial suburb of Chicago. In the classes of one teacher I was puzzled by students' frequent references to "D. M." "I think the D. M. here is . . ." "What's the D. M. of the word, Mr. Miller?" "I tried to find the D. M. in the story, but I think there's more than one." According to the coded chart I had been given, these students were in the ninth- and tenth-grade classes of below-average ability. But they were live classes, with excited discussions, wholesome differences of opinion, complete participation, many intelligent comments—despite an occasional "he seen" or "didn't have none."

Finally I figured out that "D. M." signifies "Deeper Meaning." The teacher somehow had managed to show these children that everything has a D. M.: a story, a poem, events in their own lives, each of the words they read or spoke. Each class hour was a lively search for D. M.'s, and the students seemed never to tire of the activity, which had the fascination of a series of puzzles—all different, all challenging. I have never seen more intellectually curious, intellectually alert children, though these were boys and girls whose test scores and previous marks in school had placed them just above the bottom of the barrel. I read a group of their compositions in which each student had explored "The Deeper Meaning of My Name." I'll always remember the paper of Jacqueline Smith (IQ 86, the records said). Jacqueline traced her first name back to Old French and had found that it is a feminine form of *Jacques,* which is equivalent to English *James,* and that both *Jacques* and *James* go back to Hebrew *Jacob,* meaning "supplanter"; she theorized about why anyone might ever be named *Supplanter.* She found that there are at least two alternative spellings of *Jacqueline,* and decided that some spellings are just a matter of personal preference. Turning to *Smith,* she explored the importance of smiths in earlier days,

[2] Herbert Kohl, *36 Children.* Copyright 1967 by Herbert Kohl. Reprinted by permission of The New American Library, Inc.

commenting on blacksmiths, goldsmiths, silversmiths, etc. She remembered half-facetiously "The smith a mighty man is he," and remarked about some famous Smiths in history. She even—this "subnormal," "slow" ninth-grade girl—found that *Schmidt* is German for *Smith*. Her paper was much better than many college-level themes I've read.

"How do you do it?" I asked the young teacher. He looked surprised. "Doesn't everybody?" I shook my head regretfully.

NO PANACEA

I'm not saying that the study of words, of deeper meanings, and of language history is a magic potion that will bring every class to life and will awaken every student's curiosity; it is possible to misuse and abuse such study.

Students will be bored if they're just given a list of words and told to find their etymologies. They'll laboriously copy "ME, t. L, f. Gk" and hand in their papers, and that will be the end of it. They will have wasted an hour and confirmed once more their belief that school and English are worthless.

And they will also be bored if they spend hours studying Shakespeare's language. In Shakespeare, as in all literature, the play is the thing, the story is the thing, the people are the thing, the ideas are the thing. Hit-and-run is the best way to teach Shakespeare's language. Pause a moment on an interesting word here, an archaic or a surprisingly modern phrase there. Note how Shakespeare asks questions or expresses negatives. Observe occasionally how grammar or usage has changed. Read a few lines, pronouncing the words approximately as Shakespeare would have pronounced them. And go on with the story; understanding of it will have been enriched by the short pauses.

LANGUAGE HISTORY IN THE ELEMENTARY GRADES

Grade school teachers and children have too many other things to do to attempt any systematic study of history of the language. Besides, the children usually read modern material almost exclusively, and their historical sense is being developed in other ways—through study of the Pilgrims or George Washington or Louis Pasteur or the invention of the airplane, for example.

But there can be constant inklings that language has a history, that it changes slowly but steadily. "Yes, *deaf* used to be pronounced *deef,* and some people still say that." "Sharp eyes, Carol! This article was published in England, and the English people have a *u* in words like *honour* and *armour.* People in America used to have a *u* there too." "Can you think of a lot of words that probably weren't in the language before automobiles were invented?" And remember Herbert Kohl and his sixth-graders' interest in Psyche and Cupid.

Even with such a casual approach, awareness of language and fascination with its foibles can be increased a little every day. A class studying airplanes, for example, encounters *aileron,* the name of a hinged flat piece of metal on the trailing edge of the wing, used primarily in banking maneuvers. A simple drawing shows them what it looks like and how it moves up and down, and they can see why *aileron,* which is French for "little wing," is an appropriate name: ailerons are like little wings fastened to the big wings.

A pupil from another part of the country joins the class. Some of his pronunciations and some of his words are different. Without embarrassing him, the teacher and the class talk about some of the differences and why they exist. The new student is cast as an expert; he is the "informant" who can tell everyone about the language of the area he came from. Some classes may be lucky enough to have several informants from various places. The teacher stresses that none of the variants are "right" or "wrong"—they're just interestingly different, and there are always historical explanations of the differences.

Elementary school isn't too early to build an understanding that words, like people, live in families. For instance, the *-logy* that students find in words like *biology, zoology,* and *psychology* can lead to other words and can quickly be traced back to Greek *logos* "word, speech"; students note that *zoology* is "talking about animals." And they can note that the *zoo* they are familiar with is basically the same as the first part of *zoology.* Some of them will like to play with the older, longer term: *zoological garden.*

"Play" is a fine thing to do with words. Young children like to invent odd rhymes, repeat unusual words over and over, use repetitive or alliterative sounds like "De-De-De," make up silly names for things or for one another, spell some words backwards, or try tongue-twisters like "six slick slender saplings." Simple crossword puzzles intrigue some of them. They use "big words" frequently, though often inaccurately. So there are ample foundations, motivations for teachers to build upon. If the play instinct is encouraged rather than thwarted, children may learn a great deal about words.

A point of great importance must be reiterated: all this learning about words, this play with words, results in the learning of concepts. Words represent concepts. The child who has learned much about words will find it much easier in later years to master the concepts of science, social studies, literature; he will find it much easier as an adult to make the constant adjustments that societal changes require.

LANGUAGE HISTORY IN THE JUNIOR AND SENIOR HIGH SCHOOLS

Any high school teacher of English will find it well worthwhile to read *Teaching the History of the English Language in the Secondary Classroom,* by Joseph E. Milosh, Jr., published in 1972 by the Educational Resources Information Center (ERIC) of the National Council of Teachers of English. In less than a hundred pages Dr. Milosh offers a large number of suggestions concerning rationale, content, unit-construction, and relationship of language study to literature.

Concerning the last point, Milosh says that "The most obvious help the history of English can offer to the reader of literature is on the simple level of understanding what a text literally says." He mentions as an example *buxom,* which would puzzle a reader of Middle English until he learned that in that period the word meant "submissive, compliant," not "plump" or "bosomy." Milosh recommends that when a history of literature is being taught, the study of history of the language should be concurrent. He concludes:

If his students are to understand literature as language instead of simple plot and consequently derive greater pleasure from it, the teacher must be able to demonstrate again and again in the classroom that attention to a variety of linguistic detail, reading aloud, and slowing down to catch and examine word-play are rewarding. The history of English provides a solid block of material for him to start with.[3]

As Milosh says, either a systematic or a more casual study of language in connection with the study of literature brings its rewards. It is also possible, though, to teach language history as an isolated extended unit or

[3] *Ibid.,* p. 77.

as one of the increasingly popular mini-courses. The history of the language in America may be a unit in itself.

Techniques suggested above for the elementary school may be used (in more sophisticated ways) with students in junior or senior high schools. Word play is not to be despised even on these levels, nor is such a thing as discussion of word families. Basically, as in elementary schools, it is desirable to pay very frequent attention to words, to pause now and then on an interesting word that is encountered in literature or in discussion, to wonder about the possible relationship of one word to another, to find out why a word like *pneumatic* has such an odd beginning, and so on. Interest in words should not be a sometime thing; it should be a constant in the English class.

Many high school students are studying a foreign language, usually another Indo-European language. Parallels and differences between the foreign language and English may often be pointed out in class. Reference may sometimes be made to words that appear similar in various languages, like Latin *unus,* Italian *uno,* French *un,* Spanish *uno,* English *one,* and German *eins,* and a few minutes may be spent in talking about why the similarities and the differences exist. Differences between English and another language in treatment of gender, in verb endings, or in pronunciation of vowel sounds may be discussed informatively.

In this book, the sections entitled "Classroom Activities" suggest much language history content for the classroom, and provide numerous hints on technique. Not all the suggestions will prove suitable for every class, and there are far too many of them for all to be used. Even so, ingenious teachers will think of much else that may be done, much more content that may with profit be taught, more games, more exercises, more discussion topics. The history of the English language is endless in its ramifications—so vast that one may dip in almost anywhere and scoop up material that can fascinate and inform today's young people.

2
The Ancestors
of English

HOW DID LANGUAGE BEGIN?

Obviously there were no tape recorders and cameras to portray for posterity the world of a few hundred thousand years ago. No less obviously, man is unlikely ever to invent a time machine that can carry him back through the millenniums to explore the world of his ancestors. More's the pity. We might have a better understanding of modern man if we could learn the intimate details of his ancestors' being. A few bones and an occasional shard or tool tell us much, but they leave many vital questions unanswered.

One of the most important of these questions is that of the origin of language. How did it happen that of the countless species of animal life which have inhabited this planet, only the animal called man invented a flexible, versatile language? Other animals have an instinctive, rudimentary language, consisting of essentially the same sounds repeated in the same way and in approximately the same circumstances generation after generation. Crows caw, hens cluck, dogs bark, and lions roar with no known variation from the sounds made by their ancestors for many thousands of years. Their language has not grown; today's lions can say no more than could the lions who killed the Christians in ancient Roman festivities, and probably no more than could the lions who killed our slanty-headed progenitors in a primeval grassland. Only the language of man has departed from the repetitious cry, the same few sounds instinctively uttered anew by each generation.

Assume for a moment that this departure had not occurred, that human language had never surpassed that of other animals. How would you be

10

different? Certainly you would not be reading this book, for there could be no books. You could not talk with your friends, unless you define "talk" as nothing more elaborate than the gabbling of geese or the aimless chattering of monkeys. You could not have gone to school, for language is prerequisite to schools. You might live in a cave, but not in a house of boards or brick, for people had to talk and share knowledge before they could lay bricks or saw and nail boards. You would almost certainly be naked; what animal or bird or fish weaves a garment? Your knowledge would be limited to what you observed in your own time and space. You would not know anything of people who live beyond broad waters, nor could you comprehend how broad the waters are. Just as a cow knows nothing of the history of cows, you would know nothing of the history of people. The theories of science—even the existence of science—would be as unknown to you as they are to your cat. You would live only in the few square miles over which your feet might carry you; you would live only in your few moments of time, unaware that time was before you were and that time will be after you are not.

To say it another way, without language you would greatly resemble, except in superficial appearance and habits, the apes or the horses or the hyenas; you would differ from them hardly more than they differ from one another.

But how did this human-distinguisher, this thing called language, come into being? No one knows for sure. Linguists, psychologists, philosophers, anthropologists, sociologists, and biologists have long pondered and debated the question. Of late many linguists have called it impossible to answer and therefore unprofitable to speculate about. Maybe they are right. But let's review some of the speculations and develop a hypothesis slightly different from any yet presented. It may not be tenable; unlike most of the rest of this book, it will certainly not be provable. You may be able to develop a better one, though without a time machine, you probably can't prove your hypothesis either. But it is certainly not unprofitable to think as deeply as possible about the origin of that thing which more than anything else makes man the unique creature he is.

Earlier Hypotheses

In Chapter 2 of Genesis we read,

And out of the ground the Lord God formed every beast of the field, and every fowl of the air; and brought them unto Adam to see what he would call them: and whatsoever Adam called every living creature, that was the name thereof.

Later Adam said of the newly created Eve,

. . . she shall be called Woman, because she was taken out of Man.

Even most theologians today do not take literally this Biblical account. Yet its essence seems true: human beings have attached names to almost everything with which they are familiar.

This belief in names as human in origin differs from the theory of Plato, expressed in *Cratylus,* who thought that every name "belongs by nature to each particular thing," and that human beings should attempt to perfect their language by re-discovering the original, divinely applied name. In the eighteenth and nineteenth centuries the Platonic theory was accepted by a number of linguists, who held that for each thing in the universe there is a divinely inspired word that "rings true" to that for which it stands. Later thinkers, though, have derisively nicknamed this the "ding-dong" theory, and it has few or no adherents today.

Some theorists have held that language was originally echoic, onomatopoeic. Early man, the claim is, imitated the sounds of animals or other sounds around him, and these sounds became names. Ridiculers of this theory call it the "bow-wow" theory and say, quite accurately, that only a very small proportion of the words in any language are imitative. Nevertheless, *some* words are indeed echoic, and it is at least possible that some parts of man's early language were derived through imitation.

The "pooh-pooh" theory holds that early language was interjectional, consisting of cries of pain, joy, or warning.

The obvious criticism of the interjectional theory is the difficulty of bridging the gap between interjections (which on the whole are relatively isolated phenomena in speech) and the main body of language. Indeed, it has been held that this is precisely the chasm that separates animal speech, "exclusively exclamatory," from that of men. It is difficult to see how the theory of interjections accounts for much more than the interjections themselves.[1]

Otto Jespersen, famous Danish linguist, hypothesized that emotional "songs," composed at first of repetitious nonsense syllables, may have been spontaneously uttered while men performed physical labor, rejoiced over a slain animal or foe, wooed a female, or mourned over a dead relative or

[1] Stuart Robertson and Frederic G. Cassidy, *Development of Modern English.* Englewood Cliffs, N.J.: Prentice-Hall, Inc., 1954, p. 7.

friend. But despite the high regard in which Jespersen has long been held, his theory has apparently convinced no one.

Révész's Hypothesis

Dr. G. Révész, a psychologist at Amsterdam University, distinguished the following kinds of human sounds, all of which still exist, and which he believes may have developed in this order:

1. Expressive sounds—reflex sounds, such as a squeal of pain when one is hurt. No communication with others is intended. Many animal sounds are of this sort.

2. Contact sounds—"not produced for the purpose of communication but solely for the exchange of feeling."[2] Such sounds, which animals also make (e.g., hens on a roost), "may have played a preparatory role in linguistic prehistory."

3. The cry—"The most primitive evolutionary form of communication is a message directed to the group, the non-linguistic cry. The cry is distinguished from the expressive sound by its communicative character, its signal function, and by a feeling of expectation, directed to the fulfillment of a desire. It is a biological inheritance, and is activated instinctively." (P. 224) Presumably the song of a male bird, addressed to no individuals but serving as a general warning telling others of the species to stay away from his territory, would exemplify the cry.

4. The call—"directed to definite individuals," and hence more truly a communicative device than is the cry. This stage, which may be exemplified by the differing sounds that crows make for various purposes, or by a dog's bark warning a trespasser, may be regarded, Révész says, as "the stage directly antecedent to language."

5. The word—probably first an imperative, according to Révész, because the "need of urging others of one's kind to action must have arisen earlier than the need of telling them something." (P. 224) The call probably underwent "countless transitional stages before becoming the word." (P. 172) It was a series of mutational steps, comparable to other kinds of mutational steps that biologists have described for many plants and animals. The potential for such change must have existed within primitive man, but not in other creatures. "Calls cannot have produced language by themselves; . . . new im-

[2] G. Révész, *The Origins and Prehistory of Language,* translated by J. Butler. New York: Philosophical Library, 1956, p. 223.

pulsions and particularly new creative forces must have taken effect
to bring into being the first expressions of articulate language. We
must accordingly assume that even at the cradle of language creative human activity exercised a powerful influence, that already
during man's formative period the tendency made itself felt to designate needs, wishes, thoughts, etc., with varied but constant sounds
in the interests of easier communication, and to address the individual to whom the request was directed with a particular calling
sound." (P. 179) "What is most probable is that initially cries,
calls, and primitive words overlapped, the cries and calls being predominant at first and gradually giving way to words, but without
suppressing the non-linguistic calls." (P. 179) Révész finds parallels
to this development in the language of infants, "when at the end
of the prelingual period the child begins to replace spontaneous
cries and calls by words with an imperative content and mostly expressed in an affective state." (P. 189)

Révész does not attempt to develop his hypothesis beyond the single
word, but his reasoning as far as he goes appears sound. His theory is
much more fully elaborated and much less simplistic than any we have so
far looked at. His work, however, is not widely known and has been given
little heed by linguists, who have tended of late to deal mainly with directly observable matters.

Wilson's Hypothesis

We shall conclude this rapid survey of hypotheses concerning language
origin by glancing at Richard Albert Wilson's *The Miraculous Birth of
Language,* a book that went largely unnoticed in 1937 but was brought to
wider attention when it was reprinted in 1941 with a preface by George
Bernard Shaw. Wilson, a professor of language and literature at the University of Saskatchewan, believed that early man had an inborn potential
for language—a potential perhaps similar to what linguist Noam Chomsky
was later to call "competence."

To communicate, man had to use either *form* or *sound*—a visual signal,
such as gesture, or an oral–aural signal. Charles Darwin had earlier explained the choice of sound, saying that it is easier to communicate with
sound when the hands are occupied with work, that sound can be heard in
the dark or when the sender is for some other reason not visible to the
receiver, and that sound, unlike gesture, radiates from the speaker in all
directions. Wilson adds that there could not be enough distinguishable

gestures to communicate all ideas (except when words are "spelled" as by deaf-mutes), but the number of sound-combinations is almost limitless. Further, says Wilson, "Thinking being a time process, a generating of a new world, and sound a time expression [rather than an expression of space], thought and oral expression become merely the inward and outward sides of a single time-movement." (P. 162)

The huge step forward that early man made, according to Wilson, was the conventionalizing of sounds:

Starting with his own natural sounds, which as time-expressions were the natural symbols for the time-process of intellecting the world, but which in their natural state could express time-manifestations only, man first transmuted these natural sounds into definite and conventionalized sound-symbols, which could express manifestations of space as well as of time, and in this way made the adequate biform [time-and-space] instrument for the translation of a biform world. (P. 191)

Wilson does not attempt to suggest just how this conventionalizing may have taken place, except by saying that the potential lay within man and was indeed developed. Nor does Wilson go beyond the creation of the first conventionalized sounds into the combinations of sounds that we call "sentences" and that allow us to make full use of this wondrous thing we call language. Had the sounds remained isolated, even though man would by their use have been a far step ahead of other animals, he still would not have been able to express more than simple commands or identifications; for example, he might have been able to formulate a command which in English we would express as "Run" and an identification like "Lion," but he would not have been able to put parts together so that he could say something like "We should run, because a dangerous lion is coming."

None of the theories we have examined, in fact, go much beyond hypothesizing how the first "words" were created. Those hypotheses vary, as we have seen, and it is quite possible that truth exists in more than one of them—that early "words" arose from more than a single cause. But after words were formed, man still had to effect combinations before the lid of the linguistic treasure chest could be fully opened. German psychologist F. Jodl, in his *Lehrbuch der Psychologie,* 1903, recognized this fact when he wrote, "The instant a particular call, designed to attract, warn, or frighten, takes on a form that not only describes a state of mind but also the object or activity provoking the call, in that instant language as communication of thought may be said to be born."[3]

---

[3] (Stuttgart and Berlin: J.G. Cotta), II, p. 230. In 1971, psychologists at the

A Further Hypothesis

Let us grant the assumption that in the infinitely slow process of evolution by which genera and species become increasingly differentiated, one thing that happened in man was that in his nervous system there developed the potentiality of language. Not language itself, probably not for many millenniums, but only the potential.

Scientists know that human brains today differ in many ways from the brains of other animals—in size and in complexity, for example. Whereas in simpler animals almost all of the brain's activities are devoted to sensory input and muscular output, in man no more than ten per cent of the neurons have such purposes; most of the others analyze data and select alternatives. In other words, they are constantly putting things together, eliminating, adding, storing, comparing, sorting. There are many billions of interconnections; the human brain is more complicated than any animal brain, and indeed more complicated than any computer which man can yet clearly conceive. Different parts of the brain perform different functions. The cerebral cortex receives from other parts of the brain information which those parts have grasped, sorted out, and analyzed; then the cerebral cortex, like a supreme court, makes final interpretations and decisions. The marvel of it is that the whole process—say from seeing a flame to shouting "Fire!"—takes only a fraction of a second. A simpler animal may see the flame and in a moment begin running from it, but because of the different development of the human brain, a man may choose between running and emitting a sound to warn others, or he may do both simultaneously. Because of the inbuilt and developed ways in which his brain differs from that of an animal, he has become able to translate the potential for speech into the reality of speech.

In no known way can we discover how early man first activated that potential. But it may have happened in some variation of the following completely fictional account.

Og[4] had a repertory of expressive sounds, contact sounds, cries, and calls—mostly instinctive, mostly inherited, nearly all much like the sounds made by his

---

University of Oklahoma announced that they had succeeded in teaching a chimpanzee to combine several standard gestures of sign language to construct such a message as "I want a sweet drink." So, for chimpanzees, "in that instant a communication of thought [though in form rather than sound] may be said to [have been] born."

[4] I've borrowed *Og* from Charlton Laird, who uses it (in *The Miracle of Language*, Fawcett, 1967) for the name of his primordial creature. I can't improve it, although I thought also of other sound-combinations represented by *Ug, Uh, Ho,* and *Ga*. It is of course quite possible that the earliest words made use of sounds that cannot be reflected by our Roman alphabet.

fellow human beings. He roared when he cut his finger or painfully stubbed his toe on a rock. When embracing Ogga, he made soft, gentle sounds. When he observed the approach of a dangerous animal or anything else that frightened him, he uttered a cry of warning to any of his fellows within earshot. If a hunt had been successful, he carried his dead prey to where his children were, and with a special sound called them to share the still-warm carcass with him. When one of them did something he did not like, he cuffed the child with the flat of his hand and made a guttural noise.

Often Og and his fellows engaged in crude play, running, pushing, climbing trees, or fighting, and uttering a miscellany of sounds as they did so—sounds not too different from those of the monkeys in a nearby grove. Often the same sounds repeatedly accompanied the same kind of stimulus, as when Og uttered stylized grunts in tree-climbing, cries of gleeful triumph when an adversary fled, a repetitive rhythmic chant as he swung back and forth grasping a liana with one hand. His fellows made similar sounds, but now and then there were variations as they opened their mouths a little wider or happened to hold their tongues in slightly different positions.

Once in an exuberant moment Og thumped his chest and bellowed. He liked the feeling and the sound, and he repeated it. A couple of his fellows observed him, and because they were as imitative as monkeys, they tried thumping their chests and bellowing. Still others imitated them, and there was a frenzy of chest-thumping and bellowing.

One day Og—or perhaps it was his descendant a thousand generations later— heard the roar of a lion some distance away. Had the sound been close, Og would have uttered his warning cry and then fled. But this time he did something different. He opened his mouth and made a sound like that of the lion he had just heard. His fellows opened their mouths and, imitating Og, made lion-like sounds. They had unknowingly named a thing in their environment. And, unknowingly, they had also opened the gates to true language and to man's ascent to the stars.

On another day Og—or more likely it was his far-off descendant, or *his* far-off descendant—heard a lion much closer. Og did a remarkable thing. He made the imitative sound that symbolized "Lion," and followed it with the imperative cry that meant "Run!" Og had constructed the first crude sentence. Fleshed out with later syntax, it meant, "I heard a lion, and we must run." His family had never heard a sentence before, but they knew the symbol for "lion," and the instinctive cry meaning "run" had been bred into their bones. So they understood Og, and they ran.

Still another Og, much later, killed a prehistoric elephant. He could not carry it home, but he wanted to let his fellows know what he had done. He found them, made the sound that they had all learned symbolized "elephant" and the familiar cry of triumph, thus telling them of his victory and indirectly of the availability of fresh meat. He uttered another sound that had come to mean something like "Follow me," and he led them to the fallen animal. This communication was much more complex than that of "Lion" and "Run," because this time Og had successfully conveyed information about something not physically present where and when he was speaking.

Slowly more sound-symbols entered the language. A child's vocabulary is small at first, for a while being only a word, then three, then fourteen, then thirty-five, and then growing at a rapidly accelerating rate. The early growth of words in primitive man, and the increase in putting words together, were no doubt also very slow, stretching over many millenniums. But language begot language, and with generations the words and the combinations of words multiplied.

Remember that what you have just read is pure fiction. Maybe the story should be very different to be true, or maybe the differences should be only in details. For one thing, Og certainly did not know that he was Og, because Og or any other human being had no name until many other things had names. Or maybe it was not Og at all who uttered the first real word or composed the first sentence. The great genius may have been Ogga instead.

Our story, though, is based upon what we know of early man, and combines the most likely features of earlier hypotheses. If you are a teacher, you may want your students to develop their own hypotheses, if for no other reason than the fact that it will dramatize for them how very unhuman man must have been before he began using language.

THE INDO-EUROPEAN LANGUAGES

Language Families of the World

We do not know whether language developed at approximately the same speed in various parts of the world or whether it advanced most rapidly in some one or some few parts and spread out from there. The fact that today there are many quite distinct families of languages seems to argue for the first assumption: some of the Oriental, Polynesian, African, and American Indian languages, for example, appear to be in no way related to the chief languages of Europe. But on the other hand it is quite possible that over a period of many thousands of years languages could lose whatever qualities they once had in common. Thus even though family resemblances are still apparent in the Italic languages, it took only a few centuries for Italian, French, Spanish, Portuguese, and Romanian to become highly distinct from one another and from their common parent, Latin.

Today linguists recognize a large number of language families, although not all languages (e.g., some of those in Africa) can yet be confidently assigned to specific families.

One of the largest of modern families is the Indo-Chinese, also called Sino-Tibetan, which includes Chinese in its numerous variations, as well as the languages of Tibet and the several nations making up Indochina. Japanese does not belong to this family, nor does Ainu, the aboriginal and almost extinct language of Japan. Neither does Korean.

Some of the languages of the Pacific islands have enough family resemblances that linguists refer to a Malayan-Polynesian family, encompassing not only such languages as Malayan, Indonesian, Fijian, Tahitian, and Hawaiian, but also the languages of the Philippines, Samoa, the Solomon Islands, and other places. But some island languages have no presently known relationships to any of the others.

The numerous languages of the original Australians appear to be related to one another, but probably not to other languages.

India represents a mixture of tongues, troublesome politically as well as linguistically. Southern India is the principal home of the Dravidian family, encompassing Tamil, Telugu, Malayalam, and others. Some other languages of India, as we shall see, belong to the Indo-European family.

In central Africa, north of the equator, the very diverse Negro languages have been lumped together as a Sudanese family, although many of the interrelationships are unknown and possibly nonexistent. Bantu languages, whose relationships are better understood, extend south from the equator. Hottentot and Bushman, spoken by only small numbers, are in southwestern Africa.

In northern Africa the Semitic languages include Arabic as the one most widely used today. Other branches of the Semitic are Hebrew and Ethiopic (which today includes Geez, largely a church language, and Amharic, largely a legal language, of Ethiopia). Older forms of Semitic languages, no longer spoken, are Assyrian (Babylonian), Aramaic (which Jesus spoke), Phoenician, and Moabitic.

In Europe, aside from the Indo-European languages that we'll look at later, there are the Finno-Ugric (Hungarian, Finnish, and Estonian), Turkic (Turkish; Turki, Kirghiz, Kazakh, Uzbek; Chuvash, Yakut), and Basque languages. Some scholars say that Finno-Ugric and Turkic, which extends into Asia, should be grouped with Mongolian to form the Ural-Altaic family. Basque, however, spoken in the Pyrenees between France and Spain, is a mystery language with no known relatives.

North American Indians spoke many different languages, which scholars have grouped into about fifty or sixty families and half-a-dozen superfamilies:

Algonkian-Wakashan, spoken by many tribes from eastern Canada southward, including Arapaho, Blackfoot, Cheyenne, Cree, Menominee, Miami, Mohican, Sauk, and Shawnee

Aztec-Tanoan, languages of the plateaus from the Pacific Northwest to Central Mexico, spoken by Comanche, Hopi, Pueblo, Shoshone, Ute, and other tribes

Eskimo-Aleut, in the Far North

Hokan-Siouan, languages of central North America, including those of the Assiniboin, Crow, Iowa, Kansa, Mandan, Osage, Sioux, and Winnebago tribes

Nadene, spoken in northwestern Canada and parts of southwestern United States by tribes like the Apache, Haidu, and Tlingit, and making use of changes in tone similar to those in Sino-Tibetan languages

Penutian, languages of the Pacific Coast, including the Chinook and Maidu tribes

The Indian languages of Central and South America were and are very numerous, but have not been studied sufficiently to be grouped with assurance.

Attempts, not entirely successful, have been made to classify into types the several thousand languages of the world. Some languages, including Chinese, are called *isolating;* they have no grammatical endings like the English *-s, -ed, -er,* or *-ly. Agglutinative* languages use unvarying morphemes in combination; thus Turkish *ev* is "house," *ev-ler* is "houses," *ev-den* is "from a house," and *ev-ler-den* is "from houses." *Incorporating* (or *polysynthetic*) languages go a step beyond agglutinative, running several morphemes together so that in effect a single "word" is a sentence; for instance, in some American Indian languages a sentence like "I killed a big black bear" may be expressed as a single word. *Inflectional* languages, illustrated well by Latin or Greek and less well by English, use numerous grammatical endings to show tense, number, gender, case, or other relationships.

Such classifications are only approximate, however, and cannot be relied upon completely. Thus English is classed as inflectional, but it is also in part an isolating language, since many of its words have no endings, and in part nearly incorporating, as in "the man on the street's point of view," in which the *'s* is really attached to the five preceding morphemes.

Indo-European, the Largest Family

Predominant in today's western hemisphere, prominent in the eastern, and with speakers almost from pole to pole, Indo-European languages are at present more widely used than those of any other family. About half of the world's population speak an Indo-European tongue as their first or second language. Most Europeans are included among these speakers, plus most people from North, Central, and South America, plus most Australians and New Zealanders, plus many people in India and Iran, as well as many millions scattered through other parts of Asia, much of Africa, and many of the world's islands. Four of the five official languages of the United Nations (English, French, Russian, and Spanish, but not Chinese) are Indo-European.

The Dim Beginnings of Indo-European

The wide spread of Indo-European (I-E) languages is a development that has taken place largely in modern times. Before Columbus and those who followed him, the inhabitants of the Americas spoke their own native "Indian" languages. Until 1788 only aborigines lived in Australia. Only in scattered places, such as those visited by Marco Polo, were I-E words heard in Africa and much of Asia, until European explorers and colonizers penetrated in comparatively recent times. So the last four or five hundred years have witnessed a remarkable geographical extension by people speaking English, Spanish, Portuguese, Dutch, French, German, Russian, Scandinavian, and other I-E tongues.

Many of the Indo-European forebears of these explorers and colonizers, however, were not exactly homebodies either. The Greek Alexander the Great built an empire that stretched to India, to Scythia, and to Egypt— before he died at thirty-two. The Roman Empire at its height consisted not only of most of Europe but also the whole northern edge of Africa and some chunks of Asia. Wild hordes of Germans roamed through northern Europe, and their Scandinavian brethren went far asea, reaching but not settling in the Americas centuries before Columbus. Various Slavic and Iranian tribes roved and fought through the vast lands of what we now call the Union of Soviet Socialist Republics. In the north they often encountered the Rus, a tribe that evidence suggests was related to the Scandinavians and that specialized in trading, piracy, and fighting. (It is from the name of this tribe that *Russian* comes; *Rus* meant "Norsemen," from Old Norse *Rothsmenn,* "sea-farers," from *rothr,* "to row.") To parts of

India, centuries before Christ, unknown people had brought the ancestral forms of modern Hindi, Bengali, Romany, and other I-E tongues.

Indo-Europeans, then, for several thousand years have been restless wanderers, warriors, explorers, and colonizers. Where did they come from? No one can say positively. The Garden of Eden, between the Tigris and the Euphrates, was an early nominee. Others have been parts of southwest Asia, southern Russia, the Carpathian Mountains of eastern Europe, Austria-Hungary, the Scandinavian countries, and what is now the Lithuanian Soviet Socialist Republic in northern Russia.

Most of the evidence, most scholars now believe, suggests that the early Indo-Europeans lived in a temperate zone without a seacoast, and in Europe rather than Asia. Therefore Lithuania, Austria, Hungary, or southern Germany seem more likely than other sites. The evidence is mainly linguistic. Among the cognate words in a number of I-E languages are names of trees and animals that lived in northern or central Europe but not in Asia or close to the Mediterranean. Thus there are cognate words for *beech, oak, willow,* and *pine,* but none for southern trees like the palm; there are cognates for *horse, cow, sheep, dog,* and *bear,* but none for the camel, tiger, or elephant. The numerous cognates for *mead,* a drink made from honey, suggest that the homeland had bees, which are not found in the parts of Asia that have been nominated. The absence of cognates for *ocean* seems to imply that the homeland was not a seacoast. Cognate words for *winter* and *snow* add credence to a cold climate. Professor Harold Bender, in his *Home of the Indo-Europeans,* summarizes such evidence in this way:

> There are no anciently common Indo-European words for elephant, rhinoceros, camel, lion, tiger, monkey, crocodile, parrot, rice, banyan, bamboo, palm, but there are common words, more or less widely spread over Indo-European territory, for snow and freezing cold, for oak, beech, pine, birch, willow, bear, wolf, otter, beaver, polecat, marten, weasel, deer, rabbit, mouse, horse, ox, sheep, goat, pig, dog, ant, snake, tortoise, crab, bee, etc.

Such linguistic evidence is supplemented and strengthened by historical study of migration patterns, and by evidence from anthropology and archeology.

Regardless of where the Indo-Europeans started, they have traveled far, as we have seen. They of course did not know that they were Indo-Europeans; they no doubt thought of themselves as tribes. They wandered up and down Europe, crossed Asia Minor, settled in Iran, settled in parts of India, fought with one another and with natives upon whose territory they encroached; they intermarried, traded, built great civilizations in Greece and Rome, saw those civilizations crumble and indeed helped them to crumble (since the fearsome Goths were themselves Indo-Europeans fighting with more-civilized Indo-Europeans), farmed the land and hunted and trapped, fought some more—ever restless, seldom content, always searching, always changing.

The Members of the Indo-European Family

The major members of the I-E family today are shown in the chart on page 333. Several languages spoken by small numbers of people are not included there. Not all the Indo-Iranian languages are included. Hittite and Tocharian, which could have been shown as separate branches, are not included because they are dead languages with no apparent living descendants. Also excluded from the diagram are ancestral forms of some of the modern languages—such as Old and Middle English, the forerunners of Modern English.

How do we know that the many languages shown in the diagram are indeed descended from a common source? In 1786 a prominent English orientalist, Sir William Jones, declared:

. . . the Sanskrit language, whatever be its antiquity, is of a wonderful structure; more perfect than the Greek, more copious than the Latin, and more exquisitely refined than either, yet bearing to both of them a stronger affinity, both in the roots of verbs and in the form of grammar, than could possibly have been produced by accident; so strong, indeed, that no philologer could examine all three, without believing them to have sprung from some common source, which, perhaps, no longer exists.

Following Jones's clue, "philologers" began tracing in detail the resemblances not only of Sanskrit, Greek, and Latin but also other languages. In 1816 a twenty-five year old German, Franz Bopp, took a big step with his *On the Conjugational System of the Sanskrit Language, in Comparison with that of the Greek, Latin, Persian, and Germanic Languages.* Later comparative grammarians painstakingly added details and are still doing so. Gradually they have adduced convincing evidence that not only Sanskrit, Greek, and Latin but also all the other languages in the diagram have descended from a common source, even though today they differ greatly from one another. That common source has been designated "Indo-European," a name that suggests both the Asian and the European branches. The term "Aryan," once fairly widely used, is now almost forgotten, perhaps partly because Adolf Hitler used it to designate only an idealized, "pure" German: "In Nazi ideology, a Caucasian gentile, especially of Nordic type," as one dictionary says.

Students of language refer to Balto-Slavic and Indo-Iranian as *satem* languages, and to the others as *centum* languages. An I-E *k* sound developed, in the *satem* languages, into something like an *s* sound, and this difference is one of many that differentiate Balto-Slavic and Indo-Iranian tongues from the others. *Satem* is an Old Persian word for *hundred,* and *centum* (pronounced with a *k* sound) is its Latin equivalent. *Satem* and *centum* are therefore cognate words (that is, they have the same ancestral word, the I-E *kmtóm*[5]), but like many cognates they do not now look much alike.

All I-E languages share two features: they are inflectional, and they have a sizable number of words drawn from a common source.

Inflectional, you will recall, refers to a system of varying a word to indicate such things as tense, gender, number, case, and mood. Examples typical of Modern English include the *-ed* ending to show past tense and the *-s* ending of nouns to show plurality. Old English, as we shall see, was more highly inflected; it possessed, for example, case endings for its nouns and adjectives. If you have studied German, Greek, Latin, or one of the languages derived from Latin, you are familiar with the often rather elaborate conjugations of verbs and declensions of nouns, all of which illustrate different inflectional forms. Although some non-I-E languages also make use of inflections, they differ from I-E in other respects.

To exemplify the commonality of word stock in I-E languages, examine the following table of numbers. Note that although spellings (and pronunciations) obviously differ, and that some forms are very different indeed, there are many more similarities than mere chance could explain. Note also that the non-I-E example does not share these numerous similarities.

English	one	two	three	four	five	six
German	eins	zwei	drei	vier	fünf	sechs
Danish	en	to	tre	fire	fem	seks
Latin	unus	duo	tres	quattuor	quinque	sex
French	un	deux	trois	quatre	cinque	six
Irish	aon	dhá	trí	ceithre	cúig	sé

[5] An asterisk preceding a word represents a linguistic reconstruction. Since early Indo-Europeans were illiterate, no written records remain, but scholars have reconstructed the probable forms on the basis of considerable accumulations of evidence. The Appendix of the *American Heritage Dictionary of the English Language* lists many I-E roots and words derived from these roots; it is based largely on Julius Pokorny's monumental *Indogermanisches Etymologisches Wörterbuch* (Bern: A. Franck, 1959). That Appendix also contains a concise article by Professor Calvert Watkins, "Indo-European and the Indo-Europeans," which illustrates how the language has been reconstructed, and which also discusses its grammar.

Greek	heis	duo	treis	tettares	pente	hex
Russian	odin	dva	tri	chetyre	pyat'	shest'
Slovak	jeden	dva	tri	štyri	pät	šest'
Lithuanian	vienas	du	trys	keturi	penki	šeši
Persian	yek	do	se	cahar	panj	shesh
Hindustani	ek	do	tin	char	panch	chha
Japanese (non-I-E)	ichi	ni	san	shi	go	roku

English	seven	eight	nine	ten	hundred
German	sieben	acht	neun	zehn	hundert
Danish	syv	otte	ni	ti	hundrede
Latin	septem	octo	novem	decem	centum
French	sept	huit	neuf	dix	cent
Irish	seacht	ocht	naoi	deich	céad
Greek	hepta	okto	ennea	deka	hekaton
Russian	sem'	vosem'	devyat'	desyat'	sto
Slovak	sedem	osem	devät'	desat'	sto
Lithuanian	septyni	aštuoni	devyni	dešimt	šimtas
Persian	haft	hasht	noh	dah	sad
Hindustani	sat	ath	nau	das	sau
Japanese (non-I-E)	shichi	hachi	ku	ju	hyaku

Many other words may be cited as evidence of common origin. Here are a few:

English	night	star	sun	heart	foot	mead
Old English	niht	steorra	sunne	heorte	fot	medu
German	Nacht	Stern	Sonne	Herz	Fuss	Met
Latin	noctis	stella	sol	cordis	pedis	—
Greek	nuktos	aster	—	kardia	podos	methu (wine)
Russian	noch'	—	solntse	serdtse	—	med
Sanskrit	naktam	star-	surya	hrd-	pad	medhu (liquor)

One thing that examination of these lists reveals is that in some instances certain consonants in the Germanic words (such as English, German, and Danish) differ from those in the other languages. For example, the Germanic word for *foot* starts with *f*, but in the other languages it starts with *p*. The explanation is that for unknown reasons a series of shifts occurred many years ago in the Germanic languages but not in other I-E tongues. The following examples include words in languages that did not undergo the shifts, alongside English words representing the Germanic languages in which the shifts occurred:

p = f   (cf. Greek *podos*, English *foot;* Persian *pitar*, Latin *pater*, English *father*)

t = th   (cf. Polish *tarn*, English *thorn;* Latin *tu*, English *thou*) k = h   (cf. Latin *centum,* English *hundred;* Greek *kardia,* English *heart*)

b = p   (cf. Lithuanian *dubus,* English *deep;* Greek *kannabis,* English *hemp*)

d = t   (cf. Latin *dentem,* English *tooth;* Hindustani *do,* English *two*)

g = k   (cf. Sanskrit *yuga,* English *yoke;* Latin *genu,* English *knee,* in which the *k* was once pronounced)

Also, I-E *bh* = Germanic *b, dh* = *d,* and *gh* = *g,* but illustrations are less clear here, since Greek and Latin in these instances underwent different changes of their own. For example, I-E **bhratar* corresponds to Greek *phrater,* Latin *frater,* and English *brother.* The change from *dh* to *d* may be illustrated by I-E **dhughter,* the ancestor of English *daughter.* An example of *gh* to *g* is I-E **ghans,* the ancestral form of German *Gans* and English *goose.*

Because the German Jacob Grimm (who with his brother Wilhelm also collected and popularized fairy tales) wrote about such shifts in 1822, they are referred to collectively as examples of "Grimm's Law," although the Danish Rasmus Rask had enumerated them four years earlier. In 1875 another Dane, Karl Verner, explained certain apparent inconsistencies in the application of Grimm's Law. It is not necessary to go into the technicalities of "Verner's Law," except to say that it showed how the position of the accent in certain Germanic words resulted in a *d* where a *th* would be expected on the basis of Grimm's Law, or similarly how in the word *hundred* (Latin *centum*) the expected *th* corresponding to the Latin *t* did not materialize.

THE GERMANIC BRANCH

Since English is a member of the Germanic branch of I-E, let's take a closer look at that. The chart on page 334 is an elaboration of the Germanic section of the chart on page 333.

Note that Germanic has three geographical subdivisions. East Germanic has no living offshoots. Gothic, as the name suggests, was spoken by the Ostrogoths and Visigoths who gave the Romans such a hard time. They originally lived between the Elbe and the Vistula rivers. Their language is known to us because of the survival of parts of the New Testament translated by a Christian missionary known as Ulfilas (or Ulfila or Wulfila). Dating back to the fourth century A.D., this translation is the oldest extant example of a Germanic language (except for a few runic inscriptions) and is therefore of great interest to scholars. After the Goths overran much of Italy and Spain, their language was supplanted by the Latin of those areas, although possibly the Goths may have made some contributions that helped to lead eventually to modern Italian and Spanish. The last known traces of Gothic were recorded in the Crimea in the sixteenth century.

If you will compare a few lines from the Gothic version of the prodigal son parable with the King James version (Luke 15: 11–12), you can note for yourself a few similarities in vocabulary and grammar:

Manne sums aihta twans sunums.
Jah qaþ sa juhiza ize du attin: Atta, gif mis sei undrinnai mik dail aiginis. Jah disdailinda im swes sein.

. . . A certain man had two sons.
And the younger of them said to his father: Father, give me the portion of goods that falleth to me. And he divided unto them his living.

North Germanic, as the chart shows, is itself divided. A modern Scandinavian can, sometimes with a little difficulty, understand the language of a Scandinavian from another country. Swedish differs more from Danish and Norwegian than the latter do from each other. Denmark and Norway were united for several centuries, and as a result in Norway *riksmål* or *bokmål,* a mixture of Danish and Norwegian, is the ordinary language, although national pride led some nineteenth and twentieth century Norwegians to encourage *landsmål,* a "purer" Norwegian, as the standard language. Both the Dano-Norwegian and the "New Norse" are taught in schools, in forms decreed by the parliament. There is some evidence that the two are slowly blending, especially in city speech. Newspapers are printed in Dano-Norwegian, and most children's writing is in that form.

Faroese (also spelled *Faeroese*) is spoken by some thirty or forty thousand residents of the Faeroe Islands, a self-governing part of Denmark, located in the North Atlantic. Faroese is closely related to Danish; it was given its own written form in the nineteenth century by a folklorist named Ulricus Hammershaimb.

Old Icelandic is of literary importance because of its "Eddas," distinguished poems in the heroic mold. Modern Icelandic differs much less from its Icelandic forms of a thousand years ago than does, say, Modern English from Old English. In fact, if you learned to speak and understand Old English well, you would be able to communicate after a fashion with modern Icelanders.

English, as indicated in the chart, is a West Germanic language. Its nearest relative, Frisian, is spoken by seafaring and agricultural people who live on the Frisian Islands off the coasts of the Netherlands and Germany—islands that are constantly threatened by the waves. Still more Frisians live in the province of Friesland in the Netherlands.

Dutch, which is officially called *Nederlands* and popularly *Hollands,* is spoken not only in the Netherlands but also in Belgium in a dialect called Flemish. In the fourth and fifth centuries A.D. (about the time when Angles, Saxons, and Jutes descended on the British Isles) warlike Franks from the Rhine region conquered these low-lying lands; it is a modern form of their language that is now called Dutch. Present-day Dutch is noted or notorious for the great variety of its spoken dialects: perhaps it is appropriate that the word *Dutch* means "language of the people," who presumably may do with it whatever they wish. Afrikaans is a form of Dutch spoken (along with English and surviving African languages) in the Union of South Africa.

"Low" German is a geographical designation, not a pejorative. It is spoken by residents of the low-lying areas in the north of Germany, whereas High German is spoken in the topographically higher lands to the south. Early in the Christian era many Germans worked or fought their way southward. In about the sixth century occurred the "High German shift" in their language, the shift responsible for some of the linguistic differences between Low and High. In this shift, in LG *maken* (English *make*) and similar words, the *k* sound changed to a *ch, machen;* LG *p*'s often turned into *pf*'s or *f*'s, as in *Pfeffer,* which corresponds to LG or English *pepper;* initial *t*'s became *z*'s in words like *zwei* and *zehn,* and medial *t*'s became affricates or spirants as in *sitzen* (English *sit*) or *beissen* (English *bite*). High German has become the standard for writing; this same *Hochsprache* is also normal in formal public speaking and in university use.

Yiddish, basically Germanic, is often confused with Hebrew in the popular mind. The word comes from German *Jüdisch* "Jewish." In the preface of his delightful book *The Joys of Yiddish,* Leo Rosten summarizes its history like this:

Around the tenth century, Jews from what is now northern France, who spoke Old French and, of course, Hebrew, migrated to towns along the Rhine, where they began to use the local German dialect. Hebrew remained untouched as the "sacred," the liturgical language—for reading *Tora* and *Talmud,* for use in prayer and in scholarly or theological discourse.

In the Rhineland, Jews wrote German phonetically, *using the letters of the Hebrew alphabet,* just as Jewish sages in Spain wrote Spanish (and Arabic) with Hebrew letters [and from right to left, like Hebrew].

Yiddish really took root and flowered, as a vernacular, in the ghettos. . . . This new parlance was a mélange of Middle High German, some Old German, remnants of Old French and Old Italian, Hebrew names and phrases, and local dialects.

But Yiddish did not really settle down and raise its own young until after the fifteenth century, when the Jews went to eastern Europe—Poland, Galicia, Hungary, Rumania, Russia. There the buoyant tongue picked up new locutions, adapting itself to the street and the marketplace.[6]

After reading this account of the various Germanic languages, you may well wonder, "What can all these languages, as diverse as Icelandic and Yiddish, have in common?" There are several answers.

The first is that the Germanic languages share many words, have much vocabulary in common. True, the modern forms of the words are rarely identical, but there is no denying that large numbers of the words are merely different pronunciations and spellings. English *maker,* German *Macher,* and Yiddish *macher,* or English *bones,* German *Beine,* and Yiddish *bayner* vary somewhat in sound and appearance, but so do three brothers or three sisters. Such commonality of vocabulary is much greater, say, between English and German than between English and a non-Germanic language like Persian or even French.[7]

A second common characteristic of the Germanic languages is that they underwent the sound changes previously described in the discussion of Grimm's Law, but non-Germanic languages did not change in the same ways.

Third, Germanic verbs are much less complex than those in other I-E languages. Think of the two or three pages that some Latin or Spanish grammars devote to the conjugation of a single verb. Germanic verbs, in contrast, have only two true tenses (present and past), and only a small number of personal endings; thus the typical English verb has only four forms, like *walk, walks, walked, walking,* or five forms if it is "strong," like *sing, sings, sang, sung, singing.* The existence of such weak and strong verbs is itself another characteristic of Germanic.

Still another common bond, the existence of "weak" and "strong" adjectives, has been lost in Modern English but will be discussed when we come to Old English. It can be illustrated in present-day German by the differing

---

[6] (New York: Pocket Books, 1970), pp. xx–xxi.
[7] If I were teaching German to speakers of English, or English to speakers of German, I'd begin by introducing several hundred words that are almost identical in the two languages, thus giving my students a large initial vocabulary.

forms of the adjective in *grosse Knaben* "big boys" and *diese grossen Knaben* "these big boys."

Finally, the Germanic languages employ a pattern of stress or accent different from that of most others. In English words, for example, the stress tends to be upon the base syllable regardless of the place of that syllable in the word: *lóve, lóvely, belóved;* in many other languages the stress may shift, be about evenly divided between syllables, or even (as in Japanese) be almost non-existent. The quantitative stress patterns in Germanic poetry are as a result quite different from the qualitative (musical or pitch) stress patterns of Greek, Latin, or French poetry. Strong stress on one syllable has also led in Germanic languages to the reduction or deletion of other syllables; e.g., the British pronounce *secretary* as three syllables (*secretry*) and have reduced *Cholmondeley* to something like *Chumly;* many or most Americans make *history* a two-syllable word.

CLASSROOM ACTIVITIES

The activities suggested in this section of each chapter are intended for school use, generally in the junior or senior high school, although some may be appropriate for the upper grades of elementary school. They are rather varied, and often provide opportunity for speaking, dramatizing, writing, reading, listening, drawing, etc. All are based on the belief that learning about the English language is both enjoyable and intellectually rewarding.

In college classes using this textbook, some of the suggested activities can be discussed, considering the light that they throw upon language. Some may also be takeoff points for written or oral work. Student teachers may want to try out some of the activities with their classes.

A World Without Language

Let the class imagine that for a period of twenty-four hours all human language is suspended. No one can speak, write, hear language, or read, although other physical and mental processes are unimpaired. What happens in schools, in homes, in offices and factories, at athletic events, in any places with which students are familiar? What funny things may occur? What tragic ones? (For one account, see "The Day They Turned the Language Off," in J. N. Hook, *The Story of American English,* New York: Harcourt, Brace, Jovanovich, Inc., 1972, pp. 119–21.)

Do Animals Talk?

No doubt some of your students have pets or at least have had a chance to observe certain animals or birds closely. A discussion of the "language" of animals may increase the depth of understanding of the language of man. Among possible questions:

1. Does a dog make different sounds or always the same one? Describe or imitate some of the sounds. Do they have different meanings? About how many meanings can a dog convey? About how many commands can an intelligent, well-trained dog obey? (I once knew a dog that could respond appropriately to eighty-five different signals. He reacted in one way, for instance, to "Rabbits!" and in a different way to "Rats!") What kinds of things can a dog "talk" about? What kinds of things can he not "talk" about? Does a dog ever combine two of his sounds to form a "sentence"?

2. Answer similar questions for other animals or birds that you know or know about: cats, hamsters, horses, cows, sheep, pigs, chickens, crows, dolphins, etc.

3. When a parrot says "Hello!" or "Polly wants a cracker!" or utters a burst of profanity, is it really sending a message? (The answer is *no*. Even though through coincidence the parrot may say "Hello!" when you enter the room or "Polly wants a cracker!" when it is hungry, it is equally likely to swear on either occasion. The parrot's "speech" is only imitative sounds, not used for conveying messages.)

4. Name and illustrate as many ways as you can in which human language differs from the sounds made by animals.

You Live in a Cave

A few students may put on a skit depicting human life in cave-man days before man had learned to put symbols together as sentences. They may grunt, squeal, shriek, etc., on appropriate occasions, and they may suppose that man has developed sufficiently that certain sounds may represent "fire," "tiger," etc., but they may not combine sounds to convey connected thought.

Your Own Story of Og

You may wish to read to your students the account of the fictitious Og and his descendants, pages 16–18 in this book. Groups of students may dramatize for the class their own varying versions of how the first "sentence" may have come into being. Older and more inhibited students may prefer to write their own imaginary accounts of how language began.

Theories of Language Origin

Students may write compositions explaining several of the theories of language origin such as the "bow wow" and the "pooh pooh," or may concentrate on a single theory, describing it and presenting arguments for and against it.

Language Families of the World

1. On a globe or a world map, have students locate the approximate areas in which major families of language are spoken.

2. Selected students (or volunteers) may report on the linguistic characteristics of some of the families. Many students are fascinated by learning, for instance, that languages such as some of those spoken in parts of Asia and Africa make use of sounds not heard at all in English and its relatives, or that in Chinese and related languages a change of tone may convey a totally different meaning. (One American lady in Burma, it is said, was embarrassed when her servant returned from market with a young man; the lady thought that she had ordered a head of cabbage, but she used the wrong tone.) Encyclopedias, especially the *Britannica,* provide basic information about various language families. Other sources include:

Holgar Pedersen, *The Discovery of Language.* Bloomington: Indiana University Press, 1962. (First published in Danish in 1924.)

Gary Jennings, *Personalities of Language.* New York: Thomas Y. Crowell Company, 1965. (Scattered references. E.g., pp. 8–11 on language families; pp. 54–55 on the "tweeting" language of Kuskoy, Turkey, which is useful in communicating through dense fog, and the "click" language of South African Khoi-Khoin, which has clicks and clacks and many sounds produced by breathing in rather than out.)

3. Some students may enjoy discussing the unanswerable question of whether it is more probable that all language families derived from a single source or that they developed independently in various regions. Students whose families take the Bible literally will adhere to the first belief and cite the Tower of Babel story as evidence (Genesis 11:1–9).

I-E Around the World

Provide the class with a list of living I-E languages, perhaps using the chart on page 333 as a basis. Again employing a globe or a world map, ask the students to locate places (maybe attaching removable labels) where I-E languages are spoken today. They are likely to point out first the obvious places: Europe, the Americas, India, Australia. Then they will remember that many colonies or former colonies, e.g., in Africa and some Pacific islands, still make much use of English, Dutch, French, and other I-E languages. Later someone will recall that in almost every corner of the world are people who have learned English or some other I-E tongue as a second language. At the end, almost all the earth's land areas will be seen to have at least some I-E speakers. (Labels of different colors may be used to differentiate primary I-E areas from the secondary ones.)

Counting in I-E Languages

Write the words from *one* to *ten* on a horizontal line on the board. If any students know a foreign language, ask them to write the corresponding words. (If Chinese, Japanese, or some other non-I-E language happens to be known, these words may be written at the bottom.) Fill in the counting words from other I-E languages, using the list on page 24 as a source. Have the class point out similarities they observe; the words for *two, three, six,* and *seven* are especially alike. Ask whether it is at all probable that so many similarities could be due just to chance. Contrast the I-E words with the Japanese or other non-I-E.

Advanced students may take another step, noting how Grimm's Law is exemplified in some of the words. Thus the Germanic words for *five* start with an *f* sound, but the Greek, Russian, Slovak, Lithuanian, Persian, and Hindustani keep the older *p*. The *d* to *t* shift is illustrated in *two* and *ten*. (The German language, you remember, underwent still another shift, accounting for *zwei* and *zehn*.) The *k* to *h* shift is exemplified in the initial sounds of Latin *centum* and English *hundred*.

Other Similarities in I-E Words

Several more words, like those listed on page 25, may be discussed to make the point that not only numeral words are alike in I-E languages. Actually, several hundred words could be cited, although the degrees of similarity vary. One source of additional examples is John Algeo and Thomas Pyles, *Problems in the Origins and Development of the English Language,* New York: Harcourt, Brace, Jovanovich, Inc., 1966, pp. 85–91. Algeo and Pyles include *lung, head, snow, moon, wind, beech, corn, wolf, bear, yoke, weave, sew, father, mother, brother, sister, son, daughter, widow, name, east, full, hound, tooth,* and *axle,* giving the forms of these words in Old English, German, Old Norse,

Gothic, Latin, Greek, Russian, Lithuanian, Sanskrit, and reconstructed Indo-European.

On page 86, Algeo and Pyles give an exercise that your class may enjoy. It involves sorting out related forms in eleven languages. For example, which of these Old English and I-E words correspond?

OE broþer (the þ is now *th*), dohtor, east, eax, fæder, full, hund, modor, nama, sunu, sweostor, toþ, widuwe

I-E *aks-, *ausos-, *bhrater-, *dhughter-, *dont-, *ku(o)n-, *mater-, *nomen-, *pater-, *plno-, *sunu-, *swesor-, *widhewa-

(The asterisk, you recall, indicates a reconstructed form. The hyphen shows that the I-E inflectional endings have been omitted. Application of Grimm's Law will help you with otherwise troublesome pairings like *full* and *plno-*.)

The Travels of the Indo-Europeans

Once more use a globe or a world map. Locate northern Europe (the Lithuanian area). Ask questions like these: "Assuming that the earliest Indo-Europeans first lived here, how did they probably spread, as the centuries passed? What route did they probably follow to Iran and India? (Did you realize that Iran and India are so close together?) Why didn't they settle in what is now Saudi Arabia? Why not in Africa? Why didn't they move from India into China? In general what kinds of obstacles seemed to stop them? (Chains of high mountains, large deserts, oceans, and probably the existence of firmly established peoples and cultures, as in China, were some.)

Siblings and Other Relatives

One way to help students understand the degrees of relationship of English to other languages is to pursue the family analogy. The other Germanic languages (see the chart on page 334) may be regarded as sisters and brothers of English. All other I-E languages are cousins. Non-I-E languages belong to different families, with no known relationship to English, even though we may borrow words from them or they from us, just as we may sometimes borrow a cup of sugar from someone outside our family.

The Locales of the Germanic Languages

On a large map of Europe, students may locate the homes of the modern Germanic languages: Swedish, Danish, Norwegian, Faroese, Icelandic, English, Frisian, Dutch, Flemish, Low and High German. (Afrikaans, you recall, has South Africa as its home, and speakers of

Yiddish, very numerous in Germany until Hitler's day, are widely scattered.) Students may note that on a small scale the spread of Germanic outward from a small area in northern Europe parallels the wider spread of I-E.

Sharing Information about Germanic Languages

If any of your students are familiar with a Germanic language other than English, the class may find it interesting to ask questions in order to find out both similarities and differences. E.g., "What German words do you know that are much like English words?" "Are vowels pronounced in the same way?" "How is gender treated?" "Are German verbs like English verbs?" "Does German have "odd" spellings like some in English?"

3
Alphabets and the Sounds of English

EARLY SYMBOLS FOR THE SPOKEN WORD

Remember always that language is spoken. It is a collection of arbitrarily chosen sounds that within a given speech community have been accepted as symbolic of certain "meanings." Thus in English certain sounds have come to symbolize the fruit of a particular vine. Any other combination of sounds might serve as well, but through the incidents and accidents of history man has attached the given meaning to these particular sounds. In writing, because of another set of historical incidents and accidents, the sounds are symbolized by the letters *g-r-a-p-e-s*. The written word *grapes* is then in English a symbol of a symbol—the written symbolization of sound symbols that stand for this fruit.

Spoken language existed for many thousands of years before written language appeared. Additional thousands of years passed before relatively sophisticated written symbols like *g-r-a-p-e-s* developed. In this section we'll glance at precursors of such alphabetic symbolization.

Pictographs

No doubt very early in his history man saw tracks in the damp ground and came to associate those tracks with the creatures that made them. He could recognize that some footprints were those of elephants, others those of tigers, and so on. In a sense he was "reading"; he was interpreting what were in effect pictorial symbols of an animal not at the moment physically present. Gradually he became increasingly proficient in such reading, so that he could distinguish, for example, a full-grown tiger from a kitten, or a healthy elephant from a cripple. Man must have received many such "pictorial" communications before he formed his own.

After a long period of time some brilliant prehistoric man himself created a picture of some sort. Why he did it we cannot say, nor can we guess what he pictured, for the mud or the sand, in which he drew, was soon trampled or rained upon. Maybe for his first picture he only traced around the edges of a faint track left a week before by a tiger; or maybe he responded to a vague esthetic impulse that caused him to draw a line and then another parallel to it; maybe with a finger he traced in the sand a line around the body of his child sleeping there, and when the child woke and walked away, the picture remained.

In all likelihood the earliest pictures were not symbols of language, for the chances are that they were not drawn to communicate. Language is a device used primarily to convey information or emotion to someone else. It presupposes a sender and a receiver, and is itself a medium for communication between the two. (On some occasions, the sender is also the receiver, as evidenced by such statements as "I told myself that . . . .")

But one day another brilliant ancestor of ours, in one of those flashes of insight that have recurred constantly in man's development, consciously used a picture to convey information to someone else. Perhaps, for instance, he had encountered a tiger larger than any other he had ever seen. Perhaps he stretched out his arms and uttered the sound for "big," but was still not satisfied. With his fingers he traced in the sand a rough outline to show the size of the huge beast, and his fellows, crowding around, understood at least dimly how large it was.

Although, as is true of the origins of language itself, we can do no more than hypothesize about the beginnings of pictographs, guesses like the preceding seem reasonably plausible.

As the millenniums passed, the pictorial communications became more elaborate. Just as early man had learned to combine sounds as sentences, he gradually learned to put together his pictographs so that they too formed sentence-like constructions. Examples of both simple one-figure pictographs and also multiple-figure drawings, some of them dating back to Paleolithic times, have been found in rocks and caves in Europe, Africa, North America, and elsewhere. The urge to convey thought (abetted perhaps by such other urges as to obey an esthetic drive or even to perpetuate oneself through a creation) knows no geographic boundaries. Concerning the impulses that may have led to some of the drawings, I. J. Gelb has written:

It is not improbable that several urges may have been instrumental at the same time in the origin of a drawing. When a hunter returned from a successful chase, or a warrior from a military expedition, he felt the desire to record his experience in a picture. The picture may have been drawn as a result of his artistic urge, but at the same time it may have served as a monument to commemorate past experiences. It could also have had the magic purpose of securing another good hunt or a successful razzia in the future.[1]

Professor Gelb includes a number of examples of pictorial messages. One of these (a fairly modern one) was drawn on a rock by Indians in New Mexico, close to a very steep trail. It depicts in simple lines two figures. One is a mountain goat climbing upward; the other, upside down, shows a man on a horse. The message is obvious, even eloquent: "Mountain goats can climb this trail, but horses can't."

Another of Gelb's examples, much more elaborate, is the one on page 335, taken from Henry R. Schoolcraft's 1851 volume on American Indians. It was carved on a rock on the shore of Lake Superior, and tells the story of a military expedition crossing the lake. Parts of the pictograph you can interpret for yourself: 1. How did the warriors travel across the lake? 2. How many warriors were there? 3. How many days did the journey take? (I.e., how many times did the sun cross the sky?) Some parts cannot be understood, however, without an understanding of Indian symbolization. The bird-figure at the top represents the totem or animal-symbol of the chief. The turtle symbolizes successful completion of anything. The figure on the horse may represent either the continuation of the journey on land, or the enemies to be encountered. The large bird, whose hooked beak shows that it is an eagle, indicates the bravery of the warriors. The stylized panther and serpent represent the force and cunning that the chief (or the artist) hopes will aid the warriors as they proceed.

Such picture-messages, which convey ideas and do not merely portray, are sometimes called ideographs. Ideographs, though, do not necessarily give warnings or tell stories, like our two previous examples. A drawing on a shield, perhaps appearing also on tools or a bow belonging to the same person, identifies the property of that person. The Ewe Negroes of Togo use pictures also as mnemonic devices, to remind them of proverbs; thus a drawing of a needle and a piece of cloth recalls their proverb "Small needles sew large cloths," perhaps comparable to the familiar English proverb about acorns and oaks.

---

[1] *A Study of Writing.* Chicago: University of Chicago Press, 1965, p. 26.

Hieroglyphs

In some languages pictures became used more and more for the recording of data or the transmission of messages. To facilitate the drawing, the scribes simplified the pictures so that "water," for example, might be shown merely by a wavy line, "much water" by a wavy horizontal line with two or three vertical straight lines below it, or "sun" by a circle.

The best-known form of such picture-writing is the hieroglyphic, which existed not only among the Egyptians but also among the Cretans, the Hittites, and even among the Mayans of Central America. The word *hieroglyph* is Greek for "sacred carving," equivalent to the Egyptian for "the god's words"—evidence of the high regard in which the ability to write was long held. Hieroglyphs represent a stage of transition to an alphabet.

The hieroglyph might stand for the thing pictured (circle = "sun") or for something suggested by that thing (circle = "daylight" or "the sun god," for instance). But it could also stand for the *sound* of the word. If we used such a system in English, to indicate "sunrise" we might draw a circle and an upward-pointing arrow; we could use the same hieroglyphs to indicate a bright, pleasant happening; or we could use the circle for any syllable in which the sound of "sun" appears, and the arrow in any syllable in which the sound of "rise" appears. (The last syllable of *memorize,* for example, would be shown as an arrow.)

A further development in Egyptian hieroglyphs was that some of them came to represent individual consonant sounds, bringing these symbols to the level of a partial alphabet. Thus a drawing that looked like a hand stood for the sound of [d], and one that looked like a horned snake represented the [f] sound.

The Syllabary and the Logogram

When written symbols stand for a syllable, as in the "sunrise" example, we have a syllabary, which is not an alphabet, since several sounds may be included within the syllable. Many written languages appear to have advanced from pictographs through hieroglyphs and syllabaries to alphabets.

Japanese of about fifteen hundred years ago used a clumsy syllabary called *"Man'yō-gana."* Today two syllabaries are still in use in Japan: *Hiragana* and *Katakana.* Each has about fifty characters. The Japanese word for "one" has two syllables, represented in Katakana as イチ, transliterated as "i-chi." Wherever the "i" syllable appears in Katakana, then

the ⌝ is used, so that ノく⌝ "ha-i" is "yes" and ∃⌝ "yo-i" is "good."
Wherever the "chi" syllable appears, of course, the ⧧ is used, and so on.

Another syllabary, devised in rather recent times, was that of the great
Cherokee leader Sequoyah, who in 1821 formed eighty-five written signs
for the syllables of his language—syllables which in Roman type would
have to be indicated by letter combinations such as *gi, kwo, tso, ya,* etc.
In a few years nearly the whole tribe became literate; they wrote a constitution, translated from the Bible, and in 1828 started the first Indian
language newspaper, the *Cherokee Phoenix.* One of the shameful blotches
on American history was the expulsion of these intelligent, enlightened
people from Georgia in the 1830's, with the accompanying deaths of almost
a fourth of them.

Several other syllabic systems could be mentioned, but another ancient
one is of particular interest, the cuneiform syllabaries of the Sumerians and
Akkadians, widely borrowed during the three thousand years before Christ
by other peoples of the Near East, and sometimes combined with logograms.
Cuneiform means "wedge-shaped," and the major characteristic of cuneiform symbols is their use of combinations of wedge-like forms. (Clay was
the usual writing material, and wedges were easier to draw in clay with a
stylus than were rounded forms.) Here are the cuneiform symbols for
"bird" and "go":

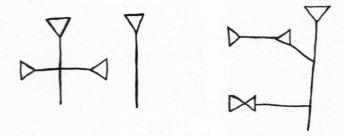

Like some of the Egyptian hieroglyphs, some of the cuneiform characters
also came to represent specific sounds and thus also were part of the movement toward an alphabet.

When the written form of a language employs symbols for whole words,
it is said to consist of logograms. Chinese, which has about fifty thousand
logograms, is the best example. To these logograms Chinese also adds a
number of syllabograms, especially for foreign words, such as three symbols
for *te-li-feng* (telephone). Possibly if the Chinese people had not been

burdened with so cumbersome a writing system, which makes literacy much harder to achieve, they would today be masters of the entire world.

EARLY ALPHABETS

The word alphabet is taken from *alpha* and *beta,* the names of the first two letters of the Greek alphabet, although the Greeks had borrowed these names from Semitic *aleph* and *beth.* An alphabet differs from the writing forms previously noted in one important way: each character or letter stands basically for one sound or one closely related group of sounds. A perfect alphabet would use one symbol for each phoneme of the language, and whenever that phoneme was to be represented, the same symbol would always be used. (In speech, a phoneme is one of the smallest units that distinguish one utterance or word from another. Thus, in *bat* and *pat,* the sounds of *b* and *p* are phonemes that enable us to differentiate the two words.) Possibly no alphabet has ever been perfect. Certainly, as we shall note later, the alphabet used for English has many imperfections, and as a result English-speaking children have more trouble than is really necessary in learning to read and to spell. Nevertheless an alphabetic system is much easier to master than is one of the older ones.

Semitic Origins

If you were to lock into a room two scholars who were well-versed in ancient languages, and if you asked them to discuss just how and where the Greeks obtained their alphabet, you might find two battered bodies when you returned in an hour or so. The scholars would likely agree that the Greeks got their basic alphabet from Semitic peoples, for the Greek letters have Semitic names and in their early forms look a great deal like Semitic characters. The scholars might also agree, although this is not certain, that Phoenician traders introduced the characters to the Greeks.

But from those points on, the scholars would be likely to disagree. Possibly Egypt was the original home of the alphabet, but maybe it was ancient Babylonia, or Cyprus, or Crete. Inscriptions found in the Sinai peninsula in 1906 apparently combine Egyptian hieroglyphics and the Semitic alphabet, but was the combination effected by Egyptians or someone else? How can one account for the fact that almost identical symbols appear widely around the edges of the Mediterranean and various inland spots, as the following table (representing early forms of *A*) shows?

Cretan	Sinaitic	Moabite	Palestinian	North Syrian
∀	⊄	⟨	⟨	⨉

Cyprian	Sardinian	Attic (Greek)
K	¢	⊁ Δ

There are still undeciphered inscriptions, which eventually may reduce scholars' puzzlement. But even though the details of development are unknown, we can be reasonably certain that the Greek alphabet, and hence eventually our own, is of Semitic origin, regardless of how the Greeks got hold of it.

Greek Contributions

In their writing (which incidentally was normally from right to left) the Semites used only consonants. The Greeks found that they could write their language more intelligibly, however, if they also included vowel symbols, so they adapted some of the twenty-two Semitic symbols to represent vowels. They also invented a few letters, including those that we transliterate as *chi, phi,* and *omega.*

For centuries there was no uniformity in writing Greek; different parts of the land (which extended into South Italy, the Balkans, and Asia Minor) followed their own customs. The number of letters differed, the symbols themselves were often not alike, and some of the surviving inscriptions (which date back to possibly the ninth century B.C.) were written from right to left, others left to right, and still others in boustrophedon style (i.e., "as the ox plows," alternately right to left and left to right).[2]

Gradually, though, as Athens became the leading Greek state in military power, social and political influence, art, philosophy, and especially literature, the Attic (Ionic) dialect became the predominant one, and its written symbols became more extensively used than the others. Thus from the fourth century B.C. this "classical Greek" may be regarded as standard. It was generally written with no spaces between words; punctuation was almost non-existent. Some writings, however, especially dramatic or poetic ones, included symbols showing breathings and accents (which in Greek were based upon pitch rather than stress). Much of our knowledge of Greek pronunciation comes from writings early in the Christian era by Apollonius Dyscolus and his son Herodian, who used an acute accent to

---

[2] A readily accessible source of further information about the Greek alphabet is "Alphabet" and "Greek Language" in the *Encyclopaedia Britannica.*

show high pitch, a grave accent (or none at all) for low pitch, and a circumflex for a pitch starting high and descending.

Changes Made by the Romans

The alphabet used in ancient Rome was based upon Chalcidic (western) Greek rather than Attic, and hence differs somewhat from the classic Greek alphabet. The Etruscans and certain Greek colonies introduced this Chalcidic alphabet into Italy, although for a time a dozen or more versions were used. As was true of early Greek, early Latin might be written right to left, left to right, or boustrophedon.

The Romans had in their language the sound of [f] which was not used in Greek. (The *ph* sound in Greek "phi" was pronounced about like a [p] sound followed by the sound of [h].) To show this sound the Romans first combined Greek F and H, later dropping the H. Since Greek F ("digamma") represented the sound of *w,* the Romans now were without a separate symbol for that; they compensated by using V for the sounds of both [w] and [u]. It is for this reason that in English printing until recent centuries a *v* often appears where the sound is that of [u].

Somewhat similar is the story of *c.* The Greek "gamma" appeared in Latin in a curved form (C); the Romans at first pronounced it [g] as the Greeks did. After a while, though, they began using C for the [k] sound, and added a line to it to form, as G, a new representation of the sound of [g].

A number of Greek letters, which were usually angular in shape, were rounded by the Romans: e.g., Greek Δ ("delta") became D, Π ("pi") became P, and Σ ("sigma") became S. The chief reason for the variation was that the angular shapes were easier to cut into stone but, as pens and ink became more widely used, the rounded forms could be made more quickly.

When Π became P, a problem arose, because P was "rho" in the Greek alphabet. The solution was to add a tail, giving R to indicate a sound resembling our [r].

Greek I ("iota") was used by the Romans for both the vowel *i* and for the semiconsonant *y* (as in English *yet*). Under the influence of Norman French, a semivocalic [i] beginning a syllable was changed to the sound of *j* that we use in words like *just*. Spellings remained confused for several centuries; thus in the First Folio of Shakespeare (1623), *abjured* is spelled *abiur'd*.

The Greek Q ("qoppa" or "koppa") was lost in Greek after the sound for which it stood disappeared from use. The Romans revived the symbol in combination with V for the sound [kw]. In today's English alphabet the sound is represented by *qu,* although since *kw* would do as well, the *q* is for us a useless letter.

The [z] sound of Greek Z ("zeta") was lost in Latin when [z] changed to [r] by a process known as rhotacism, but the letter Z was brought back into Latin at a time when the number of borrowings from Greek made it again useful.

The changes just summarized are the most significant ones made by the Romans, who showed some ingenuity in adapting someone else's alphabet to their own language. The Latin alphabet of twenty-three letters is of considerable interest to us because, with a number of adaptations, it became our own.

Further Developments

If you have seen Russian print, you are aware that its characters look somewhat like Greek. The reason is that a Greek missionary named Cyril brought the ninth century Greek alphabet to the Slavs; this alphabet, used by Russians, Bulgarians, and Serbs, is called Cyrillic in honor of the missionary. Cyril also introduced a different set of Greek letters, employed in cursive writing and called the Glagolitic, but this version of the alphabet has not been used since the seventeenth century.

Other lands than Greece adopted the Semitic alphabet in their own ways. The alphabets of India, called Kharosthi and Brahmi, are clearly related, scholars say, to South Semitic forms, probably because of the influence of Semitic traders. The alphabets of Persia and of the Arabic tongues are based upon Aramaic, a North Semitic tongue. Some of the alphabets of Asia Minor and of Armenia also have family resemblances to Greek and one or another of the Semitic alphabets, although the patterns of borrowing and adaptation have varied.

Other languages of Europe, including of course English, now make use of their own varieties of the Latin alphabet. Because sounds in these languages do not always coincide exactly with Latin sounds, various devices have been employed to make up for the differences. For example, the Scandinavian languages and German are among those that use dieresis to show the quality of a vowel: e.g., in German *flöhen* (to catch fleas) the two dots show that the sound of the *o* is not the normal one. French and several other languages make use of acute, grave, or circumflex accent marks (´, `, and ˆ) with certain vowels. The tilde in Spanish words like *cañon* shows that the *n* is pronounced like *ny* in English *canyon.* Czech uses a wedge (shaped like a rather flat *v*) to indicate a special quality of *c, e, n, r,* or *e*. French uses a cedilla below a *c* to indicate the sound of *s: garçon,* but Turkish uses it below *c* to show a sound like that of English *ch*.

Ligatures, digraphs, and specially invented or borrowed symbols also appear or have appeared in some European languages to represent particular sounds. Examples of ligatures are the æ and œ of Old English, which represented respectively the modern sound of the vowel in *cat* and the *ö* of German *horen* "to hear" (a sound that has since disappeared from standard English).

Digraphs are two or more letters used to indicate single sounds. Examples from Modern English include *ch, th,* and *sh,* which represent sounds not included in the Roman alphabet. (A perfect alphabet, remember, would have a separate symbol for each such sound.)

In Old English, as well as in early forms of Scandinavian languages, there were separate symbols for our *th,* which we shall encounter later both as þ ("thorn") and ð ("eth" or "edh"). A number of modern phonetic alphabets use these symbols to represent respectively the voiceless *th* of *thin* and the voiced *th* of *then*. (To observe the differences, pronounce the first sound of *thin* and afterward the first sound of *then;* note the vibration of the vocal cords in the latter.) The thorn came from the runic alphabet, as did another character, Ν (wynn), which at times was used for [w].

The runic alphabet just mentioned may serve as a final example of variation from alphabets of the Mediterranean area. Archeologists have found stones, dating back to the third to the twelfth century A.D., on which angular symbols called runes were cut. The number of runes in this alphabet varied from sixteen to thirty-three, with twenty-four being commonly used in early inscriptions. (The *American Heritage Dictionary* pictures twenty-six runes.) Twentieth century scholars have shown that, although the majority of the inscriptions have been found in northern Europe and in England, the runes are actually traceable to western Greek, and to Etruscan, a pre-Roman language. For example, the runes for *a, e, i, o, b, f, h, m, n, r,* and *t* all bear certain resemblances to Greek or Latin or certain other early Italic alphabets.

The word *rune* again attests to the awe in which people who could write were once held. In Germanic and Celtic languages it was a word for "magic," and in Old English it referred to secrets or mystery. (The English place-name *Runnymede* means "secret council meadow.") Anyone who could transmit messages through the carving of runes possessed secrets of magic powers withheld from common folk; traces of this belief are reflected in some of the Faust stories. *Rune* goes back to Indo-European **ruño,* which meant "mystery" or "secret."

THE ALPHABET OF ENGLISH

As we have seen, the alphabet that English uses is essentially that of the Romans, although with the passage of time certain changes were inevitable. In this section we shall look very quickly at the derivation of the twenty-six letters we now have. Note that here we are dealing only with the *shapes* of the symbols, not the *sounds* that they represent. Also, for simplicity, the discussion will concern only capital letters as they now appear in print; capitals in cursive writing, as you are aware, may differ considerably from printed forms, and lower case letters sometimes resemble capitals hardly at all. (Most ancient Greek lower case letters, in contrast, looked a great deal like the capitals.)

A. Our A is the same in shape as urban Roman of the second century B.C., and very similar to the Ionic Greek form for "alpha," although the latter sometimes lay on its side, pointing toward the right.

B. Again, like urban Roman. The Greek form for "beta" sometimes had the loops on the left, and sometimes used angular rather than curved shapes.

C. In many inscriptions the Greek form for "gamma" looks like an upside-down L or V. The Romans rounded it to the shape of our C.

D. The Greek "delta" was generally in the shape of an isosceles or equilateral triangle, although a rounded form sometimes appeared. The Roman D was like ours.

E. In ancient Greece an E ("epsilon") might have the open edges at either the left or the right. The Roman E faced in the same direction as ours.

F. The Greeks did not use the sound of [f]. However, they had derived from Semitic an F-like character ("digamma") that represented a semiconsonant [w], as in English *blow.* The Romans, as we noted on p. 43, used this symbol for the sound of [f].

G. Our G, like C, goes back to the Greek "gamma," but, as the Romans did, we use a short horizontal bar to distinguish G from C.

H. In some Greek and Roman writing, the top and bottom of the H were closed with horizontal bars. The Greeks used their "eta" originally for an [h] sound, but later for a long vowel sound. Our H is the same as the late Roman H.

I. The Greek "iota" was originally like an angular S, but later became a straight vertical line, in which form both the Etruscans and Romans borrowed it and which we still preserve. (The dot on our lower case *i* was added in medieval times to make it easier to read a word like *minimum,* which in some people's cursive might otherwise look like just a wavy line.)

J. This letter also comes from Greek "iota." At first the Romans did not differentiate the vowel sound from that of the semiconsonant sound that we represent as Y, but later they added a tail. We use J, however, for a different sound, that of *j* and *dge* in *judge.* (The dot that we use on a lower case *j* was carried over from the *i.*)

K. The Greek "kappa" at first faced left, like the Semitic "kaph." Later it and its Roman descendants looked almost exactly like our K.

L. Greek "lambda" consisted of two straight lines forming an angle, but at different times the open end faced various ways. The Romans standardized it in the form familiar to us.

M. The Semitic form of M was a wavy line referred to as "mēm," meaning "water." The Greek "mu," adopted by the Romans, was standardized as M.

N. Early Greek "nu" looked somewhat like a 7 with an extra line going up at the left end of the horizontal bar. Later it came to resemble our N. The Romans adopted this later form.

O. Since Greek times O ("omicron") has been represented as a rounded letter, although the Romans gave it the oval shape that we use. (The Semites, from whom the Greeks borrowed the symbol, used it for the sound of a consonant that does not exist in Indo-European languages; the Greeks gave it a vowel sound.)

P. Greek "pi," as we have noted earlier, became Roman P.

Q. Greek "qoppa" or "koppa," later dropped from their alphabet as useless, looked like a golf ball on a tee, and in that form the Romans borrowed it. They later moved the tee to form a tail extending from the bottom right of the ball, and it is still approximately that shape which we use.

R. Greek "rho" looked like a triangular pennant on a staff; it early faced left, later right. The Romans rounded the triangle and added a tail to distinguish the symbol from P.

S. Early Greek "sigma" looked like an angular 3 or S; the later form looked like an M on its side. The Romans borrowed the angular S form and then rounded it to the shape we use.

T. Greek "tau" and the Roman T go back to a Semitic form that looked like X or +.

U. Greek "upsilon" and "digamma" (see F) both came from a Y-shaped Semitic character called "wāw." In Greek, upsilon looked like Y, later like V. The Romans wrote it as V. The development of the curved shape to distinguish U from V is post-Roman; as we noted earlier, only in recent centuries have the two symbols been consistently distinguished.

V. Greek "upsilon" gave rise to V also. The Romans used V both for the sound of [w] as in "veni, vidi, vici" and for a *u*-sound as in IVLIVS ("Julius"). As explained under U, U and V were not clearly distinguished until fairly recent times.

W. Still another descendant of "upsilon" (and of its ancestor, the prolific Semitic "wāw") is W, which is literally "double U." (The written form looks more like two U's than does the printed one, which looks like two V's.) The Romans normally used V for [w], although the form W appears in some inscriptions.

X. For "xi" the Greeks used several shapes, including that of X, which the Romans adopted.

Y. A final descendant of Greek "upsilon" and Semitic "wāw" is Y, which looked like that in Greek. The Romans often used it interchangeably with I, and even today the differentiation is not complete, as witness British *tyre*, American *tire*.

Z. Greek "zeta" in one of its forms looked like Z. The Romans used it very little, but retained the shape, as we still do.

We have noted (pages 45–46) that still other written symbols have existed in English in the past—particularly symbols taken from runes. Some of these will be mentioned again in later chapters.

REPRESENTING THE SOUNDS OF ENGLISH

A perfect alphabet, as we commented earlier, would use one symbol for each sound (or each group of almost identical sounds) in the language. The English alphabet is much less close to the ideal than are some others, mainly because we make use of about forty phonemes (not counting numerous variants called allophones) but have only twenty-six characters to represent them. Further, in our spelling we are not consistent in using the same character for a given sound; the so-called "long i" of *kind,* for instance, may be spelled in almost twenty different ways. Some other languages, which may employ fewer phonemes, have a much closer correlation between sound and symbol. If you have studied Spanish, for example, you are aware that spelling in that language causes little difficulty, because of the consistency of orthographic representation. Finnish and Russian are other examples of consistency and close correlation. Small children who grow up using one of those languages ordinarily have comparatively few troubles either in learning to read it or in learning to spell it.

Since in this book we shall frequently need to refer to the way words have been or are pronounced, we must have a clearer method for indicating sounds than our English alphabet provides. The International Phonetic Alphabet is the most thorough, but since it is rather complex and includes some sound symbols not needed in English, we shall use a simpler system. It will be advisable for you to learn the following symbols, since they will be used frequently in the rest of this book. When a sound is being indicated, the symbol is enclosed in brackets: [b].

The pronunciations that are indicated are intended to represent those most common in the United States. When you yourself pronounce the words cited as examples, you may find some variations from what is shown, especially in the vowels. Such variations do not mean that your pronunciations are "wrong." They show only that dialectal differences exist. In fact, as an oscillograph can clearly reveal, no two persons pronounce all sounds exactly alike. Like fingerprints, no two persons' pronunciations are absolutely identical. However, unlike fingerprints, which do not change at all during a person's life, pronunciation of the same word by the same person may vary somewhat from time to time, even within a single sentence.

Consonant Sounds

[b]   the first or the last sound of *Bob*. Usually spelled *b*,[3] but sometimes *bb* as in *babble*. (For this sound and others there may also be highly unusual or even unique spellings, such as *pb*, for [b] in *cupboard*, but such eccentricities are omitted here.)

[č]   the first or the last sound of *church*. Usually spelled *ch,* but sometimes *tch* as in *witch, che* as in *niche, t* as in *feature, c* as in *cello*.

[d]   the first or the last sound of *dad*. Usually spelled *d*, but sometimes *dd* as in *add* or (very often) *ed* as in *roamed*.

---

[3] Many of the consonants occur with a final *e*, as in *jibe,* for instance. This *e* is intended to show the quality of the vowel preceding the consonant. Although such spellings are very common, they are not usually included in the examples.

[f]   the first or the last sound of *fife*. Usually spelled *f*, but sometimes *ff* as in *piffle*, *ft* as in *often*, *gh* as in *cough*, *ph* as in *phone*.

[g]   the first or the last sound of *gag*. Usually spelled *g*, but sometimes *gg* as in *egg*, *gu* as in *guest*, *gh* as in *ghost*.

[h]   the first sound of *had*. Usually spelled *h*, but sometimes *wh* as in *who*, or in borrowed words, *g* as in *gila* or *j* as in *Mojave*.

[ǰ]   the first or the last sound of *judge*. Most often spelled *j*, but sometimes *g* as in *gyrate*, *ge* as in *George*, *gg* as in *exaggerate*, *dg* as in *judgment*, *gi* as in *legion*, *d* as in *educate*, or *di* as in *soldier*.

[k]   the first or the last sound of *kick*. Usually spelled *c* as in *cat* or *k* as in *kid*, but sometimes *ck* as in *luck*, *q* as in *quit*, *que* as in *technique*, *ch* as in *school*.

[l]   the first or the last sound of *lull*. Usually spelled *l*, but sometimes *ll* as in *tell* or *Lloyd*.

[m]   the first or last sound of *mum*. Usually spelled *m*, but sometimes *mm* as in *slimmer*, *mb* as in *thumb*, *mn* as in *column*.

[n]   the first or the last sound of *nun*. Usually spelled *n*, but sometimes *nn* as in *sinner*, *kn* as in *knowledge*, *gn* as in *gnat*, *pn* as in *pneumonia*.

[ŋ]   the last sound of *ring*. Usually spelled *ng*, but *n* in *rink* or *finger*, *ngue* in *tongue*.

[p]   the first or the last sound of *pup*. Usually spelled *p*, but sometimes *pp* as in *apple*.

[r]   the first or the last sound of *rear*. Usually spelled *r*, but sometimes *rr* as in *err*, *wr* as in *written*, *rh* as in *rhyme*, *rre* as in *bizarre*.

[s]   the first or the last sound of *sis*. Usually spelled *s*, but sometimes *ss* as in *pass*, *c* as in *city*, *sw* as in *answer*, *sc* as in *science*, *ps* as in *psychology*.

[š]   the first or the last sound of *shush*. Usually spelled *sh*, but sometimes *ch* as in *machine*, *ti* as in *partial*, *ci* as in *gracious*, *si* as in *apprehension*, *ssi* as in *passion*, *shi* as in *fashion*, *s* as in *insurance*, *ce* as in *ocean*.

[t]   the first or the last sound of *tut*. Usually spelled *t*, but (very often) *ed* as in *slipped*, sometimes *tt* as in *clatter*, *tte* as in *cigarette*, *th* as in *Thames*, *pt* as in *receipt*, *bt* as in *doubt*.

[θ]   the first sound of *think*. Usually spelled *th*.

[ð]   the first sound of *that*. Usually spelled *th*, but sometimes *the* as in *bathe*.

[v]   the first or the last sound of *valve*. Usually spelled *v*.

[w]   the first sound of *wait*. Usually spelled *w*, but sometimes *wh* as in some people's pronunciation of the first sound in *when*, *u* as in *quiet*.

[j]   the first sound of *yell*. Usually spelled *y*, but sometimes *j* as in *hallelujah*.

[z]   the first or the last sound of *zoos*. Usually spelled *s* (a voiced *s*, with the vocal cords vibrating) or *z*, but sometimes *zz* as in *fizz*, *ss* as in the middle of *possess*.

[ž]   the second sound of *azure*. Usually spelled *s* as in *leisure*, or *z*, but sometimes *ti* as in *equation*, *si* as in *delusion*, *g* as in *genre*, *ge* as in *rouge*.

Vowel Sounds

[æ]   the vowel sound of *bat*. Usually spelled *a*, although with a few variations such as *au* in *laugh*, *al* in *salmon*, *i* in *meringue*.

[a]   the vowel sound of *cot*. Usually spelled *o*, but sometimes *a* as in *yacht*. (See also [ɔ] below.)

[a:]   the first vowel sound of *father*. Similar to [a] but held slightly longer. Usually spelled *a*, or *o* as in *bother*, but sometimes *ea* as in *hearth*, *e* as in *sergeant*, *ah* as in *ah*, *al* as in *palm*.

[ɛ]   the vowel sound of *set*. Usually spelled *e*, but sometimes *a* as in *any* or *fare*, *ai* as in *said*, *ay* as in *says*, *ie* as in *friend*, *ei* as in *their*. (Some phonologists differentiate an [ɛ] from a more prolonged [ɛ:], using words like *set* and *stair* as their respective examples, but in most speech the difference in length is hardly noticeable.)

[e:]   the vowel sound (actually diphthongal) of *mate*. Usually spelled *a*, but sometimes *ay* as in *pay*, *ea* as in *great*, *ai* as in *rain*, *ei* as in *rein*, *eig* as in *reign*, *eigh* as in *freight*, *ey* as in *they*, *é* as in *café*, *et* as in one pronunciation of *valet*, *er* as in one pronunciation of *foyer*.

[I]   the vowel sound of *sip*. Usually spelled *i*, but sometimes *ee* as in General American *been*, *y* as in *symbol*, *u* as in *business*, *ui* as in *built*, *o* as in *women*, *e* as in *here*, *ea* as in *hear*, *ee* as in *leer*, *ei* as in *weird*. For the unstressed final sound of words like *happy* and *lady*, some speakers use an [I] sound, but [i:] (see below) appears more common. In words like *here*, *hear*, *leer*, and *weird*, some speakers use a sound more like [i:].

[i:]   the vowel sound of *feed*. Various common spellings: *ee* as in *feel*, *ea* as in *seal*, *ei* as in *ceiling*, *ie* as in *grieve*, *e* as in *depletion* or *cede*. More rare: *i* as in *caprice*, *eo* as in *people*, *ey* as in *key*, *ay* as in *quay*. Usually spelled *i* in continental European languages, e.g., French *ici* [i:si]. (See [I] for comments on final *Y* and on words like *here*.)

[ɔ]   the sound of *awe*. Various common spellings: *a* as in *tall*, *aw* as in *saw*, *au* as in *clause*, *o* as in *long*, *oa* as in *oar*, *ough* as in *bought*. More rare: *augh* as in *naught*, *ah* as in *Utah*, *aul* as in *Faulkner*. Many speakers use [a] or [a:] and others use [ɔ] in words like *on, off, coffee, cough*. (Some phonologists distinguish a prolonged [ɔ:] from [ɔ], arguing that the sound of *awe*, for instance, is held longer than the vowel sound of *ought*, but in most speech the boundary between long and short duration is hard to detect.)

[o:]   the vowel sound of *home*. Various common spellings: *o* as in *go*, *oa* as in *toad*, *oe* as in *toed*, *ow* as in *flow*. More rare: *owe* as in *owe*, *ou* as in *soul*, *ol* as in *yolk*, *eau* as in *bureau*, *ough* as in *though*, *ew* as in *sew*.

[u]   the vowel sound of *full*. Usually spelled *u*, but sometimes *oo* as in *good*, *o* as in *wolf*, *oul* as in *should*.

[u:]   the vowel sound of *fool*. Usually spelled *u* (with a final silent *e*) as in *rule*, but often *oo*, and sometimes *ou* as in *you*, *ue* as in *sue*, *oe* as in *shoe*, *ough* as in *through*, *ui* as in *pursuit*. Some speakers use [u], others [u:] in words like *roof, proof, room, broom, root*. In words like *tune* and *news*, some speakers use [u:], saying [tu:n] and [nu:z], but others substitute a diphthong for the vowel: [tIu:n], [nIu:z].

[ə]   the last sound of *china*; occurs in unstressed positions only. (The symbol [ə] is called "schwa.") Usually spelled *a, e, i, o,* or *u* as in *about, causative,* or *Cuba; evade* (which sometimes has the [i:] sound), *remedy* (the second vowel sound); in *Cincinnati* the second vowel sound is almost always [ə] but sometimes [I], and the last sound may be [ə], [I], or [i:]; *potato* (in some speech for both the first and third vowel sounds), *melody* (the second vowel sound), *piano* (the final sound is pronounced [ə] by some, [o:] or something like [u] by others); *u* as in *suspect* or *syrup*. (One of the major reasons why English is difficult to spell is that any of the five chief vowel symbols may be used to represent [ə] in unstressed syllables, and English has thousands of such words.)

[ʌ]   the vowel sound of *cut*. Usually spelled *u*, but sometimes *o* as in *mother*, *oo* as in *flood*, *ou* as in *young*. (Some phonologists do not distinguish this sound from [ə]; others use [ə:]. However, the vowel sound of a word like *cut* is not quite like that of the *a* in *china,* and hence a separate symbol appears desirable.)

[ɝ]   the vowel sound of *earn*; appears only before [r]. Various fairly common spellings: *ea* as in *yearn,* *u* as in *fur,* *e* as in *herd,* *i* as in *bird,* *o* as in *word,* *ou* as in *journey.* In the speech of those who "drop their r's," the vowel sound in such words may be [ə] or [u]. Others may use the diphthong [əI] in words like *bird.*

Diphthongs

[aI]   the medial sound of *side.* (Note that what is popularly called "long *i*" is actually a diphthong.) Various common spellings: *i* as in *ripe,* *y* as in *why,* *ie* as in *die,* *igh* as in *might.* Less common: *eye* as in *eye,* *eigh* as in *height,* *uy* as in *buy,* *ey* as in *geyser,* *ye* as in *dye,* plus seven or eight more.

[au:]   the final sound in *cow.* Usually spelled *ow,* or *ou* as in *round.*

[ɔI]   the first sound in *oil.* Usually spelled *oi,* or *oy* as in *coy.*

[Iu]   the sound after [v] in *view.* Usually spelled *u* as in *music,* but sometimes *ew* as in *few,* *ue* as in *cue,* *ie* as in *view.*

CLASSROOM ACTIVITIES

The Ancestors of Reading

Reading is the interpretation of visual symbols. Before there were man-made symbols (writing), early human beings learned to interpret many of the visual symbols or signs found in nature. Examples: the identification of animal tracks, the recognition of smoke as a sign of fire, association of the sun with warmth, or differentiation between edible and inedible berries. Man had to have long experience with such symbols and signs before drawing, writing, and reading became possible for him.

Ask the class to make an extended list of such symbols and signs that early man probably learned to interpret. Consider with them how such interpretation was a necessary precursor of drawing, writing, and reading.

Telling a Simple Story Through Pictographs

1.   Have students try to interpret a picture story like that on p. 335, or the one below, from Garrick Mallery's *Picture-Writing of the*

American Indians (Washington: U.S. Bureau of American Ethnology, Tenth Annual Report, 1893), p. 363.

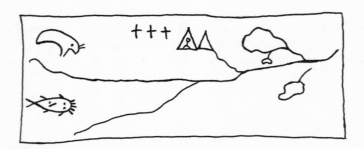

This picture is a "letter" from an Ojibwa girl to her hoped-for boy friend, telling him how to find her wigwam. She belongs to the bear totem, he to the mud-puppy. She shows the trails leading to her wigwam, and its position relative to three lakes. The crosses indicate that the (presumably three) girls who live there are Christian. The figure in one wigwam shows where the girl lives.

2. Ask students to draw similar pictures to convey messages of the sort that relatively primitive people might have used, e.g., to tell of a hunting or fishing trip, to give directions, to celebrate a military victory, to tell a sad love story, or to issue a warning.

3. Suppose that we could not write and read. Have students draw simple pictures to show something that might happen today, e.g., an automobile accident, a skiing expedition, a flight from Denver to San Francisco.

Developing Hieroglyphs

To show how hieroglyphs could develop, supply students with (or have them bring) photographs of familiar items: a man or woman, an automobile, a boat, waves on a lake or ocean, etc. Ask them to draw in a very few lines a figure that could represent one or more of these items. E.g., a man might look like an upside-down Y, or a bicycle could be a straight line with two circles under it, and an automobile a straight line with four circles below.

These pseudo-hieroglyphs would all represent nouns. Ask the class how certain verbs or adjectives could be shown hieroglyphically. E.g., how could you draw symbols for *walk, run, talk, cry, laugh,* or *happy, sad, comfortable, afraid, childish?*

Representation of abstractions is more difficult, but some students may be interested in trying to show hieroglyphically *freedom, power,* or others.

Making a Syllabary

1. This exercise is useful to show how a syllabary, such as one of those in Japanese, differs from an alphabet (and it can be fun, too). Present the students with a sentence in which several syllables occur more than once, like this:

Our cat lay like a log for an hour on an open catalog, but awoke when a nosey caterpillar crawled over her nose.

Students, alone, or in small groups or as a class, create a symbol for each of the syllables. In the example, the same symbol would be used for *our-hour, cat-cat*alog-*cat*erpillar, *a*-cat*a*log-*a*woke-*a, log*-cata*log, an-an, o*pen-*over, nosey-nose,* cat*er*pill*ar.* (The shape of each symbol may be completely arbitrary, or may be modified from certain pictographs, letter combinations, or shorthand symbols.)

2. The class may discuss the advantages and disadvantages of a syllabary in comparison with pictographs and an alphabet. They will probably conclude that a syllabary would be much simpler to learn than picture-based writing, and much better for expressing complex or abstract ideas. But for English a syllabary might not be very practical, since English uses many hundreds of different syllables, each of which would have to have its own symbol. (Even the short sentence about the cat would require about twenty symbols, and a following sentence might need twenty or so *different* symbols.)

An Imaginative Tale

Relatively young children (like those who could enjoy Kipling's stories such as "How the Elephant Got His Trunk") may have fun writing a completely imaginary account of "How the Alphabet Got Started." For instance, a student may associate the sound of [b] with "bubble," and say that the shape of B represents one bubble above another.

A Comparison of Alphabets

Some dictionaries devote a page to a table of alphabets, showing usually Semitic (Hebrew), Greek, Roman, Russian (Cyrillic), and perhaps one or two others. A student or a group of students may like to study such a table and report to the class on similarities that they observe. The report will probably make clear how our own alphabet goes back to the Semitic.

Stories of Our Letters

On the beginning page for each letter, the *American Heritage Dictionary* shows the shapes that each English letter had in the past, including Semitic, Greek, Roman, and earlier English forms, and including examples of written as well as printed forms. There is also a compact account of changes in shape and in the sound(s) represented. Each of twenty-six students may specialize in a letter, and explain how it has developed through the centuries.

Runes

1. Using an encyclopedia article as a basis, one or more students may explain what runes were, where they have been found, and what they were used for, and show some examples to the class. Runes that look somewhat like Greek letters may be especially noted. (The runic alphabet is sometimes called *futhorc* or *futhark* because its first letters represent those English sounds.)

2. Using modern spelling, some students may enjoy preparing an inscription in runes.

The Sounds We Use

If you have in your class students with rather diverse backgrounds, you may discuss and exemplify the fact that we don't all pronounce words alike, and that minor differences in pronunciation afford pleasant variety. Through historical chance, some people have come to use one pronunciation, others a different one. No pronunciation is really "wrong," although some people may consider it wrong because it differs from what they are familiar with or from what most "educated" people say.

Among the many words that may be pronounced differently by members of your class are *coffee, dance, greasy, aunt, frog, either, creek, roof, tune, pajamas, with, whether, Colorado, Iowa, Missouri, downtown, park your car*. You may write such words on the board and ask the class to pronounce each in unison; your ear will probably detect variant pronunciations of some. Talk about them, including some comments on regional variations. Your purpose should be to help students to become more acceptive of pronunciations different from their own.

Oddities of Spelling

On pages 49–53 you have a list of the usual and fairly usual spellings employed to represent the approximately forty phonemes of English. On occasion you and your class may want to play "The Odd-Spelling Game," in which groups of students may compete against one another if you and they wish.

Ask questions like "Think of any word in which [d] isn't spelled with just a *d*." "Think of a word in which [æ] is spelled *au*." "Now a word in which [e:] is spelled *eigh*." The first student or group answering correctly wins a point. (The list on pp. 49–53 will suggest countless such questions.)

Here are examples of still more unusual spellings that may be included if you teach especially bright students. The oddities are in italic type.

[b]   cu*pb*oard
[č]   *Cz*ech
[d]   *dh*arma
[f]   Chekho*v*
[h]   Don Qui*x*ote (as usually pronounced in the United States)
[ĭ]   grand*eu*r, congra*t*ulate (as commonly pronounced)
[k]   *kh*aki, sa*cque*
[n]   *mn*emonic
[p]   hiccou*gh*
[r]   cata*rrh*
[s]   *sch*ism, scien*ce*, Wor*ces*ter
[š]   *sch*napps, an*x*ious, lu*sci*ous, fu*chs*ia, nau*se*a (in which [ž] is also used)
[t]   *phth*isic, vic*t*uals
[v]   ne*ph*ew (British pronunciation)
[w]   *o*ne, *ou*ija
[j]   on*i*on, bou*ill*on
[z]   *x*ylophone, *cz*ar

[æ]   pl*ai*d, ma'*a*m, C*ae*dmon
[a]   *e*nnui, *au*nt (especially in New England)
[a:] kr*aa*l
[ɛ]   R*ey*nolds, phl*e*gm
[e:] g*au*ge
[I]   si*e*ve
[i:] am*oe*ba, m*ae*nad
[ɔ]   Arkans*as*
[o:] y*eo*man, chau*ff*eur

[u]   wo*r*sted (material)
[u:]   t*wo, to,* S*iou*x, L*ewi*s, li*eu*tenant
[ə]   Isa*a*c, fam*ou*s, vic*iou*s, fell*ow* (in some people's speech)
[ʌ]   w*a*s (in many people's speech)
[aI]   ch*oi*r, *ai*sle
[au:] sa*ue*rkra*ut*
[ɔI] R*eu*ters
[Iu] qu*eue,* f*eu*d

Learning To Transcribe Speech

You may or may not want your students to learn to transcribe spoken words. If they engage in a dialect study (which many students enjoy), it will be useful if they have a systematic method of indicating what they hear. They may, of course, simply attempt a respelling (e.g., "dahnce" for one pronunciation of *dance*), but that may be difficult for some sounds and a little less accurate than a phonemic transcription.

Some textbooks, such as *New Dimensions in English* (McCormick-Mathers Publishing Company), include their own phonemic symbols. If your text does so, no doubt its system is the one your students should learn. Otherwise you may want to introduce them to the symbols in this book.

Suggestions: 1. First have students pronounce the sound represented by the symbol, together with several words containing the sound. (Individual variations, of course, may be noted as matters of interest but should not be criticized.) 2. Given a transcribed list of words, have students study how the words are transcribed, and practice pronouncing them. 3. Given transcribed sentences, have students read them. 4. Have students transcribe words, then sentences, of their own, in the way that they themselves pronounce the words. A transcription is not wrong unless it indicates incorrectly the way that the transcriber says the word. (In some sentence contexts, the same word may be pronounced in different ways. E.g., in "I thought that that was funny," the first *that* is normally [ðət], the second [ðæt].) 5. Have students transcribe words pronounced for them by their classmates. A day later the transcriber pronounces what he has put down, and asks "Is this the way you pronounced it?"

4

Old English
and Those
Who Spoke It

THE PEOPLES WHO CAME TO THE BRITISH ISLES

The Start of the Mixture

In his ill-natured poem "The True-Born Englishman" (1701) Daniel Defoe refers to the numerous invasions and incursions that characterized the early history of the British Isles:

> He [a devil] made her [Britain's] first-born race so rude,
> And suffer'd her so oft to be subdu'd;
> By sev'ral crowds of wand'ring thieves o'er-run,
> Often unpeopled, and as oft undone;
> While ev'ry nation that her pow'rs reduc'd
> Their languages and manners introduc'd.
> From whose mix'd relics our compounded breed
> By spurious generation does succeed,
> Making a race uncertain and uneven,
> Deriv'd from all the nations under Heaven.
> The Romans first with Julius Caesar came,
> Including all the nations of that name,
> Gauls, Greeks, and Lombards, and, by computation,
> Auxiliaries or slaves of ev'ry nation.
> With Hengist, Saxons; Danes with Sueno came,
> In search of plunder, not in search of fame.
> Scots, Picts, and Irish from the Hibernian shore,

59

And conqu'ring William brought the Normans o'er.
  All these their barb'rous offspring left behind,
The dregs of armies, they of all mankind;
Blended with Britons, who before were here,
Of whom the Welsh ha' bless'd [typified] the character.

Defoe's history is a bit mixed, and his interpretation at least open to question, yet his doggerel is accurate in portraying the British as a mixture of many groups of people—as indeed most nations probably are. It is necessary to remember that as little as one to two thousand years ago wandering, fighting, invading, pillaging, taking land by force, and inter-marrying (often a euphemistic word) represented a common way of life. Few people then were pinned down by possessions; European mobility was often as great as that of tribal American Indians. Morality was frequently that of "Might makes right." The ideal man was strong, clever, unscrupu-lous; he lived hard, he fought because he had been brought up to fight, he expected to die young.

Because of the lack of written records, little is known about very early settlements in the British Isles. Probably prehistoric men made their way across the narrow Channel; evidence suggests communities of hunters and fishermen dating back many thousands of years. Archeologists have found remains which indicate that later people in the islands had long skulls, used flint for weapons and tools, and raised cattle, sheep, goats, and dogs. The long-skulls, who may have been Picts, a non-I-E people, apparently came from the Mediterranean area and from Africa and Asia. They were con-quered, perhaps between 2000 and 1400 B.C., by round-heads who may have been Indo-European, perhaps Celts. These round-heads used bronze (an alloy of tin and copper); British Cornwall, rich in tin, was useful to them. They may have had fine engineering ability, as the far-hauled massive stones of Stonehenge (c. 1800 B.C.) attest, although the Picts may have been responsible for this mammoth work. The round-heads pushed the long-skulls toward the edges of the islands and no doubt mated with many of their women.

Who were the Celts? The Greeks referred to *Keltoi,* the Romans to *Celtae,* barbarians who lived in the Iberian peninsula and north of the Alps. Later Greeks called them *Galatai,* who lived as far east as Asia Minor (Paul's epistle to the Galatians was addressed to them); in Rome of the second century B.C. they were called *Galli* (Gauls). Like others of their era, they were wanderers of mixed heritage, and at one time or another they covered much of western Europe. Their passages to the British Isles were apparently early; they must have come to the islands not at one time, but in many large or small waves whose movements may have been dictated not only by wanderlust and the search for wealth and power, but also by pressures on the Continent such as Julius Caesar's conquest of Gaul. It was Celts whom the Romans found on the islands before and after the coming of Julius Caesar. They varied widely in appearance and physique, though the Romans described them as unusually tall, strong, and fair; they were often polygamous (no doubt because so many of their men were killed in fights, leaving a surplus of women) ; they were fierce warriors and brawlers; they loved feasting and drinking, but also enjoyed music and the singing of long poems of adventure; they knew the rudiments of farming.

The Romans

Before the raids of Julius Caesar in 55 and 54 B.C., Roman traders had frequently visited the British Isles, and very early British coins with Latin words have been found. Roman emperors long regarded the islands as Roman territory, although conquest was not attempted until the middle of the first century A.D., when some forty thousand soldiers over a period of four years subdued all the people south of the Humber and east of the Severn. Roman forts, often made of stone and housing up to a thousand men, served to keep under control those whom the Romans regarded as barbarians, although there were numerous uprisings, including an exceptionally bloody one led by the warlike Queen Boadicea. Eventually Roman generals, however, conquered much of the rough country and people even of Wales and Scotland.

Besides the ruins of fortresses that each enclosed fifty acres or so, one may still see in England portions of thick defensive walls that were as much as fifteen feet high and many miles long, and segments of the Romans' durably built roads.

Some discharged Roman soldiers chose to remain in the islands, sometimes marrying native women. Some of the natives learned Latin and adopted Roman customs; some became adept at weaving, and the technology of the day. London became an important town, a hub for trading and finance; most roads led eventually to London. Celtic arts largely gave way to Roman, and native religions often became submerged in those of Rome.

But as the Roman Empire gradually declined in power, many troops were withdrawn, and those Celts who had never been willing subjects began to make life hazardous for the Romans who remained. Finally most of the

Romans were gone, though their traces remained in what they had built, in a few words that have ever since been in the language, and in many darkhaired, darkeyed people.

The Germanic Conquerors

Saxons and possibly Angles and other Germanic warriors had dared to confront the shrinking might of Rome in the fourth century A.D., at the same time that Picts and Celts in the north made frequent annoying military gestures. When the Romans removed their garrisons early in the fifth century, those Celts who had become rather soft from Roman-like living were increasingly harassed by the wild northerners. According to the Venerable Bede, who in the eighth century wrote a history that in places may be inaccurate because of the intervening years and the lack of written records, the Celts appealed to the Romans for help, but got little. They then turned to the Saxons, who with Angles, Jutes, and Frisians (the latter not mentioned by Bede, but quite powerful at the time) repelled the Picts and Scots but also made war on their hosts, the Celts, and drove them into what are now Wales, Ireland, and Scotland, or across the Channel to Brittany (French *Bretagne*).

Attracted by the rich soil and a climate milder than they had known in northern Europe, these Germanic people crossed the North Sea in considerable numbers, sometimes bringing their families along. Within a century and a half, despite some temporary setbacks, they controlled nearly all of what we call England—which is named for the Angles: "Angle-land." The Jutes, who according to Bede came from Jutland (now the mainland of Denmark), but who possibly had come from the Rhineland, settled mainly in Kent, in southeastern England. Other parts of the South came under the control of the Saxons; the names *Sussex, Essex,* and *Wessex* mean respectively "land of the South Saxons," "land of the East Saxons," and "land of the West Saxons" (in Old English Suth Seaxan, East Seaxan, West Seaxan). The Angles occupied the much larger section of England to the north of these areas.

These Angles apparently came from Angel, a district of Schleswig in northern Germany. The Saxons, some of whom had earlier conquered much of northwest Germany, were from the same general area as the Angles and resembled them in language and customs.

One additional early development should be mentioned—the coming of Christianity. In the sixth century King Ethelbert of Kent married the daughter of Charibert, the Christian king of Paris. As a result, Augustine, sent by Pope Gregory I as a missionary, was cordially received; he succeeded in Christianizing the Kentish people and prepared the way for the extension of his religion to the rest of England. Linguistically, since the missionaries spoke Latin and mingled with the people, this conversion led to the introduction of many more Latin words than had the earlier military conquest.

However, the priests did not affect greatly the basic language, which by this time was that of the people from the North. "Old English" was basically Anglo-Saxon, with a slight admixture of Celtic and Latin. The name of the language itself, "Englisc," now "English," reveals its German (Anglian) origin. The fundamental grammar and the most common words in our present vocabulary are Germanic.

The Danes

Much of English history in the ninth, tenth, and eleventh centuries is a complicated account of Anglo-Saxon battles against Danish and Norwegian invaders. Sometimes a single shipload of these northmen would swoop down and sack a village; at other times whole armies came in and seized important towns, even London. King Alfred the Great (one of the most impressive figures in history) beat them back, and for a while his descendants did well, but eventually the whole land was conquered and a Danish king mounted the throne. Considerable numbers of Danes settled permanently, often with Anglo-Saxon women as their wives.

The Normans

After Danish King Canute died in 1035, the power of the Danes diminished, and in 1042 the Oxfordshire-born Edward, later known as Saint Edward or Edward the Confessor, became king. Before his death in early 1066, since he was childless and had once been given help by the Normans, he appears to have selected William, duke of Normandy, as his successor. However, he reneged on his deathbed, naming Harold, earl of Wessex, instead. The incensed William raised an army, crossed the Channel, defeated Harold's army and killed him at the Battle of Hastings on October 14, 1066, and made England a Norman state.

The name *Norman* means "northman." The ancestors of these Normans had come down into France from Norway and Sweden, just as their brothers or cousins had come into England. Many remained in France, establishing the province of Normandy, and adopting a variation of the French language as well as many French customs and political institutions.

The Normans who followed William into England, therefore, were a blend of French and Scandinavian cultures. They effected considerable changes in English but did little to alter its essential Germanic characteristics.

The Normans were the last conquerors of England, although fairly numerous settlers from other lands have continued to come in through the intervening centuries. The English language is what it is today because of the many varieties of people who have come to the islands. It apparently shows no remains from the Picts, only a few from the Celts, some from the early Romans and more from the Roman churchmen, very many from the Germanic invaders, some from the Danes, and a considerable amount from the Normans; later, as we shall see, English contacts from around the world greatly enlarged the vocabulary and thus enriched the language.

The Role of Women in Amalgamating Languages

Early history is mainly an account of battles and conquests, filled almost exclusively with names of male leaders. Exceptions are Queen Boadicea, who led Celtic armies against the Romans, Queen Ethelfleda, who successfully beat back Danish armies, and various women who influenced history through marriage to kings or noblemen.

Historians say little of what was a more important role of women, as transmitters of culture, including language. Children, then as now, learned most of their language from their mothers. If a Danish man, for instance, married a Saxon woman, their children would learn mainly English, though with some Danish admixture. Similarly, after the Norman Conquest, women deserve much of the credit for the preservation of the basic characteristics of English. Women, in other words, represented a linguistically conservative force that helped to prevent English from giving way to a different language. Only when intermarriage was relatively infrequent, as between Anglo-Saxons and Celts, was this influence negligible.

THE LINGUISTIC CONTRIBUTIONS OF THE INVADERS

Following a roughly chronological sequence, as in the first section, we will now note the most important linguistic contributions of each of the groups.

The Celts

The Celtic language still survives as Irish Gaelic, Scottish Gaelic, and Manx (in the Isle of Man), and as the considerably different Welsh

(Wales) and Breton (Brittany, in France); the Cornish of Cornwall has only recently become a dead language. A major reason for differences in these languages is that early Celts came to the British Isles at various times and concentrated their settlements in different places.

A surprisingly small number of Celtic words, other than place-names, were taken over by the Anglo-Saxons, and of those few almost none survive: *tor* (high rock or rock pile), and perhaps *dun* (brownish gray) are examples. From the Celts who became Christians during the Roman occupation or later came *cross* (which goes back to Latin *crux*), *curse* (in the religious sense), and several other words that have since become disused. Much later borrowings, mainly from Scottish Gaelic, include *bard, clan, crag, glen, heather, plaid, slogan, whisky,* and a number of others. Among the most recent is Welsh *eisteddfod* "a gathering of poets and musicians."

Surviving place-names, however, are much more numerous, including *London, Cumberland, York, Devon, Dover, Carlisle, Cornwall,* and the names of such rivers as *Thames, Avon, Exe, Esk, Usk,* and *Wye.* If you find on the map of England or the United States names in which the following elements occur, you will be fairly safe in assuming an ultimate Celtic origin: *combe* "a deep valley" (*Holcombe*), *bryn* "hill" (*Bryn Mawr* = "great hill"), *tor* "high rock" (*Torcross*), *brock* "badger" (*Brockhall*), *pen* "hill" (*Pendleton*), as well as others with *win, salis, glou, wor,* and *lich* or *litch.*

The Early Romans

Some Latin words were borrowed by continental Germans and hence were probably already in the vocabularies of the Angles and other tribes before they came to England. A fair number of these still exist; others were used in Old English but have since died out. Here are a few survivors:

L	OE	MOD E
calx "pebble"	cealc	chalk
caupō "trader"	cēap "bargain"	cheap
cāseus	cēse	cheese
cuprum	copor	copper[1]
catillus	cytel	kettle
milium	mil	millet
mustum	must, moste	must "new wine"
pisium	pise, peose	pea
pondō	pund	pound "a weight"
vinum	win	wine

[1] In some instances there have also been later borrowings from the same Latin word. E.g., *cupreous, cupric, cupriferous, cuprite, cupronickel, cuprous.*

In England the Celts adopted a number of Latin words during the early centuries of the Christian era. Some of these were taken over by the Anglo-Saxons, sometimes partly because they may already have heard the word on the continent, but sometimes because physical evidence of the Roman occupation still remained. Thus the Roman-built military camps and fortifications (*castra*) were designated OE *ceaster*, which still survives in place-names like *Rochester, Dorchester, Gloucester, Leicester*. Latin *portus* "harbor" became OE and Mod E *port*. Roman walls (Latin singular *vallum*) were much in evidence; the word became OE *weall*, Mod E *wall*. A Roman road, or *strata via*, was known to the Anglo-Saxons as *strǣt*, Mod E *street*.

With the coming of the Christian missionaries the Anglo-Saxons encountered and adopted many more words, exemplified by:

L	OE	MOD E
abbās[2]	abbud	abbot
accentus	accent	accent
apostolus[2]	apostol	apostle
episcopus[2]	bisceop	bishop
diāconus[2]	dēacon, dīacon	deacon
metrum[2]	mēter	meter
monachus[2]	munuc	monk
pinus	pīn	pine "a tree"
presbyter[2]	prēost	priest
purpura[2] "purple cloth"	purpur	purple
schola	scōl	school
versus "a turning of the plow"	fers	verse

Still other religious words came in from Latin either early or late in the OE period; in their Mod E forms some of these (with Greek ancestry marked by an asterisk) are: *alms** (cf. *eleemosynary*), *angel*, anthem*, ark, candle, chalice, cleric, disciple, hymn*, litany*, martyr*, mass*, nun, pope*, psalm*, relic, shrine, shrive, stole** (n.), *temple*. (The Greeks had borrowed some of the starred words from Semitic languages, which therefore were also indirect contributors to the OE vocabulary.)

Household and miscellaneous words that came into the language from Latin during approximately the same few hundred years include *balsam*, beet, box*, cap, chest*, cook, elephant*, fever, lily, lobster, marshmallow, oyster*, pear, plant, radish, savory*, and *sponge**.

Later borrowings from Latin will be exemplified in later chapters.

---

[2] The Romans had borrowed this word from the Greeks, giving English an indirect Greek admixture.

A very few words reached the Germanic languages directly from Greek in the early period. *Angel* and *devil* may both belong here, but *church* (Greek *kurikon* or *kuriakon,* OE *cirice*) is the only certain one.

The Danes

If you find a rather old English word with the sound of [sk] other than one spelled with *sch,* the odds are fairly good that it entered the language during the time of Scandinavian supremacy. Examples are *bask, scrape, scrub, skill, skin, sky, whisk.* Before the coming of the Danes the Anglo-Saxons had modified [sk] to [š]. In some instances, then, parallel forms of the same word developed. Thus *skirt,* from Old Norse, and *shirt,* from OE, were originally the same word. (Such pairs, of which we'll see more examples later, are called doublets.)

Apparently only forty to fifty Scandinavian words entered written OE, although many more may have been spoken in mixed Danish-English households and worked their way up to being written in later years. Middle English used a considerable number of words evidently Scandinavian in source.

Unlike Celtic and Latin, Scandinavian influenced grammar as well as vocabulary. The sometimes troublesome final *s* in the third person singular of Mod E verbs (e.g., he brings*s*) is attributable to such influence. Middle English rules for using *shall* and *will* essentially followed Scandinavian practice. But most important, as Albert C. Baugh pointed out in *A History of the English Language,* the somewhat different inflectional endings of OE and Scandinavian words tended to be lost when Dane talked with Saxon. After a few centuries, with the further aid of Normans who didn't like to bother with word endings if they deigned to speak English at all, most such endings were lost from English, "happily simplifying English grammar," as Baugh says. (A somewhat parallel case occurred at the end of World War II, when American soldiers were still stationed in parts of Italy. These soldiers, in attempting to converse with Italians, tended to use only root words, ignoring the endings. A few Italians began to do likewise in their conversations with the Americans. Had the Americans remained there indefinitely, in considerable numbers, the Italian language might eventually have lost many of its endings, as English did almost a thousand years ago.)

In addition, Scandinavian influenced the pronunciation and the spelling of a number of words. For example, Old Norse used *systir* for OE *sweostor*; had this not been so, Mod E *sister* might be *swister.* Our pronouns *they, their,* and *them,* which in OE were *hīe, hiera,* and *him,* owe the *th* to the

Scandinavian, which first influenced the Northern dialect forms but by Chaucer's time had resulted in *th* through most of England, although Chaucer still used *hir* and *hem* for the oblique cases, along with his nominative *they*. The present form of the nominative *she* (OE *hēo* or *hīe*) may possibly be attributable to Old Norse *sjā,* although this is not certain.

The Anglo-Saxon Base

Despite contributions by Celts, Romans, Danes, and later the Normans, however, the fact remains that the base of English is the German spoken by the Angles, Saxons, Jutes, and Frisians. Of the twenty thousand most frequently used words in Mod E, about a fifth are of Anglo-Saxon origin, but that fifth includes almost all our commonly used words such as *a, and, be, for, have, in, is, it, of, on, that, the, to, we, will,* and *you*. The only non-Anglo-Saxon word that reaches the level of high frequency is *very*. The King James Bible consists of 94 per cent Anglo-Saxon-based words, 6 per cent borrowed words; in Shakespeare the proportions are 90 and 10. Of the 151 words in the paragraph you are now reading, about 82 per cent are from Anglo-Saxon or its Germanic relatives, although no special care was taken to make it come out that way.

It is true that in Mod E a higher proportion of our words are derived from Latin, and from other languages such as French and Greek, than from Anglo-Saxon. But of the borrowed words, the majority are not used at all by most people; they tend to be esoteric, specialized, more or less technical words. It is largely with Anglo-Saxon words that we talk with our friends, carry on our everyday business, write our letters and stories and poems, and make love. (The eloquently simple "I love you" consists solely of modernized Anglo-Saxon words, "Ic lufie þē.")

The sounds of English, though akin to those of other I-E languages, have their own Germanic characteristics. (See Grimm's Law, in Chapter 1.) Although many of the sounds have been modified since the coming of the Anglo-Saxons, our phonology is still at bottom what they brought with them.

Perhaps even more important than the Anglo-Saxon base of the Mod E vocabulary and sound system is the fact that Mod E grammar, with some modifications, is that brought to the British Isles by the Angles and their Germanic kinsmen. English grammar is Germanic, not Latin, in syntax and morphology. The mistake made repeatedly by many grammarians and teachers—a mistake that has misled, puzzled, and paralyzed countless millions of school children—has been to teach English grammar as if it were Latin. English is not Latin and never has been.

HINTS ON READING OLD ENGLISH

Unless sometime you take a course in Old English literature, you may never need to read it. Nevertheless it's fun to be able to read at least some of the easier passages from the fairly sizable amount of OE writings still extant. (There would have been much more, but the Danes destroyed many manuscripts during their forays. Remember that in those days, long before Gutenberg and Caxton, books were rare, since copies could be made only by laborious hand-copying.)

Once when a woman asked Edwin Arlington Robinson how she should read his poems, which seemed difficult to her, he replied, "Read them one word after another." The same advice applies to reading OE. Although some of the words have vanished from the language and most were spelled differently than they are today, you will often and unexpectedly notice that an OE word is simply a disguised form of a familiar Mod E word. The arrangement of the words seldom causes difficulty, because it was very similar to the arrangement we still use.

Most histories of the language, before presenting sample passages of OE, describe at length the phonology and the grammar. This procedure is similar to the outmoded method of teaching a foreign language. Modern foreign language teachers, however, plunge students immediately into hearing, speaking, reading, and writing the language, and perhaps move into grammar later. Since I believe that the teaching of OE needs modernizing, we'll dive at once into some reading, and after that proceed to a selective discussion of grammar and phonology.

The Voyage of Ohthere and Wulfstan

Our first piece is from King Alfred. Besides being a conqueror of the Danes, Alfred was for his time a very learned man and was eager to share his knowledge. He translated at length from Latin, and in the passage below he supplemented his translation of a world history by appending an account of the voyage of the Norwegians Ohthere and Wulfstan, a pair of Vikings who had sailed north and then east and then south from their home; their journey, which you can follow on a map, took them over the northern end of the Scandinavian peninsula and into the White Sea. Try to read the following sentences. (Punctuation and capitalization have been modernized; long vowels have been marked.)

Ōhþere sǣde his hlāforde, Ælfrēde cyninge, þæt hē ealra Norðmonna norþmest būde. Hē cwæð þæt hē būde on þæm lande norþweardum wiþ þā Westsǣ.

Are you lost? Only a few words are likely to bother you. You recognize *sǣde,* and perhaps see that you need to insert *to* or translate *sǣde* as "told." *Hlāforde* was earlier *hlāfweard* "loaf warden" or "guardian of the bread"; shortened further, *hlāforde* became *lord.* The placement of *cyninge* beside *Ælfrēde* should suggest the one-syllable form that this word now has. *Ealra* is the possessive "of all." The ð and þ, frequent in OE, are alternative symbols for the *th* sound; Đ is sometimes the capitalized form. *Būde* has left the language; it meant "dwelt." You may recognize *cwæð* by its similarity to *quoth.* Prepositions, like *on* and *wiþ,* are sometimes confusing in OE, since prepositional idioms have changed somewhat; translate each into whatever modern preposition makes the most sense. *Westsǣ* "west sea" is the part of the ocean west of Norway.

Now, except for an occasional parenthetical assist, you're on your own.

Hē sǣde þæt land sīe ("is") swiþe ("very") lang norþ þonan ("thence"), ac ("but") hit is eal wēste ("waste"), būton (Hint: Drop the ending.) on fēawum (Hint: Drop the ending.) stōwum ("places") styccemǣlum ("here and there") wīciað (live) Finnas, on huntoðe on wintra, and on sumera on fiscaþe be ("in") þǣre sǣ.

Time out to talk about *the,* represented above by *þǣre.* Today *the* is a simple, unchanging word, but in OE it shifted chameleonlike according to its surroundings, as this declension shows:

	SINGULAR			PLURAL
	Masc.	Fem.	Neut.	All Genders
Nominative (subject)	sē	sēo	þæt	þā
Genitive (possessive)	þæs	þǣre	þæs	þāra
Dative (with certain prepositions)	þǣm	þǣre	þǣm	þǣm
Accusative (direct object)	þone	þǣre	þæt	þa
Instrumental (with certain prepositions)	þȳ	—	þȳ	

To complicate your life further, you should know that these same forms are often best translated as "that." Also, þā was often a connecting word or an adverb, translated "when" or "then."

Hē sǣde þæt hē æt sumum cirre ("time") wolde ("wanted"; ancestor of our *would*) fandian (Suspect an infinitive when you see an *-an* or *-ian* ending.) hū (Hint: *cū* became *cow; hū* became *?.*) longe þæt land norþrythe ("due north"; literally, "north right") lǣge (Hint: OE *g* often became Mod E *y.*) oþþe ("or") hwæðer ænig mon de norðan þǣm wēstenne (Remember wēste) būde. þā fōr ("went") hē norþryhte be (A preposition) þǣm lande; lēt him ("he kept") ealne weg ("[the] way") þæt wēste land on þæt stēorbord and þā widsǣ on þæt bæcbord ("larboard") þrīe dagas. Þā wæs hē swā feor norþ swā þa hwælhuntan firrest faraþ. Þā fōr hē þāgiet ("still"; literally "then yet") norþryhte swā feor swā hē meahte on þǣm ōþrum ("next") þrīm dagum gesiglan ("sail"; the *ge* prefix, still present in many German verbs, has been lost in English.) Þā bēag ("bent") þæt land þǣr ("there") ēastryhte, oþþe sēo sǣ in on þæt lond, he nysse hwæðer ("knew not which"). Būton hē wisse (Hint: an affirmative form of *nysse*) þæt hē ðǣr bād ("awaited") westanwindes and hwōn ("somewhat") norþan, and siglde þā ēast be lande swā swā ("as far as") hē meahte on fēower dagum gesiglan. Þā sceolde ("must"; ancestor of *should*) hē þǣr bīdan (See bād above.) ryhtnorþanwindes, for þǣm ("because") þæt land bēag þǣr sūþryhte, oþþe sēo sǣ in on þæt land, hē nysse hwæþer. Þā siglde hē þonan sūþryhte be lande swā swā hē mehte on fīf dagum gesiglan. Ðā læg þǣr an micel ("great") ēa ("river") ūp in on þæt land, þā cirdon ("turned") hīe ("they") ūp in on þā ēa for þæm hīe ne dorston ("not dared") forþ bī ("past") þǣre ēa siglan for unfriþe ("hostility"), for þǣm ðæt land wæs eall gebūn ("inhabited") on ōþre healfe ("side"; literally "half") þǣre ēas (Hint: possessive of a noun you've read several times). Ne mētte hē ǣr ("Nor had met he before") nān (Ancestor of *none*) gebūn land, siððan ("since") hē from his āgnum ("own") hām (Hint: OE *a* often changed later to an [o:] sound) fōr. Ac him ("But for him") wæs ealne weg wēste land on þæt stēorbord, būtan ("except for") fiscerum and fugelerum ("fowlers") and huntum, and þæt wǣron eall Finnas; and him ("for him") wæs ā wīdsǣ on þæt bæcbord.

Verbs and Pronouns

Now read through the passage again as rapidly as possible.

For a breather we'll look at a few of the words you have read. Note that some of the verbs have a [d] at or near the end: *sǣde, būde, wolde, siglde.* All are in the past tense. These are examples of the rather oddly named "weak" verbs, whose chief characteristic was a dental sound [d] or [t] in the past tense and past participle; most Mod E verbs are similar: *said, dwelt, scattered, refused, laughed,* etc. In contrast, other past tense verbs, like *fōr* "went" in this passage, were "strong," forming the past tense and past participle by changing the main vowel sound instead of using a dental suffix. For example, *faran* was the infinitive for "go" or "travel," *fōr* was a past singular form, *fōron* was past plural, and *faren* was the past participle. Strong verbs were more numerous in OE than they are in Mod E, but about sixty often-used ones remain, such as *sing, sang, sung,* or *freeze, froze, frozen.*

A few comments now about pronouns, which have changed less than most other classes of words. You noted that *he, his,* and *him* look the same now as in King Alfred's day (although the pronunciations are different). Perhaps you remembered that the Scandinavians were responsible for the change of *hīe* to *they*. Here's a summary of the most common forms of the OE personal pronouns. The dual number was used in referring to two persons, but has vanished. Note the many similarities between the OE and the Mod E forms.

FIRST PERSON

	Singular	Dual	Plural
Nom.	ic	wit	wē
Gen.	mīn	uncer	ūre
Dat.	mē	unc	ūs
Acc.	mē	unc	ūs

SECOND PERSON

	Singular	Dual	Plural
Nom.	þū	git [jIt]	gē [je:]
Gen.	þin	incer	ēower
Dat.	þē	inc	ēow
Acc.	þē	inc	ēow

THIRD PERSON

	Masculine	Feminine	Neuter
Singular			
Nom.	hē	hēo	hit
Gen.	his	hire (hiere)	his
Dat.	him	hire (hiere)	him
Acc.	hine	hīe	hit
Plural (all genders)			
Nom., Acc.		hīe (hī)	
Gen.		hira (hiera, heora)	
Dat.		him	

Try to guess what the later developments in the second person pronoun have been. Also, do you find anywhere in the table a hint to explain why some Americans say "hit" for "it"?

A Selection from the Bible

The lefthand column below is the Biblical parable of the prodigal son (Luke 15:11–32) as translated into the West Saxon dialect of OE. The same story from the King James version (1611) is in the righthand column; it represents early Mod E. See first how much of the OE you can read; then refer to the Mod E for help as needed. (There are minor differences in choice of words.) Later you'll be asked to go back to the OE to look once more at certain words or constructions.

11. Hē [Jesus] cwæð: Sōðlīce sum man hæfde twēgen suna.

11. And he said, A certain man had two sons:

12. þā cwæð sē gingra tō his fæder: "Fæder sele mē mīnne dǣl mīnre ǣhte, þe mē tō gebyreþ." þā dǣlde hē him his ǣhta.

13. Ðā æfter fēawum dagum eall his þing gegaderode sē gingra sunu, ond fērde wrǣclīce on feorlen rīce, ond forspilde þǣr his ǣhta, libbende on his gǣlsan.

14. Ðā hē hīe hæfde ealle āmierrede, þā wearð micel hungor on þām rīce ond hē wearð wǣdla.

15. þā fērde hē ond folgode ānum burgsittendum men þæs rīces; þā sende hē hine tō his tūne þæt hē hēolde his swīn.

16. Ðā gewilnode hē his wambe gefyllan of þām bēancoddum þe ðā swīn ǣton; ond him man ne sealde.

17. þā beþōhte hē hine ond cwæð: "Ēalā, hū fela hȳrlinga on mīnes fæder hūse hlāf genōhne habbað, ond ic hēr on hungre forweorðe.

18. "Ic ārīse, ond ic fare tō mīnum fæder, ond ic secge him: 'Ēalā, fæder, ic syngode on heofenas ond beforan þē;

19. "'nū ic neom wyrðe þæt ic bēo þīn sunu nemned; dō mē swā ānne of þīnum hȳrlingum.'"

20. Ond hē ārās þā ond cōm tō his fæder. Ond þā gīet þā hē wæs feorr, his fæder hē hine geseah, ond wearð mid mildheortnesse āstyred, ond ongēan hine arn, ond hine beclypte ond cyste hine.

21. Ðā cwæð his sunu: "Fæder, ic syngode on heofon ond beforan ðē; nū ic ne eom wyrþe þæt ic þīn sunu bēo genemned."

22. Ðā cwæð se fæder tō his þēowum: "Bringað raðe þone sēlestan gegyrelan ond scrȳdað hine; ond sellað him hring on his hand ond gescȳ tō his fōtum;

12. And the younger of them said to his father, Father, give me the portion of goods that falleth to me. And he divided unto them his living:

13. And not many days after the younger son gathered all together, and took his journey into a far country, and there wasted his substance with riotous living.

14. And when he had spent all, there arose a mighty famine in that land; and he began to be in want.

15. And he went and joined himself to a citizen of that country; and he sent him into his fields to feed swine.

16. And he would fain have filled his belly with the husks that the swine did eat, and no man gave unto him.

17. And when he came to himself, he said, How many hired servants of my father's have bread enough and to spare, and I perish with hunger!

18. I will arise and go to my father, and I will say unto him, Father, I have sinned against heaven, and before thee.

19. And am no more worthy to be called thy son; make me as one of thy hired servants.

20. And he arose, and came to his father. But when he was yet a great way off, his father saw him, and had compassion, and fell on his neck, and kissed him.

21. And the son said unto him, Father, I have sinned against heaven, and in thy sight, and am no more worthy to be called thy son.

22. But the father said to his servants, Bring forth the best robe, and put it on him; and put a ring on his hand, and shoes on his feet.

23. "ond bringað ān fætt styric ond ofslēað; ond uton etan and gewistfullian;

24. "forþām þēs mīn sunu wæs dēad, ond hē geedcucode; hē forwearð, ond hē is gemēt." Ðā ongunnon hīe gewistlǣcan.

25. Sōðlīce his ieldra sunu wæs on æcere, ond hē cōm. Ond þā hē þām hūse genēalæhte hē hīerde þone swēg ond þæt werod.

26. þā clipode hē ānne þēow ond ascode hine hwæt þæt wǣre.

27. Ðā cwæð hē: "þin brōðor cōm; ond þīn fæder ofslōh ān fǣt cealf for þām þe hē hine hālne onfēng."

28. Ðā bealg hē hine ond nolde in gān; þā ēode his fæder ūt ond ongan hine biddan.

29. Ðā cwæð hē his fæder ondswarigende: "Efne swā fela gēara ic þē þēowode, ond ic næfre þīn bebod ne forgīemde; ond ne sealdest þū mē nǣfre ān ticcen þæt ic mid mīnum frēondum gewistfullode.

30. "Ac siððan þēs þīn sunu cōm, þe his spēde mid miltestrum āmierde, þū ofslōge him fǣtt cealf."

31. Ðā cwæð hē: "Sunu, þū eart simble mid mē, ond ealle mīne þing sint þīne.

32. "þē gebyrede gewistfullian ond blissian for þām þēs þīn broþor wæs dēad ond hē geedcucode. Hē forwearð ond hē is gemēt."

23. And bring hither the fatted calf, and kill it; and let us eat, and be merry:

24. For this my son was dead, and is alive again; he was lost, and is found. And they began to be merry.

25. Now his elder son was in the field: and as he came and drew nigh to the house, he heard musick and dancing.

26. And he called one of the servants, and asked what these things meant.

27. And he said unto him, Thy brother is come; and thy father hath killed the fatted calf, because he hath received him safe and sound.

28. And he was angry, and would not go in: therefore came his father out, and intreated him.

29. And he answering said to his father, Lo, these many years do I serve thee, neither transgressed I at any time thy commandment: and yet thou never gavest me a kid, that I might make merry with my friends.

30. But as soon as this thy son was come, which hath devoured thy living with harlots, thou hast killed for him the fatted calf.

31. And he said unto him, Son, thou art ever with me, and all that I have is thine.

32. It was meet that we should make merry, and be glad: for this thy brother was dead, and he is alive again; and was lost, and is found.

Analyzing the Selection

Answer as many of these questions as you can:

11. *a. Līce* was a frequent adverbial ending, which became our *-ly. Sōð* is the older form of the noun *sooth.* What did *soothly* mean before it became obsolete? *b.* Try to think of an expression in which we use *some* as *sum* is

used here. *c. Twegen* in OE was [twe:jən]. What word besides *two* came from it? *d.* What is the tense of *hæfde*? How could you tell without the translation?

12. How does word order differ here from that of today's English?

13. *a.* What familiar German word is cognate with *rīce*? *b.* What might be a direct translation of *forspilde* (more picturesque than *wasted*)?

14. *Micel,* translated here as "mighty" but usually meaning "much," has many relatives. What is the Scottish form? (In other guises, the I-E root **meg* appears in *magnitude* and many other *magn-* words; in *mayor, major, majority*; in *majesty, magistrate, master*; in *May* [the month]; in words from Greek starting with *mega-*, such as *megaton*; in words from Sanskrit such as *maharajah* and *mahatma*.)

15. *a.* What is the modern spelling of *folgode*? of *hēolde*? *b.* What case is *þæs rīces*? *c.* Ponder *burgsittendum* for a moment. What picture of the man do you get?

16. What Mod E word did *wambe* become?

17. *a.* What are the modern forms of *hȳrlinga, hlāf,* and *genōhne*? *b.* What now archaic form of *bepōhte* may you find in literature?

18. Comment on the OE method of showing future tense. Try to think of a modern parallel.

19. In the King Alfred passage we encountered *nysse* "knew not." What similar contraction is here, and what does it mean? Find a different example in verse 28.

20. *a.* Translate *mildheortnesse* as something "more English" than *compassion. b.* What evidence shows that a double subject was not taboo?

21. What is the modern spelling of *genemned*?

22. *a. Fōtum* is the dative plural of *fōt,* which was *fēt* in the nominative and accusative plural. What does this information tell you about the modern forms? *b.* In later OE the *h* in words like *hring* or *hræfn* "raven" was dropped. So was the [k] before [n], although it tended to remain in the spelling even though not pronounced. What are the modern forms of *cniht, cnīf, cnyttan*?

23. What would you guess are modern relatives of *stȳric* and *ofslēað*?

24. OE sentences are mainly paratactic; i.e., they follow main clauses with main clauses, and seldom subordinate one idea to another. How is this generalization illustrated here and in other verses? (The opposite of *paratactic* is *hypotactic,* which refers to subordination.)

25. *a.* How is *æcere* spelled today? *b.* In the King Alfred passage we noted that *ū* in *hū* and *cū* became [au] in later English. What example do you find here? In 28 and 29?

26. What is *ānne* today? What variant is in verse 27?

27. Comment on the use of *þīn*.

28. What form of the verb is *gān*? What are the modern forms of this verb?

29. You may have noted that the OE passages occupy a little more space than the Mod E. Look at some individual words in this verse and try to figure out why this tends to be true.

30. We have seen that many OE past tense verbs used a [d] sound. What exceptions are there? Why no [d] in these?

31. What evidence shows that the *s*-plural has not always prevailed in English?

32. *For þām* (or *for þæm*) literally means "for that." Why is it appropriate to translate it as "because"?

THE SOUNDS OF OLD ENGLISH

In this section we will not attempt a thorough coverage of OE phonology —just sufficient that you will be able to pronounce the words in the preceding passages well enough that King Alfred could understand you if he had patience and a little imagination.

In the absence of recordings, how do we know how the Anglo-Saxons pronounced their sounds? We don't, exactly. But painstaking scholars have pieced together many clues, frequently dependent upon variant spellings. To cite a simple example from later English, the seventeenth century diarist Samuel Pepys more than likely pronounced his name [pi:ps], for a number of contemporary letters referred to him as "Mr. Peeps."

Consonant Sounds

Consonants in OE were pronounced much as they are today, as the following list shows. If necessary, refer to pages 49–53 for help with the symbols.

b [b], as today. Examples: *bēon* "be," *brād* "broad."

c [k] before back vowels (such as [a], [ɔ], [o], [u]) and most consonants. *castel* "castle," *crabba* "crab."

   [č] before front vowels (such as [i], [I]). *cēowan* "chew," *cild* "child."

   [j] with *g*. *ecg* "edge," *brycg* "bridge."

d [d], as today. *dēop* "deep," *drīfan* "drive."

f usually [f], as today, but [v] between voiced sounds. Thus fǣtt was pronounced like Mod E *fat*. In *drīfan* "drive," however, and similar medial positions, the voiced [v] appeared: [dri:van].

g [g], approximately as today, before back vowels and consonants. *gan* "go," *grim* "grim."

[j] before front vowels. *gēar* "year," *gesund* "sound, safe." Also [j] after a front vowel. *dæg* "day," *līeg* "flame."

h usually like today's initial *h*. *hīeran* "hear," *hōc* "hook." In some words, though, it represented sounds no longer in English, one of which was like the sound of *ch* in German *ich*. *lēoht* "light," *cniht* "knight."

l [l], as today. *lond* "land," *leornungcniht* "pupil."

m [m], as today. *mealt* "malt," *mann* "man."

n [n], as today. *nēah* "near," *norþryhte* "northward."

p [p], as today. *papa* "pope," *plantan* "plant."

r [r], as today, though perhaps trilled a bit at the start of a word. *rīce* "kingdom," *faran* "travel."

s usually [s], as today, but [z] between voiced sounds (uttered with vibration of the vocal cords; vowels are voiced, and certain consonants, especially [b], [d], [g], [ð], [v], [z]). *syllan* "give, sell," *steorra* "star," but *cēosan* "choose," *ciese* "cheese." With *c*, pronounced [š]. *scip* "ship," *scortlīce* "shortly," *fisc* "fish."

t [t], as today. *tam* "tame," *trēo* "tree."

w [w], as today, *wæter* "water," *weorð* "worth."

x [ks], as today; rare. *weaxan* "grow, wax."

Note that the combination *sc* was pronounced like Mod E *sh*. Knowing this, you can see that *scēap* and *sceal* were much like our *sheep* and *shall*.

The combination *ng* was pronounced [ŋ], as today. The symbol þ or ð stood for [θ], or between voiced sounds, for [ð].

The letters *j, q,* and *v* did not appear in OE, although the sounds that they now represent were used: *ecg* "edge," *cwēn* "queen," *lūfian* "love." *Y* was used only as a vowel.

When consonants were doubled, as in *sittan* "sit," they were held a little longer.

Vowel Sounds

If you know a continental European language, and if you pronounce OE vowels about as they are in that language, the chances are good that your pronunciation will be close to that of OE. The following list shows the usual sounds. Since there were fewer oddities in OE spelling than in Mod E, after you learn the pronunciation of a vowel in a key word you are not likely to encounter many exceptions.

æ   [æ],   as in *fæst* "fast, secure," or Mod E *hat*.

ǣ   [æ:],   as in *ǣfre* "ever." (Essentially the same sound as that of æ, but prolonged slightly.)

a   [a]   as in *papa* "pope" or Mod. Amer. E *hot*. Many such words later developed the [æ] sound; thus OE [and] became Mod E [ænd].

ā   [a:],   as in *āc* "oak." [a:] often became [o:] in later English; thus *hām* became *home*. (The marks above long vowels, in this book and in other modern transcriptions, have been supplied to aid in pronunciation.)

e   [ɛ],   as in *menn* "men."

ē   [e:],   as in *fēt* "feet," or Mod. E *slay*.

i   [I],   as in *tin* "tin."

ī   [i:],   as in *līf* "life." (Note that an OE [i:] usually became the Mod E [aI] as the example shows.)

o   [ɔ],   as in *moððe* "moth."

ō   [o:],   as in *sona* "soon."

u   [ʌ],   as in *sunne* "sun."

ū   [u:],   as in *hūs* "house." (As we have noted, this sound tended to change later to [au:].)

y   [I],   as in *synn* "sin." (See next paragraph.)

ȳ   [i:],   as in *nȳdes* "needs." (See next paragraph.)

The *y* sounds given are not quite accurate for OE, in which they were like the umlauted German *ü,* as in *Süden* "south," or *Kühe* "cows"—a rounded front vowel no longer heard in English words. It was apparently losing the rounding in late OE, as is shown by the increasing substitution of *i* for *y* in spelling.

In a number of OE words you may also encounter the diphthongs *ēa* and *ēo,* as in *scēap* "sheep" and *sēoðan* "seethe," pronounced [ɛ:ə] and [e:ə] respectively. Later, as the examples show, these tended to become [i:]. The forms *ea* and *eo* also appear in many OE words, such as *sealt* "salt," *seolfor* "silver," *orceard* "orchard," *neoþan* "beneath," *heardheort* "hardhearted." These were probably somewhat similar, probably like [ɛə].

Two further comments: The accent in OE words was pretty uniformly on the first syllable, except for words with prefixes like *ge*. Also, a final *e* was not silent, but was pronounced as [ɛ] or perhaps more often as [ə].

For practice, you may want to go back to the selections from King Alfred and the Bible and attempt to read the passages aloud, somewhat as they would have sounded a millennium ago.

A FEW MORE NOTES ON OLD ENGLISH GRAMMAR

Inflections in Verbs

A major characteristic of I-E languages is that by inflectional endings in nouns and adjectives they indicate case, number, and gender, and in verbs may show tense, person, number, voice, and mood. This characteristic is much more evident in OE than in Mod E, which has lost the majority of endings.

OE verbs, you recall, were either strong or weak, although a few did not fit clearly into either category. The strong verbs fell into seven classes, based upon the vowels used in the root syllable. The weak verbs, characterized by a dental [d] or [t] in the past tense and past participle, fell into three conjugations. The mixed group included a number of common verbs, such as the OE equivalents of *can, may, own, be, do, go,* and *will*. (The explanation of our highly dissimilar forms of *be*—*am, is, are, was, were, being, been* —is that the OE verb form came from three different roots.)

Here are examples of the classes of strong verbs. These older forms illustrate why the modern ones are "irregular"—i.e., strong. The usual sequence of root vowel sounds is also indicated in the list, although some exceptions did occur, especially in the infinitive.

	INFINITIVE	1ST PAST SING.	PAST PL.	PAST PART.
Class I	rīsan "rise," *ī*	rās, *ā*	rison, *i*	risen, *i*
Class II	flēogan "fly," *ēo*	flēah, *ēa*	flugon, *u*	flogen, *o*
Class III	drincan "drink," *ī*	dranc, *a*	druncon, *u*	druncen, *u*
Class IV	brecan "break," *e*	bræc, *æ*	brǣcon, *ǣ*	brocen, *o*
Class V	etan "eat," *e*	æt, *æ*	ǣton, *ǣ*	eten, *e*
Class VI	scacan "shake," *a*	scōc, *ō*	scōcon, *ō*	scacen, *a*
Class VII	blōwan "blow"	blēow	blēowon	blōwen[3]

We'll glance now at the conjugation of an OE strong verb. The example is *helpan* "help," which like a number of others later became weak. (Small

[3] The root vowels in Class VII verbs varied, although *ēo* generally appeared in past forms.

children, and some older children and adults, would find the language easier to learn and use if a similar change had occurred in other OE strong verbs. One note of consolation is that the several hundred OE strong verbs have been reduced to about sixty, either through being replaced by different verbs or through becoming weak.)

PRESENT INDICATIVE			PRESENT SUBJUNCTIVE	
1st singular	helpe		1st singular	helpe
2nd singular	hilpst			
3rd singular (all persons)	hilpþ			
Plural (all persons)	helpaþ		Plural	helpen

PRESENT IMPERATIVE			PRESENT PARTICIPLE
2nd singular	help		helpende
1st plural	helpan		
2nd plural	helpaþ		

PAST INDICATIVE			PAST SUBJUNCTIVE	
1st singular	healp		1st singular	hulpe
2nd singular	hulpe			
3rd singular	healp			
Plural (all persons)	hulpon		Plural	hulpen

PAST PARTICIPLE
holpen

An awareness of the OE forms of this verb goes far to explain why even today some speakers say things like "He hulp (or *holp*) me" or "He had hulpen me." Similarly, when one knows that *climb* (OE *climban*) once had past forms like *clamb, clomb, climbon,* and *clumben,* he can understand reasons for forms such as "I clumb (or *clim*) the tree" and "I have clumb." Awareness may replace contempt with interest and compassion.

In the conjugation of the weak verb *macian* "make" that follows, you will see that the personal endings are about the same as for strong verbs but that *d* appears consistently in past forms.

PRESENT INDICATIVE			PRESENT SUBJUNCTIVE	
1st singular	macie		1st singular	macie
2nd singular	macast			
3rd singular	macaþ			
Plural (all persons)	maciaþ		Plural	macien

PRESENT IMPERATIVE			PRESENT PARTICIPLE
2nd singular	maca		maciende
1st plural	macian		
2nd plural	maciaþ		

PAST INDICATIVE			PAST SUBJUNCTIVE	
1st singular	macode		1st singular	macode
2nd singular	macodest			
3rd singular	macode			
Plural (all persons)	macodon, macedon		Plural	macoden

PAST PARTICIPLE
macod

Numerous though OE verb endings were, they were less so than in Latin and other I-E languages, in which a complete conjugation might fill a couple of these pages. The OE endings, as we shall see, were for the most part lost; survivals may be observed in the King James Bible, where forms like "thou helpest" and "he helpeth" are common. Today, except for third person singular forms like *makes,* a common past tense form like *helped,* and participial endings like *-ing* or *-en* (the latter in strong verbs only), the inflectional endings have disappeared.

Inflections in Nouns

Like the verb, the OE noun had several inflectional endings, although already the reduction of such endings had become apparent: nominative and accusative forms had merged, and the dative and instrumental (corresponding roughly to the Latin ablative case) were also usually the same.

The classification of OE nouns is complex, and no details need be presented here. Fairly representative of a declension is this for *fisc* "fish":

SINGULAR		PLURAL	
Nom., Acc.	fisc	Nom., Acc.	fiscas
Gen.	fisces	Gen.	fisca, fiscana
Dat.	fisce	Dat.	fiscum

In some nouns, especially neuter, a *u* ending signified nominative and accusative plural; a few others, like *word* "word" and *wæter* "water," had the same form in singular and plural; occasionally *e* or *a* indicated plural; and our words *oxen, kine,* and the archaic *shoon* "shoes" reflect the former existence of a number of *n* plurals.

Perhaps some of your students will sometime ask why some of our plurals, like *teeth, feet, men, women, mice, lice,* and *geese,* differ from others. Why don't we, for instance, say "foots"? As usual, there's a historical explanation: the OE plural forms in these very common words have survived. Thus OE *fōt* was pluralized as *fēt, tōþ* as *tēþ, mann* as *menn, wīfmann* "woman" as *wīfmenn, mūs* as *mȳs, lūs* as *lȳs,* and *gōs* as *gēs.*

One of the important simplifications in English grammar has been the loss of grammatical gender (largely unrelated to sex) in nouns, which led to a corresponding loss in adjectives and some pronouns, especially the demonstratives like *this* and *that*. If you have studied Latin or a modern continental language, you are aware of the need to remember whether a word like the one for *table* is masculine, feminine, or neuter. You *have* to remember, because otherwise you won't know what gender of pronoun or what form of the article or adjective to use with it. (Mark Twain, complaining about gender in German, said that every masculine noun that seems to be feminine is actually neuter.) In OE *dæg* "day" was masculine, but *niht* "night" was feminine; *wæter* "water" was neuter, but *dēaw* "dew" was masculine; *hrycg* "ridge" was masculine, but *brycg* "bridge" was feminine. Probably Anglo-Saxon children had no great trouble in learning distinctions that they had heard in the cradle, but with today's great increase in nouns the problem in learning such a non-system would be acute, and foreigners learning English would have even more difficulties than they already have. Our modern system is very simple. Most nouns are neuter, so that we can refer, for instance, to *day, night, water, dew, ridge,* or *bridge* as "it," and we can use an adjective like *pretty* before any noun without changing its form because of gender or any other reason. Only if a noun is clearly masculine or feminine in meaning, like *boy* or *girl,* do we need to use *he* or *she* instead of *it.*

Inflections in Adjectives

As has just been implied, the form of an OE adjective was determined by the noun that it described: singular or plural; masculine, feminine, or neuter; strong, used when no defining element such as an article accompanied the noun, or weak, used when there was such an element. So an adjective like *gōd* "good" had nine or ten different forms.

In OE adjectives we can see in the comparative and superlative forms the explanation of our own familiar *-er, -est* comparisons. Here are a few examples:

ceald "cold"	cealdra	cealdost
brād "broad"	brǣdra	brǣdest
hēah "high"	hīehra, hīerra	hīehst
inne "inside"	innera	innemest

Words like *innemest* developed into Mod E words with *-most*: *inmost* (or *innermost*), *northmost,* and *utmost* (from *ūt* "out"), for example.

The following list traces a few oddities of Mod E comparisons back to OE:

gōd "good"	betera, betra	betest, betst
lȳtel "little"	lǣssa	lǣst
micel "great, much"	māra	mǣst
yfel "bad"	wiersa	wierst

Simple demonstrative pronouns, which doubled as articles like our *the,* likewise had forms that varied according to gender, number, and case. We encountered these on page 70. For the equivalent of Mod E *this,* the forms were as follows:

	MASCULINE	FEMININE	NEUTER
Singular			
Nom.	þēs, þes	þēos	þis
Gen.	þisses	þisse, þissere	þisses
Dat.	þissum	þisse, þissere	þissum
Acc.	þisne	þās	þis
Inst.	þȳs, þis		þȳs, þis
Plural (all genders)			
Nom., Acc.		þās	
Gen.		þissa, þissera	
Dat.		þissum	

No doubt in everyday conversation such elaborate differentiation of endings was often ignored. There is manuscript evidence that even before the coming of the Normans, the Anglo-Saxons themselves were moving toward reduction of these inflections as well as others.

Adverbs

OE adverbs were based on pronouns, nouns, or adjectives, as ours still are. *Hēr, þær,* and *hwær* are typical of the pronoun-based group. (Note that in the spelling of words like *hwær* and *hwȳ* the order of the *h* and *w* corresponds to the order of sounds but that this is not true of our *where* and *why.*)

Often the Anglo-Saxons attached *ē* to an adjective, making it into an adverb: *soð + e = soðe* "truly," *wīd + e = wīde* "widely." Sometimes, though, an adjective such as *dēop* "deep" was enlarged to, say, *dēoplīc,* literally "deeplike"; the *e* would once more be added to form the adverb *dēoplīce* "deeply." The *līce* came to be regarded as an adverbial ending. In its shortened form, *-ly,* it has come to be the customary indicator of most of our adverbs. (As a teacher, though, be sure not to repeat the mistake of one young lady, who informed her class that an adverb is any word ending in *-ly*. She had trouble when one student gave *July* as an example. Adjectives like *lovely, lively, ugly,* and *kindly* might have caused her still more trouble.)

Some purists have objected to sentences like "He works *nights*," on the ground that a noun cannot be used as an adverb. However, the practice dates back over a thousand years, *nihtes* "by night" and *dæges* "by day" being found frequently in OE, as well as *hām* in a sentence like "He stayed *home*." Other noun-based adverbs involve combination with a preposition: *tōdæge* "today," *tōmorgen* "tomorrow" (*morgen* meant "morning"), *ofdūne* "down" (literally "off the hill").

Some adverbs were not compared at all; others used *-or* or *-ost* endings, as in *frēondlīce* "friendly," *frēondlīcor, frēondlīcost*. These endings of course became our *-er* and *-est*. The adverb *wel* "well" was compared with *bet, betst,* the ancestors of our *better, best*; and the comparisons of *yfele, micle,* and *lȳtle* were like those of their adjectival counterparts (page 83).

Word Order

Mod E sentences follow the basic word order of OE sentences, which was usually subject–verb–complement. One difference was that in dependent clauses OE placed the verb last. For example, in the King Alfred selection you encountered . . . *þæt hē ealra Northmonna norþmest būde* "that he of all Northmen farthest north dwelt." Modern German dependent clauses are still so constructed. After *þā* "then, when" the verb usually preceded the subject, as in *þā fōr hē norþryhte* "Then went he straight north." The same practice was usual after *ne* "not," as it still is after our *nor,* as in ". . . nor had he any money." Finally, when a pronoun occurred as object of the verb, it generally preceded the verb, as in verse 20 of the Biblical selection, . . . *his fæder hē hine geseah* "his father he him saw."

Dialects

The map on page 336 shows the homes of four OE dialects. Kentish, most histories of the language have said, was the dialect of the Jutes, but it is possible that Bede's *Iutae* were actually Frisians. West Saxon, in which most surviving manuscripts were written, represents the areas where most Saxons settled. Both Mercian and Northumbrian were predominantly Anglian. *Mercian* (OE Mierce) meant "men of the border," referring to the often bloodied border with Wales, to which many Celts had been driven. *Northumbrian* means simply "north of the Humber river."

The differences in these dialects were not great, but some of them have persisted in one way or another to the present. Thus, especially in uneducated speech today, a listener can hear a number of differences between the language of a person from Kent and one from Gloucestershire in the Midlands, and both of these differ from the speech of a Yorkshireman in the north. As we shall note later, the differences have also influenced dialects in the United States.

ACCOUNTING FOR SOME OF THE WORDS OF MODERN ENGLISH

Sections similar to this appear in several chapters of this book. Their purpose is to provide you with background concerning some of the unusual or historically interesting words that appear in Mod E, in order that you can answer questions raised by students or can comment on certain words encountered in literature.[4]

also, yes, no. OE *eal* "all" when combined with *swā* "so" meant "quite so." As we use *also,* it still means "quite in the same manner." It has been hypothesized that *yes* may be derived from *gēa* "yea" and *swā,* but an alternative derivation says that *yes* combines *gēa* and *sīe* "may it be." Our informal "yeah" may be just a changed pronunciation of *gēa. No* comes from OE *ne* "not" and *ā* "ever."

answer. In early OE an *andswaru* was a "swearing in reply," often a statement made under oath in reply to an accusation. Today the word has been weakened and generalized to indicate any sort of reply.

beads. One meaning of OE *biddan* (from which our *bid* is derived) was "to pray." The noun *bede,* based on *biddan,* meant "a prayer." To keep count of how many prayers had been said, people began hanging around their necks strings on which bits of wood, glass, stones, or even jewels were placed so that they could be moved. This religious significance of beads still exists, but they now more often have only a decorative function.

bedstead and its relatives. Originally a *bedstead* was just the place where a bed stood: OE *bed* "bed" + *stede* "place." Gradually it came to refer to the frame of the bed itself. *Stede* "place" still exists in *stead,* e.g.,

[4] Information in this section is in part based upon the *Oxford English Dictionary,* the *American Heritage Dictionary, Webster's Third New International Dictionary,* J.B. Greenough and G.L. Kittredge's *Words and Their Ways in English Speech,* E. Weekley's *The Romance of Words,* G. Jennings' *Personalities of Language,* C. Laird's *The Miracle of Language,* C. and H. Laird's *The Tree of Language,* G.P. Krapp and A.H. Marckwardt's *Modern English: Its Growth and Present Use,* W. Funk's *Word Origins and Their Romantic Stories,* W.B. Garrison's *Why You Say It.*

"in my stead," in the compound preposition *instead*, in *steadfast*, in *homestead*, and in *steady*, which means "firmly in place."

brand. OE *brand* was a "piece of burning wood." Someone got the idea of identifying his cattle or other possessions by burning a sign on them with such a *brand*. The word then came to refer to the sign itself. Criminals sometimes had to wear a brand; more often, it was burned on wooden kegs for liquor or fish. Today a brand name is, of course, usually just printed, technology having outmoded this use of fire. Cattle, however, are still in many places burned with a "branding iron."

brood. OE *brōd* meant "warmth," and was used to refer to the warmth necessary for eggs to be hatched by birds or, later, domestic fowls. Gradually the word came to refer to the baby birds hatched in this way, and, as a verb, to the act of sitting on eggs. A hen that sits on eggs doesn't seem to be doing anything; by extension, a person who just sits inactive is now said to "brood." In modern "brooder houses" the avian warmth is replaced by other heating methods.

clue. It may be hard to see any relationship between a clue and a ball of thread, but it may be easier if you recall the story of Theseus, who killed the monster called the Minotaur that lived in a labyrinth. To make sure that Theseus could find his way back, his sweetheart, Ariadne, gave him a ball of thread which he could unwind to mark his path. Such a ball was called *clewe* in Middle English, from OE *cliewen* or *clewen*. Today whatever may be used to help solve a problem or a mystery is called a *clue*, still sometimes spelled *clew*.

crank. In OE *crancstæf* "a weaving instrument," *cranc* referred to a part that turned. This meaning still exists in our mechanical term *crank*. But why is a person sometimes called a "crank?" Possibly because he has a twisted or "turned" personality. And when Milton in "L'Allegro" refers to "Quips and *cranks* and wanton wiles," he means unexpected "turns of words," or conceits, as the Elizabethans called them.

crib. In OE, *cribb* meant "ox stall" and was so used to indicate the birthplace of Jesus. *Cribba* were built in churches at Christmas time, sometimes containing a live ox. Gradually the meaning of the word changed to "the bed of infant Jesus," and then through generalization to the bed of any infant.

dairy, lady. An OE *dæge* was a female breadmaker. She usually had other tasks, however, such as milking and churning. In Middle English the place where she did much of her work was called in her honor a *daierie*, from which our *dairy* comes, as does the first part of *dairymaid*. The dairymaid and the lady are probably sisters under the skin, though. *Lady* is from OE *hlāfdige* "kneader of the loaf"; remember that her husband, the lord, was a *hlāfwēard* "guardian of the loaf." The last part of *hlāfdige* is apparently from the same ultimate source as *dæge*—a weakened unstressed form.

durst, dast, holp, clumb. As noted on page 80, there are historical reasons (OE forms of the verbs) that explain why some people say "holp," "clumb," etc. Similar is *durst,* which often in the nineteenth century and still in some places today, was and is pronounced "dast." In the Alfred passage you encountered *dorston,* a verb form meaning "dare," which suggests why *durst* or *dast* is an occasional form of *dare, dares,* or *dared.*

elder, eldest, older, oldest. For *old* OE used both *eald* and *ald*. Different spellings of the comparative and superlative degrees also existed. For many years after that, *elder* and *eldest* were generally used, but *older* and *oldest* have gradually superseded them, so that today *elder* and *eldest* are unusual if not archaic.

English. As indicated earlier, *England* and *English* come from *Angle,* the name of some of the Germanic conquerors. They came from Angel or Angul, which got its name from *angul* "fishhook," which in turn came from an Old German verb meaning "to bend." In Holstein, Germany, a river valley had the shape of a fishhook, so the area was called *Angel* or *Angul*. In the British Isles, possibly because of Celtic influence, *Angle* became *Engle*. If we adhered to earlier meanings, *England* would mean "land of the fishhook," and *English* would mean "like a fishhook." Modern *angler* and *angling* come from the same source.

enthrall. Today, if you are *enthralled* by something, you are held spellbound, charmed, or captivated by it. Thus one may be enthralled by a painting, by a symphony, or by a person of the opposite sex. Historically, one who was enthralled was made a slave. The OE word for "slave" or "bondage" was *þrǣl*.

fret. OE *fretan* meant "to devour." (Modern German *fressen* still has that meaning.) One still-current meaning of *fret* is "to gnaw or wear away," and another is "a hole made by abrasion or erosion." More commonly, though, it means "to worry." This represents a figurative extension of the original meaning; i.e., one who *frets* is devoured by worry.

gossip. In OE a relative or a very good friend was a *sibb*. (Our *sibling* comes from this source.) *Gōd* meant "good." A *gōdsibb*, like a *godparent* today, was a "good relative," a sponsor of an infant. *Gōdsibba* of the same child or of children in the same family were often close friends who talked long and frequently together. The word gradually came to refer to them as talkers—sometimes slightly malicious talkers perhaps—and then to the conversation itself: our *gossip*.

grit and its relatives.   I-E had a root **ghreu-* "to rub or grind," which has a varied progeny. OE *grēot* "sand or gravel" was one of them, today's form being *grit*, such as chickens need; a person who has *grit* "pluck" may be said to have traction or stick-to-it-iveness such as sand gives a car on slippery surfaces. OE *grytt* gave us *grits*, referring to ground grain that is somewhat sandlike before cooking (and sometimes after). Our *gruel* comes from the French form of **ghreu-*. OE *grēat* "coarse, large" gave us *great*. A Middle Dutch *grūwen* "to abhor" was a cousin of Middle English *grue*, which gave us *gruesome*. The ancient Greeks spelled **ghreu-* as *khrōs* and *khrōma* "texture, skin, complexion, color"; from that source we get words like *chromatic, chrome, chromium, Kodachrome*. Finally, it seems that the Celts used **graw-* for "coarse sand," corresponding to French *grave*, the ancestor of our *gravel*.

Halloween.   In OE, *hālga* was used to refer to a holy person, a saint. The word was closely related to *hālig* "holy," *hālgian* "to consecrate," and several others. Later, All-Hallows Day (with *Hallows* still meaning "Saints") came to be celebrated on November 1. The evening before it was *All-Hallow-even,* shortened to *Halloween*. It is ironic that this religious eve has come to be regarded by some as a time to raise hell, although there is precedent in the fact that for the ancient Celts this night was "the night of all the witches."

heathen.   Rivalry or distrust between urban and rural dwellers has long existed. In OE times the term *hǣðen* was used by town folks to designate people who lived on the *hǣþ* "heath." Christianity reached the *hǣðen* later than it did the townspeople, who began to use the term to show contempt for the country dwellers' lack of religion—an unChristian attitude, perhaps.

homonyms.   Most homonyms are the result of chance. A few of those with OE background are the following:

ere, air, heir, e'er.   *Ere* was in OE *ǣr* "before." *Air* entered the language later through Old French from Latin and Greek. *Heir* also came in through Old French from a different Latin word. *E'er* is a now seldom-used contraction of *ever*.

gilt, guilt.   OE *gyldan* meant "to cover with a thin layer of gold." *Gilt* comes from its past tense and past participle. *Guilt* comes from another

OE word, *gylt* "responsibility for a wrong-doing." When *y* changed from an umlauted pronunciation, the words became homonyms.

hail, hale. *Hail* referring to ice pellets came from OE *hagol*. *Hail* meaning "to greet" or "to summon" (e.g., a taxi) is from an old greeting, "Wæs hæl," meaning "Be healthy." *Hale* as in "hale and hearty" is from the Northern or Scottish form *hāl* "whole or sound." *Hale* as in "haled into court" is from a Norman French word, *haler*. The four once-different pronunciations merged in Middle or Modern English.

there, their. OE *þ̄ær* meant "there." One form of the word for "their" was *hiera*. Under Danish influence, the latter became *their,* which even in medieval times sounded almost like *there.*

to, too, two. *Tō* "to" and *twegen* or *twa* "two" were obviously not homonyms in OE. However, the latter went through a series of changes in pronunciation in ME, emerging as a homonym of *to*. *Too* entered ME as an emphatic form of *to,* meaning "in addition to."

hussy. Nearly any housewife would resent being called a "hussy," but *hussy* and *housewife* are basically the same word, OE *hūswȳf*. Perhaps because some housewives had characteristics that other people considered undesirable, the word achieved low reputation. But since *housewife* was a needed word and most housewives did not want to be slandered, the pejorative term gradually acquired a different pronunciation.

last. The Mod E adjective *last* was *latost* in OE, the second consonant being dropped later as it also was in *betst* or *betost,* although the *t* remains in *later* and *better*. The verb *last* is from a different word, the OE verb *lǣstan* "to continue." And the noun *last* (a footlike shape used by shoemakers) comes from a related but different source, OE *last* "sole, footprint."

let. Tennis or table tennis players may refer to a "net ball," but technically and officially it is a "let ball," one whose flight during serve is hindered or altered by hitting the top of the net. In OE, *lettan,* the source of this *let,* meant "to hinder." A different word, *lǣtan,* meant "to permit." They became confused and eventually merged, so that today *let* has two opposed meanings: "to hinder" and "to permit." The meaning of "hinder" also appears redundantly in the legal phrase "without *let or hindrance.*"

lewd. Today a *lewd* act or person is lustful, licentious, "dirty." Not so in the past. OE *lǣwede* simply meant "lay," i.e., pertaining to laymen, anyone not a member of the clergy. Perhaps the use of the word by the clergy brought the word to its present low estate. For example, when clergymen referred to laymen's actions as "lewd" they often had to censure those actions, so that *lewd* gradually came to be a word of dispraise.

names of days.   Our names of days are of mixed origin.

Sunday.   OE *Sunnandæg* "day of the sun," translated from the Latin *dies solis.* It became a holiday (which is from OE for "holy day") because Christ was resurrected on that day.

Monday.   OE *Mōnandæg* "day of the moon," translated from Latin *lunae dies.*

Tuesday.   OE *Tīwesdæg* "day of Tīw." The Old Norse god *Tyr* or *Tiw* was the son of Woden.

Wednesday.   OE *Wōdnesdæg* "day of Woden." The name of Woden, a Norse god comparable to Mercury, is preserved here.

Thursday.   OE *þuresdæg* "Thor's day." Norse Thor was the equivalent of Jupiter or Jove. The Latin name for the day was *dies jovis* "day of Jove."

Friday.   OE *frīgedæg* "day of Frigg." Frigg, or Freya, was a Norse goddess approximating Venus. Her husband was Woden, her son Thor. The Romans called the day *dies veneris* "day of Venus."

Saturday.   OE *sæternesdæg* "Saturn's day," adapted from the Latin *saturni dies* "day of Saturn." He was a Roman god of sowing.

names of flowers.   Although many names of flowers are of Latin origin or, like *fuchsia,* are based on people's names, some are of OE origin, often descriptive of the imagined appearance.

cowslip.   OE *cū* "cow" + *slyppe* "slime, dung." Though the cowslip is praised in romantic songs and other poetry, its name obviously has a decidedly unromantic origin, perhaps attributable to the fact that the flower grows frequently in pastures. Mod E *slip, slippery, slop,* and *sloppy* may also be derived from *slyppe.*

cranesbill.   OE *cran* "crane" + *bile* "beak."

crowfoot (which includes the *buttercup,* also from OE). OE *crāwe* + *fōt.*

daisy.   OE *dæges* "of the day" + *ēage* "eye." Chaucer wrote:

> Wele by reson men it calle may
> The *dayeseye* or ellis the eye of day.

forget-me-not.   OE *forgietan* "forget" + *mē* + *ne;* however, the flower probably got its name as a translation of Old French *ne m'oubliez mie.*

names of months.   All our names of months come from Latin. The Anglo-Saxons, as an agricultural people, called them by the following earthy names:

January.   W*ulf-mōnaþ* "wolf-month," because hungry wolves entered villages then.

February. *Sprote-Kalemōnaþ* "the month when cabbages sprout."

March. *Hlyd-mōnaþ* "boisterous month," because of the wind.

April. *Ēaster-mōnaþ.*

May. *þrīmilce-mōnaþ* "month of three milkings," because cows eating plentiful grass could be milked three times a day.

June. *Sēre-mōnaþ* "dry month."

July. *Mǣd-mōnaþ* "meadow-month," since meadows bloomed then.

August. *Wēod-mōnaþ* "weed-month."

September. *Hǣrfest-mōnaþ* "harvest-month."

October. *Wīn-mōnaþ* "wine-month."

November. *Blōt-mōnaþ* "sacrifice-month," because cattle were sometimes sacrificed then; also *Wind-mōnaþ.*

December. *Midwintra-mōnaþ* "midwinter month," or, by Christians, *Hālig-mōnaþ* "holy month."

naughty. OE *nāwiht,* which became *naught,* meant "nothing," "not at all." The Middle English *nauhty* had a related meaning, "worthless." That which is worthless is supposedly bad, so the idea of "evil" crept in. When Shakespeare referred to "a good deed in a *naughty* world," he was calling the world not so much worthless as evil, wicked. Since his time, though, the word has relaxed its meaning to "mischievous." Today we may refer to a child as "naughty," but not to a murderer, as Shakespeare might have done.

near, neighbor. *Near* is historically a comparative, though now used as a positive, with *nearer,* which historically means "more nigher," as our comparative. The OE word for "nigh" was *nēah,* comparative *nēahra* or *nēarra,* superlative *niehst. Near* and *next* come from these forms, literally "nigher" and "nighest," but these meanings have been forgotten. The first part of *neighbor* comes from *nēah;* the whole word was *nēahgebūr* "nigh-dweller," so its meaning has not changed.

nickname. OE *ēaca,* "also, in addition" developed into Middle English *eke. An ekename* was "an additional name" applied to someone. The *n* from *an* got moved to the noun, giving *a nekename,* which developed into our *nickname.* (See also *nonce.*)

nightmare, mermaid. *Mara* "evil spirit" and *mearh* "female horse" are confused in *nightmare,* which should have no equine associations. Supposedly a nightmare is caused by an evil spirit (*mara*) that comes in the night. The unrelated OE word *mere* "lake, sea" is preserved in Mod E *mermaid.* (Incidentally, OE *mere* shows cousinship with Latin *mare* "sea" and French *mer* "ocean," but is not borrowed from either. All go back to

IE *mori- "body of water," as do Mod E *morass, marsh, meerschaum, marine, maritime, Muriel,* and other words.)

nonce. A nonce word is one coined for a particular occasion and perhaps not used again; e.g., *boxucopia* for a box filled with goodies. The word *nonce* is shortened from a phrase *for then once,* which through misunderstanding became *for the nonce.* Similarly a child may say "a napple" for "an apple." Misunderstanding may also result in the movement of *n* in the other direction: *an adder* was formerly *a naddre* (OE *nædre* "snake"). Similar is the story of *apron* and *umpire,* and, from foreign languages, *orange* and *alligator.*

nostril, thrill. These seemingly unrelated words come from the same source, OE *þyrl* "hole." A *nōsþyrl* was a "nose hole." A Middle English verb based on *þyrl* was *thirlen,* later *thrillen* "to make a hole, to pierce." (A similar example of making a noun into a verb occurs in the modern golfer's expression "He *holed* out.") Someone observed that strong emotion has a piercing quality, at least figuratively, and *thrill* took on that meaning, "pierce with emotion."

once, twice, thrice. These words are based on the genitives of the OE words for *one, two, three: ānes, twȳes, þrȳes.* Thus adjectival forms are used as adverbs. The adverb *needs,* meaning "necessarily," as in a James Fenimore Cooper-like sentence such as "he must needs pay for this dastardly deed," is also based on a genitive case, *nȳdes* "of need."

penny. The oldest known coin was called the *penig,* a word possibly related to Latin *pannus,* a piece of cloth that might be used as a medium of exchange. It was a silver coin that at one time was supposed to equal in weight thirty-two grains of dry wheat. In England its abbreviation for many centuries was *d.,* so that a sixpence, for instance, was *6d.* Why *d.?* When Anglo-Saxon scholars translated the Bible, they did not know how to translate the name of the Roman coin *denarius,* so they called it *penig,* but also used the Latin term, which gave rise to the abbreviation.

quick. OE *cwic* meant "alive"; that meaning is retained in the Biblical "the quick and the dead." At one time a pregnant woman could be described as "quick with child." But since that which is alive may move rapidly, that meaning entered and has largely superseded the older one.

rather. OE *raþe* meant "quickly" or "ahead." Today when a student says he'd *rather* go swimming, he means that he puts swimming ahead of something else.

shrew. A smelly, mouse-shaped, pugnacious, and persistent little animal once abundant in England was called *scrēawa* in OE, *shrewe* in Middle

English. Since some women in the past apparently shared certain characteristics of the shrew, the word was often applied to them. The best-known
example is Shakespeare's Kate.

starboard, larboard. On Anglo-Saxon ships the *stēorbord* (literally
"steering-board") was the side of the ship from which the steering was
done. *Board* with the meaning of "side" still exists in our *seaboard*. OE
used *bæcbord* to refer to the left side of the ship; in Middle English this
became *ladborde* "loading side," which became our *larboard*. The words
laden and *load* are related.

step-. *Step-* in *stepchild, stepdaughter,* and *stepson* is from OE *stēop*
"bereaved, destitute." The *stepfather* or *stepmother* is not bereaved, but is
the new parent of the bereaved one.

uncouth, unkempt. Our dislike for the unfamiliar is reflected in *uncouth.* OE *cūþ* meant "known" or "familiar," and *un* made it negative.
But when people referred to something or someone as "uncouth," they
often showed distaste, just as many people in the 1960's considered long
hair on men "uncouth" because they had not been familiar with it. The
reference to hair brings us to *unkempt,* which is based on an OE verb form
for "combed"; an unkempt person is probably uncombed, though we now
also consider him dirty or disheveled. (*Dishevel,* incidentally, came into
Middle English from Old French for "hair disarranged.") *Uncouth* and
unkempt are two of the words with rare affirmative forms; no one is
likely to be called "couth" or "kempt." Another such word is *inept.*

wench. OE *wencel* could mean a child of either sex, or a maid. Even in
Shakespeare's day *wench* was still sometimes a neutral word for a girl or
young woman, but was most often applied to someone of the servant class.
(In an Elizabethan-style restaurant in London today, the buxom waitresses
ask to be addressed as "wenches.") But since some wenches became prostitutes, the word degenerated in meaning.

window. To let smoke escape from their early houses, the Norse would
cut a hole in the roof or high on a side. Since wind whistled through the
hole, they called it a *vindr auga* "wind eye." To the Anglo-Saxons this was
a *windēage.* Now we've relocated the window and covered the hole with
glass, but we still use the same term, modified in pronunciation and spelling.

world. I-E **wiros-* meant "man." (Cf. Latin *vir.*) In Germanic languages, including English, this was combined with *ald* "old" or "age." OE
weorold, from which our *world* derives, therefore literally meant "the age of
man," a rather egocentric view of the planet.

wormwood, vermouth. An English name for the plant *Artemisia absinthium,* from which absinthe and certain flavorings for wines are made, is *wormwood.* It has nothing to do with worms or wood. In medieval times the OE name *wermōd* was changed, through a misunderstanding typical of folk etymology, to *worm* plus *wood.* The French borrowed their word *vermout* from the German form of the name, *Wermut,* which is about the same as the OE word.

CLASSROOM ACTIVITIES

Note: It is unlikely that in the elementary or secondary schools you will ever teach anything written in OE (unless you use a modern translation) or that you will have occasion to teach OE phonology or grammar. The material in this chapter, then, has been intended largely for your background as a teacher, especially since it may prepare you to cope with some language questions that you might not otherwise be able to answer. Nevertheless, some of your especially able and advanced students may enjoy working on or playing with some of the activities below. Doing so will help them in gaining a deeper understanding of the language than most high school (or college!) graduates possess.

Who Are the English?

In a course in English literature some students who are interested in history may attempt to trace the conquests and immigrations that have made the British people as mixed as they are today. The early part of this chapter may be one source for them, as well as encyclopedia articles, histories of England, and other histories of the English language such as the excellent one by Alfred C. Baugh. Defoe's "True-Born Englishman," of which only a fragment is quoted above, is a satirical poem attacking popular prejudice against a foreign-born king; some bright student might want to read more of it.

A Prehistoric Courtship

Suppose that a long time ago a young soldier was strongly attracted to a girl in a country conquered by him and his fellows. How could they converse? As he learned parts of her language and she learned parts of his, what kinds of linguistic adjustments would probably have to be made? For example, how might each of them attempt to simplify his own language to make it more comprehensible to the other? If they married, what might their children's language be like? If many soldiers and native girls married, what permanent effects on the language might there be?

A discussion of this sort will help students to understand what actually happened, after a fashion, in England during successive invasions. (It also had happened earlier when Indo-European tribes moved into territories new to them.)

Why *England*?

How suitable are the names *England* and *English*? To what extent might any of these names be justified instead: *Celtland* and *Celtic, Romanland* and *Romish* (or *Latin*), *Saxonland* and *Saxon, Normandy* and *Norman*?

Place-Names from *Castrum*

Castrum, the "armed camp" or "fort" of the early Romans in England, gave rise to many place-names using *chester, caster,* or *cester.* Students may recall many such names in England and the United States or Canada. Among them: *Chester, Chesterfield, Doncaster, Dorchester, Gloucester, Lancaster, Manchester, Rochester, Winchester, Worcester.* Why are there more such names in the Eastern United States than farther west?

Danish Place-Names

On a large map of England, students may find numerous place-names that show how widespread the Danish settlements were. The easiest means of identification are these elements in town names: *-by* "farm" or "town," as in *Derby, Rugby*; *-thorp(e)* "village," as in *Bishopsthorpe*; *-thwaite* "isolated piece of land," as in *Langthwaite*; and *-toft* "piece of ground," as in *Lowestoft.* (The *-by* in *by-law* is from the same source as *-by* in *Derby,* etc.; a by-law was originally a "town law.")

Fossils

Fossils are often found in words, not just in rocks. Thus the *i* in *handiwork* is the surviving form of the prefix *ge-*: *hand + geweorc*; *handicraft* was formed by analogy to *handiwork.* The *t* in *amidst, amongst,* and *against* reflects illiterate pronunciations in ME and Early Mod E; a similar addition is heard today in some people's *oncet* and *twicet. Once, twice,* and *thrice* (page 92) are survivals of an old genitive case; Chaucer spelled them *ones, twyes, thryes* "of one, of two, of three." *Since* goes back to OE *sith then* "later than" which became *sithenes* and *sithence* before being shortened to *since.* OE *gār* "spear" survives in *garlic* (literally "spear-leek") and in the name of a long fish. Some of your ablest students may be interested in looking up these fossils and others.

How We Changed the Latin Words We Borrowed

Here is a list of some early borrowings from the Romans, most of them attributable to the coming of missionaries in 597 A.D. and later. Students may try to guess what each became in modern English, using hints like those below. For your own comfort, answers are provided here in brackets.

ancora (This will hold you!)   [anchor]
apostolus   [apostle, etc.]
arca (It's still raining!)   [ark]
balsamum (It grows rather tall.)   [balsam]
butyrum (From happy cows?)   [butter]
cāseus (Ditto.)   [cheese]
circulus   [circle, circular, etc.]
comēta (Faster than a jet.)   [comet]
coquīna (You might eat *cāseus* there.)   [kitchen]
crispus (The way you like *lactūca*.)   [crisp]
crystallum   [crystal]
daemōn   [demon]
dīaconus (Title of a certain religious person.)   [deacon]
disc (Found in the *coquīna*.)   [dish]
furca (Ditto.)   [fork]
hymnus   [hymn]
lactūca (A vegetable.)   [lettuce]
monachus (Another religious man.)   [monk]
monasterium (Home of the *monachus*.)   [monastery]
papa (Probably more religious than your father.)   [pope]
peru (A fruit.)   [pear]
portus (It's wet here.)   [port]
pund (A weight.)   [pound]
schola   [school, scholar, etc.]
secula (It should be sharp.)   [sickle]
sēcūrus   [secure]
strata via (Now often one way.)   [street]
vallum (Romans made it big.)   [wall]
templum   [temple]
vīnum (Not *vine*, but you're close.)   [wine]

Some Irregularities

1. *The American Heritage Dictionary* is one that gives the principal parts of OE strong verbs that still remain strong ("irregular") today. Students who look up the OE forms of the following verbs, among others, will learn why they do not follow our usual pattern in the past

tense and past participle: *bear, begin, bid* (command), *bind, bite, blow, cling, come, drink, drive, eat, fall, fight, find, fly, freeze, grow, hold, know, ride, rise, see, shake, sing, sink, swear, take, tear.*

2. As suggested earlier in this chapter, the unusual plurals *teeth, feet, men, women, geese, lice,* and *mice* can be accounted for by reference to OE plurals.

3. The expression *willy-nilly* "whether desired or not" is literally "will I will I not." *Nill* was in OE a contraction like *nysse* and *neom,* which you noted in this chapter. It consisted of *ne* plus *will.* Another somewhat later contraction of interest is *don* "to put on," from *do* plus *on. Won't* is a contraction of *woll* (an old form of *will*) plus *not. Shilly-shally* was "Shall I? Shall I?"

Tracing Pronunciations and Spellings

In discussing how spellings change, you may want to comment on a few rather consistent changes from OE to later English. In this chapter you noted that OE *hām* [ha:m] became Mod E *home* [ho:m], and that *hū* [hu:] became *how* [hau]. Ask your students what these words became:

āc	[oak]	cū	[cow]
ār	[oar, ore]	hūs	[house]
bār	[boar]	lūs	[louse]
gād	[goad]	mūs	[mouse]
hāl	[whole]	tūn	[town]
stān	[stone]	ūt	[out]

OE *ē* as in *tēþ* [te:θ] moved to [i:] as in Mod E *teeth* [ti:θ]. OE *i* or *ȳ* as in *īs* [i:s] and in *hȳdan* moved to [aI] as in Mod E *ice* [aIs] and *hide* [haId]. Given this information, your students should be able to say what each of these words became in Mod E:

cwēn	[queen]	fīf	[five]
hē	[he]	fȳr	[fire]
nēd, nēod	[need]	līf	[life]
stēpel	[steeple]	mȳs	[mice]
		pīn	[pine]
		wīf	[wife]

German and English

As one bit of evidence that English is a Germanic language, those of your students who know German may point out some of the similarities in vocabulary. In some instances, like *sauerkraut* in both languages, relatively recent borrowing is involved, but in many, the OE form came in with the Anglo-Saxons. Here are a few examples.

MODERN GERMAN	MODERN ENGLISH	OLD ENGLISH
Sohn	son	sunu
Hund	hound	hund
Feld	field	feld
Freund	friend	frēond
Buch	book	bōc
Weib	wife	wīf
best	best	betst
Land	land	land, lond
Licht	light	lēoht
weis	wise	wīs
Pfennig	penny	penig

Reading Old English

Some of your better students may enjoy reading the two OE selections given earlier in this chapter.

5

Middle English

A NATION WITH TWO LANGUAGES

Immediate Effects of the Norman Conquest

Even before the Norman Conquest in 1066, the Anglo-Saxons had ties with their Scandinavian-French cousins across the Channel. King Ethelred's wife, whom he married in 1002, was Norman, and the king and queen lived in Normandy after the Danes drove them out of England. Their son, who was to rule as King Edward (the Confessor) was brought up in Normandy, and as king he was considerably influenced by Normans to whom he gave important posts.

The duke of Normandy, William, was dubbed William the Bastard and William the Great before he became William the Conqueror. An illegitimate child (his mother was the daughter of a tanner of hides), he became duke at the age of six and while still a young man had successfully defended his dukedom against ambitious noblemen and avaricious rulers of other parts of France.

William, at age thirty-nine, won the Battle of Hastings by faking a retreat that pulled the English from an almost impregnable position. A well-aimed arrow killed English King Harold, and other English leaders were also killed in the battle. William followed the initial victory at Hastings by ravaging southeast England until the people of that area, including London, decided that they would have to give up. They crowned William king on December 25, 1066. In the next few years William overcame the resistance of the rest of England, replacing one by one the English earls with Normans. For several centuries Normans and their cohorts held the most important positions in England, as Robert of Brunne wrote in 1338:

To Frankis [French] & Normans, for þar grete laboure,
To Flemminges & Pikardes, þat were with him in stoure [battle],

He gaf londes bityme [betimes], of whilk [which] per successoure
Hold git [yet] þe seysyne [power], withe fulle grete honoure.

Normans also held most of the top posts in the church, and were not just
the major landholders. To the victors belonged the spoils.

Among the lower classes, however, the majority were still English. This
was true despite the fact that many Norman soldiers settled in the islands,
and many Norman shopkeepers came over and established businesses.

The Persistence of English

Given the complete domination of England by the Normans, why did the
English language survive? Why was it not completely replaced by Norman
French? Several major reasons may be adduced.

One is that the English outnumbered the Normans. Even though they
lacked military, political, and economic strength, they were still numerically
strong. They were the tillers of the soil, the common laborers; some of
them still held small plots of land. Population figures are not available, but
there must have been several times as many Englishmen as Normans.

Furthermore, unlike previous conquerors, the Normans did not drive the
English to the outskirts of the islands. They allowed them to remain, in
order to profit from their labor. They did not attempt to eradicate English,
although some of them regarded it superciliously as a crude, unpolished,
inferior language used by an inferior people. The Normans themselves were
linguistically flexible, as their quick adoption of French in Normandy had
already shown. English continued to be spoken in all parts of the country.
The Normans did not insist that their menials learn French; when they
had to communicate with them, they often made use of bilinguals.

The role of women, mentioned in Chapter 3, was again important. When
an English woman married a Norman, their children generally learned first
their mother's tongue; many, of course, learned both languages and no doubt
incorporated some French words into their English and vice versa. But
most English women continued to marry English men, thus preserving the
language with only incidental dilution by French.

Over a period of time, however, it was inevitable that the English language would be affected by the French presence. Most notable of the
changes was the loss of many inflections. This loss had already begun before
the Conquest, but was unquestionably accelerated after it. If a Norman who
knew a little English deigned to use it, he tended to slur or ignore the
endings of words, and some Englishmen no doubt began to do the same
thing in talking with the Normans. In mixed households the children per-

haps often used neither "pure" English nor "pure" French, but a simplified mixture of the two, with few inflectional endings.

A second major effect of Norman French upon English was the gradual introduction of more and more French words into the English vocabulary. Since the Normans were the powers in the land, and since their words reflecting military, political, and economic power were different from English words, it is easily understandable why words like *army, captain, lieutenant, sergeant, government, administer, crime, prince, duke, salary, carriage,* and *voyage* were adopted by the English, who had to live under a regime in which such words were important.

The Status of the Languages in the Twelfth and Thirteenth Centuries

For many years kings of England doubled as dukes of Normandy. They usually divided their time between their two realms. Some of them, as well as some of their noblemen, spoke both French and English, others, French only. The courtly literature—all literature, in fact, except possibly some oral folk songs and tales—was in French. Members of the clergy, particularly those above the lowest orders, spoke and wrote Latin and French, more rarely English. In the legal profession, too, French and Latin were dominant, although some weird amalgams of French, Latin, and English have been preserved in legal records.

As time went on, though, more speakers of French found it advantageous to know at least a little English. As Professor Baugh has said, ". . . among those whose activities brought them into contact with both upper and lower classes, the ability to speak both languages was quite general." Among the lower classes, on the other hand, a late thirteenth century poet estimated that no more than one person in a hundred knew French:

> Lewede men cune Ffrensch non,
> Among an hondryd vnneþis on.
> (Common men know no French,
> Among a hundred hardly one.)

Cherchez les Femmes

If the rulers of England had remained permanent rulers of Normandy, the future of the language of the British Isles might have been different. French influence, at any rate, might have been even greater than it was.

But a pretty face, as so often happens, helped to shape history. In 1200 King John of England became enamored of a French girl, Isabel of Angoulème, who was engaged to a nobleman named Hugh of Lusignan. When John married her, the king of France became so angry that he induced a court to declare that Normandy should be confiscated in reprisal. John fought the verdict on the battlefield, but lost, and Normandy was no longer under the rule of a king of England.

Further confiscations followed. The king of France took over the French estates of English nobility, and King John seized the British estates of Frenchmen whom he mistrusted. Only a few of the nobility managed to hang on to their possessions on both sides of the Channel, and eventually all had to become, in effect, either Frenchmen or Englishmen.

However, French influence did not cease at once. In the middle of the thirteenth century, waves of Frenchmen from farther south than Normandy came into England. Again feminine beauty played a part. The son of King John and his French Isabel was Henry III. He married the daughter of the count of Provence, in southern France, and brought to England many of her relatives and friends and their adherents, and bestowed upon them honor and rich holdings. Moreover, after the death of John, Isabel had married her original betrothed, Hugh of Lusignan; the generous Henry showered her five sons, his half-brothers, with titles and riches.

Many of the English, and of the Normans who more and more were considering themselves English, objected, complaining, "They hold your castles and the strength of your dominions in their own hands, as though you could not place confidence in your own people." The concerted opposition to the foreigners, combined with the earlier loss of Normandy, was a factor in building a sense of British unity. The Baron's War of 1258 to 1265 was a symbol of the opposition to whatever was not English.

Although the upper classes still, for the most part, spoke French as their first language, and although French was still regarded as the language of culture, more and more of the wealthy also learned English—partly for ease in communication with the majority of the inhabitants, partly because of the reduction of ties with France. Henry III (1207–1272) probably knew English; his son, Edward I (1239–1307), unquestionably did. But Frenchmen who learned English would still interlard their conversation with French words; in this way, great numbers of additional French words entered English.

At the height of Norman influence, almost nothing approaching the literary was written in English. But the author of *Cursor Mundi* (c. 1300) wrote his long poem in English, explaining:

> þis ilk [same] bok es translate
> Into Inglis tong to rede
> For the love of Inglis lede [people],
> Inglis lede of Ingland,
> For the commun at [to] understand . . .
> Give we ilken [each one] þare langage,
> Me think we do þam non outrage.

Oxford University, alarmed at the decrease in French, enacted in the fourteenth century a requirement that students translate in both English and French, so that French would not "be entirely disused." But little by little, that was what was happening.

The Victory of English

In the fourteenth century still more evidence was accumulating that English would indeed survive the onslaughts of Norman French, though it would be far different from the English of King Alfred. Geoffrey Chaucer's contemporary, John Gower, wrote in Latin, French, and English, partly because he was uncertain about which language would give his writings the greatest chance of permanence. But wise old Geoffrey wrote in English, as did many of his contemporaries and nearly all of his fifteenth century successors. William of Nassyngton had testified in c. 1325:

> Boþe lered [learned] and lewed [lay], olde and yonge,
> Alle vnderstonden english tonge.

It was because of this general understanding of the "english tonge" that its victory was assured. Even the courts of law, traditionally conservative, began late in the fourteenth century to conduct cases in English.

All this, of course, does not mean that French was suddenly abandoned. The shift was slow; there were many diehards. The Hundred Years War (1337–1453), much of which was fought in Normandy, showed that the English kings even yet had not given up continental ambitions. But one of many significant indications of the near-completeness of the shift was the occasional appearance in fifteenth century England of books of French instruction, with French taught as a foreign language. When that happened, England had virtually ceased being a nation with two languages.

Dialects

ME dialects were a mixed lot. Each was based, of course, on the OE dialect from which it grew, but in some places Danish influence was more considerable than in others, and Norman French influence also varied from

place to place. Furthermore, in a largely illiterate society with little inter-
communication, dialectal differences are likely to be greater than in a literate,
mobile one; people living on opposite sides of a river or a chain of hills
may develop a number of peculiarities in their speech—pronouncing words
differently, sometimes using different names for the same object, and
occasionally varying in at least small matters of grammar and usage.

Scholars have attempted to group ME dialects, although much work using modern linguistic techniques remains to be done before the classification
can be definitive. The usual groupings, subject to later refinement, are
Northern (north of the Humber River), West Midland, East Midland,
and Southern; some scholars find the Kentish of southeast England sufficiently different to call it a fifth dialect. Of these, East Midland was to
become most important, largely because of London, which already was and
was due to remain the literary, cultural, and commercial center.

Thousands of dialectal variations could be cited, but a few examples
will suffice. Here are some still significant today:

1. Southern and Midland *ch* was often *k* in Northern. Hence even today *kirk* is used for *church* in the North and in Scotland.

2. Southern used a voiced sound in *f* words: *vor, vox, vrom.* We call
   a female fox a *vixen* because of this Southern influence.

3. For the third person singular of verbs, Northern used an *-es* ending (*rides*), Midland an *-en* (*riden*), Southern an *-eth* (*rideth*).
   The *-es* gradually worked its way southward, in the time of the
   King James Bible (1611) was still battling with *-eth,* and eventually won.

4. A similar battle was fought in endings of the present participle.
   Northern used *-and(e)*, the Midland used *-ende* and *ing(e)*, and
   Southern used *-inde* and *ing(e)*. Finally, of course, *-ing* was the
   victor.

5. In West Midland OE *ȳ* and *y* retained more of their rounded quality than they did in East Midland, being characteristically spelled
   with a *u* in West Midland ME (*fur* or *fuir* "fire," *fullen* or *fyllen*
   "fill"), and with an *i* in East Midland ME (*fir* [fI:r], *fillen* [fIlən]).
   Later the East Midland forms won, although the [i:] was diph-
   thongized to [aI]. Consequently we say [faIr] and [fIl] rather than
   something with a *u* sound.

6. In the South and parts of the Midlands OE *ā* developed into an *ō*
   sound as in Mod E *stone* and *home,* but in parts of the North one
   may still hear *stane* and *hame.*

7. For our *these* the North, unlike the rest of England, used an *r: þir* or *þer*. If London had been in Northumbria, we might today use *thire* or *there* for *these*.

THE RESULT OF THE MIXTURE: READINGS IN MIDDLE ENGLISH

Examples from Chaucer

In *Chaucer and His Poetry* (Harvard University Press, 1915) George Lyman Kittredge said:

. . . Chaucer was born in London. His native dialect was that which was to become, in the natural course of events, the English of literature. And it was a critical moment, when nothing was needed to determine the tendency but a poet of commanding genius. Chaucer did not make the English language. His service was to write the Midland dialect with an ease, a polish, and a regularity which commanded immediate and unanimous admiration, and to use it as a vehicle for first-rate poetry. Nothing more was needed. Those who came after him now had an accepted standard. (P. 7)

F. N. Robinson, editor of *The Poetical Works of Chaucer* (Houghton Mifflin, 1933) partly concurred, but added:

It is doubtful if Chaucer had any important part in making the East Midland the dominant dialect. The speech of the capital would have become standard English if he had never written a line. But he did add greatly to its prestige and distinction. The very fact that he wrote in English instead of French was significant. He developed the resources of the language for literary use, and set an example which was followed by a long line of poets. (P. xxvi)

You will find Middle English (ME) much easier to read than OE. One reason is that the loss of most inflections makes words look much more like their Modern English (Mod E) equivalents. Another is that some OE words with which you would not be familiar have dropped out and been replaced by words from Norman French, even though the proportion of such words is not very high. In the following two passages from the Prologue to *The Canterbury Tales,* the words taken from French are italicized. (Try first to read the passages without any help; then refer if you must to the brief glossary that follows.)

> With hym [the Knight] ther was his sone, a yong *Squier,*
> A lovyere and a lusty *bacheler,*
> With lokkes crulle as they were leyd in *presse.*
> Of twenty yeer of *age* he was, I gesse.
> Of his *stature* he was of even lengthe,

And wonderly *delyvere,* and of greet strengthe.
And he hadde been somtyme in *chyvachie*
In *Flaundres,* in *Artoys,* and *Pycardie,*
And born him weel, as of so little *space,*
In hope to stonden in his lady *grace.*
Embrouded was he, as it were a meede
Al ful of *fresshe floures,* whyte and reede.
Syngynge he was, or *floyting,* al the day;
He was as *fressh* as is the month of *May.*
Short was his *gowne,* with sleves longe and wyde.
He koude songes make and wel *endite,*
Juste and eek *daunce,* and weel *purtreye* and write.
So hoote he lovede that by nyghtertale
He sleep namoore than dooth a nyghtyngale.
Curteis he was, lowely, and *servysable,*
And carf biforn his fader at the *table.*

. . .

Ther was also a Nonne, a *Prioresse,*
That of hir smyling was ful *symple* and *coy;*
Hire greetest ooth was but by Seinte Loy;
And she was cleped *madame Eglentyne.*
Ful weel she soong the *service dyvyne,*
Entuned in hir nose ful semely,
And Frenssh she spak ful faire and *fetisly,*
After the scole of Stratford atte Bowe,
For Frenssh of *Parys* was to hire unknowe . . . .
Ful semyly hir wympul *pynched* was;
Hir nose *tretys,* hir eyen greye as glas,
Hir mouth ful smal, and therto softe and reed;
But sikerly she hadde a fair forheed;
It was almost a spanne brood, I trowe;
For, hardily, she was nat undergrowe.[1]

GLOSSARY

bacheler—a candidate for knighthood (Cf. our "bachelor's degree.")

carf—carved (A duty of a squire was to cut the knight's meat.)

chyvachie—cavalry expeditions (Like *chivalry,* from the French for "horse.")

cleped—called, named (Often appears as *yclept,* with *y* surviving from OE *ge-.*)

coy—quiet (The implication of coquetry came later.)

crulle—curly (An example of metathesis, transposition of letters.)

---

[1] The text, including the supplied punctuation, is that of F. N. Robinson.

delyvere—active, agile

eek—also

embrouded—embroidered (May refer to the squire's clothing, but possibly to his pink and white complexion.)

endite—compose the words (For his "songes.")

evene—moderate, average

fetisly—gracefully

floyting—whistling, or playing a flute

hardily—(as used here) certainly (Related to *hardly.*)

hoote—hotly

juste—joust

koude—knew how (Ancestor of *could.*)

lokkes—locks, hair

lovyere—lover (Southern dialect; usual Midland form was *lovere.*)

meede—meadow

nyghtertale—night-time

presse—(as used here) probably an instrument for curling

purtreye—draw

sikerly—certainly

space—amount of time

spanne—span (About nine inches, the distance from thumb to little finger.)

Stratford atte Bowe—a nunnery at Stratford-Bow, Middlesex

tretys—well-formed

trowe—believe, declare

wonderly—wondrously

wympul—wimple, a cloth wound around the head

The borrowings from French in these passages are fairly representative of some of the types of words that were introduced a century or two after the Conquest. For example, *Squier, bacheler, chyvachie,* and *juste* reflect Norman military concepts and terminology. Even more words reflect the courtly, cultured life of upper-class Normans: *grace, embrouded, fresshe floures, floyting, gowne, endite, daunce, purtreye,* and *curteis* (derived from the word for *court*)—such words suggest some aspects of the kind of life that wealthy Normans enjoyed. Words like *Prioresse* and *dyvyne* show additions to the religious vocabulary the Anglo-Saxons had earlier taken over from Roman missionaries. And a word like *stature* shows that sometimes a French word came into the language without displacing its English equivalent—*height,* in this case. Today such words still co-exist, although their denotations or connotations may have separated somewhat: we may say "a poet of stature," but not "a poet of height."

Perhaps you noticed a considerable number of final *e*'s in the passages. These generally represent all that was left of many of the OE inflectional endings. In the first line, for example, is *sone,* the ME version of OE *sunu.* The ME final *e* was usually pronounced as a separate syllable, with the vague schwa sound [ə]. Before scholars discovered that these *e*'s were usually pronounced (rather than silent as so many final *e*'s are now), the true quality of Chaucer's meter was not realized, since the number of syllables in a line obviously depended in part upon whether or not the *e*-syllables were counted. One result of pronouncing the *e*'s is many feminine rhymes, with an unaccented final syllable in the line.

Here are the first four lines of the description of the Clerk (a student) with the accented syllables marked and a dieresis above the pronounced final *e*'s:

> A Clérk ther wás of Óxenfórd alsó,
> That únto lógyk háddë lónge ygó.
> As leénë wás his hórs as ís a rákë,
> And hé was nát right fát, I úndertákë.

(In *longe* the *e* was elided because of the following vowel sound.)

Other Examples

In the left-hand column below is a late fourteenth century version of Matthew 2: 1–9, a translation ascribed to John Purvey, a follower of Wycliffe. The right-hand column is from the King James Bible (1611), this time presented without any modernization of the spelling. You should be able to read almost all the ME without reference to the Early Mod E, but you may want to make some comparisons.

1. Therfor whanne Jhesus was borun in Bethleem of Juda, in the daies of King Eroude, lo! astromyenes camen fro the eest to Jerusalem,

1. Now when Jesus was borne in Bethlehem of Judea, in the dayes of Herod the king, behold, there came Wise men from the East to Hierusalem,

2. And seiden Where is he, that is borun King of Jewis? For we han seyn his sterre in the eest, and we comen to worschipe him.

2. Saying, Where is he that is borne King of the Jewes: for we haue seene his Starre in the East, and are come to worship him.

3. But King Eroude herde, and was trublid, and al Jerusalem with hym.

4. And he gaderide to gidre all the prynces of prestis, and scribis of the puple, and enqueride of hem, where Crist shulde be borun.

5. And thei seiden to hym, In Bethleem of Juda; for so it is writun bi a profete.

6. And thou, Bethleem, the lond of Juda, art not the leest among the prynces of Juda; for of thee a duyk schal go out, that schal gouerne my puple of Israel.

7. Thanne Eroude clepide pryueli the astromyens, and lernyde bisili of hem the tyme of the sterre that apperide to hem.

8. And he sente hem in to Bethleem, and seide, Go ge, axe ge bisili of the child, and whanne gee han foundon, telle ge it to me, that Y also come, and worschipe hym.

9. And whanne thei hadden herd the Kyng, thei wenten forth. And lo! the sterre, that thei sigen in the eest, wente bifore hem, til it cam, and stood aboue, where the child was.

3. When Herod the king had heard these things, he was troubled, and all Hierusalem with him.

4. And when he had gathered all the chief Priests and Scribes of the people together, hee demanded of them where Christ should be borne.

5. And they said vnto him, In Bethlehem of Judea; For thus it is written by the Prophet;

6. And thou Bethlehem in the land of Juda, art not the least among the Princes of Juda: for out of thee shall come a Gouernour, that shall rule my people Israel.

7. Then Herod, when he had privily called the Wise men, enquired of them diligently what time the Starre appeared.

8. And he sent them to Bethlehem, and said, Goe, and search diligently for the yong child, and when ye haue found him, bring me word againe, that I may come and worship him also.

9. When they had heard the King, they departed, and loe, the Starre which they saw in the East, went before them, tell it came and stood ouer where the young childe was.

It may be useful for you to attempt to answer these questions about the ME version:

Find several words that would probably have had inflectional endings in OE but have lost them in ME. What verb ending do you see (several times) that had not been lost in the dialect of this scribe? What are examples of inflectional endings that still survive in Mod E?

How do the ME pronouns differ from those of Mod E?

What words do you find that have since dropped out?

What historical evidence do you see that can explain the occasional modern pronunciation [æks] for ask?

Compare the ME word order with that of Mod E and of OE. Can you find any evidence of change from OE word order?

Trevisa and Layamon

Middle English was by no means a standardized language. The language was still in flux. It was spoken differently in various parts of the country, as we have noted, and each scribe followed his own preferences or idiosyncrasies in spelling. The printing press, a great standardizer, had not yet been invented. The OE þ was still used by some writers; others used *th* regularly; some used both. The letters *u* and *v*, and *i*, *y*, and *j* would not be regularized in use for another few centuries.

As an example of ME that differs in a number of respects from those we looked at first, here are a few sentences from John Trevisa's translation of the Latin *Polychronicon* of Ralph Higden, who had attempted to combine several early histories of Britain. The date of Trevisa's work is 1387.

For þis ilond is beest and bringeþ forþ trees and fruyt and reþeren [cows] and oþer bestes, and wyn groweþ þere in som place. þe lond haþ plente of foules and of bestes of dyuers manere kyndes; þe lond is plentevous and þe see also. þe lond is noble, copious, and riche of nobil ryueres wiþ plente of fische; þere is grete plente of small fische, of samon, and of elys. . . þere beeþ ofte i-take dolphyns, and see calues, and baleynes [whales], grete fisches as hit were of whales kynde, and dyuers manere schelfische. . . . þis ilond is plentevous of veynes of metals, of bras, of iren, of leed, of tyn, of sylver also . . . . The kyngdom of Bretayne was somtyme i-hight [usually "called"; here perhaps "renowned"] wiþ eigte and twenty noble citees, wiþ oute [not counting] many castelles þat were wiþ walles, wiþ toures, wiþ gates, wiþ barres, stalworþliche i-buld. And for þis lond lieþ vnder þe norþ nolle of þe world, þey haþ ligt and brigt nygtes in þe somertyme, so þat ofte tyme at mydnygt men haueþ questiouns and doute where [whether] it be euentyde or dawenynge.

The examples so far have been of fairly late (fourteenth century) ME. To understand clearly the transitional nature of the changes from OE, however, you should look at some earlier ME. All language change is gradual; people didn't wake up one morning in 1100 and say "Now we'll start talking a different kind of English." The following lines are from a huge, 32,000-line poem called *The Brut,* composed by a priest named Layamon in c. 1205; about a third of the whole is devoted to the legendary King Arthur and represents the first telling of the story in English. The excerpt concerns Arthur's death.

Arður wes forwunded [sorely wounded] wunder ane swiþe
　　[wonderfully much].
þer to him com a cnave [boy] þe wes of his cunne [kin];
He wes Cadores sunu, þe eorles of Cornwale;
Constantin hehte [was called] þe cnave, he wes þan king deore.

Arður him lokede on þer he lai on folden [the ground],
And þas word seide mid sorhfulle heorte:
"Constantin, þu art welcume; þu weore Cadores sone.
Ich þe bitache [bequeath] here mine kineriche [kingdom]
And wite [guard] mine Bruttes [Britons] a [ever] to þine lifes
    ende,
And hald heom [uphold for them] alle þa lagen [laws] þa habbeoð
    istonden a mine dagen,
And alle þa lagen gode þa bi Uðeres [King Uther's] dagen stode.
And ich wulle varen [fare] to Avalun, to vairest alre [of all]
    maidene,
To Argante þere quene, alven [fairy] swiðe [very] sceone
    [beautiful; cf. German schön],
And heo scal mine wunden makien alle isunde,
Al hal [whole] me makien mid haleweige [healing] drenchen
    [draughts; cf. drink];
And seðe [afterward] ich cumen wulle to mine kineriche,
And wunien [live] mid Brutten mid muchelere [great] wunne
    [joy].

Note that in this passage a considerable number of inflectional endings still remain; for example, in the third line, *eorles* is genitive to agree with *Cadores,* but late ME and Mod E would use here the simple form *earl.* In the last half of the fourth line we must translate *þan kinge* as "to the king," but the inflectional forms made *to* optional for Layamon. You can find several other examples of inflections that have since been lost. No doubt you also noticed a higher proportion of unfamiliar words than in Chaucer, Purvey, or Trevisa.

Layamon's poetry, unlike Chaucer's, has no regular rhymes. Instead, it uses the alliterative system of OE, in which a sound or sounds in the first half of each line alliterate with a sound or sounds in the second half. As examples, see the *w*'s in the first line, the *c*'s in the second. Layamon does, however, play a bit with rhyme or near-rhyme between half-lines, as in *lagen-dagen, gode-stode,* and *wunden-isunde.*

As a final example of ME, here is a short anonymous poem dated c. 1450. If you contrast it with the early thirteenth-century lines from Layamon, or even with Chaucer's work of c. 1387, you will observe that it seems much closer to Mod E.

What is this worlde but oonly vanyte?
Who trustith fortune sonnest hat a falle.
Ech man tak heed of prodigalite;
Welth that is past no man agayn may calle.

The grenowst [greenest; i.e., rawest] wounde that ever
     man had or schalle
Is to thynk on welth that is gon and past,
And in olde age in mysery to be cast.

THE PRONUNCIATION OF MIDDLE ENGLISH

Once more we shall not attempt a thorough analysis of phonology, but
instead shall be content with a generalized description. The examples will
be taken from the East Midland dialect, which included the speech of
London, the most influential of its day and destined to remain the literary
standard and to be the ancestor of the Received Standard of the present.
If we looked at examples from other areas, we would notice countless
variations.

Consonant Sounds

The sounds of consonants did not change greatly from OE to ME. Here
is a summary of the chief shifts.

1. In OE a number of words began with *hl, hn, hr,* and *hw,* as in *hlāf*
"loaf," *hnīgan* "to bow," *hrīm* "frost" (preserved today as one meaning
of *rime*), and *hwīl* "while." In OE the *h* was pronounced, but in ME the
h sound was generally lost, though it sometimes remained in the *hw* combination, as it still does in some people's pronunciation of words like *while*
and *when.* For unknown reasons, in spelling the *h* and *w* changed places
in these words, probably after the *h* had ceased being pronounced.

2. The sound of *w* disappeared in words like OE *twā* "two," *swā* "so,"
sweord "sword," and *andswarian* "to answer." This ME change accounts
for our Mod E pronunciations, even though the *w* remains in the spelling
of a number of such words.

3. The sound of *v* (spelled in OE with *f*) disappeared before a consonant
in some words. Thus OE *hæfde* became *hadde* or *had, hlāford* became *lord,*
and *hēafod* became *hed* (today's *head*).

4. The sound of *-ch* disappeared late in ME in unstressed syllables. You
recall that in OE a frequent adverbial ending was *-līce,* which sometimes
came to be spelled *-lich.* Gradually this became reduced to [lI] or [li].
Chaucer spelled *lively* as *lyfly* or *lyvely.* Had this reduction not occurred,
most of today's adverbs might end in *-lic.*

5. As some of the literary examples have illustrated, the OE prefix *ge-*
was reduced in ME to *i-* or *y-,* representing a corresponding change in

pronunciation. Later the prefix disappeared. Thus OE *gefæstnan* appears in some ME manuscripts as *ifasten* but today is *fasten*.

6. The distinctions between [f] and [v], [s] and [z], and [θ] and [ð], which had been slight in OE, became more definite in ME—probably because of French influence.

It should also be noted that *gn, kn* (or *cn*), and *wr* still consisted of two sounds. Thus ME *gnawen* "to gnaw" was [gna:wən], *knee* was [kne:], and *wrong* was [wroŋ]. There is some evidence from spellings, though, that simplification was under way, especially in *wr*.

Vowel and Diphthong Sounds

The major results of changes in vowels and diphthongs from OE to ME may be illustrated like this:

OLD ENGLISH			MIDDLE ENGLISH		
ā [a:]	hām "home"	[ha:m]	[ɔ]	ham, hom	[hɔm]
æ [æ]	þæt "that"	[θæt]	[a]	that	[θat]
ēa [ɛ:ə]	drēam "joy"	[drɛ:əm]	[ɛ:]	dreem	[drɛ:m]
ea [æə]	earc "ark"	[æərk]	[a]	ark	[ark]
ēo [e:o]	dēop "deep"	[de:op]	[e:]	deep	[de:p]
eo [ɛo]	heorte "heart"	[hɛortə]	[ɛ]	herte	[hɛrtə]

In addition, the sounds of *y,* which in OE were rounded like certain sounds of *u* in French or German, became unrounded to [i:] or [I]. Thus OE *mys* "mice" was in ME pronounced [mi:s], and LE *mylen* "mill" became ME [mIl].

In reading ME aloud, as was true of OE, you will not be far wrong if you give vowels their usual continental values. Thus *ham* rhymes with *Tom,* and *deep* with *shape.*

Some Lines for Practice

Here is a phonemic transcription of the opening lines of Chaucer's "Prologue." Try reading the passage aloud three or four times, and then turn back to the earlier examples of ME to see what you can do with them.

Whan	that	Aprille	with	his	shoures	soote
hwan	θat	a:prIlə	wIθ	hIs	šu:rez	so:tə

The	droghte	of	March	hath	perced	to	the	roote,
ðə	dru:xt[2]	of	Martš	haθ	pɛrsəd	to:	ðə	ro:tə

[2] The symbol *x* represents a sound like that of German *ch.*

And	bathed	every	veyne	in	swich	licour
and	baðəd	ɛvəri	ve:n	In	swItš	liku:r[3]

Of	which	vertu		engendred	is	the	flour;
ɔf	hwItš	vɛrtIu:		ɛndjɛndrəd	Is	ðə	flu:r

Whan	Zephirus	eek	with	his	sweete	breeth
hwan	zɛfIrus	e:k	wIθ	hIs	swe:tə	bre:θ

Inspired	hath	in	every	holt	and	heeth
Inspi:rəd	haθ	In	ɛvəri	holt	and	he:θ

The	tendre	croppes,	and	the	yonge	sonne
ðə	tɛndrə	krɔpəz	and	ðə	juŋə	sunə

Hath	in	the	Ram	his	halve	cours	yronne,
haθ	In	ðə	ram	hIs	halvə[4]	kurs	Irunə

And	smale	foweles	maken	melodye,
and	smalə	fu:ləz	makən	melodiə[5]

That	slepen	al	the	nyght	with	open	ye
θat	slepən	al	ðə	nIxt	wIθ	opɛn	iə

(So	priketh	hem	nature	in	hir	corages);
so	prIkəθ	hɛm	natu:r	In	hIr[6]	koradjɛz

Thanne	longen	folk	to	goon	on	pilgrimages.
θan	lɔŋən	folk[4]	to	go:n	ɔn	pIlgrImadjəz

MORE GRAMMAR

Grammatical changes in ME are not usually attributed directly to French influence, since many of them, including the very important loss of inflectional endings, were already beginning before the Normans came. It seems probable, though, that the linguistic mix-ups resulting from having two widely used languages accelerated the changes.

Nouns

The numerous endings of nouns dwindled so much that in effect nouns were declined about as they are today, with only a common singular form, like *boy,* a common plural form, like *boys,* and possessive forms like *boy's* and *boys'* (although the apostrophe was not used until later). For a while, especially in the South, *-en* battled with *-s* and *-es* as the typical plural

[3] Unlike our *liquor,* is accented on the second syllable.
[4] Note that in words corresponding to our *half* or *talk,* the *l*'s were pronounced.
[5] Four syllables in ME; *ye* "eye" is two syllables.
[6] The vowel sounds before *r* had not yet changed to the ɝ of Mod E *her, first, word,* which were [hIr], [fIrst], [wɔrd].

ending; it still survives in *oxen, children,* and *brethren,* and in the rare use of *kine* "cows" and *shoon* "shoes." Gradually, though, -*s* and -*es* were accepted throughout England, as the old dative and accusative forms died away. If you remember that OE nouns existed in several declensions, with often quite distinctive inflectional endings, you can readily see that these changes in nouns resulted in considerable simplification.

A few nouns did not become regularized in their plurals, though. As noted in Chapter 3, that is why we still have the plurals *men, women, teeth, feet, geese, lice,* and *mice.*

Accompanying the loss of inflections was the loss of grammatical gender, also previously noted. As a result, Chaucer and his contemporaries, like us, did not have to worry about whether they should use *he, she,* or *it* to refer to a noun, and did not have to vary their determiners and adjectives to make them agree, as the French and Germans still do. (Gender, though, is by no means a universal characteristic of grammars; some languages make no such differentiation at all, though some may vary word forms to indicate relative size, or age, or honor and respect, or some other characteristic instead of sex.)

Adjectives and Determiners

In ME, adjectives slowly lost their complex patterns of endings. For a time both singular and plural forms remained, but then these too merged. An *e*-ending, typical of many adjectives, remained for a while with the pronunciation [ə], but gradually it too disappeared from speech, though it survives in the spellings of many Mod E adjectives like *fine, whole, white, brave.*

The determiners (articles) *the* and *a,* which you will recall had many forms in OE, became simplified in ME to approximations of our *the, a,* and *an. This* and *that* did retain plural forms, now our *these* and *those;* another plural of *that, tho,* persisted into the age of Shakespeare and even now may be heard occasionally in some uneducated British speech.

Pronouns

The dual number, used in OE to refer to two persons, vanished presumably because it seemed unnecessary. The other personal pronouns, especially *she* and *them,* took a long time to settle down. A recent map prepared by Professors Angus McIntosh of Edinburgh and Michael Samuels of Glasgow shows the varied forms of *she* they found in late ME manuscripts from the English shires surrounding Gloucestershire. Included are some forms like *heo, hea, hoe, hoa, ho, he, hu,* and *hue,* all of which are no doubt derived from OE *heō;* but the map also shows *she, shee, sche, sho, scho, sheo, che, scheo, ssche, shoe, scheghe,* and others. Almost certainly these many spellings also represent a number of different pronunciations. *Hem* for *them* was usual in ME and was not largely replaced until late in the period; Chaucer, as we have noted, customarily wrote *they,* but *hire* or a variant for *their* and *hem* for *them.* Scandinavian influence probably led to the ultimate adoption of the *th.*

The second person pronoun was still regularly differentiated for singular and plural, with *thou* (OE ðū) and *three* (OE ðē) still being fairly regularly distinguished as singular subject and object, and with *ge* or *ye* as a customary plural.

The first person singular appears as *ich, ic, ik,* and sometimes as *I* or *Y.*

Verbs

In verbs, as in nouns and adjectives, the loss of inflections led to considerable simplification. Today, you recall, a typical verb has only four forms, such as *walk, walks, walked, walking,* but in OE it often had several times that number. By late ME, forms similar in number to our own had largely replaced the OE forms.

In addition, about a third of the approximately three hundred OE strong verbs disappeared early in ME, another thirty or so later in ME, and still others in later centuries, so that today only about sixty such verbs, like *ring, rang, rung,* are still widely used. Some of the strong verbs were superseded by different verbs; others simply switched from strong to weak forms, with the two existing side by side for a time. For example, both *stope* and *stepped* and both *oke* and *ached* may be found in late ME manuscripts. Some of today's students are repeating the old process when they say "blowed" or "knowed," and most small children say "singed," "runned," etc., before they learn the socially approved strong forms. Past participles of some strong verbs are still used, like *swollen,* even though the past tenses (*swelled*) have become weak.

THE GROWTH OF THE VOCABULARY

A major result of the Norman Conquest was, as has been suggested, numerous borrowings by English from Norman French (as well as a smaller number of reverse borrowings). In the next section we'll look at a few of the more colorful or odd results. In this section we'll be concerned with describing and exemplifying the major types of borrowings from Norman French, as well as those from Latin and the Low Countries.

Military and Governmental Words

Since almost all military officers in England for many years after the Conquest were of Norman descent, it is easy to understand why many military terms entered the English language. Here are a few:

Military titles: *archer, captain, garrison, guard, lieutenant, sergeant, soldier*

Equipment: *banner, buckler, dart, harness, hauberk, lance, mail*

Fortifications: *barbican, moat, portcullis*

General: *ambush, army, battle, besiege, combat, defend, enemy, navy, peace, retreat, skirmish, stratagem*

For similar reasons the majority of words relating to government came over with the Normans, although *king, queen, earl, lord,* and *lady* are exceptions. Examples:

Titles: *ambassador, baron, chamberlain, chancellor, constable, count, countess, courtier, duchess, duke, governor, marshall, mayor, minister, noble, peer, prince, princess, squire*

Feudal terms: *bailiff, bondman, demesne, homage, manor, peasant, serf, servant, slave, subject, vassal*

General: *alliance, assembly, council, crown, empire, exile, liberty, parliament, public, rebel, record, repeal, revenue, sovereign, state, tax, traitor, treason, tyranny, usurp*

Legal: *adultery, advocate, arson, assault, bail, bar, bill, convict* (verb), *defendant, fine, forfeit, fraud, heir, indictment, inquest, judge, jury, pardon, petition, plaintiff, proof, ransom, sentence, suit, summons, verdict*

Church Words

Although, as we saw in Chapter 3, most of the basic religious words entered English after the coming of missionaries from Rome, many others came in from medieval French. Examples:

Titles: *abbess (abbot* was in OE), *cardinal, chaplain, clerk*, dean, friar, hermit, legate, novice, parson*, pastor, prelate, sexton, vicar*

Words referring to service or buildings: *abbey, baptism, censer, chancel, chantry, chapter, cloister, communion, convent, confession, cro-*

---

* Words marked with an asterisk are discussed in the following section.

sier, crucifix, hermitage, homily, incense, lectern, miter, orison, prayer, preach, priory, sacrament, sanctuary, sermon, surplice

Theological: *absolution, contrition, creator, damnation, devotion, faith, heresy, immortality, miracle, mystery, penitence, reverence, sacrilege, saint, salvation, savior, trinity, virgin*

General: *charity, mercy, piety, pity, religion, sacrifice, theology*

Words in Science and the Arts

Although the Normans brought in the word *science,* for a long time it meant only "knowledge," as its Latin ancestor *scientia* did. Not until the eighteenth century did it approximate the modern definition. Of the Norman words pertaining to science in its modern sense, most refer to medicine. The Normans also are responsible for many of the words still used in the arts.

Medical: *anatomy, apothecary, arsenic, balm, contagion, distemper, gout, jaundice, leper, malady, medicine, ointment, pain, physician, pleurisy, poison, pulse, remedy, sulphur, surgeon*

Literary and linguistic: *chapter, clause, gender, grammar, lay, literature, noun, paper, pen, poet, preface, prose, rhyme, romance, story, title, tragedy, treatise, volume*

Artistic and architectural: *art, beauty, cathedral, ceiling, cellar, chamber, chimney, color, column, figure, garret, image, joist, lattice, mansion, melody, music, palace, pillar, pinnacle, porch, tower*

Social and Domestic Words

For a few centuries the social and domestic importations of the Normans showed only slight influence in many English households, but eventually they affected food, clothing, furnishings, and pastimes—in fact, almost every phase of English life.

Culinary: *appetite, beef, biscuit*, boil*, blanch, cruet, feast, fry*, grate, goblet, jelly, mutton, mince, plate, platter, poach*, pork, saucer, veal,* and the names of dozens of specific foods and spices

Words for apparel and ornamentation: *apparel, attire, boots, buckle, button, cape, chemise, cloak, coat, embroidery, garter, garment, gown, habit, lace, ornament, petticoat, pleat, robe, veil,* as well as names of many jewels and the colors *blue, brown, russet, saffron, scarlet,* and *tawny*

Words for furnishings: *basin, blanket, chair, chandelier, closet, couch, curtain, cushion*, lamp, lantern, quilt, screen, towel*

Words for recreation: *carol, checkers, chess, dance, fool, jolly, joust, joy, juggler, leisure, minstrel, revel, ribald, tournament,* plus many words relating to riding and hunting as sports.

Doublets

English has a number of pairs of words that come from the same ultimate source but have come to differ in spelling and usually in meaning. Thus *camera* "room," a Latin word, was *chambre* in French. We use both *camera* and *chamber;* the legal phrase *in camera* "in chambers, in privacy" retains the early sense of *camera.*

Gentile comes from Latin *gentilis,* but *gentle* and *genteel* come from its French derivative, *gentil.*

Latin *taberna* "shop, tavern" gave rise to French *taverne,* our *tavern.* But we borrowed *tabernacle* directly from Latin and gave it a special religious sense.

Bench and *bank* go back to the same Germanic word. But the French borrowed it as *banc,* and the English borrowed it back as *bank,* while retaining the OE *benc* that became *bench.*

Latin *arcus* "bow" gave us *arc,* but its French variant gave us *arch.* Similarly Latin *legalis* "according to law" gave us *legal,* and its Old French variant *loial* is responsible for our *loyal. Regal* and *royal* both came from Old French, where they had already diverged; both go back to Latin *regalis,* which was a derivative of *rex* "king."

Norman French and Central French were different dialects, and English has a few doublets reflecting borrowings from both. For example, Normans are responsible for our *cattle,* Central French for *chattel.* Perhaps the most interesting pair is *chase* and *catch,* almost opposite in meaning; Central French *chacier,* from Latin *captāre* "to seize" gave us *chase,* and the Norman French variant *cachier,* from the same Latin word, gave us *catch.*

A Summary of Middle English Borrowings from French

Studies by the Danish Otto Jespersen and the American Albert C. Baugh have indicated that the rate of ME borrowing from French was slow at first, but that it accelerated after 1250 and reached a peak followed by a decline in the fourteenth century. (These studies should be replicated with the *Middle English Dictionary* at hand, a tool not available to Jespersen and Baugh.) It is apparent, as might be expected, that only when the Normans and the English began to associate fairly closely did the French English begin to affect English substantially. And given examples like those we have noted, we can see how the hundreds of borrowings reflected considerable change in the lives of the English.

One interesting development resulted in the combination of English and French components within the same word. Thus the English suffix *-ly* was often added to French adjectives, giving us words like *courteously* and *royally*. The same comment applies to OE *-ful* and *-ness,* resulting in words such as *beautiful* and *faithfulness.* The French-derived *battle* combined with English *ax* to give *battle-ax.* When such assimilation occurred, the two languages were obviously becoming one.

Along with gains came losses. Some English words were simply replaced, as these examples show: *ādl—disease, earm—poor, gōdian—improve, lyft* (cf. German *Luft*)*—air.* It is partly because of losses during this period that a number of OE words are now unfamiliar to us.

In other instances, though, both the English and French remained, as synonyms or near-synonyms. Professor Baugh (*A History of the English Language,* page 225) includes these examples: *deed—exploit, spell—enchantment, ask—question, goodness—virtue,* and *holy—sacred.*

Borrowings from Latin

Since French is a language derived from Latin, clearly almost all of the examples of borrowings from French can be traced back to earlier Latin forms. Some of these, in turn, go back to ancient Greek.

It is not possible to say positively whether a few medieval borrowings were from French or from Latin. However, religious writers in particular are known to have gone back to Latin directly; thus most of the thousand or so Latinate terms used by Wycliffe and his followers were borrowed without French intervention, though some of them did not survive. Also, scholars, semi-scholars, would-be-scholars, and pseudo-scholars in the fifteenth and sixteenth centuries often Anglicized Latin into weird forms, "inkhorn words" as they are sometimes called. Thomas Wilson (1553), who apparently coined the expression "ynke pot termes," objected to Latinate spawning, quoting as an example a letter containing *adepted* "attained," *splendidious* "splendid," *adnichilate* "reduced to nothing," and *Archgrammacian* "Chancellor."

Despite the needlessness and ridiculousness of thousands of such words (most of them now completely forgotten), Latin in medieval times as well as earlier and later did add countless useful words to the English vocabulary. Here are a few examples, mostly from the fourteenth or fifteenth century, from the many listed by Baugh (p. 223):

adjacent, custody, genius, history, index, individual, inferior, inmate, lunatic, mechanical, necessary, polite*, popular, promote, solar, solitary, submit, temperate, tributary, zenith.

ACCOUNTING FOR SOME OF THE WORDS OF MODERN ENGLISH

In this section we'll look at a number of English words, most of which entered the language in medieval times, and attempt to explain some of their interesting qualities or their oddities of meaning or form. When you and your students encounter some of these words in literature, a comment about them may add a little color to your discussion, even if offered only as a casual aside, and may help to increase interest in language. In addition, word stories show a great deal about the life of the time, and clarify the notion that words reveal the life of a people.

abed, alive, aside, a-running. OE *on bedde, on sīde,* and *on life* meant "in bed," "on the side," and "in life." The *on* was sometimes contracted in late OE or in ME to *a,* giving us the modern *abed, aside,* and *alive. On purpose* is still sometimes pronounced *a-purpose. On* sometimes also preceded participles. From this *on,* or sometimes from the unstressed *ge-* common in many verbs (with *g* having a sound like that of our *y*), came the *a-* prefix still common in uneducated speech, as in "a-running" or as in a folk song with the phrase "a-wanderin' and a-wonderin'."

aboveboard. Something is "aboveboard" if it is not concealed. In medieval times, a wheel somewhat like a roulette wheel was manipulated by unscrupulous gamblers so that with a concealed treadle they could stop the wheel wherever they wished. Honest gamblers put the wheel above a board to show that there was no hidden mechanism. At various times, also, shufflers of cards were told to shuffle "above the board" so that they could not cheat.

alias. Lawyers have long been addicted to the use of Latin expressions. In medieval courts one such expression was *alias dictus* "otherwise called," as "John Johnson, *alias dictus* James Jameson." The term was heard so often that, reduced to *alias,* it entered the common language. A person with an "alias" thus actually has an "otherwise."

bedlam.   In 1247 a priory called the Hospital of St. Mary of Bethlehem was established in London. It served both as a place to house visiting religious dignitaries and as a place where poor, ill people could be helped. When Henry VII confiscated church property in 1536, Bethlehem became an insane asylum. The pronunciation was corrupted to "Bedlam." For a while it was fashionable for visitors to go to Bedlam to observe and laugh at the wild antics of the inmates. Eventually *bedlam* came to mean any scene of wild confusion.

biscuit, Zwieback.   On early wooden ships, there were no ovens, because of the danger of fire, and bread brought from shore quickly became moldy. A Roman baker discovered, though, that he could re-bake thin slices of unleavened bread and thus dry it out enough that it would not spoil during a voyage. To the Romans this was *biscoctum panem* "twice-cooked bread." In Old French it became *bescoit* or *bescuit;* the word was borrowed in ME, and for a few centuries was usually spelled *bisket*. Today biscuits are no longer twice-baked, but the name remains. German *Zwieback* is a literal translation of the Latin *biscoctum*.

blow one's own horn.   When medieval dignitaries rode through town streets, heralds often preceded them, blowing horns to warn people to get out of the way. Peddlers or street salesmen also sometimes used horns to draw attention, but since they had no heralds, they had to blow their own horns.

bonfire.   A bonfire is literally a "bone fire"; although both words were in OE, the combination seems not to have been recorded before 1483. The usual explanation is that a bonfire was a large fire of bones, but since bones don't burn well, perhaps it referred instead to burning at the stake, leaving only the bones of the victim. That may be Christopher Marlowe's implication in "Ere I die, those foul idolaters / Shall make me bonfires with their filthy bones."

bridegroom.   OE *guma* "man" survived for a time in ME *bridegome* "recently married man" but then became confused with *grom* "man who takes care of horses"; the confusion resulted in *bridegroom*. The suggestion has been made, though, that the substitution was intentional, since at the wedding feast, several days in length, the newlywed man was expected to act as servant for his bride.

bring home the bacon.   *Bacon* or *bacoun* was one of a number of food-words borrowed by the English from the Normans. Almost annually for about five hundred years starting about 1445, a church in Essex awarded a side of bacon to the couple married one year who could prove they had lived most harmoniously. A jury of twelve unmarried men and women made the decision. The winning couple "brought home the bacon." Through generalization, success in any enterprise is now figuratively said to "bring home the bacon."

broker. The original *broker,* from French *brocher,* was one who broached or opened a new cask of wine. The *Oxford English Dictionary* says, "The *broker* was lit. a tapster who retailed wine, and hence, any retail dealer, a second-hand dealer, middleman, agent, etc." The modern *stockbroker* is a specialized kind of middleman.

burglar. Norman French *burgler,* assisted by Medieval Latin *burgulator,* gave us *burglar.* Earlier Latin, however, had borrowed from German the word *burgus* "a fort," and apparently early burglars were men successful in breaking into a fort. Burglary must have been common in medieval England; a document dated 1268 says that the most common varieties of criminals were "morditrores & robbatores & burglatores."

cardinal. In the early Catholic Church a certain type of official was called a *cardinal,* from Latin *cardin* "a hinge," possibly because much of the work of the church hinged on him. Cardinals grew in importance until they became second in importance only to the pope. In 1245, Pope Innocent IV recommended that they choose a distinctive garb. All-red outfits, including red hats, resulted. The American bird, *cardinal,* was so named because its color was like that of the churchmen's clothing. Today most people associate the name only with the color; certainly the idea of "hinge" has disappeared.

clerk. Chaucer's Clerk (still pronounced [klark] in England) was a scholar, learned in books. Clerks were also often *clerics,* or churchmen. As literacy increased, many people who could write took positions as correspondents, bookkeepers, etc. Dickens's Bob Cratchit was a nineteenth-century example of such a clerk. In today's America, most clerks work in stores, and because of cash registers may never need to write anything.

cooking terms. A number of our familiar cooking terms came into ME or E Mod E from Norman or later French.

baste, probably an early sixteenth-century borrowing from French.
boil, ME *boillen,* from Old French *boillir* "to bubble up."
braise, a late borrowing, from French for "hot charcoal."
broil, ME *bruyle,* from Old French *bruiller* "to broil, burn."

fricassee, a sixteenth-century borrowing from French *fricasser* "to mince and cook in sauce."

fry, ME *fryen,* from Old French *frire.* (But *fry* referring to fish or children, as "small fry," is from Old Norse.)

grill, from French *griller,* seventeenth century.

poach, a fifteenth-century borrowing from French *pochier* or *pocher.*

roast, a medieval borrowing from Old French *rostir.*

Devil, however, as in "deviled egg," goes back ultimately to Latin and Greek. Apparently, early stuffed eggs contained so much pepper that they were hot as hell.

coward. Of uncertain origin. A frightened dog often runs away with his tail between his legs. Old French *couard* may refer to this fact; it perhaps comes from *coue* "tail." An alternative possibility, given credence by the ME spelling *couherde,* is that a coward was a "cowherd," often a young boy who would usually run for help rather than fight in case of an attack by predators. A third explanation is that the word comes from *Coart,* the hare in an Old French story of Reynard the Fox.

curfew. To save wood while still preserving a little warmth in cold medieval houses, it was customary at night to cover the fire with ashes; the logs would smolder all night and flames could be revived in the morning. In some French and English towns a bell was rung to remind people that it was time to cover the fire; this signal in Old French was *covre-feu,* in Anglo-French *coeverfu.* Later the bell was a signal that it was time to come in off the streets. Today many places still have a *curfew*-hour for youngsters, though no bell is rung and no fires need banking.

cushion. Latin *coxa* meant "hip." A pad to protect the hips was a *coxinum.* French called it *couissin,* and ME spelled the borrowed word in several hundred ways, including *cuisshin, cusshyn, cushin,* and *quisshen.* Obviously a pad could protect more than just hips. Eventually the term took on figurative senses; today, for instance, an athletic team with a large lead is said to have a "good cushion."

debonaire. ME took the three French words *de bon aire* "of good disposition" and wrote them as one. Since a person of good disposition seldom showed unpleasant emotions that he may have felt, the word took on the connotations of urbanity or nonchalance that it now has.

derby. The ancestor of the earls of Derby who figure so prominently in Shakespeare's plays and in much English history came over with William the Conqueror. The word is usually pronounced [darbi] in England. The twelfth earl of Derby in 1780 established a horse race that has become the world's most famous. Americans attending a derby in 1888 liked the hats worn by some of the spectators, called them *derbies* (Americanizing the [a] to [ɜ·], and popularized them in the United States; such hats are still worn by brisk young Englishmen who, umbrella in hand, stride proudly down Piccadilly Street on their way to the office or shop.

double-cross. Some of Chaucer's pilgrims told of selling fake religious relics, such as pieces of the cross of Jesus, and Mark Twain attested that the practice continued in the last century. "Giving the cross" became thieves' slang for cheating. When a cheater was himself cheated, he was said to be "double-crossed."

dun. Though you do not like to be *dunned* for what you owe, the process is probably less noisy than it once was. Apparently ME *dun* is a variant of *din,* from an Old Germanic root meaning "to thunder." In medieval times town criers would beat drums to attract attention, and then shout names of debtors who were being sought. At that time *dunning* was hardly a private matter, so obviously invasion of privacy is not just a modern problem.

dunce. John Duns Scotus (Duns, in Scotland, was his home) was a noted theologian who died in 1308. His followers, called *Dunsmen* or *Dunses,* were very influential, but their teachings were discredited during the Renaissance. So today, despite the learning of these gentlemen, a *dunce* is ignorant and stupid.

falsehood, thinking cap. Medieval clergymen, doctors, and other professional or trades people often wore hoods that symbolized their occupations. It was obviously easy, though, for anyone to put on a "false hood" and merely pretend to be qualified for a particular type of work. Hence *falsehood* came to mean deceit or a lie. Scholars wore a square-cut cap, which ignorant people believed helped them to be great thinkers; the cap was therefore dubbed a *thinking cap,* which everyone would like to put on occasionally.

farce. ME *farse* meant "stuffing," such as was put into fowls for baking. It came from Old French *farce,* derived in turn from *farcire* "to stuff." In late medieval times when miracle or morality plays were presented, amateur actors would sometimes put on humorous skits between the regular acts. These served as "stuffing" or "filling," and hence the term *farse* or *farce* was applied to them. The word *forcemeat,* still found in some cookbooks to mean ground meat used as stuffing, retains the early meaning.

garble. Something is "garbled" if it is badly mixed, as a message may be. The word goes back to Arabic *gharbala,* the act of sifting to separate good spice from bad. ME *garbelen* meant "to sift, to select," but its meaning reversed to refer to the act of mixing.

George.   *George,* a man's name, was introduced into ME by the Normans, who generally used the form *Georges.* The name can be traced back much further, though, to ancient Greek *geōrgos* "farmer," the first part of which is the same *geo-* that we find in words like *geography, geology,* and *geometry,* as well as recent words like *geophysics* and *geopolitics.* Vergil wrote a long poem, the *Georgics,* concerning agriculture and country life.

grocer.   A medieval *spicer* sold spices, which he bought from a *spicer en gross,* or wholesaler. The latter became known as a *grosser,* and the distinction between retail and wholesale faded. Later *grossers* or *grocers* no longer confined themselves to spices; they sold *groceries* in a *grocery store,* usually unaware of the history of their occupation or its relationship to the current meanings of *gross,* except that they looked carefully at *gross* profits and bought some items by the *gross* and maybe *grossly* overpriced them.

gyp.   In late medieval times bands of swarthy people roamed England and the continent. They were Hindus (Romany), but the English miscalled them *Egyptians* or *Gypsies,* and distrusted them. When a person was cheated, he was said to have been "gypped," regardless of whether or not the "Gypsies" were responsible. *Gibberish,* referring to their "odd" language, may come from the same source, but probably is onomatopoeic, related to *jabber.*

hoax, hocus pocus.   Medieval swindlers often impressed illiterate peasants by use of Latin phrases such as those in the Mass. One of these was *hoc est corpus Domini* (This is the body of the Lord), which sometimes was distorted into something like *hocus pocus.* When the swindlers were found out, their language or "hocus pocus" was associated with their trickery. *Hoax* is apparently a shortened form of *hocus pocus.* (See also *hokum,* page 278.)

jail, gaol, jailbird.   It is well known that American *jail* is frequently spelled *gaol* in England. ME used two words for it, *jaiole* from Old French and *gayole* from Norman French; both variants remained in the language, as *jail* and *gaol.* A *jailbird,* usually a woman, was originally a prisoner who instead of being placed in stocks was kept in a cage a few feet off the ground.

jimmy (v.).   In ME *James,* nicknamed *Jemmy,* was one of the most common names. It was applied to most helpers or apprentices, regardless of their real names, just as in some cities today almost any man may be called "Mac." When burglars invented a short crowbar as a "helper," they referred to it as a "jemmy." The term is now often used both as a noun and as a verb: to "jimmy" a lock.

maudlin. A ME pronunciation of *Magdalen* was [mɔdlən]. Since pictures of Mary Magdalen almost always showed her weeping, in the seventeenth century the word became a synonym of "extremely tearful," "highly emotional," or "crying drunk." The noun *maudlinism* "state of being maudlin-drunk" is now seldom used.

mess. William the Conqueror's Norman soldiers called food *mes,* which today is French *met.* American soldiers still may eat in a "mess hall." In early England, *mess* came to refer to a mixed, soupy mixture such as porridge. By extension any sort of unsystematic mixture, not just of food, is a *mess.*

noon. *Noon,* ME *none* or *noon,* is associated with Latin *nona hora* "the ninth hour after sunrise," the time when Jesus is believed to have died. Many churches and monasteries held religious services, called *nones,* at three P.M.; afterward the monks ate their main meal. Perhaps because they got hungry long before then, the "noon hour" was gradually advanced to about twelve, or even eleven A.M. "High noon" designated the time when the sun was highest in the sky.

parson, person. One of Chaucer's pilgrims was "a povre [poor] *Persone*" who was rich in "hooly thoghte and werk . . . a lerned man, a clerk." The form *persone* is part of the evidence that *parson* and *person* were once the same word; the parson was "a person of the church." Both words go back to Latin *persōna,* referring to the mask worn by actors in ancient plays. Everyone, person or parson, wears his own mask.

patter. The ME form was *patren* or *patern.* When people recited their prayers or Pater Nosters (Our Fathers), or anything else, very rapidly and thoughtlessly, they were said to "patern," later *patter.* Another *patter,* however, referring to a repetitive sound like that of raindrops, is simply a frequentative form of *pat.*

pay the piper. Medieval amusements were simple, including street dancing, with music often supplied by a strolling flutist or "piper." At the end a collection would be taken up to pay the piper. By extension, whenever we have fun of any kind, we may later have to "pay the piper."

pedigree. French genealogists frequently indicated lines of family descent by use of a three-pronged mark. Some of them noticed the similarity of this mark to the track of a crane, and hence called it *pié de grue* "foot of crane." In late ME this was borrowed as *pedegru* or *pee-de-grew.*

penitentiary. In a penitentiary it is hoped that prisoners will be or become *penitent;* both words go back to the Latin for *penitent.* ME *penitenciary* was a penance officer; the word later changed its meaning to that of the place over which such an officer presided.

piggy bank. In late ME one meaning of *pig* or *pygg* was "an earthenware pot, pitcher, jar, or crock." Housewives sometimes used one such pig as a place to deposit small coins. Later someone got the idea of shaping this kind of pig like its coincidental namesake.

please. ME *plaise, pleise,* or *plese* came from Old French *plaisir* "to give pleasure," as in the archaic "It pleasured him." In "if you please," the *you* is an old dative case; the meaning is "if it pleases you." Our *please* in a polite request is a shortening of some such phrase as "may it please you" or "if it be pleasing to you."

polite. *Polite* is related to *polish.* Both come from Latin *polire* "to smooth, polish." In late medieval times churchmen very painstakingly polished their ecclesiastical ware; when it was properly done it was said to be *politus,* from the Latin participle. In the form *polite* or *poylte* it came to be used figuratively to refer to smoothness and pleasantness of manners.

pretty penny. The expression "I'd give a pretty penny for that!" seems odd, since pennies seem much alike and not really very valuable. But in 1257 King Henry III minted some gold pennies, worth twenty shillings. Anyone who bought something with one of these pretty pennies was giving a great deal.

rack one's brains. ME *rekke* or *rakke,* a framelike instrument of torture on which prisoners were stretched, apparently came from Middle Dutch *rec* "framework." Today if you "rack your brains" you are supposedly stretching them to the limit.

ringleader. Medieval dances generally started with the dancers in a ring; afterward a ringleader would lead them through various conventionalized group movements. By extension a ringleader became a leader of any enterprise including some that were unlawful.

salary. Salt, now cheap, was once expensive. Ancient Roman soldiers were provided a *salarium* "money to buy salt." A Roman road over which much salt was transported was the *Via Salarium.* In Anglo-French, the word for payment to a soldier or an employee was *salarie,* which came into use in England in late ME. Even then the idea of "salt" had been lost, although we may still say of an inefficient employee, "He's not worth his salt."

season, seasoning. *Season* goes back to Latin for "sowing time." Old French *seison,* however, meant any time of year, as does our noun *season,* ME *sesoun.* When wine or cheese was kept for a period of time, its flavor improved. The French called the process *saisonner.* English housewives found that adding salt, spices, etc., to food also improved the flavor, so they began using *sesoun* or *season* for that process also, even though the time factor was no longer involved.

spendthrift. One old meaning of *thrift* is "accumulated wealth." Often however, painfully accumulated money is spent in prodigal fashion by a person's heirs, who "spend his thrift."

surnames from occupations. A number of familiar modern surnames are derived from medieval occupations largely unknown today or changed in spelling:

Baxter = Baker
Chapman = "merchant"
Day = "dairyman"
Fletcher = "arrow-maker"
Latimer = "interpreter, Latiner"
Lorimer = "maker of bits (for horses)"
Sumner = "summoner" (one of Chaucer's pilgrims)
Wagner, Waggoner = "wagon-maker"
Webster = Weaver

tags. In an old poem for children, beggars are described as wearing "rags and tags." ME *tagge,* probably from a Scandinavian source, referred to slashes or small triangular cutouts at the hems of garments; later, small ornaments replaced these *tagges.* Still later, *tags* of parchment were used to seal official papers. Merchants finally saw how useful tags might be to them, although the custom of attaching price tags or other informative tags did not become very widespread until our own century.

talent. In Matthew 25: 14–30 Jesus tells the story of the "talents," which were amounts of money. The word is from Greek *talanton,* a sensitive scale for weighing valuables. Medieval Latin *talentum* referred both to a unit of money and to mental aptitude. Although *talente* for money existed in OE, the second definition apparently first showed up in late ME or early Mod E.

tell, teller, tale, talk, tail. ME *tellen* meant "relate" but also "count," as a nun might "tell her beads." Today a *teller* in a bank or in an election is a person who counts money or ballots. *Tale* and *talk* go back to the same I-E root as *tell*. *Tail* is from a different source and did not become a homonym of *tale* until late ME or early Mod E.

tennis, love. Like so much else, the game of tennis (ME *tenetz* or *tennys*) was brought to England from France. The French name apparently comes from *tenez* "take, receive," a call once made by the server to alert his opponent. But why is a score of zero called "love"? One explanation, not verified, is that a zero is shaped like an egg, which in French is *l'oeuf*.

thorough, through. These were originally the same word, OE *þurh*. The two meanings began to separate fairly early, but the separation was not yet complete in ME, or even in the Elizabethan age, when Shakespeare wrote "thorough bush, thorough brier." A *thoroughfare* is actually a *throughfare* or *throughway*.

train. ME *trayne* came from Old French *train,* which goes back to Latin *trahere* "to draw, pull." A "train" of wagons or sleds consisted of one drawn behind another. By analogy, the long, trailing portion of a lady's dress was called a train, as were the long tailfeathers of a bird or the retinue of a nobleman. With the invention of railroads in the nineteenth century, the word was naturally applied to the cars drawn by (and including) the locomotive.

varnish. ME took *vernisch* from Old French *vernis,* from Medieval Latin *veronix,* said to be from Greek *Berenikē,* a city in Libya where varnish was first made. Nothing unusual so far. But Berenikē was named for the beautiful wife of Pharaoh Ptolemy III of the third century B.C.; she sacrificed her lovely amber hair as a religious offering to bring him back safely from war. So in this roundabout way an Egyptian queen gave her name to a common household item.

villain. An ancient Roman farm was a *villa,* and in Medieval Latin one who lived on a farm was a *villānus,* which became Old French *vilein* and ME *vilain,* a term used for any lowborn rural person. The life of serfs was so difficult that many of them turned to crime, so gradually the word degenerated to mean a criminal or scoundrel, regardless of where he lived.

wink. Today a *wink* requires a quick lowering and raising of an eyelid. Earlier it meant to close the eyes. That early meaning remains in *wink at:* if a person winks at corruption, he figuratively closes his eyes to it, pretending it isn't there.

with. One old meaning of *with* was "against," a meaning still current in "fight with someone." This meaning also survives in *withstand* "to stand against" and less obviously in *withhold* "to refrain from giving."

year (plural). OE *gēar* "year" was one of a number of nouns with no inflectional ending in the plural nominative or accusative. Others included the words for *word, breast, sword, thing, woman, wild animal (dēor), house.* Chaucer, when the *s*-plural was becoming common, used both *yeer* and *yeeres* as a plural. Today many uneducated people still say things like "ten year ago"—a survival that shows that the changes in inflections were never totally completed. Similarly we may hear "six foot tall," "weighs twelve pound," "two mile from here." In other contexts, such expressions are standard: a "three-year delay," "a six-foot rule," "a twelve-pound weight," "a two-mile walk."

CLASSROOM ACTIVITIES

Books about Medieval Life

Some of your students may enjoy reading:

Beers, Loran. *The Book of Hugh Flower.* A mason in the fifteenth century.

Bolton, Ivy May. *A Son of the Land.* A young fourteenth-century serf.

Chute, Marchette. *Geoffrey Chaucer of England.* Vivid. For older students.

Doyle, Arthur Conan. *The White Company.* The time of Edward III and the Hundred Years' War. For older students.

Gilbert, Jane. *Imps and Angels.* Boys in thirteenth-century England.

Gray, Elizabeth J. *Adam of the Road.* Thirteenth century—boy-and-dog-centered.

Hartman, Gertrude. *Medieval Days and Ways.*

Hewes, Agnes. *A Boy of the Lost Crusade.* French boy in the Children's Crusade.

Jones, Gwyn and Thomas. *The Mabinogion.* Welsh medieval romances.

Kent, Louise A. *He Went with Marco Polo.*

MacLeod, Mary. *King Arthur and His Noble Knights.* A simple retelling of the Thomas Malory stories.

Muntz, Hope. *The Golden Warrior*. About King Harold.

Porter, Jane. *Scottish Chiefs*. Scottish and English in 1296.

Price, Christine. *Three Golden Nobles*. A young serf in fourteenth century England.

Pyle, Howard. *Men of Iron*. A boy in the age of knighthood.

Schoonover, Lawrence. *Burnished Blade*. The continental adventures of a thirteenth-century orphan.

Scott, Sir Walter. *Ivanhoe*. Rather hard reading at times, but a great adventure story.

Sedgwick, Henry D. *Dan Chaucer*. For older students.

Stevenson, Robert Louis. *The Black Arrow*. Set in the War of the Roses, 1485 and later.

Tappan, Eva M. *When Knights Were Bold*. Old (1911), but readable.

Twain, Mark. *A Connecticut Yankee in King Arthur's Court*. A delightful spoof.

Any of the stories or poems about Robin Hood and his Merry Men, reputed to have lived in the twelfth century, may also be suitable. One very easy one is *Robin Hood's Arrow,* by Eugenia Stone. A novel about the Norman Conquest, difficult for most high school students but more historically credible than many, is Charles Kingsley's *Hereward the Wake,* written in the nineteenth century.

Poems of Linguistic Interest

Here are the titles of a few frequently anthologized medieval short poems that have both literary and linguistic interest. The arrangement here is roughly in order of difficulty.

"Get Up and Bar the Door" (one of the few humorous ballads)
"Johnnie Armstrong" (gallant fight by a robber band against odds)
"The Wife of Usher's Well" (a ghost story)
"Thomas Rymer" (the queen of Elfland takes Thomas to her domain)
"Sir Patrick Spens" (a fatal voyage)
"Lord Randal" (young man poisoned by his sweetheart; told in questions and answers; good for choral reading)
"Edward" (tale of a patricide; told in conversation)
"Kathrine Jaffray" (the source of Scott's "Lochinvar")

(Most ballads are from northern England or Scotland, and date back to Norman times, but in their existing forms the language is usually sixteenth century or later. Hence they are easier to read than the lyrics listed next, but give a less accurate idea of ME.)

"Alysoun" (love poem; *Alysoun* is ME for *Alice*)
"Cuckoo Song" (spring poem)

Here are excerpts from two harder-to-find poems that may also be looked at for their language. The first, written by a Yorkshireman named Edward Minot, ridicules the flight of French King Phillip.

> Our king and his men held the felde
> Stalworthy [stalwart], with spere and schelde,
> And thoght to win his right.
> With lordes, and with knightes kene,
> And other doughty men bidene [enlisted]
> That was ful frek [eager] to fight.
> When Sir Philipp of France herd tell
> That King Edward in feld walld [would] dwell,
> That gaynéd him no glee.
> He trusted of no better boot [course of action]
> But both on hors and on foot
> He hasted him to flee.

A Lancastrian poet denounced the luxury of the court of Richard II (1367–1399) in this excerpt:

> . . . And rest on the daies,
> And spend of the spicerie [spices, expensive foods]
> More than it nedid,
> Both wexe [candles] and wyn
> In wast alle about.
> With deyntis ydoubled,
> And dannsing to pypis,
> In myrthe with moppis [moppets; refers to courtiers'
> lust for youngsters],
> Myrrours of synne.

Long metrical romances flourished during the medieval period, some written in French and translated into English. The following excerpt is from a *lai* written by Marie de France, born in France but a resident of England; it concerns the flight of a young woman with her baby, and is given here in a medieval translation.

> The maid took the child her mid [with]
> And stale away in an even tid,
> And passed over a wild heath,
> Throgh fild and thorough wood she geth
> All the winter longe night.

The weather was clear, the moon was light.
So that she cum by a forest side;
She wox all weary, and gan abide.
Soon after she gan heark
Cockes crow and dogges bark,
She arose, and thither wold;
Near and nearer she gan behold
Walls and houses fele [many] she seigh;
A church with steeple fair and high.
There was there nother street nor town,
But a house of religioun;
An order of nonnes, well y-dight [equipped]
To serve God both day and night.
The maiden abode no lengore,
But yede [hied, went] her to the churches door,
And on knees she set her down,
And said, weepand, her orisoun.

The next excerpt is a sentimental one from *Floris and Blanchefleur;*
it concerns a very young pair of lovers who are about to be decapitated
by a Saracen prince.

His sword he braid [snatched] out of his sheath
The children to have done to death.
Blanchefleur put forth her swire [neck],
And Floris agen [against] her did tire [pull].
"I am a man, I shall go before,
Thou mightest nought my death acore." [feel so grievously]
Floris forth his nekke bet [bent]
And Blanchefleur withdrew him yet.
Neither might the other thole [endure]
That the other deide before.
Alle that y-seen this
Therefor sorry were iwis [I know].
Though the Amiral [ruler] wroth he were
Yet he changede his cheere [attitude],
For either would for the other die,
And he saw many weeping eye.
And, for he loved so much that may [girl],
All weepinge he turned away.
His sword fell out of his hand to grounde
Nor might he hold it in thikke stounde [at that time].

Chapter I of *Ivanhoe*

Although the reading of *Ivanhoe* is unfashionable in schools today
(largely because many students find Scott's vocabulary too unfamiliar), a class may at least read the first chapter to get some background

on the linguistic and other differences between Anglo-Saxons and Normans of the late twelfth century. That Scott was an Anglophile is revealed by sentences such as "In short, French was the language of honor, of chivalry, and even of justice, while the far more manly and expressive Anglo-Saxon was abandoned to the use of rustics and hinds, who knew no other."

The differences between Norman French and English are epitomized in the following conversation between Gurth, the swineherd, and Wamba, the jester or fool. Your students may be led from it to an exploration of some of the other differences between the two languages. (It is rather amusing that in this conversation Scott—unknowingly or unthinkingly—put some forty Norman-based words into the mouths of the two Saxons.)

"Why, how call you those grunting brutes running about on their four legs?" demanded Wamba.

"*Swine*, fool, swine," said the herd; "every fool knows that."

"And *swine* is good Saxon," said the Jester; "but how call you the sow when she is flayed, and drawn, and quartered, and hung up by the heels, like a traitor?"

"Pork," answered the swineherd.

"I am very glad that every fool knows that, too," said Wamba, "and *pork*, I think, is good Norman-French; and so when the brute lives, and is in the charge of a Saxon slave, she goes by the Saxon name; but becomes a Norman, and is called *pork,* when she is carried to the castle hall to feast among the nobles . . . . Nay, I can tell you more," said Wamba in the same tone: "there is old Alderman *Ox* continues to hold his Saxon epithet while he is under the charge of serfs and bondsmen such as thou, but becomes *Beef,* a fiery French gallant, when he arrives before the worshipped jaws that are destined to consume him. Mynherr *Calf,* too, becomes Monsieur de *Veau* [*veal*] in like manner: he is Saxon when he requires tendance, and takes a Norman name when he becomes a matter of enjoyment."

"By St. Dunstan," answered Gurth, "thou speakest but sad truths; little is left to us but the air we breathe, and that appears to have been reserved with much hesitation, solely for the purpose of enabling us to endure the tasks they lay upon our shoulders. The finest and fattest is for their board [table]; the loveliest is for their couch; the best and bravest supply their foreign masters with soldiers, and whiten distant lands with their bones [a reference to the Crusades], leaving few here who have either will or the power to protect the unfortunate Saxon."

How Much Study of Early Pronunciations?

Joseph E. Milosh (*Teaching the History of the English Language,* pp. 46–48) recommends that high school students be armed with only a few general principles for pronouncing Chaucer and other early writers, since minute attention to the sounds of the period might result in boredom and take time away from more interesting and useful items such as an understanding of how vocabulary developed. If students, in reading aloud, pronounce each ME consonant (e.g., *kn* in *knee*) and give continental values to the vowels, they will be approximating Chaucer's pronunciation well enough.

Parallel Passages

Reading of some lines of Chaucer side by side with one or more modern translations can reveal some of the changes that have occurred in word order, word endings, etc.

Doublets

Students who look up the following words will discover that they go back to the same source, but because they entered the language through different channels and at different times, have different meanings:

annoy, ennui	feeble, foible
arc, arch	fragile, frail
banjo, mandolin	gentle, jaunty
bank, bench (See page 119.)	jealous, zealous
camera, chamber	legal, loyal
courtesy, curtsy	ratio, ration, reason
dike, ditch	regal, royal (nearly synonymous)

An Imitation of Chaucer

"A common exercise for the individual student asks him to write a portrait like those in the *General Prologue,* though in Modern English and perhaps of a modern figure. Here a student might want to experiment with archaisms, imitate Chaucer's use of doublets or manner of phrasing, and in general play with his language."
(Joseph E. Milosh, *Teaching the History of the English Language,* p. 74.)

Chaucer's Fear

Near the end of *Troilus and Criseyde,* Chaucer addresses his 'litel bok,' hoping that it will not be misread or faultily scorned:

> And for ther is so gret diversite
> In Englissh and in writyng of oure tonge,
> So prey I God that non miswrite the[e],

Ne the[e] mysmetre for defaute of tonge.
And re[a]d wherso thow be, or elles songe [sung],
That thow be understonde, God I biseche!

Ask your class whether today a writer of English ever need fear misinterpretation as Chaucer did, and if so, in what circumstances.

6

Early
Modern English

THE INFLUENCE OF THE RENAISSANCE UPON LANGUAGE

Internal vs. External History

Some language scholars devote nearly all their attention to the anatomizing of a corpus of language. They study its syntax, its morphology, its phonology, and (though this is largely a recent development) its semantics. They analyze texts—sentences or parts of sentences—as independent entities, just as the "new critics" in the middle third of the twentieth century analyzed each literary work as though it were an authorless, self-contained arrangement of words. Scholars of language history who concentrate upon such kinds of anatomizing are concerned with *internal* history, and their research has contributed much to our awareness of linguistic details. Both the philologists in the Germanic tradition, who carefully counted and classified and compared, and the more recent grammarians who analyze older forms of the language in light of the doctrines of transformational grammar, have made readers aware of language characteristics that otherwise would have escaped notice.

In contrast, other scholars have been more interested in *external* history. They regard language as a reflection of the time when it was produced: language, they say, changes because of what happens to people. Thus while the "internalists" are content to describe what they find in English manuscripts of, say, about 1600 A.D., the "externalists" are especially interested in how the language got that way: how it reflected recent and current events and attitudes, and how the people lived and how the styles of their lives

138

influenced the language they spoke and wrote. The externalists do not deny the worth of the scholarly contributions of the internalists, but they argue that one cannot accurately describe language as a thing in isolation: it must be observed in the context of its time. For example, Italian, French, German, and English of the period from 1400 to 1700 must be looked at from the standpoint of what was happening to people in those years. Since the Renaissance, with the spirit that typified it, produced great impact upon the people of that era, at least an inkling of that impact is essential to an understanding of linguistic developments.[1]

What the Renaissance Was

Two definitions of *Renaissance* are frequent. The narrower of these equates *Renaissance* with its root meaning, "rebirth." In this definition *Renaissance* is virtually the same as the Revival of Learning, the rebirth of awareness of the philosophy, science, literature and other arts of the ancients, especially the Greeks and Romans.

The other definition, which I prefer, is much more inclusive. The Revival of Learning is an important part, but the Renaissance is, more than anything else, a spirit, a climate, an environment, that encouraged people to look not only to the past but also at themselves in the present. A whole new attitude toward life prevailed. Whereas in the Middle Ages human life was regarded as mainly preparation for a potentially richer life beyond the grave, in the Renaissance it was thought of as valuable in itself: every day could be an opportunity, an adventure.

Not that the Middle Ages were as dark, as unenlightened, as the term *Dark Ages* suggests. Chaucer lived in the Middle Ages, but he possessed much of the *joie de vivre* and the spirit of adventure that were to characterize the Renaissance a little later. Nevertheless, life in the Middle Ages, under the pressures of feudalism and the medieval church, was hard and confining. Most people seldom ventured more than a few miles from their places of birth, they were isolated from most of humanity, they had little sense of the past and almost none of the future except the peril of Hell and

---

[1] Best-known of the English-language histories that devote considerable space to external history is that by Albert C. Baugh (*A History of the English Language.* New York: Appleton-Century-Crofts, second ed., 1957). Numerous popularized books by Mario Pei (e.g., *The Story of English.* Philadelphia: J. B. Lippincott Co., 1952) are also in this tradition. Representative of the internal histories are Morton W. Bloomfield and Leonard Newmark's *A Linguistic Introduction to the History of English* (New York: Alfred A. Knopf, 1963) and Robert A. Peters' *A Linguistic History of English* (Boston: Houghton Mifflin Co., 1968).

the possibility of Heaven, and each person for generations tended to repeat the sort of life his or her parents had known—for most, a life of incessant toil in the fields, in the house, or in the smithy or other place of employment.

The change to the Renaissance was not abrupt and certainly not universal: the lives of some people in 1600 differed only a little from the lives of their forebears. But the small changes piled up, and for many people became big changes. Sailors, aided by the new mariner's compass, returned from across an ocean and told gaudy tales of a previously unknown world. English people who could afford it traveled widely on the continent, especially in Italy, where they found art and architecture such as they had never seen. International commerce added to the acquaintance with other lands. The stranglehold of a monolithic church was lessened, and abuses of the sort typified by some of Chaucer's churchmen abated. The invention of the printing press made learning available to many who otherwise would never have learned even to read. Humanism in literature contrasted with dull religious argumentative tracts, and cast new light on what being human means. In education, the medieval trivium and quadrivium were slowly supplanted by humanistically based studies (which were, perhaps unfortunately, too narrowly confined to classical literature). Theaters opened, presenting plays much more ambitious and literary than the earlier "morality" and "mystery" plays. Life was more comfortable for many people, and less threatening and fearful. There was a little more time to think, to experiment, and to explore, and more inclination to do so.

The Beginnings of Printing

Until the fourteenth century every European book was a manuscript in the etymological sense of that word—written by hand. Copyists, usually monks, spent long periods of time on each copy, inscribing it letter by letter and word by word on parchment or vellum. The slow process made books too expensive for most people, and education could hardly be widespread until a better copying procedure was found.

In the fourteenth century Europeans introduced block printing from China, where it had been known for centuries. This process involved cutting pictures or words in relief on a block of wood; when inked, whatever was cut upon the block could be reproduced on a page at a time—the way you perhaps made "potato prints" in childhood. Once the cutting had been done, this early form of printing was relatively speedy, but the carving required great care and much time, very small letters were especially hard to form, and an error on a block could be corrected only by recarving the whole block. Despite the problems, in eighth-century Japan a Buddhist charm was printed from wood blocks or cast-metal plates in an edition of one million copies; no such extensive use of the block method, however, existed in Europe.

Other materials that would eventually lend themselves to mass production of printed matter were available before the fifteenth century. The Chinese had known for more than a thousand years how to make paper from rags and fibers, and paper-making came to Italy, and from there to the rest of Europe, in the twelfth century. Ink composed of lampblack and linseed oil was available. Metalworkers had created alloys that would prove suitable for metal type. Presses used for making wine or cheese could be adapted to printing.

Movable Type

Unknown to Europeans, the Chinese also had invented the one additional item needed for rapid printing—movable type—and had experimented with such type made of hard earthenware, then tin, and then wood. The Japanese and the Koreans also knew the system. Europeans invented movable type independently; had there been contacts with the Orient, they might have borrowed the idea much earlier, and perhaps European history and world history would as a result have been different. Some historians call the Dutch Lourens Janszoon Coster the European most responsible for movable type, in about 1430; some credit Frenchmen or Italians; others say that the German Johann Gutenberg was the inventor, in the 1440's. At any rate Gutenberg was the first European to bring all the pieces together and make extensive use of the method; the Bibles that he printed are today among the word's most renowned and most expensive books.

The early center of printing was the German city of Mainz, where Gutenberg lived. In 1462, though, a couple of archbishops went to war against each other, and residents of Mainz were on the losing side. Among the many inhabitants driven into exile were the printers, who carried their young trade into other cities and even into other countries. The first printers in Italy, France, Switzerland, and Spain were Germans—some of them apparently refugees from Mainz.

Hunger for books was keen not only in England but throughout Europe; by 1500, according to some estimates, Europe had printed 40,000 books or editions in copies totaling some 15,000,000 to 20,000,000. By that year the printing center had shifted from Germany to Italy, where, along with other printers, the great Aldus Manutius lived. He founded the Aldine

Press, standardized punctuation, invented italic type, perfected the casting of small sizes of type that were to make possible easily portable books, published works ranging from Aristotle and Aristophanes to Dante and Petrarch, and had enough spare time to found an academy for Greek studies. His son Paulus continued his father's work, publishing most of the Latin classics.

Caxton

The first English book, the *Recuyell* (summary) *of the Historyes of Troye,* was published at Bruges, Belgium, in 1475 by Colard Mansion and William Caxton. In 1476 Caxton moved his press and type to Westminster, England, and during the next fifteen years issued almost a hundred books, of which he himself was the translator of twenty-four, from French, Latin, and Dutch. He was as remarkable a man as Aldus Manutius. After an apprenticeship to a dealer in textiles in England, he had moved to Bruges, prospered, served as the influential "Governor of the English Nation of Merchant Adventurers," negotiated commercial treaties for England—and had become enamored with literature. In Cologne he learned about printing because in translating the *Recuyell* his "pen became worn, his hand weary, his eye dimmed" from all the copying. So he set up the press in Bruges, printed the *Recuyell,* then a book about chess, and then a couple of French books. In England, in the remaining years of his life, his press brought out not only translations of classic literature but also books on chivalry, morality, history, and philosophy, and—even more important—English literary works including the poetry of Chaucer, Gower, and Malory. The first illustrated English book, *The Myrrour of the World,* came from his press.

Caxton was sharply aware of linguistic change. In the preface to his *Eneydos* (a translation of a French paraphrase of Virgil's *Aeneid*) he makes the point both clearly and amusingly:

... And also my lorde abbot of westminster ded do shewe to me late, certain evydences wryton in olde englysshe, for to reduce it in-to our englysshe now usid. And certaynly it was wreton in suche wyse that it was more lyke to dutche than englysshe; I coude not reduce ne brynge it to be understonden. And certaynly our langage now used varyeth ferre [far] from that whiche was used and spoken whan I was borne. For we englysshe men ben borne under the domynacyon of the mone, whiche is never stedfaste, but ever waverynge, wexynge one season, and waneth & dyscreaseth another season. And that comyn englysshe that is spoken in one shyre varyeth from a nother. In so moche that in my dayes happened that certayn marchauntes were in a shippe in tamyse [Thames], for to have sayled over the see into zelande [Zeeland], and for lacke of wynde, thei taryed atte forlond, and wente to lande for to refreshe them. And one of theym named Sheffelde, a mercer, cam in-to an hows and axed for mete; and specylly he axyd after eggys. And the goode wyf answerde, that she coude speke no frenshe. And the marchaunt was angry, for he also coude speke no frenshe, bot wolde have hadde egges, and she understode hym not. And thenne at laste a nother sayd that he wolde have eyren. Then the good wyf sayd that she understod hym wel. Loo, what sholde a man in thyse dayes now wryte, egges or eyren? Certaynly it is harde to playse every man by cause of dyversite & chaunge of langage.

In the same passage, Caxton says that a translator must choose between "curyous termes whiche coude not be understande of comyn peple" and "olde and homely termes." Since the *Eneydos* is intended not for "a rude uplondyssh man" but for "a clerke [i.e., a learned man like Chaucer's Clerk] & a noble gentylman that feleth and understondeth in faytes of armes, in love, & in noble chyvalrye," he says he decided to translate "this sayd booke in to our englysshe, not ouer rude ne [nor] curyous"—in other words, to attempt some sort of compromise. Caxton here hints at a problem that was to vex many writers in the next century: to what extent should they admit Latinate or other foreign words, and to what extent should they use only native, "pure" English? We'll say more of this a bit later.

Within a few decades of Caxton's first book, the number of titles published in England reached into many hundreds, and by 1640 had passed 20,000. The chief effect that so much printing activity had upon the language was to move it toward standardization; punctuation is one example. The British took over, with little change, the system of punctuation (or "pointing," as many Englishmen still call it) developed by Aldus Manutius; with minor variations we employ the same system today.

Problems with Spelling

In pre-printing days, few writers tried to spell consistently; Caxton himself, as the passage quoted above reveals, would often spell the same word in two or more different ways. Early printers took advantage of such flexibility by spelling some words so that a line would come out the right length: *bin,* for example, might fit where *beene* would not. But in general, printing had a standardizing effect on spelling. Readers who had noticed the same spelling several times began to feel that a variation was at least "odd" if not "wrong," and eventually almost every word was thought to have only one "right" spelling. Owners of printshops began telling their printers which spellings to use; today all large publishing houses have their own stylebooks that inform editors and printers about the house's regulations concerning preferred spelling, preferred punctuation, preferred usage, etc.

Reaching a consensus regarding spelling was not easy, though. For instance, Sir John Cheke, a Biblical translator of the mid-sixteenth century, used doubled vowels to indicate length: *see* for "sea," *sijd* for "side," *boot* for "boat," *maad* for "made," etc. But *An A.B.C. for Children,* published at almost the same time, consistently used a final *e* to show length: *side, made;* this system ultimately prevailed, though with many exceptions. Today's spelling would be a little simpler if we wrote *bote, fite, fale, kined,* and so on for *boat, fight, fail, kind,* and other words with so-called long vowels. Some sixteenth-century men and women advocated spelling each word as it sounded (in their own speech and to their own ears), not realizing that pronunciations would ever change. A number of scholars thought that when a word was derived from Latin or Greek, its spelling should reveal that derivation even though its pronunciation might not; thus they insisted upon *debt* and *doubt,* although no sound of *b* was present in either the English pronunciations or in those of the French from whom we borrowed these words after the French had altered the Latin to suit themselves. Still other scholars wanted to reform the alphabet. The alphabet of Thomas Smith (1568) contained thirty-four letters; that of John Hart (1570) included separate characters to represent the sounds of *th, sh,* and others; William Bullokar (1580) required hooks above and below letters according to the sounds they represented. None of these revised alphabets aroused much enthusiasm; as Richard Mulcaster argued, they were all "to combersom." Mulcaster himself preferred to eliminate unnecessary letters as in *shutte* or *tubbe,* and to use a final *e* as a signal that the preceding vowel is long; he liked *daie* and *trewelie* but *defy* and *try;* and he argued in favor of similar spellings for similarly pronounced words: *hear, dear, fear, rear.* But whenever a spelling already seemed pretty well established, he would not change it. In his *Elementarie* (1582) he included a list of the spellings he recommended for 7,000 words—a list that was highly influential despite such oddities (as they seem to us) as *gest* ("guest")[2] and *dable* ("dabble"); many printshops apparently followed most of his recommendations. Mulcaster believed that pronunciation and spelling would never be

---

[2] Some of the oddities of today's spelling are attributable to the fact that many early English printers came from Holland. They often used a *gh,* as in *ghost* and *gherkin* (as we still do), in *ghospel* and *ghossip* (where we have dropped the *h*), and in *ghess* and *ghest* (which because of French influence we now spell *guess* and *guest*).

in complete harmony because "When the age of peple, which now vse the tung so well, is dead and departed there will another succede, and with the peple the tung will alter and change"—a surprisingly modern insight.

Other Effects of Printing

Inevitably the existence of printed materials also aided in standardization of usage, even though complete standardization has never been attained and perhaps cannot and should not be. *You were,* as print generally had it, slowly crowded out *you was;* some strong verbs, like *help* and *climb,* came to be treated uniformly in print as weak; double negatives, comparatives, and superlatives eventually became rare in print and therefore became considered "wrong." Printing, unlike the spoken word, is tangible; moreover, it is presumably based upon a carefully written, carefully edited manuscript. Therefore whatever appears in print seems to the layman to be "correct" even though not sacrosanct. If printed material says "you were," then that usage must be the one approved by the supposedly well-educated persons responsible for the writing and printing of books. Over a period of centuries, then, printing serves to make readers and writers conform to essentially the same usages, even though their less literate contemporaries habitually employ other forms. Even today, much of the effort of teachers of English is devoted to an often vain attempt to make students' usage conform to that usually found in print, since the students have often grown up in families and among friends whose usages are "wrong" in terms of the conventions of print.

The spread of printing unquestionably also contributed to a substantial increase in the number of English words. If there had been no printing presses, even if as much writing had been done (a doubtful assumption), there would have been few people who would have had a chance to read the thousands of newly coined words, and in consequence not many of them would have found a permanent place in the language. As a result we today might not have had such useful words as *allusion, appendix, encyclopedia, expectation, figurative, penetrate, scientific,* and *spurious,* which (along with many others that will be exemplified later) entered the language during the Renaissance.

Printing no doubt had its influence upon speech, also—partly by introducing into speech words that were first written, and more subtly and gradually by influencing sentence structure. ("Eye-pronunciations," such as using the *th* sound in *author,* which earlier had a *t* sound, are less significant.) W. F. Bolton comments, in *A Short History of Literary En-*

glish, that by the end of the sixteenth century a "literary dialect" had been created, and that "forms of literary origin would increasingly influence those of everyday speech," whereas before the coming of printing such an effect was very slight.

The influence of printing upon education, and hence upon the spread of familiarity with words of ink rather than of air, is obvious. In Chaucer's day most of the highborn could read and write a little, and so could some of the middle class whose work or inclinations required literacy, but the great majority of people were unlettered. In contrast, perhaps as many as half of Shakespeare's London contemporaries, a century after Caxton, could read. Many early printed materials were textbooks; Shakespeare learned his "small Latine and lesse Greeke" from some of them. Earlier, in Deventer, the Dutch town where Erasmus first studied, 450 books were published between 1480 and 1500, and most of them were textbooks. Across much of Europe the story was essentially the same: printing provided materials for teaching, schools developed that used these materials, and children who in an earlier day would have had no formal education went to the schools and learned to read the print and to write their names and to translate their thoughts into squiggles on paper. If some kind of mass printing had never developed, even today perhaps only an eighth or a tenth of the population would be literate, and our lives might differ but little from life in the Middle Ages.

The Linguistic Impact of the Revival of Learning

Later in this chapter we'll note the influence of the Revival of Learning upon the English vocabulary. Here we'll consider a few less obvious results.

As increasing numbers of Englishmen became acquainted with the writings of the ancients, a whole world of unfamiliar ideas opened to them. Unthought-of concepts of art, literature, science, politics and government, and ethics and other branches of philosophy came into their minds. Often English had no words for these concepts and therefore could express them only indirectly or, as we shall see, by adapting words from older tongues. Even the metaphors of the classics were sometimes unfamiliar. (A parallel case is that of the Eskimo tongue, in which Bible translators had to say "the *baby seal* of God" because Eskimos did not know *lamb*.)

The literature of Greece and Rome also increased interest in literary polish. Although Chaucer and a few others certainly worked hard to polish their works, most pre-Renaissance writing was relatively crude. But when Greek and Roman dramatists and poets became widely known, they influenced both the thought and the form that English writers were to employ. Shakespeare, for instance, often went to Plutarch for his stories and to Plautus or Seneca for his dramatic structure. Orators or would-be orators studied the speeches of Cicero as prime examples of the art of speaking. Writers of prose sought to emulate the literary characteristics of Aristotle, Plato, and the Greek historians. Poets like Ovid and Horace were imitated for two or three centuries.

The increase in classical knowledge also had, in a sense, a plateau-spreading effect upon the English people. That is, it raised· the general level of education so that what had previously been the property of no more than a few became the property of the many. This increased commonality of knowledge tended toward a lessening of class distinctions: if the son of a butcher or even of a heath-dweller came to know Vergil and Aristotle, the differences between him and a nobleman were significantly reduced. Among other things, his level of language approximated more closely that of his "betters."

Oddly enough, the Revival of Learning also contributed to a rise of interest in the vernacular and even to an increased national consciousness. Although some writers asserted that the English language could never attain the perfection of Latin, others disputed the claim. Richard Mulcaster, for instance, said that English was "excellentlie well fined," and Sir Philip Sidney, in his "An Apologie for Poetrie" (1583) said that for "the right use both of matter and manner . . . [English is] indeed capable of any excellent exercising of it." Sidney went on:

I know, some will say it is a mingled language. And why not so much the better, taking the best of both the other? Another will say it wanteth Grammer. Nay, truly, it hath that prayse, that it wanteth not Grammer: for Grammer it might have, but it needs it not; beeing so easie of it selfe, and so voyd of those cumbersome differences of Cases, Genders, Moodes, and Tenses, which I thinke was a peece of the Tower of *Babilons* curse, that a man should be put to schoole to learne his mother-tongue. But for the uttering sweetly, and properly the conceits of the minde, which is the end of speech, that hath it equally with any other tongue in the world: and it is particulerly happy, in compositions of two or three words together [compound words], neere the Greeke, far beyond the Latine: which is one of the greatest beauties can be in a language.

Sidney and others were proud, too, of some of the literature their country had already produced, although they recognized that it was not free from defect. Sidney, for instance, said:

Chaucer, undoubtedly did excellently in his *Troylus and Cresseid,* of whom, truly I know not, whether to mervaile more, either that he in that mistie time, could see so clearely, or that wee in this cleare age, walke so stumblingly after him. Yet had he great wants, fitte to be forgiven, in so reverent antiquitie.

The Linguistic Impact of Foreign Travel and Commerce

Although the most obvious linguistic influence of England's rapidly growing overseas interests was upon vocabulary, less tangible was the effect upon the spirit. Professor Frederick C. Dietz has this to say:

. . . New words were taken from every language under heaven and were added to the English language to describe the new materials. New scenes, heroic deeds, and characters were given to writers of literature. Thus Shakespeare laid the scene of The Tempest in Bermuda, and Dryden wrote one of his best dramas around Aurengzebe, the Emperor of India. More generally, the new lands opened up strange vistas of things to be seen and known, and their first reaction was an impulse of activity to search out and discover "the sundry sights and shapes of strange beasts and fishes, the wonderful works of nature, the different manners and fashions of divers nations . . . strange trees, fruits, fowls and beasts, the infinite treasure of pearl, gold and silver, the new found lands, the sundry positions of the sphere and many others." Interest in the next world was lessened, and the greatest curiosity was aroused in all sorts of things in this. While this led in one direction to the invention and acceptance of the most extravagant tales, it also led to the formation of collections of curiosities in botanic gardens and in museums . . . . Collection inevitably resulted in classification of information, and the development of the scientific spirit. . . . Finally, the new geographical explorations, combined with epochal astronomical discoveries, led to changes in men's whole outlook on life . . . .[3]

This new outlook led in part to perhaps the most exuberant use of language that England has ever known. Thousands of words were borrowed, experimentation with sentence structure was frequent, and stylistic experimentation no less so. Language play abounded (e.g., Shakespeare's puns and Lyly's linguistic extravaganzas). Language was little more fettered than were the explorers who boldly sailed into unknown waters.

VOCABULARY GROWTH

Borrowings from Latin

Greenough and Kittredge once estimated that "a full quarter of the Latin vocabulary" has been borrowed for English, much of it during the Renaissance. Many of these borrowings are now such familiar words that it seems difficult to believe that they have been in the language only three

[3] Frederick C. Dietz, *A Political and Social History of England*, New York: The Macmillan Company, 1935, p. 279.

or four hundred years; besides the ones mentioned on page 145, they include *animals, appropriate, area, climax, consult, democracy, education, expend, extra, fertile, gradual, imitate, item, janitor, medium, modern, native, pacific, series, splendid, sponsor, strict, urge,* and many, many more. Charles C. Fries estimated that between 1475 and 1700 the English vocabulary grew from about 45,000 items to 125,000; of these 80,000 or so additions, the great majority were taken from Latin or from Latin's child, French.

Not all these words remained alive. Of the words that died out, many were of the sort referred to contemptuously as "inkhorn" words, coinages that seemed unneeded or too artificial. In *Love's Labour's Lost* Shakespeare ridicules Holofernes, the pedantic schoolmaster who speaks pompous nonsense like this:

You find not the apostrophas, and so miss the accent. Let me supervise the canzonet. Here are only numbers ratified; but for the elegancy, facility, and golden cadence of poesy, caret. Ovidius Naso was the man. And why, indeed, Naso, but for smelling out the odoriferous flowers of fancy, the jerks of invention? Imitari is nothing.

Thomas Wilson, in his *Arte of Rhetorique* (1553), attacked inkhorn terms by composing a burlesque letter in which *ingent* means "huge," *ingenie* "mind," *accersited* "brought," *adjuvate* "aid," *obtestate* "call upon," *invigilate* "watch for," and so on. Some semi-learned fools did indeed attempt to show off their erudition by needlessly twisting Latin words into English forms even when simple English equivalents already existed.

In direct contrast to users of inkhorn terms, some Renaissance writers argued that no borrowing at all was needed. Sir Thomas Chaloner (1549) criticized those who "shew two tongues, I mean to mingle their writings with words sought out of strange langages." Sir John Cheke, in translating the New Testament, tried, though not with complete success, to use Anglo-Saxon terms exclusively: *hundreder* for "centurion," *foresayer* for "prophet," *byword* for "parable," and *gainrising* for "resurrection."

Eventually a compromise was reached. Words from Latin that filled a need in the language were borrowed and retained. Thus English had no word for *catechism,* so the sixteenth century adapted the Latin *catechismus.* Military words like *catapult,* from Latin *catapulta,* came in at about the same time. Other examples include *cremation, cumulate, culmination, debilitate, decimal, reverberate, roseate, ruminate, salacious,* and *sinuous.* (In all, several thousand such useful words could be listed.)

Inevitably, though, some of the additions duplicated meanings already in the language, so that Mod E often has both a Latinate and an Anglo-

Saxon way of saying the same thing: Latin-based *lunar* and *solar*—Anglo-Saxon "of the moon" and "of the sun," *agrarian*—"land," *mariner*—"sailor," and many more. (See page 173.) Whether this duplication hurts or helps the language is debatable, although it certainly provides opportunity for varied style: any educated writer or speaker chooses, consciously or not, the degree of Latinity he desires to employ.

Borrowings from French

Often it is difficult to decide whether a Renaissance borrowing was made directly from Latin or from a French form of the Latin. The *Oxford English Dictionary* has many etymologies like this:

> **Revolution**. . . . late ME [a. OF., or ad. late L. *revolutionem*, f. *revolvere* to REVOLVE.]

This means that *revolution* may have entered the language either as an adoption from Old French or an adaptation of the Latin word, but that in either event it goes back to the Latin *revolvere*.

Some of the borrowings, though, definitely have French forms, even though many of these can also be traced back to Latin. Here are a few examples:

> *prejudge*—from French *prejuger;* Latin provided the doublet *prejudicate*.
>
> *blaspheme*—from Old French *blasfémer,* and traceable to Latin and Greek.
>
> *blanch* "to whiten"—from French *blanchir,* from French *blanc* "white."
>
> *chief* and the later *chef*—from Old French, going back to Latin *caput* "head."
>
> *change*—a medieval borrowing from Old French *change,* taken from Latin *cambire* "to change." (This word is representative of the very common words in Mod E that were taken at one time or another from French—words like *city, close, course, large, pay, place, please,* and *state*. Such words account for about 300 of the 1,000 most commonly used words in English, according to a study by Lawrence Faucett and Itsu Maki.)

Borrowings from Greek

Most Greek words that entered English during the Renaissance came in by way of Latin: *antipathy, atmosphere, chronological, critical, dogmatic, emphasis, enthusiasm, pathetic,* and *system,* for example. Since, however,

Renaissance scholars knew both Greek and Latin, it is not surprising that some of the borrowings from Greek came in directly: *anonymous, catastrophe, criterion, idiosyncrasy, lexicon, tantalize, thermometer, tonic,* and a number of others.

Borrowings from Around the World

Before the Renaissance, as we have seen, few words entered English from languages other than the native Germanic stock plus French, Latin, and Greek (except when one of those languages had itself borrowed from Hebrew or something else). But the Renaissance English vocabulary came from more than fifty languages, even though some languages might be represented by only a word or two each. The reason, of course, was that English people were no longer stay-at-homes. They traveled extensively on the European continent and elsewhere, and their sailors and explorers roamed the globe. In addition, French of this period was also increasingly indebted to other languages, and the English took secondhand a number of words the French (or other nationalities) had borrowed first.

So Italian contributed, for example, *algebra* (which goes back to Arabic), *balcony* (which the Italians had themselves borrowed from Old High German), *cupola, stanza, trill, violin,* and through the French, *battalion, carat, charlatan, gazette,* and *parakeet.* Spanish offered *alligator, armada, cocoa, potato,* and *sombrero,* plus *grenade, cavalier,* and others by way of France. *Anchovy, mosquito,* and *mulatto* may be either Portuguese or Spanish.

Guinea (Congo) gave us *banana,* Haitian *canoe,* Carib *hammock,* Cuban *maize,* and American Indian *tobacco,* all through Spanish or Portuguese.

Scud "to move briskly" is apparently of Scandinavian origin, as is *rug,* which in the sixteenth and seventeenth centuries referred to a rough woolen material like the Norwegian *rugga. Mug* "a drinking vessel" is associated with Swedish *mugg,* Norwegian *mugge.* The seafaring skill of the Dutch is attested by English *buoy, cruise,* (page 169) *deck, luff, marlin, scow, skipper, sloop, yacht,* and *yawl,* whose dates of entry into English ranged from the fifteenth century to the nineteenth. Low German contributed over a span of years *brake, pickle, spool, brandy, duffel, easel, frolic, gin, skate,* and *wagon.*

A number of English words starting with *al* go back to Arabic, in which *al* is used as a definite article. Thus *almanac* entered ME from Spanish, which had taken it from Arabic *al-manōkh* "calendar." Other examples, with the time of first known use in English, are *albacore* (1579), *alchemy*

(ME), *alcohol* (1543), *alcove* (1623), *alembic* (ME), *algebra* (1541), *algorism* (ME), *alkali* (ME), plus others where the *al* is hidden: *admiral* (ME), *elixir* (ME), *hazard* (1530). Other words from Arabic, with no *al* involved, include *apricot* (1551), *assassin* (1531), *candy* (1769), *coffee* (1598), *garble* (1483), *giraffe* (1594), *harem* (1634), *henna* (1600), *lemon* (ME), *magazine* (1583), *sherbet* (1603), and *tariff* (1591). Only a few words were taken directly from Arabic; most came by way of French, Spanish, Italian, or Turkish.

From Hebrew, either before, during, or after the Renaissance, English has taken words particularly familiar to readers of the Bible: *amen* (OE), *behemoth* (ME), *cherub* (OE), *hallelujah* (1535), *jubilee* (ME), *rabbi* (OE), *Sabbath* (OE), *seraph* (1667), *shekel* (1560), *shibboleth* (ME).

Anglicizing the Borrowings

When a word was borrowed, its form usually was changed to make it seem "more English." The process may be exemplified by what happened in the Renaissance and at other times to a few Latin suffixes (although there was no complete uniformity in such changes):

-*alis* usually became -*al*: *casualis* → *casual, naturalis* → *natural*

-*aris* usually became -*ary*: *militaris* → *military*

-*icus* often became -*ic*: *publicus* → *public*

-*ivis* usually became -*ive*: *primitivus* → *primitive*

-*tio* usually became -*tion*: *portio* → *portion, ratio* remained but also → *ration.*

-*ura* usually became -*ure*: *natura* → *nature,* but *future* is from *futurus*

-*us* or -*osus* usually became -*ous*: *magnanimus* → *magnanimous, curiosus* → *curious*

Sometimes English suffixes were added to foreign words to form different parts of speech. Thus -*ish* attached to Latin *modus* (French *mode*) gave us *modish.*

Occasionally, though, a foreign word was borrowed without a change of spelling; e.g., *militia, nausea, adieu, addendum, cello, aide-de-camp, maestro.* The attempt to retain the foreign pronunciation was less frequent; it is illustrated in French *chic,* which if anglicized would sound like the name of a young fowl.

Revival of Older English Words

"E. K." (Edward Kirke) wrote of Edmund Spenser, ". . . he hath laboured to restore as to their rightfull heritage such good and naturall En-

glish words as have ben long time out of use and almost cleane disherited."
E. K. objected to writers who "patched up the holes [in the English lan-
guage] with pieces and rags of other languages, borrowing here of the
Frenche, there of the Italian, everywhere of the Latine . . . so now they
have made our English tonge a gallimaufray or hodgepodge of all other
speches." In contrast, as Professor H. S. V. Jones reported in *A Spenser
Handbook,* "When Spenser consciously undertook to enrich the language
of poetry, he acted in full accord with E. K.'s critical doctrine by reviving
obsolete words. He was careful to maintain the essentially English character of his idiom."

So Spenser brought back to life words like *astound* and *doom* as well as
others that have died again, like *displeasance, nathemore* "nevermore," and
whilere "some time before." From the Northern dialect he took words like
filch and *freak.* Some he created on older models, e.g., *blatant, delve.* And
he added suffixes to other old words, with results like *baneful* or *sunshiny,*
or he shortened older words, as in *drear* for *dreary.* OE-based affixes like
with-, un-, under-, up-, and *-dom, -ful, -ish, -ly, -ness* were used by Spenser
and others not only with native words but also with imports: *unciville,
ceremonially.*

Despite all the Renaissance borrowings from abroad, Spenser and his
contemporaries continued to use a language that was largely Germanic in
word frequency. Of each hundred consecutive words employed by Shakespeare, according to H. S. V. Jones, only an average of 10 were "foreign";
for Spenser, the average was 14; for Milton, 19. The borrowed words did
often fill gaps in English, and they added to a speaker's or a writer's range
of choice. They are like raisins in a bread pudding, adding variety and
flavor, but most of the pudding still consists of bread.

THE SOUNDS OF EARLY MODERN ENGLISH

The major sound changes in E Mod E may be illustrated by the word
name. In Chaucer's day *name* [na:mə] almost rhymed with Mod E *comma*
[ka:mə]. But not much later, as part of the Great Vowel Shift, [a:] became [e:], the vowel sound in Mod E *mate* or *name.* And the final unaccented vowel in ME *name* and hundreds of other words simply disappeared.

The Great Vowel Shift

During Late ME and Early Mod E, for unknown reasons, English-
speaking people began pronouncing their long vowels differently. The low
ones became higher, and the high ones changed to diphthongs that glided

from low to high. Not all the changes were completed in the same period, and two or more distinctly different pronunciations of the same common word could exist side by side for many years. The following list, then, is only approximate, and shows tendencies rather than completions:

CHAUCER		SHAKESPEARE		TODAY'S ENGLISH		
[i:]	[li:f]	[əI]	[ləIf]	[aI]	[laIf]	"life"
[e:]	[swe:tə]	[i:]	[swi:t]	[i:]	[swi:t]	"sweet"
[ɛ:]	[klɛ:nə]	[e:]	[kle:n]	[i:]	[kli:n]	"clean"
[a:]	[na:m]	[e:]	[ne:m]	[e:]	[ne:m]	"name"
[ɔ:]	[hɔ:m]	[o:]	[ho:m]	[o:]	[ho:m]	"home"
[o:]	[fo:d]	[u:]	[fu:d]	[u:]	[fu:d]	"food"
[u:]	[hu:s]	[əu]	[həus]	[au]	[haus]	"house"

This list shows that in Shakespeare's day the pronunciation of the vowel sounds in words like *life, sweet, name, home,* and *food* was about the same as ours and considerably different from Chaucer's. In words like *clean* and *house* the pronunciation was moving toward that of today but was not yet there.[4]

On the continent of Europe no such vowel changes occurred. So German *Name,* for instance, is still pronounced about as Chaucer pronounced the cognate word. In the Romance languages, too, the sounds of the long vowels are about as they were in ME.

Changes in Unaccented Vowels

The final unaccented *e* as in [na:mə] was already being lost in pronunciation of Chaucer's time, though it was to remain in spelling. (In contrast, in words with short vowels like Chaucer's *hadde* "had" it also dropped from the spelling.) When the process was completed in E Mod E, it represented the final disappearance of large numbers of the inflectional endings that had characterized Old English before being reduced to the noncommittal [ə].

Other unaccented vowels did not vanish but were gradually leveled to [ə]. The italicized letter in each of these Mod E words represents this sound: *a*mong, ben*e*fit, eas*i*ly, gall*o*p, croc*u*s. One of the reasons for modern spelling difficulties is that any one of several letters may stand for [ə] ; a modern writer must simply memorize which letter is used in each

[4] Varying intermediate steps between fourteenth and sixteenth or seventeenth century pronunciations are not shown in the list. For example, [a:] was probably [o:] [æ:], and [ɛ:] before it became [e:]. Shakespeare and his contemporaries probably, as individuals, used all five of these sounds, but with [e:] showing signs of winning.

word. If the leveling to [ə] had not occurred, pronunciation would have afforded more clues to spelling.

Short Vowels

In general, short vowels in accented syllables changed little in the transition from ME to E Mod E. One exception is Chaucer's [a] as in [man], which by Shakespeare's time had generally become [æ] as in [mæn], the same pronunciation we use today. Another is Chaucer's [u], which in *sun, but,* etc., had a sound such as we use in *pull,* but which became [ʌ] by Shakespeare's day.

Until the nineteenth century in words like *nature* or *gesture* the unstressed *-ure* was pronounced [ɜ·r] as in modern *earn;* in fact, Noah Webster defended this pronunciation, and Lowell illustrated it repeatedly in his *Biglow Papers.* Today in TV Westerns, "creatures" are sometimes called "critters"—a survival from previous centuries.

Consonants

Although no substantial changes occurred in pronunciation of consonants between ME and E Mod E, a number of small ones are worthy of note.

ME [x].   A sound like that in German *ich* still remained in ME words like *thouht* "thought" and *niht* "night," but disappeared a little later, or in some words like *cough* changed to [f]. (This helps to explain the often-noticed oddities in our *-ough* and other *-gh* words.)

[d], [ð], Some words during the Renaissance vacillated between [d] and [θ].   and [ð]. Shakespeare's plays have both *murder* and *murther,* and he and his contemporaries had not yet settled finally upon *burden* or *burthen,* but most of them had moved from *fader* to *father, moder* to *mother.* Also, the present distinctions between [ð] and [θ] were being reached; thus ME [θiː] "thy" became E Mod E [ðʌI] or [ðəI] (which today is [ðaI] with a different initial consonant from that of "thigh" [θaI]).

[ž].   The sound of [ž] as in *azure* did not exist in ME, but developed in E Mod E as a result of French influence.

[I] to [j].   In words with *-ion* and *-ious,* the vocalic [I] was changing during the Renaissance to the consonantal [j], which we generally use in words like *stallion* and *curious.* Shakespeare often made the *i* a separate syllable, though not uniformly, since the change was in progress.

Loss of Consonant Sounds

During the fifteenth century, *wr-* as in our *write* lost the sound of *w*, probably because [r] alone is easier to pronounce. Similarly, *wl-* (ME *wlispen* "lisp"), *-mn* (*hymn, damn, column*), *-lm* (*calm, palm*), and *-mb* (*limb, thumb*) lost one of the consonant sounds. In the sixteenth century the same thing occurred with *gn-* (*gnash, gnat*) and with *-lk* (*talk, folk*). A little later *kn-* (*knife, know*) was similarly simplified. Since the lost letters remained in the spelling, we have here an explanation of a fairly large number of spelling oddities in Mod E.

In late ME and E Mod E the [r] was often lost in words like *burst* and *horse*, thus providing a clue for the still occasionally heard *bust* and *hoss;* this loss antedated the more widespread loss of [r] still noticeable in much British speech and in that of New England and certain other American regions. The presence or absence of medial or final [r] has long been one of the best indications of dialectal variation.

[ŋ]. Chaucer pronounced words like *thing* with [ŋg] at the end— somewhat as we pronounce [ŋg] in *finger* or *stronger*. Gradually the un-needed [g] was lost, giving E Mod E [θIŋ], for instance. In words like *running,* though, the final sound in Shakespeare's day and later was usu-ally just [n]. James D. Gordon's *The English Language* quotes this rhyme from Swift as evidence:

> All mad to speak, and none to hearken,
> They set the very lap-dog barking

And Jespersen's *Modern English Grammar* has these examples: Words-worth's *Helwellyn/dwelling,* Byron's *children/bewildering,* Shelley's *pur-suing/ruin,* and Tennyson's *treading/wed in.* The present school insistence upon [ŋ] (often ignored by public speakers) arises from the belief that the *-ing* ending should be consistent with the [ŋ] in words like *thing* or *sing*—even though the participial ending is unstressed and therefore might well follow a different pattern.

[z] In OE in an inflected form like *fæderas* "fathers" *s* was pronounced [s]. As inflections disappeared, however, a syllable was usually lost in the pronunciation, as *fathers* illustrates. Influenced by the preceding sound, this [s] usually became [z]. Such sound changes are called assimilation; they result from the fact that some sounds are easier to pronounce together than others are. For example [kIds] is harder to say than [kIdz], so the easier combination prevailed. The change from terminal [s] to [z] in many words had begun in ME or even earlier but was largely complete in the

Renaissance. Today we retain the -s spelling but use the sound [z] in forming plurals of almost all nouns except those ending in [k] as in *tracks,* [f] as in *staffs,* [p] as in *caps,* and [t] as in *pits.* Similarly, verbs like *lobs, bids,* and the like end in [z]; the few exceptions are similar to those for nouns: *picks, whiffs, sips,* and *hits,* for example. The usual pronunciation of an -es ending has become [əz], not [əs]. In short, our very frequent use of terminal [z] or [əz] is largely attributable to the virtual departure of inflectional endings in English.

An Example of Shakespeare's Pronunciation

Although some questions about pronunciations of Shakespeare's time still exist, and although many variations could have been heard on the streets of his London, the work of Helge Kökeritz[5] and others has shown that Shakespeare probably would have pronounced the first part of Antony's funeral oration about like this:

Friends,	Romans,	Countrymen,	lend	me	your	ears:
[frɛndz	ro:manz	kuntrImɛn	lɛnd	mi:	jər	Irz
I	come	to	bury	*Cæſar,*	not	to	praiſe	him:
əI	kum	tə	buri	si:zɝr,	nɔt	tə	pre:z	hIm
The	evill	that	men	do,	lives	after	them,
ðe	i:vIl	ðæt	mɛn	du:	lIvz	æftər	ðɛm
The	good	is	oft	enterred	with	their	bones,
ðə	gud	iz	ɔft	ɛntɛrəd	wIð	ðɛr	bo:nz
So	let	it	be	with	*Cæſar.*	The	Noble	*Brutus,*
so:	lɛt	It	bi:	wIð	si:zɝr	ðə	no:bl	bru:təs
Hath	told	you	Cæſar	was	Ambitious:
hæθ	to:ld	ju:	si:zɝr	wəz	æmbIsIəs
If	it	were	ſo,	it	was	a	greeuous	Fault,
If	It	wɛr	so:	It	wəz	ə	gri:vəs	fɔlt
And	greeuouſly	hath	Cæſar	anſwer'd	it.
ænd	gri:vəsli:	hæθ	si:zɝr	ænsɝrd	It.
Heere,	vnder	leaue	of	*Brutus,*	and	the	reſt
hIr	undɝ	li:v	ʌv	bru:təs	ænd	ðə	rɛst
(For	*Brutus*	is	an	Honourable	man,
fər	bru:təs	Is	n	a:nərəbl	mæn
So	are	they	all;	all	Honourable	men)
so:	a:r	ðe:	ɔ:l	ɔ:l	a:nərəbl	mɛn

[5] *Shakespeare's Pronunciation,* New Haven: Yale University Press, 1953.

Come	I	to	ʃpeake	in	Cæʃars	Funerall.[6]
kʋm	əI	tə	spi:k	In	si:zɝrz	funərɔl]

Note that most of the words in the passage were pronounced about as in today's usual English. Exceptions include *I, come, not, under, were,* and *ambitious,* and possibly a few others. (It has been said that a modern Irish brogue probably sounds much like sixteenth-century English.)

GRAMMATICAL CHARACTERISTICS

In contrast to the luxuriant growth of vocabulary and the significant changes in pronunciation, the conservatism of English grammar during the Renaissance is noteworthy. There are no major developments like the earlier decline in inflections, the loss of grammatical gender, or the sizable reduction in the number of strong verbs. The points to be noted in this section, then, though numerous, are all relatively small. They will serve the teacher, however, in explaining many features of the language of Shakespeare's time in contrast to that of today.

Sentence Structure

In our discussion of OE we noted that word order in sentences was essentially that which we still use, with most sentences following a subject–verb–complement (SVC) arrangement. Minor variations existed even in King Alfred's day, and in Chaucer's, and still in the sixteenth century through the twentieth. Inversions in which V precedes S may have been a little more common in the Renaissance that at any other time. Here are some examples from Shakespeare and Sidney:

There's scarce a Bush. (*King Lear,* II, iv, 304–5. The *there*-transformation almost always requires V before S.)

Went he hence now? (*Othello,* III, iii, 50. Today we use a *do*-transformation, as Shakespeare did occasionally: "Did he go hence now?" in which the S comes between the Aux and the V.)

Then is Doomes Day neere. (*Hamlet,* II, ii, 242. Today we'd be more likely to say "Then doomsday is near." However, some initial adverbs even today usually are followed by V or Aux: "Here is your coat," "Seldom does he come this way.")

---

[6] *Julius Caesar,* Act III. This text, including spelling, punctuation, and the like, is taken from the Norton Facsimile of *The First Folio of Shakespeare* (1623), prepared by Charlton Hinman (New York: W. W. Norton, 1968). Note the frequent use of the elongated *s,* a symbol often used initially and medially.

Upon the backe of that, comes out a hidious Monster . . . (Sidney, *Apologie for Poetrie*. The phrase, used adverbially, is followed by V and S; today the SV order would be more likely.)

An adjective used as a complement sometimes opened a sentence, and may still do so. An example is Sidney's "True it is," in which the order is CSV. Such a sentence could also be arranged in CVS order: "True is it," especially if a *that*-clause followed. Today "It is true" is most common.

The position of *not* was more flexible in E Mod E than it is today:

I like not that. (*Othello*, III, iii, 35. *Not* comes between V and C.)

I ſaw him not. (*Much Ado*, II, i, 2. *Not* follows SVC.)

. . . it not appears to me . . . (*2 Henry IV*, i, 107. *Not* comes between S and V.)

Today's much more general use of the *do*-transformation would in all these instances result in *do + not + V*: "I do not like that," "I did not see him," "It does not appear to me." In Shakespeare this transformation is paralleled in ". . . doe not mock me, fellow ſtudent." (*Hamlet*, I, ii, 177) (See page 166 for further discussion of *do*.)

Participial phrases at the beginnings of sentences were rather rare before E Mod E, in which their increase was rapid. The "dangling participle," much condemned by modern handbooks because it seems to modify the wrong substantive or none at all, became fairly frequent. Thus Shakespeare has " . . . ſleeping in mine Orchard, / A Serpent stung me" (*Hamlet*, I, v. 35–36)—a construction that would cause most teachers today to grab their red pencils indignantly, since obviously the serpent was not asleep but the speaker (Hamlet's father) allegedly was. A more elaborate dangler is Sydney's:

. . . they tell you they will make you immortall, by their verses. *Thus doing*, your name shal florish in the Printers shoppes; *thus doing*, you shall be most fayre, most ritch, most wise, most all, you shall dwell upon Superlatives.

Not until the nineteenth century was there a sustained attack upon such constructions; purists continue the attack today, but most experts on usage now object only when the construction results momentarily in a ludicrous misinterpretation.

Today, the use of subordinate clauses (hypotaxis) is considered one mark of a mature style. In OE it was rare, as we have seen. ME employed more subordinate clauses, and E Mod E still more, largely because the store of relative pronouns and relative adverbs had been increased to *who, which, that, when*, and *where*, and subordinating conjunctions by that time included *because, until, if, though* or *although,* and a number of others. As a result, in a single speech by Katherina in *The Taming of the Shrew* (Folio IV, i), we find

> Beggars *that come vnto my fathers doore* . . .
> But I, *who neuer knew how to intreat,* . . .
> And that *which ʃpights me more then all theʃe wants* . . .
> As who ʃhould say, *if I ʃhould ʃleepe or eate* . . .
> I care not what, ʃo *it be holʃome foode* . . .

Nouns

In E Mod E the *-s* or *-es* plural became ever more firmly fixed in the language, even in dialects that for a while had clung to some older forms. Exceptions, some of which have been previously mentioned, included the few plurals in *-en,* the survivals of OE *fēt* "feet" and a few other words, some unchanging plurals like *sheep* and *swine* (today's sportsman catches *fish* and shoots *quail* rather than *fishes* and *quails*), and a few borrowed words that retained (and sometimes still retain) foreign plurals, such as *algae* (1551), *alumni* (1645), *criteria* (1613), *data* (1646), *fungi* (1527), and *rondeaux* (1525). English has not been systematic in the pluralizing of its borrowed nouns, but retention of the foreign plurals has been more often the exception than the rule.

The Middle English genitive ended in an unaccented *-es,* often written *-is* or *-ys.* This sounded like "his," which, as is often true today, was pronounced without the [h] in unstressed positions. As a result, *his* became a fairly common indicator of the possessive form of nouns: "her father his house" or "as red as Mars his heart" (Shakespeare). The usage caused problems with a noun like *woman* or *girl,* or a plural like *winners,* but nevertheless was quite common. Eventually an apostrophe was used to represent the *hi* that supposedly had been left out; our apostrophes in possessives therefore go back to the *his* that originally was used only because of a misunderstanding.

Another interesting genitive is typified by the modern "man in the street's opinion," which seems to make *street* rather than *man* the possessor. But the alternative "man's in the street opinion" would pose its own problems. Before the Renaissance "the king's crown of England" was usual, but Renaissance Englishmen slowly changed this to "The king of England's crown" and the like. Thus our "man in the street's opinion" has a heritage of about four hundred years. Related is "somebody else's," which some people even in our century have argued should be "somebody's else."

Adjectives

Today we ordinarily form the comparative and superlative degrees of one-syllable adjectives by affixing -er and -est, and of longer adjectives by prefixing *more* and *most.* This custom was still not systematized in E Mod E: Shakespeare and his contemporaries wrote "more tall," "beautifullest," "anxiouser," "nothing certainer," and the like, as well as the alternative "taller," "most beautiful," etc.

The present disapproval of double comparatives ("more rarer") and double superlatives ("most rarest") had not yet come into being. Shakespeare's "moʃt vnkindeʃt cut of all" (*Julius Caesar,* III, ii, 187) is the most famous example, but his "moʃt boldest and beʃt hearts of Rome" (ibid., III, i, 121) and other expressions are similar. Only a few decades later, however, John Dryden criticized Ben Jonson's "Contain your spirits in more stricter bounds" as a "gross way of two comparatives."

Far is an interesting adjective. We may compare it by means of either *further, furthest* or *farther, farthest.* The explanation is that the comparisons developed from those of both OE *fore* "before" and ME *fer* or *ferre* "far." The comparison *fore, furðra, fyrrest* gave us *further,* and when *fyrrest* became *first,* the new word *furthest* was developed by analogy to *further.* In *fer, ferther, ferthest,* the *er* changed to *ar* in the fifteenth century.

Today some people write "an historical novel," but others prefer *a* on the ground that *historical* starts with a consonant sound. The advocates of *an* can find adequate precedents in the sixteenth century, when "an hermitage," "an historic sight," and the like were common, because the *h* in unstressed syllables was then rarely pronounced.

Adverbs

The -*ly* ending of adverbs was firmly entrenched by E Mod E times, but "flat" adverbs without the -*ly* were more common than they now are. Dozens of them are in Shakespeare: "drink *deepe*," "*wondrous* strange," "How *strange* or *odd* so'er I bear myself," "*new*-lighted," "shee'l *sure* speake," etc.

The now-maligned double negative was about as common in E Mod E as it had been in ME. Caxton, for instance, wrote "Ne *never* shal *none* be born fairer than she," and Shakespeare was capable of "*Nor* this is *not* my nose *neither*" or even the quadruple "Man delights *not* me; *no, nor* woman *neither.*"

Pronouns

Perhaps the most interesting development in E Mod E pronouns involves the second person. The singular forms of late ME were *thou* (nominative), *thee* (objective) and *thy* and *thine* (possessive), but already there was a tendency to regard *ye* (nominative), *you* (objective) and *your* (possessive) as more formal or respectful than the *th-* forms. (The parallel with the two second person forms, intimate and respectful, of modern French, Spanish, Italian, and German has often been noted.) In *Hamlet* III, iv, 9–11, Shakespeare uses the distinction with dramatic effect. Hamlet's mother addresses him with the familiar *thou:* "Hamlet, thou haſt thy Father much offended." But, thinking her an adultress, he responds with the formal, distant *you:* "Mother, you have my Father much offended." Angered, she adopts the same formality: "Come, come, you anſwer with an idle tongue."

The King James Bible (1611) makes considerable use of *thou, thee, thy,* and *thine* but without any implication of informality: the pronouns are used to refer even to God. *Ye* and *you* also appear consistently nominative and objective respectively: e.g., "And as ye go, preach" (Matthew 10:7) and ". . . let your peace return to you" (Matthew 10:13). But many writers used *ye* and *you* interchangeably, as Shakespeare often did, probably because in unstressed positions they were pronounced alike as [jə].

It remained for the seventeenth century to abandon the *th-* forms and *ye,* although traces persisted in some dialects for considerably longer.

Mine and *thine* continued to be used as possessives before vowel sounds, *my* and *thy* before consonant sounds. This distinction remained in speech until the eighteenth century and sometimes showed up in nineteenth-century poetry: "*Mine* eyes have seen the glory . . . ."

In the third person pronouns, *a* sometimes was written for *he:* in the Second Quarto version (1604) Hamlet says of Claudius, ". . . now a is a-praying,/And now Ile doo't, and so a goes to heaven," but the First Folio (1623) changes each *a* to the more normal *he. Hem* and *em,* Southern dialectal forms, sometimes were used for *them. His* for the neuter possessive was general, as in the biblical "if the salt have lost his savour." Sometimes, though, *it* was used as a possessive, as when the Fool in *King Lear* says, ". . . it had it head bit off by it young." When *its* began creeping in, late in the sixteenth century, the usual spelling was *it's* (a form that teachers to this day find necessary to combat) ; no doubt the apostrophe that was beginning to be used—though inconsistently—in the possessives of nouns simply carried over to *it's.*

The distinctions of pronoun case that teachers have stressed so much in the past century were by no means uniformly observed by Shakespeare and his contemporaries. Modern editors of Shakespeare's plays tend to correct silently "errors" like these in the First Folio (here italicized):

I pray thee chide me not, *her* I Loue now
Doth grace for grace, and Loue for Loue allow.

(Romeo and Juliet, III, iii, 85–86)

And damn'd be *him,* that firſt cries hold, enough.

(Macbeth, V, viii, 34)

You know my Father hath no childe, but *I,* nor none is like to have.

(As You Like It, I, ii, 18–19)

. . . all debts are cleered betweene you and *I* . . .

(Merchant of Venice, III, ii, 322)

Is he as tall as *me*?

(Antony and Cleopatra, III, iii, 13)

Sir Andrew Aguecheck, in *Twelfth Night,* uses both *me* and *I* as a subjective complement: "That's mee I warrant you." "I knew 'twas I." (II, v. 87, 89)

Similarly, distinctions now made between simple and compound personal pronouns had not yet hardened in the sixteenth century. Chaucer had written ". . . *myself* have been the whippe," and Shakespeare paralleled that usage, as in "Myself have letters" (*Julius Caesar,* IV, iii, 171) and in "Her Father and *my ſelfe* . . . will ſo beſtow our ſelues . . . (*Hamlet,* III, i, 33–34). Conversely, Shakespeare wrote "Let euery ſouldier hew *him* downe a Bough," (*Macbeth,* V, iv, 6) where modern usage prefers *himself.*

We have already noticed (page 159) that relative pronouns were more numerous in E Mod E than before. *That* was used to refer to both things and persons (as it still may be); it also appeared where today we would use *that which,* as in "Meane while I am poſſeſt of *that* is mine" (*Titus Andronicus,* I, i, 408). Somewhat similarly, *who* sometimes appears where today *he who* would be used; "*Who* ſteales my purſe, ſteales trash" (*Othello,* III, iii, 157). *Whose* was a possessive form of both *who* and *which;* only modern purists object to constructions like Hamlet's ". . . Playing, whoſe end . . . is, to hold, as 'twer, the Mirrour up to Nature" (III, ii, 23–24). *Who* and *whom* were often used in ways that modern purists deplore, as in the King James Bible's "Whom do men say that I the Son of man am?" In fact, throughout the whole Mod E period there have been countless departures, in "good" writing, from the prescription of nominative *who,* objective *whom.*

Prepositions

In reading OE, we noted that prepositions of a thousand years ago often have to be translated with different prepositions today. Prepositions became increasingly important when inflections were reduced, because what had formerly been shown by case endings often required prepositions. Instead of adding a large number of new prepositions, however, the language tended simply to employ each existing preposition for more and more meanings, and sometimes meanings shifted from one to another (e.g., OE *on* must now often be translated by *in* or some other word). Today's unabridged dictionaries may distinguish literally scores of different meanings or shades of meaning for any of the most common prepositions, such as *of*.

In general, E Mod E prepositional usage was close to ours, but exceptions may be found, as in these examples cited by Pyles (pages 222–23): ". . . looke on [at] the divell" (*Othello*, II, i, 229), ". . . come of [on] an errand" (*Merry Wives*, I, iv, 80), "As dreames are made on [of]" (*Tempest*, IV, i, 157), "Then speake the truth by [of] her" (*Two Gentlemen*, II, iv, 151), and ". . . that our armies joyn not in [on] a hot day" (*2 Henry IV*, I, ii, 234). When your students encounter a prepositional use that seems strange to them, ask them merely to substitute whatever word makes best sense.

The preposition *to* was often omitted before the indirect object, even when the direct object came first. Examples include:

Dromio my man did bring them me.

(*Comedy of Errors*, V, i, 385)

I could not for my heart deny it him.

(*Merchant of Venice*, V, i, 165)

Today Americans and most British would insert *to* before *me* and *him*.

Late ME and E Mod E saw the development of a few new prepositions: *during* and *concerning*, both derived from participles (though the verb *dure* has been lost, as have its derivatives *dureful* and *dureless*), *except*. Phrasal prepositions such as *owing to, because of, in connection with*, the still controversial *due to*, and many more began also to appear in the language.

Verbs

Most easily noticed of the characteristics of the E Mod E verb is the frequency of *-eth* as a third person singular ending in the present tense: ". . . a man's life consisteth not in the abundance of the things which he possesseth" (Luke 12:15). *Doth* and *hath* remained and flourished for another two hundred years. The *-est* (or *-st*) second person ending also still existed, as in "Soul, thou hast much goods laid up" (Luke 12:19). The *-eth* was gradually being displaced by the present *-es* or *-s,* however, and the *-est* or *-st* ending was increasingly rare.

In the past tense, the *-ed* ending was often pronounced as a separate syllable, as we still pronounce it in "a learned man." When it was not syllabic, printers often inserted an apostrophe in place of the *e;* the First Folio abounds in examples like "vrg'd" and "ſupply'd."

The conjugation of *be* in E Mod E was like this:

PRESENT SINGULAR	PRESENT PLURAL
1. (I) am	(we) are *or* be
2. (thou) art	(you) are *or* be
3. (he, she, it) is	(they) are *or* be

PAST SINGULAR	PAST PLURAL
1. (I) was	(we) were
2. (thou) were, wast, werst, *or* wert	(you) were
3. (he, she, it) was	(they) were

The strong verbs, less numerous than they had been earlier, sometimes appeared in forms unfamiliar to us but explainable as parallels to other verbs. Thus we find in sixteenth-century writers past tense forms like *flang,* "flung," *gat* "got," *chese* "chose," *writ* "wrote," *stale* "stole," *spake* "spoke," *sate* "sat," *drave* "drove," and *builded* and *catched* "built" and "caught." Survivors of earlier past participles included *holpen* "helped," *snowen* "snowed," *speken* "spoken," *waxen* "waxed," *lorn* "lost" (which still survives in *lovelorn*), *frore* "frozen," and *broke, spoke* and *wrote* where today's English has *broken, spoken,* and *written.* Some of these examples show that the language had not yet decided whether a given verb should be treated as strong or weak.

Present participles preceded by *a-,* as in the nursery rhyme "Daddy's gone a-hunting," reflect the survival of *on* from OE: "He wæs on huntunge," literally "He was on hunting." The unstressed *on* weakened to *a;* Shakespeare has *a-feasting, a-hanging,* and other instances.

Such uses of the participle, with or without the *a-,* resulted in the development of progressive tenses, like "She is weeping," which had existed only embryonically in OE and were slightly more developed in ME. Shakespeare was still likely to write "She weepeth" instead of the progressive, even though the latter was in his syntacticon (syntactic repertory). In a study of progressive tenses in selected British writings from 1466 to 1932, Leah Dennis found the following slowly growing numbers of instances.

1466–1499	3	1633–1665	16
1500–1532	3	1666–1699	15
1533–1565	5	1700–1732	14
1566–1599	14	1733–1765	24
1600–1632	6	1900–1932	60[7]

The verb *do* is of special interest. Of its use in "Affirmative sentences" (definition 25), the *OED* says:

Originally, simply periphrastic, and equivalent to the simple tense. Found in OE, frequent in ME, very frequent 1500–1700, dying out in normal prose in 18th C; but still retained in S.w. dialects; also as an archaism in liturgical and legal use, and as a metrical resource in verse.

An example from 1615 is "I do pity the case in which I do see they are."

In interrogative sentences with *do*, the earliest *OED* citation is Chaucer's "Fader why do ye weep?" More normal, though, from the fourteenth to the sixteenth centuries, was "Why weepest thou?" Similarly with the negative: Shakespeare could choose, for instance, between "I do not know" and "I know not," but more often chose the latter. *Do* was frequent but optional with imperatives; Spenser's "Arise, and doo thy selfe redeeme from shame" illustrates both possibilities.

The reason for so much attention to *do* is that it has become one of the most important words in the language. Today we use it over and over in questions (e.g., "*Do* you understand?") and with negatives ("He *did not* understand"), as well as for emphasis ("He really *did* go") and as a full verb ("She *does* her work well"). The first two of these uses were only occasional in the sixteenth century, but since then have largely ousted the *do*-less questions and negatives; today "Understand you?" and "He understood not" might be greeted with "Huh?"

ACCOUNTING FOR SOME OF THE WORDS OF MODERN ENGLISH

abracadabra. "Abracadabra, a Mysterious Word, to which the Superstitious in former times attributed a Magical power to expel Diseases, especially the Tertian-Ague, worn about their neck," said Aubrey's *Miscellanies* (1696). First recorded in a Latin poem of the second century, the word goes back to a Greek Gnostic group that believed in 365 deities.

---

[7] Leah Dennis, "The Progressive Tense: Frequency of Its Use in English." *PMLA*, LV (September, 1940), 855–65.

Repeating the 365 names was reputedly health-giving, but obviously difficult. *Abracadabra,* when numerical values are assigned to its Greek-letter components, adds up to 365, and hence was considered a shorthand version of all the names, especially when written in this form:

```
A   B   R   A   C   A   D   A   B   R   A
  A   B   R   A   C   A   D   A   B   R
    A   B   R   A   C   A   D   A   B
      A   B   R   A   C   A   D   A
        A   B   R   A   C   A   D
          A   B   R   A   C   A
            A   B   R   A   C
              A   B   R   A
                A   B   R
                  A   B
                    A
```

Today *abracadabra* is a nonsense word used, for example, by amateur magicians.

antenna. A Greek verb meaning "to stretch out" was adopted by the Romans as *antenna* to refer to the bars or "yards" which stretched out from masts to support sails. As an extension of this meaning, Theodorus Gaza, a fifteenth-century translator of Aristotle, used *antennae* to refer to the "horns" which stretch out in front of insects; biologists still use the term in this way. The *antennas* that stretch their arms over modern houses bear some resemblance to the old "sail-yards" or *antennae.*

bankrupt, mountebank. First used by English in the sixteenth century, *bankrupt* is from Italian *banca rotta* "bench broken." Lombard money changers of medieval Venice sat in St. Mark's Square with their coins on a bench (*banca*) in front of them. If they were robbed or for some other reason had to give up their business, they traditionally broke their benches. Italian *rotta* is from the same Latin source (*rumpere* "to break") as English *rupt* in *rupture, interruption, abrupt,* etc. In English usage even a person who owns no bench may become *bankrupt. Mountebank* is also associated with the Italian word for "bench." A *montambanco* "mounted on a bench" stood on a bench while he amused the crowd and sold his generally useless medicine or other wares.

bitter end. Does not refer to taste, but is a sailing term. *Bitts* were pairs of posts used to hold cables such as anchor cables. Captain Smith's *Seaman's Grammar* (1627) says: "A Bitter is but the turne of a Cable about the Bits, and veare [wear] it out by little and little. And the Bitters end is that part of the Cable doth stay within boord." Sometimes the "bitter end" would be reached without the anchor's having taken hold, so that the ship continued to drift—a possibly dangerous situation.

bombastic. French *bombace* was cotton, often used for padding clothing. The English borrowed the word, usually spelling it *bumbaste* at first, as in Gascoigne's "to stuff thy doublet full of such bumbaste" (1572). But language, too, may be padded, as when Iago criticized Othello's language as "a bumbaſt circumstance/Horribly stufft with Epithites of warre." The *OED*'s first citation for the derivative *bombastic* is dated 1704.

calico and other cloths. An example of early linguistic borrowing from the Orient, *calico* is traceable to the Indian city *Calicut*. A sixteenth century work refers to "iiij yards of Callaga." The cloth was also called *Calicut, Callicute,* and *Collaca;* as well as *Cal(l)ico(e)*. Other cloths of Oriental origin include *nankeen* (Nanking), *organdy* (Urgandi, a city in Uzbek), *shantung* (a Chinese province), and *pongee* (from Chinese for "home loom"). The Near East has given us *damask* (Damascus), *gauze* (Gaza, in Palestine, through French), *muslin* (Arabic *Al-Mawsil* or *Mosul,* through French and Italian), *seersucker* (Hindi *sirsakar,* from Persian *shir-o-shakar* "milk and sugar"), and *taffeta* (Persian *tāftah* "woven," through Italian and French).

canary. The Canary Islands are so named because ancient Romans found there many large dogs (Latin *canis* "dog"). But when Renaissance sailors went there, they captured and brought back many bright little yellow birds, which became known as *canaries*. (At about the same time, or earlier, a dance called "the canaries" was borrowed from the inhabitants; Shakespeare says ". . . and make you dance Canari" [*All's Well,* II, i, 77].)

cartridge, musket. Cartridge goes back to Latin *charta* "paper," through Italian and French, but was invented only during early modern times. A definition dated 1611 says "a Cartouch [French *cartouche*], or full charge, for a pistoll put vp within a little paper to be the readier for vse." Before the invention of cartridges a musket had to be fired by two men, one of whom loaded and aimed, the other applying fire to the gunpowder at the aimer's signal. *Musket* came through French from Italian *moschetto,* originally a sparrowhawk; the moschetto or musket was comparatively small, light in weight, and quickly moved, thus somewhat like the small, agile sparrowhawk. Early muskets discharged arrows, not bullets.

coconut. Portuguese sailors first found the fruit in India, and were surprised at its resemblance to a human head. Portuguese *coco* referred to a grinning or grimacing face; Portuguese parents would frighten their children by telling them that a *coco* would get them. Early texts in English used various spellings, e.g., Robert Burton's "Coquernuts," John Smith's "Cokar nuts," Thomas Heywood's "Cocker-nutts," Samuel Purchas's "Coquo-Nuts," and Samuel Pepys's "Coco-nutts."

could. The *l* came in in E Mod E because of the influence of *would* and *should.* Chaucer generally wrote *coud* or *coude,* and *cuð* was also frequent. Like the present tense *can* (OE *cunnan* "to know"), *could* originally meant "knew" or "knew how to." What one knows, he presumably is able to do something with. So in one syllable *can* or *could* suggests the saying "Knowledge is power."

crestfallen. When a rooster or hen is ill or when a rooster has lost a fight, its crest or comb droops. Shakespeare realized that people, too, at least figuratively, can be crestfallen: "Let it make thee Creſtfalne," says the Duke of Suffolk as he recalls the lowly origins of a man who threatens to kill him (*II Henry VI,* IV, i, 59).

cruise. Dutch sailing terms are fairly numerous in English. *Cruise* is ultimately the same as the verb *cross.* Dutch pirates used to cross and re-cross shipping lanes looking for rich merchant ships. Such sailing without a precise destination was indicated by the Dutch verb *kruisen,* as in "kruys-syn op de Zee." In more recent times, a *cruise* may follow a rather flexible time-table. American sailors looking for girls or adventure sometimes say that they are "just cruising."

dandelion. In the Middle Ages speakers of Latin referred to this flower as *dens leonis* "tooth of the lion" because they fancied that the petals resembled lions' teeth. The French borrowed the name as *dent de lion,* and by the sixteenth century the word was familiar in English as *dandelion.*

derrick and other words from proper nouns. A hangman named *Derrick* became so well known in early seventeenth-century London (at Tyburn prison) that his gallows was called by his name. A little later a hoisting apparatus that looked something like a gallows was invented and was also called a *derrick.* Today thousands of workmen operate such machines, generally no doubt unaware of the grisly history of the name.

Gargantuan comes from *Gargantuan,* the huge central figure in *La Vie Très Horifique du Grand Gargantua,* by Rabelais (1534).

Guy is from *Guy Fawkes,* who in 1605 tried to blow up Parliament because of the stringent anti-Catholic laws of James I. In British parades on Guy Fawkes' day, people burned his effigy, or *guy* as it came to be called. In America, where these political implications are not important, any man can be a "guy."

Nicotine recalls Jean Nicot, who in about 1600 introduced tobacco to France. A name for the plant, *Nicotiana,* also honors him.

Solecism reflects the fact that residents of the ancient Greek colony of Soloi didn't speak Greek "correctly." Athenians described the dialect as *soloikos,* with the noun form *soloikismos,* which became Latin *soloecismus.* By 1577 some English people were critical of others' *solecisms,* thus further immortalizing the otherwise forgotten early inhabitants of Soloi.

discount. From French *descompte,* one of many English borrowings from sixteenth-century French. The word rapidly acquired most of its present meanings, but first apparently meant "not counted." If, for example, you bought eleven items but were required to pay for only ten, the item not included represented a *discount.*

doll, Hal, moll, Sally. These are respectively nicknames for Dorothy, Harry (or Harold or Henry; e.g., Shakepeare's Henry V is called "Prince Hal"), Mary, and Sarah. As early as the sixteenth century, a doll was a female pet, a mistress, but the earliest *OED* reference to the doll as a toy is dated 1700. "Moll" Flanders was a prostitute-protagonist in Defoe's novel of 1722, and earlier, in 1611, Middleton and Dekker had used "Moll Cutpurse" in their *Roaring Girl;* the modern "gangster's moll" comes from this illustrious lineage. The uncapitalized verb or noun *sally,* as in "to sally forth" or "a sudden sally," is from a different source, the French *saillir,* "to leap, bound, or dance."

earshot. Anything within hearing range is said to be within *earshot.* When measurement of land was less precise than it is today, distances were sometimes indicated in terms of "bowshots," about two hundred yards. E.g., the *OED* includes from 1450 "more than fowre *bowschote.*" By analogy *earshot* developed. Beaumont and Fletcher (1607) say, "Hark you Sir, there may be some within Ear-shots."

embarrass. The French *embarrasser* meant "to block, obstruct," and was related to *embarrer,* "to embar, imprison." A character in Dryden's *Marriage à la Mode* (1673) probably reflected the present meaning in "Pray do not Embarrass me," calling the term a "delicious French word."

far-fetched. Literally, "fetched from afar." Early explorers brought back many curiosities from the New World, but also frequently told unbelievable stories. Hence for a while both useful products and lying inventions were described as "far-fetched." Today the term is restricted to things imaginary or improbable, but in the sixteenth century ladies were accused of excessive liking for any items "farrefetched and deare boughte."

fender. *Fend* and *fender* are shortened forms of *defend* and *defender,* as a 1440 quotation from *OED* reveals: "Fendowre, or defendowre." (*Fence* is related.) As sailing ships became large and numerous, they tended to scrape against crowded wharfs or each other; to prevent damage, heavy ropes or other materials were hung over the sides. A book for seamen, published in 1627, says "Fenders are peeces of old Hawsers called Iunkes hung ouer the ship sides to keepe them from brusing." The meaning was later broadened to include, for example, automobile fenders.

flour, flower. Ultimately the same word. Originally the word was used just for a blossom, but then added the idea of "the finest part of grain"; the French have a similar "fleur de farine." By the seventeenth century we find sentences like "They make flower also of fish dryed in the Sun," where the word obviously refers to ground meal. The differentiation in spelling was slow in coming; ME generally used *flour,* or *flur,* although *flowre, flower,* and other spellings were also common; Samuel Johnson in the eighteenth century had no entry for *flour* in his dictionary, but by the nineteenth century *flower* and *flour* had separated.

fork. An Anglo-Saxon ate with a knife (*cnif*) and sometimes a spoon (*spon* "chip of wood"), but to him a *forca* (from Latin *furca*) was only a tool for use in making hay. Not until the Renaissance did Englishmen use forks at the table. Ben Jonson's *Volpone* (1605) says, "Then must you learn the use/And handling of your silver fork at meals"; the speaker, Sir Politic Would-Be, is telling Peregrine what he needs to know to live in Italy, where table forks were used earlier than in England.

gas. Dutch chemist J. B. Van Helmont (1577–1644) wanted a word to signify an occult principle that he believed all bodies contained and that was an ultrararefied condition of water. Using Greek *chaos* as his inspiration, he named it *gas.* Later the term became less occult, more physical, but since the movements in a gas seemed to early observers to be chaotic, there was no reason to seek a new word.

gazette. Many modern newspapers are named *Gazette.* One of the earliest newspapers, published in Venice in the sixteenth century, was available to a reader for a *gazetta,* a coin worth about a half-cent. The name became transferred to the newspaper itself, and entered English as *gazette;* there are numerous early seventeenth-century references to *gazetti, gazets,* or *gazetts.* The earliest official governmental journal was the *Oxford Gazette,* 1665, which carried public notices. "To be in the gazette" came to mean "having one's name listed in the *Gazette* as a bankrupt."

grenade, grenadier, grenadine, pomegranate. In Latin, *pomegranate* was *pomum granatum* "apple with seeds." The French borrowed the name as *pome* (later *pomme*) *granate,* and Wyclif used it in fourteenth-century England as *poom-garnet.* In the sixteenth century the French invented an explosive shell shaped like a pomegranate; they dropped the first part of the name and called it a *granate* or *grenade,* which the English borrowed at once. *Grenadier,* originally "one who throws grenades," entered English in the seventeenth century, and *grenadine* "thick, sweet syrup made from pomegranates" in the eighteenth.

helpmeet, helpmate. When God decided to create a woman for Adam, according to Genesis 2:18, He said "I will make him an helpe meet for him" (1611). *Meet,* as sometimes used in Shakespeare, was here an adjective meaning "suitable." But that meaning was disappearing, so that the verse became hard to understand. In 1675 it was printed as *help-meet,* thus creating a compound noun. But that still seemed puzzling, and *helpmate* began to replace it; thus in 1722 Defoe admonished, "A woman is to be a *helpmate,* and a man is to be the same." Today *helpmeet* and *helpmate* are used interchangeably, with the latter seemingly more frequent.

infant, infantry. Both words go back through French to Latin *infans* "unable to speak." Why should foot-soldiers (who are often loquacious) be called *infantry?* The usual explanation is that the older soldiers usually had horses to ride, but the neophytes had to walk; therefore the word for babies was applied derisively to them, with no reference to their ability to speak.

jeans. *Janua* was a medieval spelling of *Genoa,* which specialized in making a strong cloth called *ieen, gene, jene, jane,* etc. Henry VII ordered "262 Cables of Jeane makyng" in 1495. The name was later transferred to the garments, especially trousers, made from the cloth. The present usual blue color is relatively recent.

kibitz, kibitzer. In German a *Kiebitz* is a plover or lapwing, a bird named for its cry; its noise sometimes frightens away game sought by hunters. The German verb *kiebitzen* came to mean "to look on in bothersome fashion, to meddle," as the Kiebitz did. The Yiddish verb was *kibitsen,* and one who performed the action was a *kibitser.* Largely because of their extensive use among Yiddish-speaking people, *kibitz* and *kibitzer* are frequently heard in America, especially with reference to a meddlesome on-looker. Leo Rosten, in *The Joys of Yiddish,* tells of a sign that read:

Dr. Joseph Kipnis—Psychiatrist

Dr. Eli Lowitz—Proctologist

Beneath the sign a kibitzer had written "Specialists in Odds and Ends."

Latin adjectives for English nouns. Otto Jespersen, in *Growth and Structure of the English Language,* pointed out that for the adjective companions of many nouns that go back to OE we rely upon Latin-based words:

book—literary	town—urban	house—domestic
man—human, virile	eye—ocular	mind—mental
(but also *manly*)	mouth—oral	nose—nasal
moon—lunar	star—stellar	sun—solar
son—filial	worm—vermicular	

Latin and English adjectives paired. Jespersen also reminds us that many Latin-based and OE-based adjectives exist side by side, with the same or closely related meanings. Examples:

daily—diurnal	brotherly—fraternal	earthy, earthly—terrestrial
fatherly—paternal	heavenly—celestial	motherly—maternal
timely—temporal	truthful—veracious	watery—aquatic, aqueous
old—venerable		

Jespersen says that we don't really need the "cold" words *frigid, gelid,* and *algid,* since the native words *cold, cool, chilly, icy,* and *frosty* are sufficient. But sometimes, as with *timely—temporal,* the meanings have diverged: *readable* and *legible* don't mean quite the same thing as a rule, nor do *youthful* and *juvenile* or *wretched* and *miserable.*

locomotive. Long before the invention of trains, *locomotive* existed in English—one of the thousands of Renaissance borrowings from Latin. *Loco* was the ablative case of *locus* "place," and *motivus* meant "moving." Hence anything *locomotive* could move from place to place. A book of 1612 referred to "command over the locomotiue facultie"; a person who had no such command could not walk. After trains were invented in the nineteenth century, the locomotives were first called "locomotive steam engines" or "locomotive engines," but the adjective became a noun a little later.

milliner. Originally a resident of Milan, a city famous for making and selling ladies' hats, ribbons, and the like. Later a *milliner* was anyone who dealt in such items, regardless of where she (occasionally he) lived.

musical scale. Singers in the Renaissance did not practice "do-re-mi" quite as moderns do. They used instead a "hexachord" consisting of six notes, sung on an ascending scale, as illustrated in this Latin hymn for St. John the Baptist's Day:

UT queant laxis
RE sonare fibris,
MIra gestorum
FAmuli tuorum,

SOlve polluti
LAbii reatum
  Sancte Joannes

Later, *ut* changed to *do,* and *ti* was added.

names of vegetables. Our tables would be poorer if it weren't for importations of the plants and with them, of course, their names; some of these borrowings occurred several centuries ago, others more recently.

asparagus. Known to the Anglo-Saxons. The name was taken from the Romans, who had adopted it from the Greeks.

broccoli. First mentioned in 1699. The word is Italian, meaning "little stalks."

cabbage. ME *caboche,* French *caboche* "head," ultimately Latin *caput* "head." Frenchmen now call it *chou cabus* or simply *chou.*

cauliflower. Called *cole-florye* or *colie-florie* in the sixteenth century. From French *chou-flori* (now *chou-fleur*) "flower of the cabbage."

gherkin. 1661, from a Dutch word for "little cucumber." May be ultimately of Slavic origin.

mushroom. Though the fungus has always been known in Britain, the word came in in late ME from French *mousseron,* probably from *mousse* "moss."

pumpkin. First *pompion* (1545) from French, Latin, and ultimately Greek *peptein* "ripen in the sun." The diminutive ending *-kin* may have been applied humorously to this sometimes huge fruit.

radish. Known to the Anglo-Saxons, who took the name from Latin *radicem* "root" (also the source of our *radical*). Our spelling reflects the French form, *radis.*

rutabaga. A comparatively recent borrowing, from Swedish *rotabagge.* "The ruta-baga has been sown in small quantities by a few individuals, most of whom approve of it," according to an agricultural publication of 1800.

spinach. Perhaps ultimately from Arabic *isfanakh.* Widely grown in Europe, and in its early days in Renaissance England considered a treat for the wealthy, ". . . helps inflammations . . . of the Stomach," said a 1671 writer; "not very nourishing" was a verdict in 1732.

squash. Thanks to the Narragansett Indian *asquutasquash* (1643). The English form is the same as that of earlier *squash* "unripe peapod," 1590.

turnip. Called *næp* in OE. The first syllable probably came in during the Renaissance from French *tour* "round."

pecuniary, peculiar. Ancient Romans, in determining the value of a share in an estate, often expressed it in terms of the number of cattle (*pecu*) it was worth. Their *pecunia* "money, property" came from this source. *Pecu* is a cognate of OE *feoh,* the ancestor of modern *fee.* (See Grimm's Law, page 26.) In the Middle Ages and later, *pecu* was borrowed in a variety of forms, some of which are now obsolete:

pecunarious "pertaining to cattle" (1656)

pecudiculture "the raising of cattle" (1885)

peculate "to embezzle" (1649). (Also *peculation,* 1658, and *peculator,* 1656)

peculiar "pertaining to that which is one's own," e.g., one's own cattle (1460). (Also *peculiarism,* 1836, *peculiarity,* 1610, *peculiarize,* 1624, *peculiarness,* 1561)

peculiate "to provide with a peculium" (1656) ; *peculium* "a private possession" (reported in 1681, but no doubt earlier)

pecunial "pecuniary, pertaining to money" (used by Chaucer in 1386 as *pecunyal*)

pecuniar, pecuniary "pertaining to money" (1530, 1502). (Also *pecuniarly, pecuniarily*)

pecunious "having money" (1393). (Today used mainly in the negative *impecunious;* also *pecuniosity,* 1883)

pecuny "money" (1393; "Be þe pecunie y-payed")

perfect, verdict, and other French-Latin words. ME and E Mod E borrowed many words from French but later changed them in spelling and pronunciation to bring them closer to the ancestral Latin. Here are a few examples:

This Modern English word	was borrowed in this form	from this French word.	The Latin original was
adventure	aventure	aventur	adventurus
advice	avis	avis	ad + visum
equal	egal	egal	æqualis
language	langage	langage	lingua "tongue"
perfect	perfet, parfet	parfit	perfectus
picture	peynture	peinture	pictura
verdict	verdit "say true"	veirdit	verus + dictum

pineapple. *Apple* was early a general name for many kinds of fruit (as *corn* was for grain). The pine cone was referred to by Trevisa in 1398 as "þe pinappel . . . þe frute of þe pine tre." A seventeenth century Italian traveler to the New World, Petro della Valle, found that natives ate an "ananas," which he said "resembles in shape our common Pine-Apple." In 1666 J. Davies said "The Pine-Apple is accounted the most delicious fruit . . . of all America." Scientists refer to the low-growing plant as *Ananassa* *sativa,* retaining the native name, but the popular name still suggests the completely unrelated pine tree.

pocketbook, purse. Compact, pocket-sized books containing mathematical tables and the like were invented by the versatile Aldus Manutius about 1510. The *OED* first records the word in English in 1617, as a synonym for *manual* (i.e., *handbook*). People began putting a few of their banknotes or other valuables between the leaves; then someone got the idea of making for such valuables a container that looked like a book but had no pages: hence the *pocketbook* as a holder of money. Many of today's ladies' pocketbooks have, of course, far outgrown the ladies' pockets. The word *purse* goes back to OE *purs,* apparently adapted from late Latin *bursa* "purse," to which our *bursar* and *reimburse* may also be traced.

profanity. Pre-Reformation Englishmen were notorious for swearing; as Chaucer attests, even the ladies swore "grete othes." After the Reformation, the name of God in oaths was often changed to *gad, gosh, gog, gom* (later *gum,* as in "by gum"), etc. *Lord* became *law, laws, lawks,* etc. *God's* was sometimes reduced to *'s: 'sblood, 'snails, 'slight, 'zounds* (or *zounds*) "God's wounds." *Drat it* is from *God rot it. Goodness, my goodness, goodness gracious,* etc., were other euphemisms. The Puritans passed laws against swearing—laws more easily enforced for printed than for oral matter; nevertheless, the laws did have influence, and until recent years comparatively little profanity was heard in England and still less was seen in print.

rummage. Today a rummage sale is a sale of miscellaneous items, e.g., a rummage sale held by a church. The word goes back to Medieval French *arrumage,* the arranging of items in the hold of a ship. An English publication of 1526 refers to the "Romage and Carridge of Wine," and Hakluyt's *Voyages* (1598) uses the word as a verb: "To give the Master . . . a good reward for his labour to see the goods well romaged." However, despite care in "romaging," goods were often damaged and had to be sold at reduced prices. Later *rummage* came to refer to various odd or old or damaged items put up for sale.

salesman. OE had the noun *sala* "sale," but the first use of *salesman* recorded in *OED* is from 1523: "It is not conuenient that the salesman, that selleth the wod [wood], shuld be partener with the bier [buyer]." The reference is to the woodcutter whose representative, the salesman, sold wood to townsfolk. Eventually any such middleman became known as a salesman.

sign. The growth of literacy is reflected in the verb *sign.* In the Middle Ages, when most people could not read or write, they "signed" documents by affixing some distinguishing mark or "sign" on them. By 1596, however, signing usually meant the affixing of one's name; this is what is meant by Shylock's speech in *Merchant of Venice* (IV, i, 397): ". . . send the deed after me,/And I will signe it."

slipper, slipshod. A writer in 1555 said, "They vse a maner of slippe shooes, that may lightly be putte of and on." Earlier (1478) the Paston Letters referred to "a peyer of sclyppers." Slippers were for inside wear only; a person who carelessly wore them outdoors was "slipshod" when he should not have been. By extension *slipshod* came to mean careless in anything; e.g., *King Lear* (I, v, 12) "Thy wit ſhall not go slip-shod."

spelling oddities. We have already accounted for the spellings of *debt* and *doubt* and *perfect* and several other words. Here are a few more explanations:

> **comptroller.** *OED* says "An erroneous spelling of CONTROLLER, introduced c. 1500." Influenced by French *compt-*.
>
> **fault, vault.** *Fault* had no *l* in ME or in French; the *l* is attributed to association with *false* (Latin *falsus*). Not until the eighteenth century was the *l* pronounced. The story of *vault* (ME *vaute*) is similar.
>
> **island.** The ME word was *ilond,* but the *s* crept in by association with French *isle* and Latin *insula*.
>
> **programme, catalogue, quartette.** The useless letters (now often dropped in American spelling) are there because of French *programme* and *catalogue,* and Italian *quartetto*.
>
> **receipt.** The *p,* not pronounced, is attributable to Latin *recipere* "to receive."
>
> **sovereign, foreign.** We took *sovereign* from Old French *sovrain,* but erroneous association with Latin *regnare* "to rule" resulted in the *g*. Then *foreign,* formerly also *g*-less, got its *g* from *sovereign*.
>
> **subtle.** *Sutil* was good enough for medieval people, but Renaissance scholars traced the word to Latin *subtilis* "thin, fine" and decreed that English must conform to the ancestral word in spelling if not in pronunciation.
>
> **tongue.** OE *tung* or *tunge,* sometimes *tounge* in ME; the transposition of the *u,* says the *OED,* is "neither etymological nor phonetic, and is only in a very small degree historical." Just a linguistic accident!
>
> **victuals.** ME *vitaile,* but scholars traced the word to Latin *victualis,* with predictable consequences. The *c* has probably never been pronounced—especially by people who eat good "vittles."

stave off, bulldog, bullfrog. The cruel medieval sports of bear-baiting and bull-baiting, still popular in the sixteenth century, endangered the dogs as well as the larger animals. Sometimes to save his dog's life the owner would beat it away from the infuriated bear or bull by using a barrel stave; he "staved it off." The way that the expression was extended is illustrated by T. Adams (1633): "He [a man] is like an old bitten curre, that being fleshed to the game, will not be stav'd off." *Stave* is derived from OE *stæf* "staff," in the plural of which the *f* was pronounced [v]. The bulldog was developed specifically for bull-baiting; hence its name. *Bullfrog,* however, is an Americanism; a writer in 1698 said that it "makes a roaring noise, hardly to be distinguished from that well known of the Beast, from whom it takes its name."

unstrung. In Mod E if a person is "unstrung," he is fearful, disorganized, nervous. In medieval and later times, it was necessary to loosen a bowstring when the bow was not in use, to preserve the resilience of the weapon. If an archer unexpectedly met an enemy when his own bow was unstrung, he was understandably nervous. As archery declined in importance, *unstrung* remained to describe the trepidation, even when no bow was involved.

CLASSROOM ACTIVITIES

Encouraging Play with Language

The Renaissance was a time of widespread experimentation with language—much of it very playful. Try to encourage your students, too, to play with language. (The younger they are, the more they'll enjoy it.) For example:

Make an occasional pun, or read some puns that you like. Encourage your students not to repress their puns.

Look at the far-out rhymes used by Ogden Nash: *swallow that— habitat, extinct—thinked, better for—metaphor, experience— Assyrians, many things—anythings, interpolate them—purple ate them,* etc. Ask your students to write some verses with their own funny rhymes. Talk about words that supposedly have no rhymes, like *orange* and *chimney;* students may come up with something like *orange juice—gore'n'juice* or *chimney—Jim-n'- he.*

Encourage experimentation with unusual, even original, metrical forms.

Talk often about oddities of the language. This book provides much material.

Make up a factual quiz of two (on any classwork) in a simple crossword puzzle form. Encourage students to try their hands at solving crossword puzzles, Double-crostics, and other word games. The magazine *Word Ways,* though intended for adults, always has some games and puzzles that interest students; it should be in the school library.

Talk about English expressions (like those in Peggy Parish's poem "Amelia Bedelia") that might seem ambiguous to a foreigner. E.g., "Dress the chicken" sounds as though clothing is to be put on it, or "Draw the drapes" suggests making a picture.

The Origins of People's Surnames

Until the Renaissance most people had only one name: *John, Mary,* etc. To distinguish one John from another, it was customary to say something like "John the smith," "John the long," "John from Kent," "John the son of John," etc. Thus in Shakespeare's *Midsummer Night's Dream* we find Bottom the weaver, Quince the carpenter, etc. The word *the* gradually dropped out, so that John might become John Smith, John Long, John Kent, or John Johnson, etc. As these examples suggest, most surnames originally indicated occupation, physical appearance, or location, or were patronymics like *Johnson.* A person whose name is *Noble* or *King* doesn't necessarily have a noble or a royal ancestor: the name may have been chosen only because the characteristics or the wealth of noblemen or kings seemed appealing. When ghetto Jews were belatedly allowed to choose surnames, they often selected names of things they considered pretty: *Bloom* (German *Blum* "flower"), *Gold, Stein* (German for "stone" or "gem"). At the end of slavery, some black people chose the names of their former masters or names of persons they had heard about (e.g., *Washington*), but others selected names of places, occupations, or physical characteristics.

Your students may enjoy guessing the origins of these common names: Brown, Williams (short for *Williamson*), Jones (a Welsh version of *Johnson,* and equivalent to *Jansen, Hansen, Ivanovich,* and many other names that mean "son of John"), Miller, Davis (short for *Davidson*), Anderson (son of Andrew), Wilson (same as *Williams*), Taylor, Moore ("from the moor").

They may have more trouble with the following names because the occupations represented are now rare or extinct or have changed in designation: Bailey (bailiff), Bauer (German for "peasant, farmer"), Baxter (baker), Chapman (merchant), Day (dairyman), Fletcher (arrow-maker), Foster (forester), Gruber (engraver), Lambert (lamb herdsman), Latimer ("Latiner," interpreter), Reeder (thatcher), Turner (woodworker), Wagner (wagon-maker) Ward (watchman), Webster (weaver), Wheeler (spinner), Zimmerman (German for "carpenter"). Gray, Armstrong, and Longfellow are easy, but the personal qualities represented by these names are less so: Blount (blond), Boyd (yellow-haired), Cameron (twisted nose), Campbell (crooked mouth), Cruikshank (crooked leg), Dunn (dark), Gross (German for "large"), Schwartz (German for "dark"). Among old place names represented in surnames are Bach (German for "brook"), Baum (German for "tree"), Baumgarten, Churchill, Ford, Holt (wood), Hurst (wood), Steinberg (German for "stone mountain"), and Thorpe (village). Names of nationalities are pretty obvious: Deutsch, English, French, El Greco, Hollander, Inglis (English), Scott, Welsh.

If a student's name is foreign, he may be able to supply a translation, e.g., Leblanc (French for "the white"), Schmidt (German for "smith"). Your students may have fun tracing as many as possible of the names represented in their class. (They will probably not be able to trace some of them, especially non-English names.)

The Meanings of Given Names

Until the Renaissance, the number of given names used was relatively small, but acquaintance with Latin and Greek added to the total, and literacy also increased knowledge and adoption of Biblical names. Several dictionaries (including Webster's *Collegiate*) give extensive lists of the meanings of today's given names. E.g., *Adam* is "man" and *Eve* is "life, living." For a dollar you can get from the U.S. Government Printing Office a booklet "Foreign Versions of English Names" (Order Number M-131), which gives the equivalents of several hundred English given names in some twenty other languages.

More Renaissance Words

The preceding section on "Accounting for Some of the Words" provides considerable ammunition about words that came in or were interestingly modified during the Renaissance. Some of your students may enjoy reading a number of the entries. The following list names others that have interesting histories, most of them introduced in the Renaissance, but a few at other times. Your students may divide the list, each looking up one or two words for selective reporting. Etymologies may be found in dictionaries; unabridged dictionaries or especially the *OED* provide most information. The stories behind these thirty words (plus others) are given interestingly in Helene and Charlton Laird's *The Tree of Language,* World, 1957; a number of them are also reported in other books on etymology, such as Ernest Weekley's *The Romance of Words,* Dover Publications, 1961, or Wilfred Funk's *Word Origins and Their Romantic Stories,* Grosset & Dunlap, 1950.

amphibian (-ious)	delirious	hippopotamus
ballot, ballet (ball)	dollar	humor
bus (omnibus)	echo	magazine
calendar	electric	money
card	explode	music
caterpillar	fool	poison
circus	good-by	pupil, puppet, puppy
cosmetics	gun	romance
coward	handicap	travel
curfew	handkerchief	umbrella

Words Whose Meanings Have Changed

John Algeo and Thomas Pyles, in *Problems in the Origins and Development of the English Language* (Harcourt Brace Jovanovich, 1966, page 250) have concocted the following paragraph in which the italicized words must be interpreted in an older sense for the paragraph to have meaning. Your students may enjoy looking up older meanings and "translating" the passage by substituting modern equivalents.

He was a happy and *sad girl* who lived in a *town* forty miles from the closest neighbor. His unmarried sister, a *wife* who was a vegetarian member of the WCTU, ate *meat* and drank *liquor* three times a day. She was so fond of the oatmeal bread made from the *corn* her brother grew that she *starved* from over-eating. He fed nuts to the *deer* that lived in the branches of an *apple* tree which bore pears. A *silly* and wise *boor* everyone liked, he was a *lewd* man whom the general *censure* held to be a model of chastity.

Algeo and Pyles also call attention to these and other expressions in sixteenth- and seventeenth-century literature: *addressed* himself "prepared himself" (Bunyan); *approved* the dignitie of his Science "proved . . ." (Raleigh); we *prevent* the last great day "anticipate . . ." (Herbert); ships are safely come to *road* ". . . harbor" (Shakespeare); *portly* emperess "stately, dignified" (Marlowe); *unvalued* jewels "priceless . . ." (Shakespeare); that false *worm* ". . . serpent" (Milton).

Words from Mythology

The Renaissance familiarized many people with classical mythological characters. In a unit on mythology you may want your students to try to think of some of the words that English has taken from mythological characters. Here is a partial list:

Achilles—Achilles' heel, Achilles' tendon
Andromeda, Argo, Pegasus, Perseus—(constellations)
Amazon—amazon, amazonian, amazonite (a mineral), Amazon river
Apollo—apollo (handsome young man), appollonian
Argonauts—Argonaut (California gold-seeker), argonaut (a mollusk)
Argus—argus pheasant
Atlas—atlas
Aurora—aurora, aurora borealis
Bacchus (Greek *Dionysus*)—baccate (berry-like), bacchanal(-ia) (-ian), bacchant(e), dionysian
Calliope—calliope
Ceres—cereal
Cupid (Greek *Eros*)—cupid, Cupid's bow, erotic(ism, -ally), erogenous
Hercules—herculean, Hercules (a constellation)
Hyacinthus—hyacinth
Hymen—hymen, hymeneal
Iris—iris, iris diaphragm
Jove (Jupiter)—jovial, Jovian, the planet Jupiter
Juno—Junoesque
Mars (Greek *Ares*)—martial, the planet Mars, the constellation Antares "opposite Ares"
Mercury (Greek *Hermes*)—mercury, mercurial, mercuric (and other words in chemistry), the planet Mercury, hermetic(-ally)
Odysseus—odyssey
Pan—panic, pan-pipe
Pluto (Greek *Hades*)—the planet Pluto, plutonic, plutonium, pluton (igneous rock), Hades
Proteus—protean
Saturn—Saturday, saturnalia, saturnid (a moth), saturnine, saturnism, the planet Saturn
Siren—siren
Tantalus—tantalize
Titans—titanic

Uranus—the planet Uranus, uranium (and other words in chemistry)

Venus (Greek *Aphrodite*)—the planet Venus, Venus's fly-trap (and other plants and animals), venereal, venery, aphrodisiac, aphrodite (a butterfly)

Vesta—vestal, vesta (matches)

Vulcan—vulcanize, volcano, volcanic

Words for Houses

Glimpses of social and family history are available in the stories behind the words for *house* (OE *hūs*) and for parts of houses. Some of the words in the following list entered the language during the Renaissance, others earlier or later. Brief oral or written reports on a selected group of them can be interesting.

apartment, bungalow, castle, dwelling, hotel, hovel, igloo, mansion, palace, residence, shack, shanty, tepee, wigwam.

attic, basement, cellar, conservatory, dining room, drawing room, garret, kitchen, library, parlor.

Household Words

We have discussed *fork* and *rug;* other household words of interest appear in the following list. Words with asterisks can be traced, with the aid of the *American Heritage Dictionary,* all the way back to Indo-European, although the meanings may have changed. Each date in parentheses represents the first use recorded by the *OED.*

andiron (ME), *basin* (ME), *bellows* ("fireplace tool"; note that one definition is "lungs"; (OE), *billiards* (1591), *bowl** (ME), *bureau* (1742), *cabinet* (1549), *carpet** (ME), *chair** (ME), *chaise longue** (1825), *chiffonier* (1806), *cup** (OE), *davenport* (Not in *OED* in the sense of "sofa"; *A Dictionary of Americanisms* dates it 1902), *desk* (ME), *dish* (OE), *divan* (1586), *dumb-waiter** (1755), *furniture** (1529), *glass** (OE), *iron** (OE), *lamp** (ME), *picture** (1489), *plate** (ME), *pool** ("game"; 1848 in this sense), *refrigerator** (1611), *saucer** (Look up *sauce,* too; ME), *settee** (1716), *sink** (as a noun, 1440), *sofa* (1625), *spatula** (1525), *stove** (1456), *table* (OE), *toilet* (1540), *tureen** (1706).

Shakespeare's Language

In reading a Shakespearean play (or any other piece of literature, for that matter), obviously most attention should be paid to the literary qualities such as the portrayal of people. Nevertheless, understanding may be enriched by looking at the language, too. Often no more than a moment need be given to an unusual word, an archaic meaning, an "odd" sentence structure, or the like. But on occasion fifteen minutes or a half-hour can be spent profitably in a careful look at the language of a scene, with attention paid both to vocabulary and to sentence structure, and perhaps to brief comments by the teacher on the pronunciation formerly used.

With reference to words that have changed in meaning since Shakespeare's time, your students may be able to add to this list compiled by Otto Jespersen, in *Growth and Structure of the English Language:*

bonnet—man's hat
to charm—to use spells or witchcraft on
notorious—well-known (for either good or bad deeds)
success—(could be either good or bad)
sheer—pure
politician—("seems always to imply intriguing or scheming")
remorse—pity or sympathy
now-a-days—("a vulgar word")
also—("nearly always puts it in the mouth of vulgar or affected persons")

A Useful Recording

Beowulf, Chaucer, Shakespeare, and the Gettysburg Address, by Harry M. Ayres, a recording distributed by the National Council of Teachers of English, presents brief illustrations of the pronunciations during four periods of history. An informative leaflet accompanies the record.

Suggested Topics for Class or Group Discussion

What was the Renaissance?
How our lives would be different if no one had invented movable type
The advantages and disadvantages of borrowing foreign words
The importance of Latin words in the English vocabulary
Spelling (or Usage) should (should not) have been allowed to remain anarchic
How Shakespeare's English differed from (or was similar to) ours

English Words from Latin

The roots listed below are some of those from which English, at one time or another, has derived numerous words. (Several, but not all, of the progeny are listed.) Study of such derivations may add words to your students' vocabularies and show them previously unsuspected interrelationships. The forms vary, especially those taken from verbs, since borrowings could be from infinitives, participles, or other forms. One interesting exercise is to give the Latin word, its common forms, and its meaning, and ask students to try to create English words from it. They may add affixes as needed.

agere "to drive, to do" (*act, ag, ga*): act, action, active, activity, actuary, agent, agility, agitate, enactment, prodigal, reaction.

anima "breath, life" (*anim, anima*); animal, animation, animosity, equanimity, inanimate, unanimous.

cadere, caedere "fall, cut, kill" (*cad, cas, cis, cid*): accident, cascade, circumcise, decadent, excise, incisive, incisor, occasion, patricide, precise, scissors.

capere "take, hold" (*cap, capt, cip, cep*): capable, capacity, captivate, capture, deception, except, forceps, inception, participant, perception, recipient.

cedere "move, withdraw, yield" (*ced, ceed, cess*): accede, access, accessory, antecedent, cede, concession, proceed, process, recede.

currere "run" (*cur, curr, curs, cours*): concur, course, currency, current, curriculum, cursive, cursory, excursion, occurrence, precursor, recur.

dicere "say" (*dict, dic, dex*): addict, benediction, contradiction, diction, dictionary, edict, index, indictment, malediction, predicate, predict, verdict.

ducere "lead" (*duc, duct*): conducive, deduct, educate, induce, induction, produce, reduction, seduction.

facere "make, do, build, prepare" (*fac, fact, fect, fic, fy*): affect, artifact, confection, defect, efficient, facility, facsimile, factory, fortification, magnify, manufacture, petrify, rectify.

frangere "break" (*fract, frag, fring, frang*): fraction, fracture, fragile, fragment, infraction, infrangible, infringement.

gradi "walk, go, step" (*grad, gress, gred*): aggression, congress, degrade, digression, grade, gradation, graduate, ingredient, regress, retrograde.

jacere "throw" (*jac, ject*): abject, adjective, conjecture, dejected, ejaculation, eject, inject, interjection, object, projection, rejection, subject.

jungere "join" (*junct, jug*): adjunct, conjugal, conjunction, junction, juncture, subjunctive.

magnus "great, large" (*magn, major, maxim*): magistrate, magnanimous, magnate, magnificent, magnify, magniloquent, magnitude, major, majority, maxim.

malus "bad" (*mal, male, pair, pessim*—from the comparative and superlative): *impair, malady, malefactor, malevolent, malicious, malign, pessimism.*

mittere "send" (*mit, miss, mis*): *admit, commission, dismiss, emissary, missive, promise, remit, submission, transmit.*

plicere "fold" (*plicat, plicit, plic, plex*): *application, complex, complication, explicate, implicate, imply, simplicity.*

scribere "write" (*scrib, script*): *ascribe, description, circumscribe, inscription, postscript, prescribe, scribble, script, scripture.*

specere "see, look at" (*spec, spic, spect*): *aspect, conspicuous, inspect, prospect, perspicacity, retrospection, species, specimen, spectacular, spectator, specify, suspicion.*

stare "stand" (*stan, stat, sist, stitut, sta*): *constant, distant, establish, insist, stable, stationary, stature, status, substance.*

tendere "stretch, strain" (*tend, tens, tent*): *attend, extensive, intention, ostensible, portend, pretentious, tendency, tension.*

tenere "hold" (*ten, tent, tain, tenac*): *content, detain, lieutenant, pertain, retention, tenacious, tenant, tenement, tenor.*

venere "come" (*ven, vent*): *advent, adventure, circumvent, convene, covenant, eventual, intervene, invention, prevent.*

videre "see" (*vid, vis*): *evident, improvise, provident, revise, supervise, television, visage, visible, vista, visualize.*

vivere "live" and *vita* "life" (*viv, vit*): *convivial, revive, survive, vital, vitality, vivacity, vivid, vivify, vivisection.*

volvere "roll, turn around" (*volv, volut, volu*): *convolutions, devolve, evolution, involve, revolution, revolver, volume, voluminous.*

English Words from Greek

As is true of the Latin roots just listed, the following Greek roots have been responsible for considerable numbers of English words.

arche "beginning, first" (*arch*): *anarchy, archaic, archangel, archbishop, archduke, archeology, monarch, patriarchal.*

chronos "time" (*chron, chrono*): *anachronism, chronic, chronicle, chronology, chronometer, synchronize.*

graphein "write" (*graph, gram*): *anagram, biography, epigram, epigraph, geography, grammar, graph, grapheme, graphic, graphite, telegram.*

kosmos "world, universe" (*cosm*): *cosmic, cosmopolitan, microcosm, microcosmic.*

logos "speech, word, reason" (*log*): *logic, zoology,* (and scores of other words ending in -*logy*).

onyma "name" (*onym*): *anonymous, antonym, homonym, pseudonym, synonym.*

pathein "feel, suffer" (*path*): *antipathy, apathy, empathy, pathetic, pathological, sympathy.*

philos "loving" (*phil*): *Philadelphia, philanthropy, philology, philosophy.*

phone "sound, voice" (*phone, phon*): *cacophonous, euphonious, megaphone, microphone, phonetic, phonics, telephone.*

phos "light" (*phos, phot*): *phosphorus, photograph, photostat, photoplay, telephoto.*

polys "many" (*poly*): *polyandrous, polygamy, polysyllable, polytheism.*

thermos "hot" (*therm*): *thermal, thermometer, thermos, thermostat.*

Latin Prefixes in English Words

The following list includes a number of the Latin prefixes often used in English. Awareness of their meanings will often enable your students to interpret English words. A few minutes of dictionary-searching for words with each prefix can be rewarding. (Caution: Not every English word starting with these letters contains the prefix; for example, *bicuspid* and *binocular* start with the prefix *bi-* or a variant, but *biology* does not, since *bio* is from the Greek word for "life.")

ab- "from, away from, down" (appears in English as *ab-, abs-, a-*)
ad- "to, toward, for" (*ad-, ap-, at-*)
ante- "before" (*ante-*)
bi- "two" (*bi-, bin-*)
contra- "against" (*contra-*)
cum- "with" (*com-, con-, col-, cor-, co-*)
de- "down, down from, away" (*de-*)
dis- "apart, away, not" (*dis-, dif-, di-*)
ex- "out, out of" (*ex-, e-*)
in- "in, into, on" (*in-, im-, il-, ir-*)
in- "not" (*in-, im-, il-, ir-*)
inter- "between, among" (*inter-*)
intra- "within" (*intra-*)
intro- "inward, inside" (*intro-*)
ob- "against, toward, before" (*ob-*)
per- "through" (*per-*)
post- "after" (*post-*)

prae- "before" (*pre-*)
pro- "for, in favor of, on behalf of" (*pro-*)
re- "back, again" (*re-*)
sub- "under, below, beneath" (*sub-, suc-, suf-, sup-, sur-, sus-*)
super- "over, above, beyond" (*super-, sur-*)
trans- "across, through" (*trans-, tra-*)

Greek Prefixes in English Words

As is true of the Latin prefixes, short periods of dictionary study of words beginning with the following Greek prefixes can help in vocabulary building.

an- "not, without" (*an-, a-*)
anti- "against, opposite" (*anti-, ant-*)
auto- "self" (*auto-, auth-*)
deka- "ten" (*deca-, dec-, deci-*)
dia- "through, across, between" (*dia-*)
hemi- "half" (*hemi-*)
homo- "same" (*homo-*)
kata- "down, wholly, against" (*cat-, cath-, cata-*)
meta- "between, with, after" (*meta-, meth-*)
neo- "new" (*neo-*)
para- "beside, near, beyond" (*para-, par-*)

If English Hadn't Borrowed Any Words

Ask students to write a couple of sentences (say a total of thirty to forty words) on any subject. Then have them check a dictionary to discover which of their words were borrowed. Next have them rewrite their sentences using only words not traceable to a foreign tongue, and compare the two versions. This exercise should illustrate how dependent we are on our borrowings.

Learning Words in Related Families

Charlton Laird (*English Journal,* November, 1970, pp. 1110–11) argues that students' vocabularies can grow rapidly if students learn much about word-relatives. He says that as a child he had trouble in remembering that *mega-* implies bigness, but that if any teacher had told him it comes from the same source as *much,* the difficulty would have vanished. "The untutored layman cannot be expected to guess that *much, maharajah, mayor,* and *megaton* all stem from the same old expression, and that they accordingly have a common foundation in the idea of bigness . . . . Most people who have never been taught better methods try to learn words one by one, whereas usually they could learn a dozen words, or scores of words more easily and in ways that will help them to understand better and to remember longer if they will learn words in related families." (Be sure to read Laird's whole article.)

For Indo-European roots and lists of related words from those roots, useful in following Laird's recommendation, see the appendix of the *American Heritage Dictionary*. There you will find, for instance, that I-E *gheu "to pour, pour a libation," which was nasalized in Latin to *fundere,* gave us *font, funnel, fuse, effusive, profuse, refund,* as well as *gust, gush, geyser,* and other words, all of which can be seen to have some relationship to the I-E meaning.

Words from the Same Root

As a fun exercise, students may compose sentences containing a number of words from the same root. Florence A. Mattingly illustrates with words from Greek *biblos* "book": "A born *bibliophile* browsing in a *bibliotheca,* bewilders a *bibliographer* by *bibliolatry* bordering on *bibliomania,* but a *bibliothec* benefits *bibliology,* bewails *biblioclasts' biblioclasm,* berates *bibliopoles' bibliopolism,* bewares banal *bibliopegy,* and becomes blatant *Biblical bibliomancy.*" (*Word Study,* December, 1937, p. 8)

Musical Terms

Most technical musical directions were borrowed from Italian in the sixteenth and seventeenth centuries. Your musically inclined students (or others who can never remember, for instance, whether *allegro* means "fast" or "slow") may look up the Italian and earlier Latin meanings. Here are a few:

adagio: Italian for "at ease," from Latin *ad* "at" and *agio* "ease"

allegro: Italian for "lively," from Latin *alacer* "lively, quick"— also the source of *alacrity*

allegretto: the Italian diminutive of *allegro;* consequently not quite so fast

andante: Italian for "walking," going back ultimately to Latin *ambulare* "to walk," which has given us *ambulate, perambulate,* etc.; an andante tempo is moderate, between adagio and allegretto

crescendo: Italian for "increasing," from Latin *crescere* "to grow" —also the source of *crescent*

diminuendo: Italian for "diminishing," from Latin *deminuere* "to diminish"—also the source of *diminutive,* etc.

pizzicato: Italian for "pinching, plucking," from Latin *pizzare* "to pinch, to pluck"—also the source of *pizza, pizzeria presto, prestissimo:* Italian for "rapid" and "most rapid," from Latin *praestus* "ready," from *praesto* "at hand," and hence associated with "nimble-fingered"; presto is faster than allegro

Seventeenth Century Spellings

By the seventeenth century most but not all English spellings had settled into their present forms. If you have available a literary work (say *Pilgrim's Progress*) in an edition in which spellings have not been modernized, students may spend a few minutes in noting some of the differences between the seventeenth and twentieth centuries. E.g., *cloathed, sinck, threatned, perswade, exprest, missled, gon, bogg, slow* [slough], *dispond* (all from a few pages of the 1678 edition of *Pilgrim's Progress*). Several additional examples may be found in this book, page 194. Discuss: Do any of the seventeenth-century spellings appear more reasonable or desirable than the ones we use?

7
English from 1650 to 1800

THE BUILDING OF AN EMPIRE

In the middle of the seventeenth century, England was still a small, mainly agricultural country with a population of some four million, concentrated chiefly in the southeastern quarter or third of the island. Although her foreign interests were developing (as witness tiny colonies in North America and elsewhere), few if any Englishmen could envision anything like the empire that was to develop in the next century and a half. Simultaneously with empire would come substantial growth in England's population (though this was still only eight or ten million in 1800), greater ease of transportation and communication, an industrial revolution that signaled a transition to a largely urban economy and style of life, and the replacement of old class distinctions by new ones between management and labor. Of special importance—from a linguist's point of view—was the continued expansion of knowledge and the need for vocabulary to express that knowledge. There was a feeling in the air that England was in the forefront of change; hustle and bustle had succeeded the more leisurely pace of the past: "Everything wears the face of dispatch," Henry Homer wrote in 1767.

The process of change did not bring happy results to everyone; some people suffered whenever someone else gained. Wars were almost constant—with the Dutch, the French, the Spanish, with the natives in those places where the colonists went, and finally with some of the colonists themselves. But England was economically a winner in most of the wars; her fur trade and her slave trade, for instance, profited tremendously from the Treaty of Utrecht in 1713, and the sugar interests profited no less from the Peace of Paris in 1763. British merchants were often unscrupulous exploiters: colonies in continental North America supplied food for slave laborers on British islands, the islands grew cane for molasses that the colonists made into rum, British traders used the rum in Africa to buy more slaves, and the merchants pocketed a profit from each stage of the transaction. Such "merchants," though, were not just a handful of rich men. Stockholders became increasingly numerous in the British East India Company, the Royal African Company, and the Hudson's Bay Company, and in the eighteenth century the huge South Sea Company, before its bubble broke, could secure investors for even its wildest schemes, such as insurance against death from rum or against female unchastity.

Increasing Prosperity

The colonies occupied increasingly important roles in England's prosperity. They sent in, for example, tobacco, tar, pitch, hemp, and masts for the growing navy, and in return England sold them the goods she was producing in ever-increasing quantities. "You have sought to raise up a nation of customers in the colonies," said Adam Smith. Laws governing the colonies were often dictated by the mercantile class—laws, for instance, against colonial production of iron or even against the making of beaver hats, so that British industry would not suffer from such competition.

The English became a people on the go, with thousands emigrating to foreign soil and other thousands going abroad as sailors, soldiers, or sometimes just as sightseers. The ten million speakers of English in the England of 1800 were approximately matched in number overseas. Movement accelerated in England too: new roads were built and were traversed by swift coaches and long wagon-trains; canals threaded the countryside. A letter could be delivered anywhere in London for a penny (on the same day it was mailed), and from 1638 on there was a royal post serving all of England.

The Industrial Revolution brought blast furnaces, steam engines, spinning jennies, and other technological innovations. It spelled the virtual end of cottage industry, replacing it with the noisy, dirty ancestors of today's factories. "The whistling of birds is not for us," said a labor pamphlet in the late eighteenth century; "our melody is the deafening noise of the engine." Factory workers, many of them previously farm people, were crowded into hovels near their places of work.

Agriculture itself was becoming mechanized with new tools for tilling and harvesting. The use of fertilizer increased, and England soon could supply food for export as well as for its own growing population. Agricultural publications were numerous. Farming was becoming scientific.

The Arts and Language

Literature flourished, as names like those of Milton, Bunyan, Dryden, Defoe, Swift, Pope, Fielding, Johnson, and Goldsmith remind us. Inigo Jones and Christopher Wren were outstanding architects. The theater was popular from the Restoration on. Henry Purcell brought his church music and his opera to an England that was fast acquiring a taste for such things. The names of the furniture designers of the time—Chippendale, Sheraton, Hepplewhite—still live. England's prosperity (at least for those who shared in it) made possible a sturdy and intelligent interest in nearly all the fine and applied arts.

Near the end of the period, though, there were already indications that the empire that was growing so rapidly might in the future diminish almost as quickly. Recurrent wars, troubles in India, and especially the success of the American Revolution were among the signals. But before those events, the English flag and with it the English language had been carried to many of the land areas of the world; in the nineteenth century they would be carried even farther. The language was in most places destined to remain longer than the flag. As a result of the empire's growth, English is today the predominant language not only in England but also in North America and Australia, and in parts of Asia and Africa and South America and on islands scattered around the globe.

A PERIOD OF LINGUISTIC CONSOLIDATION AND GROWTH

No More Major Changes

The second half of the seventeenth century has gone relatively unstudied by philologists or modern linguists. Probably the chief reason is that, though as always the language continued to change, there were no developments as dramatic or far-reaching as some that had occurred previously. There were, for instance, few further changes in inflections, no new technology that affected language as much as the invention of printing had, no great vowel or other phonological shift, no second Renaissance.

Instead, the late seventeenth century and much of the eighteenth are noteworthy for consolidation of changes already made—especially for a gradual approach toward a regularity or uniformity greater than any the users of the language had previously conceived. Not that uniformity was actually attained, then or later. Dialectal variations in British speech were (and are) easily noticeable, and not all users of a "standard" dialect employed exactly the same verb or pronoun forms in their speech.[1] But as the London literary influence became stronger and stronger, and as printing styles became more and more standardized, and as more children went to school and learned from printed books, writers increasingly adopted the same spellings, the same principles of punctuation, the same habits of capitalizing; and they tended to settle on one verb or pronoun rather than another, one type of sentence transformation rather than another. The changes were not sudden: in 1800 many variants still existed, though fewer than in 1650 or 1600 and much fewer than in 1400, the date of Chaucer's death. (Even today the language is far from uniform, but particularly in printed matter the differences are not generally great.)

Parallel Passages

A careful reading of the following paragraphs will reveal examples of minor changes that occurred between the beginning of the seventeenth century and the end of the eighteenth, but will show no really substantial differences.[2]

1. *Translation by "I. T.," 1609*

First therefore wilt thou let me touch and trie the state of thy mind by asking thee a few questions, that I may vnderstand how thou art to be cured. To which I answered, aske me what questions thou wilt, and I will answere thee. And then shee said, Thinkest thou that this world is gouerned by happe hazard and chance? or rather doest thou belieue that it is ruled by reason? I can (quoth I) in no manner imagine, that such certaine motions are caused by rash chance. And I know that God the Creator doth gouern his worke, neither will I euer thinke otherwise. It is so, saith shee, for so thou saidest in thy verse a little before, and diddest not doubt, but that they were gouerned by reason. And surely I cannot chuse, but exceedingly admire, how thou canst be ill affected, holding so

1 For example, the past participial forms of some strong verbs were less fixed than most of them are today. Thomas Gray's "Elegy Written in a Country Churchyard" (1751) was originally entitled "Elegy Wrote in a Country Churchyard."

2 The passages are from three translations of the same part of Boethius' *Consolation of Philosophy*. The texts followed are those in *A Sourcebook in the History of English*, published by Holt, Rinehart and Winston, 1969, and edited by Anthony E. Farnham to preserve the spellings, etc., of the originals.

wholesome an opinion. But let vs search further, I gesse thou wantest something, but I know not what.

2. Translation by Richard Graham, Viscount Preston, 1695

Phil. First then wilt thou suffer me to try the Estate, and feel the Pulse of thy Mind, by a few Questions; that so I may better understand thy Malady, and prescribe the Methods of thy Cure? *Boet.* Ask me what thou pleasest, and I will answer thee. *P.* Thinkest thou that this World is manag'd by blind Chance and Fortune? or dost thou believe that Reason hath any share in the Government of it? *B.* I do by no means believe or imagine, that things, so certain in their Methods, and so regular in their Motions, should be mov'd and informed by so unsteady a Cause; but I know that God, the Master-workman, doth preside over his Work; nor shall any Time or Accident ever move me from the Truth of this Opinion. *P.* So 'tis indeed; and of this a little before, thy Muse did sing when thou didst also deplore the Misfortune of Man, whom alone thou didst believe, not to be under the Care of Providence; though, that every other thing was govern'd by Reason, thou didst not doubt. But it is miraculous to me, that thou, who hast so just notions of all things, shouldst be in so ill a State of Health; I will therefore search further, for I believe thou yet labourest under some notable Defect.

3. Translation by Richard Ridpath, 1785

First then allow me, continues she, to ask you a few questions upon the present state of your mind, that I may know in what manner I ought to proceed in your cure. Ask me what you please, replied I, I shall most willingly answer you. Tell me then, says she, do you believe that the affairs of this world are under the direction of blind fortune, or conducted by a wise and rational intelligence? I can by no means believe, answered I, that the beautiful order we every where observe in nature, could proceed from the caprice and irregularity of chance. I know certainly that God, the creator of the universe, presides over his work. There never was a day in my life, in which I hesitated a moment with regard to the certainty of this comfortable truth. I believe you, says she; for a little while since you declared you were of this opinion, when deploring in your moving verses the unfortunate state of the human race, as alone destitute of the divine care, you allowed that all other things were guided by a rational intelligence. Ah! continued she, I am above measure surprized, that you should despond, when upheld by so comfortable a sentiment! But we must search farther; I am afraid that there is some imperfection, some defect in this conviction.

If you think in terms of what changes would need to be made in each of these passages for it to be idiomatic twentieth-century printed English, it is obvious that 3 would require very little modification, 2 somewhat more, and 1 still more. Note in 1, for instance, the use of *thou, thee,* and *thy,* the later discontinued verbs like *wilt* and *diddest,* spellings like *answere, shee,* and *chuse,* the occasional retention of *v* for *u* and vice versa, the slightly heavy punctuation, the use of now archaic or obsolete words like *quoth,* the lack (at least here) of the *do*-transformation which eventually became customary in expressions to replace "I know not what," etc., examples of word order or word choice not quite like ours (e.g., "I can . . . in no manner imagine"), and occasional use of words in senses unusual today (e.g., *admire* still retained its earlier meaning of "wonder at," and *wantest,* as the later translations show, meant "lackest" or "art defective in"). In 2, some but not all of these are changed, but in 3 most of the "old-fashioned" touches have vanished.

Growth of Vocabulary

The English vocabulary continued to grow from 1650 to 1800, although many of the additions were simply different parts of speech, taken from words borrowed earlier. The first few pages of *OED* offer the following examples:

New word	OED date	Parent language	Earlier borrowing	Type of shift
abdominal	1746	Latin	abdomen, 1541	adj. from n.
abhorrence	1660	Latin	abhor, 1449	n. from v.
abnegate	1657	Latin	abnegation, 1554	v. from n.
absolutism	1753	French, Latin	absolute, ME	n. from adj.
absorbent	1718	Latin	absorb, 1490; absorption, 1597; absorptive, 1664	adj. from v.
academician	1749	French, Latin	academy, 1474	n. from n.
accentuate	1731	Latin	accent, 1538	v. from n. or v.
accuracy	1662	Latin	accurate, 1612	n. from adj.
acidulous	1769	Latin	acid, 1626, from French	adj. from n.
acoustics	1683	French, Greek	acoustic, 1605	n. from adj.
adjectival	1797	Latin	adjective, ME	adj. from n.

But some words were completely new. Increased knowledge of the medical sciences, for example, gave *abducent* "drawing away or out, as muscles," 1713; *acupuncture,* 1684; *adductor* "muscle that pulls toward," 1746; *adipose* "fatty," 1743; and many more. The words *aeronautics* and *aerostatics,* from Greek, entered the language in 1753; about thirty years later, interest in flying by balloon added *aeronaut,* 1784; *aerostat,* 1784; *aerostatic,* 1785; *aerostation* "the art of raising and guiding balloons," 1785.

The same few pages of *OED* show other borrowings from 1650 to 1800, some of which are rare or obsolete but others still in use. Examples include *abbé,* 1780, from French; *abele* "white poplar," 1681, Dutch; *achromatic,* 1766, Greek; *acrid,* 1712, Latin; *adept,* 1663, Latin; *adroit,* 1652, French; *aesthetic,* 1798, Greek.

Words from more exotic languages, such as those of the American Indians, continued to enter the language. A mid-eighteenth century Englishman, Richard Owen Cambridge, said that a glossary was needed to explain expressions used in accounts of wars with Indians, mentioning as examples *sachem* "chief," *calumet* "peace pipe," and *wampum* "shell beads used as currency," as well as English phrases like *take up the hatchet.* Dr. Samuel Johnson, though, refused to admit to his dictionary any Indian words (or any terms that he considered Americanisms), although he used *tom-ax* (for *tomahawk*) in one of his essays.

Countless examples of changes in meaning or additions of meaning could be cited. The word *æsthetic,* mentioned earlier, was first used with the meaning "received by the senses"; not for several decades did it approximate the present meanings of "pertaining to the criticism of taste" or "pertaining to the sense of the beautiful" or "having a love of beauty"; in 1842 *Æsthetics* was described in an encyclopedia of architecture as "a silly pedantic term." In form, the word even yet has not settled down, sometimes (though rarely) preserving the ligature: *æsthetic;* sometimes separating the *a* and *e: aesthetic;* and sometimes abandoning the *a* as useless: *esthetic.* *Actress,* derived from *actor* in 1589, at first meant only "a female doer [of anything]," but by 1700 meant "a female player on the stage." *Academician* was originally restricted to a member of an academy such as the Royal Academy; only gradually did its meaning expand so much that today the term is sometimes applied to a professor of any academic subject, as in the perhaps pejorative phrase "educationists and academicians."

Pronunciation

William Shakespeare (1564–1616) and Alexander Pope (1688–1744) could have understood each other's pronunciations with little difficulty, and Pope's pronunciations would appear only slightly odd if we in the twentieth century could converse with him. Most of the differences between eighteenth and twentieth century pronunciations are in a few vowel sounds.

A well-known couplet from Pope's *Rape of the Lock* goes like this:

> Here thou, great Anna! whom three realms obey,
> Dost sometimes counsel take—and sometimes Tea.

A single example of such a rhyme would not prove conclusively that Pope said either [te:] for *tea* or [obi:] for *obey,* for he might have been satisfied by an approximate rhyme. But when we find that he also rhymes *tea* with *away* and *obeys* with *sways* and that his contemporaries used similar rhymes, we can be reasonably sure that he did say [te:] and that *obey* was pronounced about as it is today. Other evidence from rhymes indicates that many additional words that now have an [i:] sound were then pronounced with [e:]. Thus rhymes like *take/weak* suggest [we:k] for the latter. *Shade/dead* suggests that *dead* must have approximated [de:d], and when we also find *dead/tread* we suspect that *tread* also shared the [e:].

Similarly, when Pope rhymes *sphere* with *there, bear,* and *fair,* we may conclude that the vowel of *sphere* was [ɛ]. *Hair/ear, ear/repair,* and *care/ were* suggest that [ɛ] also was used in *ear, were,* and other words that now have other vowel sounds. *Obliged/besieged* and similar rhymes show an [i:] in *obliged* rather than our [aI]. Pope's *join/nine, join/shine, joined/mind,* and *line/join* attest to an [aI] in *join,* and perhaps recall that nineteenth century writers of dialect often spelled the word *jine.*

The following list of selected rhymes from Pope (which could be supplemented by examples from other writers) shows that still other sounds have changed at least slightly in the past two hundred years.

> *preferred/guard, desert* (v.)/*heart, reserve/starve* (The [a] before [r] is best known in the still-surviving British [klark].)
>
> *wind* (n.)/*unkind, wind* (n.)/*mind, find/wind* (n.) (The pronunciation [waInd] is now regarded as poetic.)
>
> *give/believe, feel/mill, chagrin/spleen, been/seen* (The present [I] was often [i:] in the eighteenth century.)
>
> *race/grass, mast/placed, glass/place*
>
> *mourns/burns, born/return*
>
> *long/tongue, young/long*
>
> *doom/come, foredoom/Rome, home/come*
>
> *lost/boast, tost/coast*
>
> Also Swift's *warm/arm; dizen'd/poisoned; thoughts/draughts; figure/ digger, figure/vigour/bigger, lecture/hector*

Tendencies in the Sentence

Many lines of influence converged . . . to persuade the writers of the time [the period after 1660] to free their style of obscurities, baroque complexities, and erudite irrelevancies, to use the simple word instead of the unusual or highly colored one, to employ matter-of-fact imagery, practical similes . . . . The clear style was dwelt upon by a succession of Anglican divines. . . . Simplicity and clarity of expression, and directness and homeliness of imaginative and emotional appeal were the indispensable condition of the appeal of Baxter, and still more Bunyan, to the masses of the population. In this movement the scientists played a highly important role, as the remarks on language delivered by Sprat in his *History of the Royal Society* serve to remind us.[3]

It is certainly true that the labored or even tortured prose sometimes found in the sixteenth and early seventeenth centuries was simplified, and that stylistic excesses like those of Lyly in *Euphues* vanished. Writers like John Bunyan and Izaak Walton introduced to English a new standard of readability. But the change was less abrupt and less complete than the quotation suggests. Although few writers after Milton emulated the sometimes awesomely long sentences of his *Areopagitica* (1644), Jonathan Swift not infrequently managed to get two hundred words into a sentence, and Dr. Samuel Johnson's prose was highly Latinized (28 per cent, compared to Milton's 19, Shakespeare's 10, and the King James Bible's 6). Nevertheless, two or three centuries before the Fowlers recommended clear, simple, straightforward English, many writers were moving in that direction, and the tendency continues even today.

As we have seen, until the Renaissance the use of participial phrases and subordinate clauses was comparatively infrequent. Then, partly because the elaborate, architectonic sentences of Cicero were so much admired ("Ciceronian periods," they were called), some writers began building tremendous sentences of their own—gigantic structures, intricately formed, balanced, antithetical, with phrases and clauses upon phrases and clauses. As architecture the sentences were often estimable, but as devices for communication of thought they frequently failed. Like hungry children in a candy store, their authors showed too little restraint. Later writers, more conscious of their roles as communicators, split their thoughts into smaller segments, pruned verbiage, moved directly rather than wander through verbal labyrinths. The contrast may be illustrated by these sentences, the first from Robert Burton's *Anatomy of Melancholy* (1621), the second from John Bunyan's *Grace Abounding to the Chief of Sinners* (1666):

Or else we are insulted over, and trampled on by domineering officers, fleeced by those greedy *Harpyes* to get more fees; we stand in feare of some precedent Lapse; we fall against refractory, seditious Sectaries, peevish Puritans, perverse Papists, a lascivious rout of Atheisticall *Epicures*, that will not be reformed, or some litigious people (*those wild beasts of Ephesus,* must be fought with) that will not pay their dues without much repining, or compelled by long suit;

[3] Helen C. White, *et al., Seventeenth-Century Verse and Prose,* Volume Two: 1660–1700, New York: The Macmillan Co., 1952, pp. 10–11.

for *Laici clericis oppido infesti* an old axiome, all they think well gotten that is had from the Church, and by such uncivill, harsh dealings, they make their poore Minister weary of his place, if not his life; and put case they be quiet, honest men, make the best of it, as often it fals out, from a polite and terse Academick, he must turne rustick, rude, melancholise alone, learne to forget or else, as many doe become Maulsters, Grasiers, Chapman, etc. (now banished from the Academy, all commerce of the Muses, and confined to a country village, as *Ovid* was from *Rome* to *Pontus,*) and daily converse with a company of Idiots and Clownes.

After I had been in this condition some three or four days, as I was sitting by the fire, I suddenly felt this Word to sound in my Heart, *I must go to Jesus;* at this my former darkness and Atheism fled away, and the blessed things of Heaven were set within my view.

Of course not all sentences by Burton and his contemporaries were as complicated as the first example, and neither Bunyan nor his contemporaries and followers always wrote with the simplicity of the second. Nevertheless, the two quotations illustrate the fact that the English sentence had moved from brevity and straightforwardness in Old English to great complexity in much Renaissance and post-Renaissance writing, and then started back again. Modern writers have not gone all the way back to the frequently stark simplicity of Old English, however; they have learned to use effectively the devices of subordination that the Anglo-Saxons largely ignored and that Burton and others employed to excess. Modern writers pack their sentences tightly but do not overload them.

A Few Matters of Grammar and Usage

The important *do*-transformations, used only occasionally by Shakespeare and his fellows, moved toward their present frequency between 1650 and 1800. Although Dryden in the late seventeenth century could still write "I alter not . . ." and "Think you that . . . ?" he was at least as likely to write "I do not alter . . ." and "Do you think that . . . ?" A century later, in the writings of men like Edmund Burke and Horace Walpole, the *do*-transformations had almost eliminated the older forms.

Thou, thee, thine, thy, and *ye* nearly vanished during this period except in certain dialects and (because of Biblical influence) in certain religious contexts. The fact that *you* was now employed as both singular and plural caused problems with the past tense of *to be; you were* was soon widely used for both singular and plural, although printed instances of *you was* are not rare. The frequency of *you was* in personal letters suggests that it was probably quite common in conversation. (Several early Presidents of the United States used *you was* in familiar correspondence.) Interestingly enough, the comparable present tense *you is* has rarely been observed in print and apparently has been spoken by relatively few people. It could be argued that if language were consistent and logical, *you is* and *you was* would both be standard singular forms, showing subject–verb agreement and differentiation from the plural forms *you are, you were*. But it might be argued contrarily that since other verbs such as *walk, walked* are the same in form after both singular and plural *you, be* should behave similarly. Linguistic arguments based on logic, though, are profitless, because language is no more logical than its users. Only a concocted language, like Ido or Esperanto, is likely ever to be logical and consistent.

In the seventeenth and eighteenth centuries the strong verbs continued their erratic course. Earlier, as you will recall, many of the rather numerous OE strong verbs had either dropped out or had switched to weak forms. Shakespeare and his contemporaries might use either *gat* or *got, span* or *spun, spake* or *spoke,* etc. In the mid-seventeenth century Samuel Pepys wrote "the King had *spoke* to the lady," "we . . . *drunk* whey," "I stopped to hear news of the fleete, but none *come*," and "I have *wrote* to her." In the eighteenth century Lady Mary Wortley Montague wrote "My sex is usually *forbid* studies of this nature," "I *writ* a letter," and "For P. *has wrote* upon their tomb."

But despite such evidence that the language was not "fixed" (a favorite eighteenth century word in linguistic discussion), and despite the fact that dialectal variations were very great, the language was much more nearly uniform than it had ever been before. There were no longer almost limitless options in spelling and there were few in punctuation; pronouns and most verbs had settled into the forms familiar to us; adjectives and adverbs were treated essentially as we treat them.

Some writers, though, wanted uniformity to be complete, and they criticized those people whose ideas of what was "correct" differed from their own. It is this influential group of writers that we shall next consider.

THE DOCTRINE OF "CORRECTNESS"

Philosophical and Literary Background

The eighteenth century is often called "The Age of Reason." Its roots go back into the seventeenth century, to Francis Bacon, who argued in favor of inductive processes rather than intuition or revelation, and to the French philosopher–mathematician René Descartes, who stressed methodical reasoning as an abstract instrument that functioned best when freed from custom, prejudice, and idiosyncrasy. Descartes' *Discourse on Method* was translated into English by 1649 and was strongly influential in the development of abstract systems of economics, politics, criticism, statistics, and even religion. The Deists, for example, argued against the revelations of Christianity and its dependence upon faith, and in favor of a religion whose conclusions were arrived at through supposedly rational processes.

The doctrine of reason was an argument against individuality, for all people who reason correctly must reach the same conclusions, as they do, for example, in proving a theorem of geometry. As Professor Francis Gallaway has said in *Reason, Rule, and Revolt in English Classicism,*

> The aesthetics based on symmetry, proportion, and fulfillment of function; the supremacy of the judgment over the imagination; the emphasis on realism; the attempt to find a universal foundation for taste; and the effort to re-establish the Rules on the basis of reason are all more or less intimately connected with the basic temper of the Age of Reason.

Everything in the universe is subject to the same laws; any attempt at departure from the laws results in error, it was supposed. A correct uniformity must therefore be a goal to be sought continuously in everything.

Under the influence of the doctrine of reason, Abraham Cowley shifted from metaphysical conceits to straightforward prose, and John Dryden tried to develop a rational rather than an individualistic style of criticism. Works of literature, many critics came to believe, were not inspired but methodically thought out. Ancient writers had discovered most of the essential rules of literary construction, and success in writing required only that those rules be followed. As Pope said,

> These Rules of old discovered, not devised,
> Are Nature still, but Nature methodized.

Ben Jonson had said a century earlier,

> . . . what other men did by chance or custom he [Aristotle] doth by reason; and not only found out the way not to err, but the short way we should take not to err.

And Pope's contemporary, John Dennis, declared in 1704,

> In short, poetry is either an art, or whimsy and fanaticism. If it is an art, it follows that it must propose an end to it self, and afterwards lay down proper means for attaining that end: for this is undeniable, that there are proper means for the attaining of every end, and those proper means in poetry we call the rules.

If poetry and other forms of literature demanded that rules be followed, then clearly the language in which literature is composed must likewise follow rules. Many eighteenth-century Englishmen tried to find and state such rules.

Proposals for an Academy

Under the patronage of Richelieu, L'Académie Française was incorporated in 1635, with the aim of guiding literary effort and controlling French grammar, orthography, and rhetoric; in 1694 it published a dictionary designed to create uniformity in the language. (The Academia della Crusca had published a similar Italian dictionary, called *Vocabulario,* in 1612.) England had no such academy, but before his death in 1666, the "historiographer royal," James Howells, praised the concept as worthy of emulation, and Robert Hooke (1635–1703) of the Royal Society wrote in favor of an English academy that would license books, check on accuracy of translations, prepare a dictionary, and "purify" the language. The Royal Society, even before Hooke became a member, had established a committee on language reform (in 1664), but nothing came of it. Thomas Sprat's *History of the Royal Society* (1667) argued that the English language "has hitherto been a little too carelessly handled," even though the Society's members themselves attempted "a close, naked, natural way of speaking, positive expressions, clear senses, a native easiness, bringing all things as near the mathematical plainness as they can, and preferring the language of artisans, countrymen, and merchants, before that of wits and scholars."

In the early eighteenth century both Swift and Addison advocated the creation of an academy, and were supported by such lesser writers as Matthew Prior and Thomas Tickell. Swift approached members of Queen Anne's cabinet with his plan, and a list of twenty prospective members was drawn up; had Queen Anne not died in 1714, it is at least possible that an academy would have been established. The proposal was revived later in the century, with Joseph Warton and Oliver Goldsmith among its supporters, but once more no academy resulted.

Proposals for something like an academy have been made from time to time in the United States too. John Adams argued in 1780 for an academy that would "correct and improve" the English language and keep it from changing. "It will have a happy effect upon the union of the States," he said, "to have a public standard for all persons in every part of the continent to appeal to, both for the signification and pronunciation of the language." As late as the 1960's a congressman from California unsuccessfully introduced in each session of the House of Representatives a bill that would have led to an official American dictionary and grammar; those in charge of these publications would in effect have constituted an American academy.

The Kinds of Reforms Desired

John Dryden complained in 1679 that his countrymen wrote "barbarously," and feared that he himself used "false grammar." In 1693 he lamented the lack of "a tolerable dictionary, or a grammar, so that our language is in a manner barbarous." He noted, for instance, that a Latin infinitive such as *amare* "to love," being a single word, is never divided, and argued that in English a split infinitive like *to really love* must be bad because it does not conform to Latin grammar. Swift in 1712 said that "our language is extremely imperfect" and regretted what he considered its "daily corruptions" and the "abuses and absurdities" of which its users were guilty. He felt that some authoritarian group should obliterate the "gross improprieties," saying "They will find many words that deserve to be utterly thrown out of our language, many more to be corrected, and perhaps not a few long since antiquated, which ought to be restored on account of their energy and sound." He would admit new words only if they were approved by an academy, and would allow no approved word to "be afterwards antiquated and exploded."

Swift did not realize that the French Academy was not succeeding in "fixing" the French language, which continued to change (and still changes) despite the officially sponsored conservative force. Classical Greek and Classical Latin, of course, were indeed fixed—but only after they became languages with no native speakers; both had changed, as all languages do, while they were languages of the household and the street and not just of the scholar's study, and they had changed to different kinds of Latin and Greek when they were used in medieval monasteries.

Dr. Samuel Johnson once thought that his dictionary might "fix our language," but said in the Preface of the work when it came out in 1755,

[I] now begin to fear that I have indulged expectation which neither reason nor experience can justify. . . . [A lexicographer may with justice be derided if he] shall imagine that his dictionary can embalm his language, and secure it from corruption and decay, that it is in his power to change sublunary nature or clear the world at once from folly, vanity, and affectation.

Writers and editors of the *Critical Review,* despite what Johnson had learned, apparently decided to condemn all words that caused them displeasure. The list of their dislikes, expressed over a period of years, might run on for pages. It would include *abandonment, adroitly, aggrandizement bilious, devastated, emanate, foibles, generalized, insistence, intermediary, occident, orient, paternity, population, simplification,* and *tranquilly,* as Robert D. Spector noted in *Word Study* in 1951. Sometimes, as with *insurgents,* the *Review* granted that the word "may be convenient on many occasions," but then added, "if this reason were admitted for the coining of new words, we should hardly have any standard of language remaining." What reasons for word-coinage might be "admitted" is not stated.

Some of the would-be reformers accused the English language of lacking grammar. It did not, of course, except in the sense that it lacked long conjugations and declensions like those of Greek and Latin, having lost most of its inflections at an earlier time. The reformers did their best to remedy the supposed defect, identifying the nominative, genitive, dative, accusative, ablative, and vocative cases of nouns (thus following the Latin pattern), and preparing two-page conjugations of verbs (even though most English verbs by the late eighteenth century had only four commonly used forms). They managed to find active, passive, and neuter verbs, as well as regular, irregular, and defective; and indicative, imperative, potential, subjunctive, and infinitive moods; and tenses as numerous as those in Latin; and not only gerunds but also gerundives. They formulated grammatical principles for schoolboys to learn: "The conjunction disjunctive has an effect contrary to that of the conjunction copulative," to quote a slightly unfair example from Lindley Murray. They made very definite statements: "Two negatives, in English, destroy one another."

Some grammarians, largely ignored, wanted to improve the language only by reducing its irregularities. Thus Thomas Cooke, in "Proposals for Perfecting the English Language" (1729), urged that all the strong verbs be made weak (a proposal that if adopted would eventually have made easier the lives of countless millions), wanted to get rid of irregular comparisons of adjectives, and pleaded that every plural noun should end in *-s* or *-es.* Other grammarians, such as William Loughton (1734), were sufficiently perspicacious to realize that English differed enough from Latin that it could not be forced "to the Method and Rules of the Latin Grammar." Loughton did not even admit Latin terms like *noun* and *verb* to his *Practical Grammar.*

Thomas Sheridan, father of the author of *The School for Scandal,* felt that "the study of our language" could contribute to curing "the evils of immorality, ignorance and false taste," especially if someone could "refine, ascertain, and fix" it, as he said in *British Education,* 1756. Most influential of the fixers was Bishop Robert Lowth, whose *Short Introduction to*

English Grammar (1762) was to go through twenty-two editions before 1800 and was to be responsible for offspring and descendants of offspring even to the present time.

Lowth and Other Prescriptivists

Lowth probably applauded Dr. Johnson's statement "I found our speech copious without order, and energetick without rules: wherever I turned my view, there was perplexity to be disentangled, and confusion to be regulated." Lowth appointed himself a regulator. He saw his task as that of preparing a grammar that would "enable us to judge of every phrase and form of construction, whether it be right or not. The plain way of doing this is, to lay down rules, and to illustrate them by examples. But, beside shewing what is right, the matter may be further explained by pointing out what is wrong." So Lowth looked at the work of "our most esteemed writers" and found much that, in his judgment, was very wrong indeed. Chaucer, Spenser, Shakespeare, and Milton were among the offenders. Lowth's view was not too unlike that of the twentieth century schoolboy who innocently said, "Shakespeare wrote tragedies, comedies and errors."

Lowth was echoed steadily; for example, James Buchanan puffed his own 1767 book by saying, ". . . considering the many grammatical Improprieties to be found in our best Writers, such as Swift, Addison, Pope, etc., *A Systematical English Syntax* is not beneath the Notice of the Learned themselves." From 1700 to 1750, according to a count made by Sterling Leonard, fewer than fifty English books were published on grammar, rhetoric, criticism, and linguistic theory, but from 1750 to 1800 there were over two hundred, and "most of these were concerned in whole or in part with solecisms, barbarisms, improprieties, and questions of precision in use of English."

Many of the opinions, biases, and rules still current in textbooks can be traced back to the language preferences held by the authors of some of these books. The rules for use of *shall* and *will,* for example, although first suggested in 1653 by John Wallis in *Grammatica Linguae Anglicanae,* were elaborated by Lowth in 1762 and by William Ward in 1765 in order to cover for instance the form "Shall you accept?" (where *shall,* they said, is needed in the question because it is the form expected in the answer). The matter of *shall–will, should–would* eventually became so complicated that the Fowlers devoted to it twenty pages in *The King's English,* concluding that anyone not to the manor born could not hope to use these verbs correctly.

The prescriptions for *who* and *whom*, the proscription of the double negative, the condemnation of *this here book* or *that there book* (but the acceptance of *this book here* and *that book there*), the demand for *taller of the two* (not *tallest*), the differentiation of *between* from *among*, the insistence upon *you were* even when *you* was singular, the objection to comparisons like *more perfect*—all these and many other pronunciamentos, largely arbitrary, have echoed through hundreds of thousands of classrooms since Bishop Lowth's time. If these prescriptions and proscriptions had been accurate in describing the ways that educated people actually used the language, they would be less subject to criticism. But most of them were actually only statements about how the self-anointed grammarians believed the language *should* be used.

Why was the doctrine of correctness so widely accepted? Partly, of course, because it was a natural outgrowth of the basic beliefs of the Age of Reason. But remember, too, that great social changes were occurring in eighteenth-century England; particularly, a sizeable middle class was emerging. One way for them to conceal the lowness of their background was to learn to talk as their "betters" supposedly did. So they eagerly bought the books that presumed to instruct them in "correct" English. Across the Atlantic, Americans wanted to learn to talk and write as well as their British cousins. So Lindley Murray in 1795 adapted Lowth's book for American use; edition after edition of his *English Grammar* appeared, with total sales exceeding a million copies during a period when the median population of the United States was only nine or ten million. In 1808 Murray added a second volume, consisting of "Appropriate Exercises"— the forerunner of countless books in which students have been required to correct someone else's sentences.

Application to Vocabulary

Vocabulary, and not just grammar, was of much concern to those who wanted firm standards of correctness. We have already noted some of the words disliked by the men responsible for the *Critical Review*. Swift had earlier objected to *banter, sham, bubble, bully,* and *shuffling,* and to shortenings such as *mob* (from *mobile vulgus*). Rhetorician George Campbell, although he thought that "The ears of some critics are immoderately delicate," believed that these words are "pleonastic": *unto, until, selfsame, foursquare, devoid, despoil, disannul, muchwhat, oftentimes, nowadays, downfall, furthermore,* and *wherewithal,* for which he preferred *to, till, same, square, void, spoil, annul, much, often, now, fall, further,* and *where-*

with; it is noteworthy that all but three or four of the words he disliked are still active. Campbell also thought it ridiculous that a ship should be referred to as "she," especially when the ship was a *man of war* or a *merchantman.*

Just as during the Renaissance some persons objected to borrowings from foreign languages, so did some writers in the eighteenth century. Addison was echoing earlier comments by Dryden and Defoe when in 1711 he wrote that it would be desirable "to hinder any words of a foreign coin, from passing among us; and in particular to prohibit any French phrases from becoming current in this kingdom, when those of our own stamp are altogether as valuable." (It is interesting to note that six of the words Addison uses in this comment had been borrowed by English from Old French: *foreign, coin, passing, particular, current,* and *valuable.*) Campbell, too, feared "an inundation of foreign words." But French, a prestigious language with which most educated Englishmen were familiar, inevitably continued to enrich the English vocabulary, giving us during this period such useful words as *ballet, cartoon, champagne, coiffure, dentist, negligee, patrol, publicity, routine,* and *syndicate.* And other languages, as we have already noted, made their own contributions, especially names of things formerly unfamiliar to the English: *alpaca, condor, llama, pampas, puma,* and *quinine* from Peru; *cayenne, jaguar, petunia,* and *tapioca* from elsewhere in South America; *bandana, calico, cashmere, chintz, coolie, cot, curry, juggernaut, jungle, jute, polo, rajah, thug,* and *veranda* from India; *banana, boorish, chimpanzee, gorilla, guinea, gumbo, hoodoo,* and *zebra* from Africa; and so on. The protests against such infiltration were unavailing, just as in the twentieth century Charles De Gaulle could not keep his French countrymen from adopting or adapting English words that they found useful.

An Opposing Doctrine

A few small voices opposed prescriptions of "rightness" and "wrongness" in grammar and vocabulary. These few persons realized that language inevitably goes its own way and cannot successfully be encaged. In ancient Rome Horace had declared that "use is the only arbiter and norm of speech." The Earl of Chesterfield echoed him, saying, "Every language has its peculiarities; they are established by usage, and whether right or wrong, they must be complied with." George Campbell, although ambivalent in his own practice, wrote in 1776,

Language is purely a species of fashion. . . . It is not the business of grammar . . . to give law to the fashions which regulate our speech. . . . [Grammar] is no other than a collection of general observations methodically digested, and comprising all the modes previously and independently established, by which the significations, derivations, and combinations of words in that language, are ascertained. . . . [The] grammarian's only business is to note, collect, and methodise [the modes and fashions].

Loudest of the small voices, though, was that of the remarkable Joseph Priestley, a theologian and a scientist, discoverer of oxygen and several other gases, author of a history of electricity, pioneer in the study of photosynthesis, and supporter of the American and French revolutions. At the age of twenty-eight (1761), he wrote *Rudiments of English Grammar,* in which he declared that language will never be controlled "by the arbitrary rules of any man, or body of men whatever." Usage, particularly that of established writers and speakers, determines what is good English. So, when he wrote his book, "The best and the most numerous authorities have been carefully followed. Where they have been contradictory, recourse hath been had to analogy, as the last resource. If this should decide for neither of two contrary practices, the thing must remain undecided, till all-governing custom shall declare in favour of one or the other." A year later he declared, "The general prevailing custom, whatever it happen to be, can be the only standard for the time that it prevails."

In such statements Priestley was directly opposed to Lowth and his followers. But the temper of the age preferred the definite *thou shalt* and *thou shalt not* of the Lowthians, rather than the less precise and more difficult-to-apply principle that Priestley advocated. Because of his outspokenness in political matters, Priestley's house, church, and laboratory were burned in 1791, and he had to flee in disguise, later emigrating to America. His comments on grammar, a relatively harmless topic, had caused him no serious trouble, but his views on that subject were no more accepted than were his views on the French Revolution.

Influence on the Schools

It is easier to teach something definite and prescriptive than to teach something relativistic. It is easier, for example, to declare firmly that a double negative is always wrong than it is to observe whether authors and other people ever use it, and, if so, in what circumstances. It is easier to grade papers in which each item is definitely "correct" or "incorrect" than it is if flexibility exists. So busy teachers, who themselves were seldom well informed about the language and its history, welcomed the prescriptions of the Lowths and ignored the Priestleys. And when Lindley Murray wrote his "Appropriate Exercises," which spawned a vast progeny, teachers also welcomed the opportunity to keep their pupils occupied in picking out predicate nominatives or gerunds or whatever, in correcting columns of wrong sentences, and in choosing between *shall* and *will*. And the children came to assume that such things are what English is all about; some of them learned and applied the rules; some of them went through the necessary motions and then promptly forgot; and some couldn't or wouldn't learn the stuff at all. Later, as parents, most of them assumed that their children should be exposed to the same kinds of English study as they themselves had been (whether they had learned it or not), and so the custom was perpetuated.

The language does, of course, have rules, or principles, which it is the duty of a grammarian to describe. Most of these rules have to do with word order, deep and surface structure, and transformations; a few concern morphology; many concern the lexicon—the ways in which it is customary to use certain words. But the Lowths and the Murrays, by devoting so much attention to *shall–will, who–whom,* and the like, sowed in the minds of teachers and the public an idea that trivia are the most important determinants of goodness and badness in language use. As a result, much English instruction for many years was mainly negative: don't split infinitives, don't say "I will" unless you are expressing determination or promise, don't end a sentence with a preposition. Children came to believe that good writing was itself a negative thing: merely the avoidance of error. They learned little about tone, color, and force, little about style and organization and content, and almost nothing about dialects, semantics, and history of the language. They were grossly cheated. And the overriding irony of all this was that the Lowthian precepts to which hundreds of millions of child hours had to be devoted were for the most part insignificant personal preferences of a few not very scholarly eighteenth-century Englishmen who set themselves up as the arbiters of language.

DICTIONARY-MAKING COMES OF AGE

Early Dictionaries

Ernest Weekley, in the *Atlantic Monthly* for June, 1924, said, "The earliest lexicographical efforts were probably made by Roman students of the Greek and Latin culture. . . . Teachers naturally compiled lists of words and phrases for the use of their pupils, and such vocabularies would be copied and attain some circulation; but it is obvious that what we call a dictionary was made possible only by the invention of printing."

The word *dictionarius,* referring to a collection of "dictions" (words and phrases) appears in thirteenth-century England, *dictionarium* in the fourteenth century. Scholarly monks sometimes wrote in margins of manuscripts simple translations or "glosses" of difficult Latin words; collected, these notations became a *glossarium,* today's *glossary.* An English–Latin *glossarium* appeared in 1449, called *Promptorium Parvulorum* "a storehouse for young clerks." Other names included *Ortus Vocabulorum* "garden of words," *Catholicon Anglicum* "English universal remedy," and *Gazophylacium* or *Thesaurus* "treasure house." Most of these books, instead of being arranged alphabetically, grouped words under headings such as *animals, music,* or *herbs.* Sir Thomas Elyot's *Dictionary* (1538) was the first book to use that name; it was expanded in 1542 as *Bibliotheca Eliotae* and became part of Thomas Cooper's *Thesaurus* in 1565. English–French, English–Italian, and English–Welsh wordbooks began appearing, and early in the seventeenth century men named Calepino and Minsheu published polyglot dictionaries giving synonyms in eleven languages; Minsheu's *Ductor in Linguas or Guide into the Tongues* was the first dictionary to attempt etymologies—sometimes quite imaginative ones.

Early makers of English–English dictionaries thought it unnecessary to define presumably familiar words. (In contrast, as Weekley pointed out, the *OED* devotes thirteen pages to *take* and explains and illustrates fifty-two separate meanings for *take up.*) One of the first of these books was a tiny one by Robert Cawdrey, *Table Alphabeticall of Hard Words* (1604). Also typical of the early practice was the work of a medical doctor, John Bullokar, who in 1616 used the title *An English Expositour teaching the Interpretation of the hardest Words used in our Language, with sundry Explications, Descriptions, and Discourses.* It was a much smaller book than its title suggests, and so were most of its immediate successors, like Henry Cockeram's *The English Dictionarie: or, An Interpreter of hard English words* (1623), which promised "Elegant Perfection of the English Tongue" to "Ladies and Gentlewomen, young Schollers, Clarkes, Merchantes, as also Strangers of any Nation."

One book that reflected the widespread vocabulary borrowings of the English was Thomas Blount's *Glossographia: or a Dictionary, Interpreting all such hard words whether Hebrew, Greek, Latin, Italian, Spanish,*

French, Teutonick, Belgick, British, or Saxon, as are now used in our refined Tongue (1656).

John Milton's nephew, Edward Phillips, brought out a considerably larger dictionary in 1678, *New World of Words or a General English Dictionary*. Revised and expanded several times by John Kersey (who was called on the title pages "J. K. Philobibl."), this book is sometimes considered the first true English unabridged dictionary, even though its definitions of common words were quite skimpy; e.g., *"dog,* a well-known creature."

Eighteenth-century Dictionaries before Johnson's

Kersey's revisions of Phillips were the most important dictionaries in the early part of the eighteenth century. Then in 1721 Nathaniel Bailey brought out the dictionary which, in revised or enlarged forms, was to be most widely used until Dr. Johnson's much superior volumes appeared. Bailey was a schoolmaster first, a lexicographer second. He ended his preface with this advertisement:

Youth boarded and taught the Latin, Greek, and Hebrew Languages, Writing, Accounts, and other parts of School Learning, in a Method more easy and expeditious than is common; by the Author, in his House in Stepney, near the Church.

The 1730 edition of Bailey's *Dictionarium Britannicum* was a 950-page folio volume accurately described on the title page as "a more Compleat Universal Etymological English Dictionary Than any Extant." Bailey listed cognate or ancestral forms from many languages and sometimes included little essays, such as one on "Mother Tongues." He was also the first lexicographer to indicate syllabic stress in words, the progenitor of today's elaborate diacritical systems.

A New General Dictionary; Peculiarly calculated for the Use and Improvement Of such as are unacquainted with the Learned Languages, by Thomas Dyche and William Pardon (1735) was most noteworthy for its long and chatty definitions. John Wesley, founder of Methodism, prepared in 1753 a small dictionary concerning which, according to the title page, "The Author assures you he thinks this is the best English Dictionary in the world."

These dictionaries and others prepared the way for the greatest of all lexicographical feats—the almost singlehanded compilation of a dictionary that reflected the best earlier practices and rejected the worst.

Dr. Johnson's Dictionary

Samuel Johnson (1709–1784) was well qualified for lexicography. Son of a bookseller and himself an avid reader, he was told by the Master of Pembroke at Oxford that he was "the best qualified for the university that he had ever known come there." Johnson taught for a while (actor David Garrick was one of his pupils), worked for *Gentleman's Magazine,* translated and did other hackwork, wrote prose and poetry, earned a much-needed £300 with his tragedy *Irene,* and wrote the bi-weekly *Rambler* for two years. Later he was to edit Shakespeare and write his *Lives of the English Poets.* From 1747 to 1755 he was at work simultaneously on some of these tasks and on his dictionary, for which he had unsuccessfully sought financial backing from Lord Chesterfield. Part of the time he had up to six ill-paid assistants, but most of the writing came from his own pen. The completed *Dictionary of the English Language* appeared in two volumes, nearly 2,300 folio pages, more than twice the bulk of Nathaniel Bailey's. The 40,000 entries, though fewer than Bailey's 48,000, were in general more accurate and more nearly complete ; thousands of them were illustrated with representative quotations distilled from Johnson's wide reading.

The use of quotations is significant, for it showed that Johnson generally built his definitions on actual citations rather than on just his memory. Today's lexicographers, with their large staffs, follow his practice, collecting literally millions of citations on index cards, using them to determine inductively the meanings and other features.

Johnson's etymologies, though not always correct, were among the best yet prepared, although many of them were based on a 1671 book by Stephen Skinner, *Etymologicon Linguae Anglicanae.* Most of his definitions were clear and complete, with different senses of the same word numbered— another practice still followed today.

All lexicographers borrow from one another, and Johnson was no exception.[4] He interleaved a copy of Bailey, and obviously used Bailey to remind him of words he might otherwise not have thought of. But he eliminated a number of Bailey's words that he considered unimportant,

---

[4] Johnson received from an unknown correspondent a suggestion about the origin of *curmudgeon,* to the effect that it was a mispronunciation of French *cœur méchant* "wicked heart." Johnson said, then, "It is a vitious manner of pronouncing *cœur méchant,* Fr. an unknown correspondent." True to the tradition of borrowing, but sleepily misinterpreting Johnson, a later lexicographer, John Ash, LL.D., in his 1775 dictionary said that *curmudgeon* is "from the French *cœur,* unknown, and *méchant,* a correspondent." (Ernest Weekley, *The Romance of Words,* pp. 157–58.)

rewrote and added to definitions, corrected etymologies, and, as just mentioned, supplied illustrative quotations.

The work did contain errors, misjudgments, and idiosyncrasies. The most famous error was his definition of *pastern* as "the knee of a horse"; it is actually part of the foot. Asked how he happened to make this mistake, Johnson said, "Ignorance, Madam, pure ignorance." Simple things were sometimes defined polysyllabically: "*Cough:* A convulsion of the lungs, vellicated by some sharp serosity." In politics an ardent Tory, he brushed off *Whig* with this definition: "Name of a faction," but then followed the definition with a long paragraph of etymology, concluding like this: "from Scotland the word was brought into England, where it is now one of our unhappy terms of disunion." A *lexicographer* he defined as "A harmless drudge." Frequently he condemned words as "low," saying of *job,* for instance, "A low word now much in use of which I cannot tell the etymology." He quoted disapprovingly Pope's "Increase of years makes men more talkative, but less *writative,*" saying "A word of Pope's coining, not to be imitated." *Swop* was also "low," and *wabble* (our *wobble*) was not only "low" but also "barbarous"; *row* "a disturbance" was "a very low expression," and *chaperon* was "an affected word of very recent introduction." He included some of the slang of his time, but avoided words that he considered indecent; when a woman complimented him for doing so, he twitted her because she obviously had been looking for them.

Although Johnson was not successful in "fixing" the language as he at first had thought possible, he influenced it more than almost anyone else ever has. Most of the spellings we now use are those favored by Johnson; we accent most words where he said they should be accented; we accept most of his definitions, even when, as was infrequently true, they were incorrect in his own time;[5] we still believe that some words are "low," although our choices are not always the same as Johnson's. Lord Chesterfield, even though he had not helped Johnson financially, suggested that Johnson should be made Dictator of the language; Thomas Sheridan thought the dictionary the "corner stone" for fixing the language, and Boswell declared that Johnson "had conferred stability on the language of his country." For a century or more Johnson's book was the arbiter most frequently consulted when questions about language arose. "Johnson says"

---

[5] An example is *internecine,* as Weekley pointed out. The word meant "murderous, destructive," but Johnson defined it as "endeavouring mutual destruction," and that is the meaning it now has in expressions like *internecine war.*

was an expression as frequently used as the "Webster says" of today's American schoolboy who has to write a composition.

There are no scales to tell us whether Johnson's contributions were more helpful or more harmful. Certainly there are values in a degree of linguistic uniformity, and Johnson contributed heavily to that. But there is harm in the belief that individuals can dictate the linguistic usages of others, and harm in the belief that a dictionary should prescribe what is right and wrong rather than just describe objectively how the language is used.

ACCOUNTING FOR SOME OF THE WORDS OF MODERN ENGLISH

Adam's apple. John Craig's dictionary, 1847, said that the *Adam's apple* is "so called from a superstitious notion that a piece of the forbidden fruit stuck in Adam's throat, and occasioned this prominence." Samuel Johnson, in 1755, had merely called it "a prominent part of the throat." (Dissection of cadavers for the learning of anatomy was illegal until rather recent times; hence folklore explanations like the name for this part of the larynx were widely believed.)

attic. The adjective *Attic* comes from the Latin *Atticus* "pertaining to Attica or its capital, Athens"; thus we may speak of "Attic architecture" or "Attic art." In seventeenth-century England some buildings had Attic-style columns placed above larger ones. The name *Attic* was used for this decorative structure and then for the space it surrounded; since this was ordinarily at the top of a building, *attic* became the name of the topmost room even when, as was usually the case, it had no pillars at all. Then, humorously, the term was sometimes used for "head": "He has bats in his *attic*."

begonia, dahlia, magnolia, zinnia. A seventeenth-century Frenchman, Michel Bégon, was a governor of Santo Domingo and was much interested in the bright-colored flowers there. Transported to England in 1777, one of these was given an adaptation of his name, *begonia*. Similarly the *dahlia,* native to Mexico and Central America, was named for a Swedish botanist, Anders Dahl, and reached England in 1789. The *magnolia,* found originally in both the Western Hemisphere and Asia, was named for Pierre Magnol (1638–1715), a French botanist. And the hardy and prolific *zinnia,* from the American Southwest and Mexico, got its name from a German botanist and physician, J.G. Zinn (1727–1759).

bigwig. Wearing of wigs by men was stylish in the eighteenth century, and the more important the man thought himself, the larger his wig was likely to be. So *bigwig* became a humorous or contemptuous term for a person of importance. In twentieth-century American slang, *big shot* replaced it.

bonus. Almost everyone likes to get a bonus, which is Latin for "good," changed to a noun. Rather surprisingly, the earliest *OED* citation is not until 1773, in "all the political bonuses," although *OED* says the word was "Prob. originally Stock Exchange slang." In 1855 Macaulay used it in this sense: "Every proprietor received as a *bonus* a quantity of stock equal to that which he held." The plural noun *goods* "possessions," based on the adjective *good,* was already in use in Chaucer's time. Oddly enough, the language even yet has no single word meaning "good things of any sort"; neither *goods* nor *bonuses* has such a broad meaning. A word like *bads* "bad things of any sort" is also needed.

cologne. *Colonia Agrippina* "the colony of the Emperor Agrippina" was the early name of a German city, later shortened by the French to *Cologne.* In 1709 the inhabitants began manufacturing a perfume called *eau de Cologne* "water of Cologne." As it became widely used, *eau de* and the capital letter were lost, leaving the common noun *cologne.* So etymologically speaking, a user of cologne dabs a Roman colony in appropriate places.

Fahrenheit. An inventor, like a prophet, may be without honor in his own country. The German Gabriel Fahrenheit invented in 1714 the thermometer that bears his name, but Germany uses the centigrade thermometer, which it calls *Celsius,* the name of its Swedish inventor. Fahrenheit also lived in Holland and in England, and within a few decades his thermometric scale was in use in England.

flu. In 1743 the *London Magazine* reported "News from Rome of a contagious Distemper raging there, call'd the *Influenza.*" The Italian word goes back to Latin *influentia* "influence," but came to mean "an epidemic," and specifically the epidemic of *la grippe* which ravaged Europe in 1743. We still have *influenza* but frequently shorten the name to *flu*—a disease whose "influence" can be serious or even fatal.

funny bone. The *humerus* is a long bone extending from shoulder to elbow. When the ulnar nerve at the base of the humerus is struck sharply, a strong tingling sensation occurs. Some unknown comic, punning on *humerus,* called the place of such impact the *funny bone*—or so one explanation goes. A more prosaic one is that the bone "feels funny" when struck.

groggy. British Admiral Edward Vernon wore an expensive cloak of *grogram,* which caused his sailors to refer to him as "Grog" or "Old Grog." In 1740 he issued an order that sailors' rum should be diluted with water, and in his dishonor the seamen called the mixture *grog.* The *Gentleman's Magazine* in 1770 listed eighty words meaning "having drunk too much"; one of these was *groggy.* By the nineteenth century the adjective meant "unsteady, shaky," even when the unsteadiness did not result from grog or other drink.

humor. In the fourteenth century *humour,* from Latin *humorem* "fluid," meant "moisture" or "fluid," and also any of the four chief fluids of the body (blood, phlegm, choler, and melancholy), which were supposed to rule one's temperament. References to disposition appear in Ben Jonson's title *Every Man in His Humour* and in Shakespeare's "Thus Ile curbe her mad and headstrong humor" (*Taming of the Shrew,* IV, i, 212). During this same time it could also mean a temporary state of mind or feeling, as it still does in expressions like "in bad humor." Not until late in the seventeenth century did it refer to amusement, jocularity, facetiousness, as in "Humour in its perfection is allowed to be much preferable to wit" (1728); this definition narrows the meaning of the word to a particular sort of disposition.

landlubber. Most of the Germanic languages have words like *lob* or *lubb* to refer to a person or thing that is heavy, clumsy, or flabby. The English William Langland in the fourteenth century referred to fat, lazy men as "grete *loburs.*" A couple of centuries later the word *lubber* meant an inferior servant or drudge, or a clumsy seaman. By the eighteenth century *land lubber* was used contemptuously by seamen to refer to landsmen or to sailors who did not seem to belong at sea.

lark, skylark. The name of this bird was *laferce* or *laewerce* in OE, but the application to fun or frolic, "We'll have a lark," came only in the eighteenth and nineteenth centuries, perhaps because of the fun associated with hunting larks, which were formerly considered gamebirds. The comparable verb *to skylark* was common among sailors at about the same time, perhaps because they imagined that the bird was as carefree as they liked to be.

lothario. A fashionable, unscrupulous seducer of women, *Lothario* was the leading male character in Nicholas Rowe's play *The Fair Penitent* (1703). He served as the model for Samuel Richardson's Lovelace in *Clarissa* (1747). Gradually the name was applied to any love-'em-and-leave-'em man.

magazine.   From Arabic *makhzan* "storehouse," and used in that sense in English in the sixteenth century. However, today's most common meaning goes back to 1731, when the *Gentleman's Magazine* was founded, with this explanation: "This Consideration has induced several Gentlemen to promote a Monthly collection to treasure up, as in a Magazine, the most remarkable Pieces on the Subjects abovemention'd." The magazine was so successful that it inspired countless imitators.

malapropism.   Mrs. Malaprop, a character in Richard Brinsley Sheridan's *The Rivals* (1775), often confused words, referring for instance to "contagious [contiguous] countries" and to "a progeny [prodigy] of learning." Sheridan took her name from French *mal à propos* "inopportune" or "inappropriate." Since students sometimes misuse words as Mrs. Malaprop did, the word *malapropism* has become a standard one in English teachers' vocabularies.

maroon.   Dampier's *Voyages* (1699) says, "I began to find that I was (as we call it, I suppose from the Spaniards) *Morooned, or Lost,* and quite out of the Hearing of my Comrades Guns." *Brice's Weekly Journal* (1726) says, "He farther says, that Lowe and Spriggs were both maroon'd, and were got among the Musketoo Indians." The use of marooning as a punishment by eighteenth century buccaneers made the term generally familiar. This *maroon,* a verb, is believed to be a corruption of Spanish *cimarron* "wild." The adjective *maroon,* however, comes from French *couleur marron* "brownish-crimson color."

minuet, minute, menu.   One of the most fashionable dances of the late seventeenth century and all of the eighteenth was the *minuet,* slow and stately and requiring short steps. The word is French *menuet* "small, delicate," from Latin *minuta* "small," which is also the source of our *minute* (n. and adj.) and, interestingly enough, *menu.*

nickel.   In German a mischievous demon was called a *Nickel,* from *Nicholas.* Miners had named a copper-colored ore *Kupfernickel* "copper demon" because it often fooled them by its resemblance to copper. But, says the *Gentleman's Magazine* for 1755, Swedish mineralogist Alex F. von Cronstedt found that Kupfernickel was actually a noncuprous metal, which he decided to name *nickel.* The American coin was originally worth only one cent, and was called *nickel* or *nickle* because the bill authorizing its issuance, in 1857, said that it should contain twelve per cent of that metal. A quarter of a century later the coin became worth five cents, and consisted of three parts copper and one part nickel, which lent hardness. Some twentieth-century nickels have contained much less of the metal. (The word *cobalt* comes from a different name for a demon.)

nostrum. Quack doctors have long sold their own homemade concoctions of herbs and other ingredients. *Nostrum* is from Latin *noster* "our," and signifies "our own remedy." A medical book of 1602 refers to "Setting for sale their witlesse nostrums," but the quack doctors and their worthless medicines were especially numerous in London's Great Plague of 1665–66, described so vividly by Daniel Defoe.

palaver, parable. Portuguese traders used to bargain with Africans, and used *palavra* "word, speech, talk" for their discussion. *Palavra* is related to French *parole* "word" and Latin *parabola* "parable, story, word." Eighteenth-century sailors borrowed the word; e.g., Goldsmith reports a sailor as saying, "I'll try to make *palaver* with them though." Later, landlubbers borrowed the term, and its meaning gradually changed to "talk intended to cajole or flatter" or, contemptuously, "idle talk." *Palaver* and *parable* are cousins, but their only similarity is that both refer to speaking.

paraphernalia. In ancient Roman law, *parapherna* was the name applied to all property owned personally by a married woman, and in English common law as early as the fifteenth century *paraphernalia* meant specifically her personal belongings such as clothing and jewelry. But in the eighteenth century the word broadened to include small belongings of any sort, regardless of the owner's sex. Thus Fielding said (1736) that thunder and lightning "are indeed properly the *paraphernalia* of a ghost" on the stage, and a 1791 writer referred to "equestrian paraphernalia."

praline. The cook of French Marshal Duplessis Praslin (1598–1675) delighted his employer with a candy made by browning almonds or other nuts in boiling sugar; unfortunately the employer rather than the cook is remembered in the name, which at various times has been spelled *praslin, praleen, prawleen,* and *prawling.* The ingredients have varied. Today the word is considered mainly an Americanism; the New Orleans pralines, round patties of brown sugar and pecans, are especially famous.

roué. A *roué* is a dissolute person. The French Duke of Orleans (for whom New Orleans is named) joyed in the companionship of profligate rogues, many of whose actions made them deserve to be "broken on the wheel," i.e., tortured. *Roué* is the past participle of *rouer,* "to break on the wheel," and the Duke laughingly called his fellow revelers by that name in about 1720. The word entered English some decades later.

rubber.   The versatile Joseph Priestley got hold of a piece of *caoutchouc* (a South American word) about 1780, found that it would rub out pencil marks, and hence named it *rubber*. It took several more decades, though, before Europeans used the substance for boots, shoes, bottles, and water-proof cloth, as people living near the Amazon had done for centuries. Even when the substance became so widely used, Priestley's limited name for it remained.

run amuck.   In 1672 Andrew Marvell wrote, "Like a raging Indian . . . he runs *a mucke* (as they call it there) stabbing every man he meets." A century later Cook's *Voyages* explained, "Jealousy of the women is the usual reason of these poor creatures running *amock* (or *amuck*)." *Amuck* is adapted from Malaysian *amoq* "engaging furiously in battle, rushing in a state of frenzy to the commission of indiscriminate murder." An older noun, borrowed from the Portuguese *amouco* or *amuco,* referred to a frenzied Malay.

sandwich.   The Earl of Sandwich (1718–1792) was a passionate gam-bler. According to unauthenticated stories, he ordered that slices of bread with roast beef between them be brought to him so that he need not leave the gambling table; hence our *sandwich*. The Hawaiian Islands were for-merly called the Sandwich Islands, after him. His ineptitude as First Lord of the Admiralty contributed to the British defeat in the American Revolu-tion. No wonder that sandwiches are the favorite food of many Americans!

silhouette.   Louis XV of France had a treasurer, Étienne de Silhouette (1709–1767), who used cheap outline drawings rather than expensive oil paintings to decorate the chateau the king had given him. His stinginess is immortalized in the name now given such drawings.

simon-pure.   In 1717 Susanna Centlivre wrote a play called *A Bold Stroke for a Wife*. A virtuous character in it was a Pennsylvania Quaker named *Simon Pure,* but an impostor who used Simon Pure's name made things difficult for him. Since that time, something is simon-pure if it is authentic, not faked. The capital letters were lost in the nineteenth century.

tunnel.   In late ME we find "*Tonel,* to take byrdys," a net with a wide opening that gradually narrowed until the birds were entrapped. Later the *tonell* or *tunnell* was the shaft of a chimney or any kind of pipe or tube. When an underground passage cut by a small stream was observed, it was called a *tunnel*. Some such natural passages were later enlarged to allow boats to pass through. In 1790 we find, "We went through what they call a Tunnel—a passage through the Earth for the convenience of carrying

Coals by Water: it is two miles and a half long, fifteen feet wide, the same high." Later, with the coming of railroads, tunnels were blasted and bored through mountains.

yarn. Referring to spun fiber, *yarn* (*gearn*) goes back to OE. In the eighteenth century, however, *yarn* came also to refer to a long, improbable story, and the verb *to yarn* developed from the noun. What's the connection between spun fiber and a story? Well, sailors not otherwise occupied often had to make rope from *yarns* "threads." To amuse themselves during the boring task they would often tell true or imaginary stories, and the term *yarn* was transferred from the task to the pastime. A slang dictionary of 1812 has this definition: *"Yarning or spinning a yarn,* signifying to relate their various adventures, exploits, and escapes to each other."

CLASSROOM ACTIVITIES

The Poetry of John Gay

When your students are reading eighteenth-century literature, they can learn much of London life, and painlessly about the language of the time, by reading in John Gay's *Trivia: Or, The Art of Walking the Streets of London* (1716). Here, for instance, is a warning about beggars and torchbearers who are actually criminals:

> Where Lincoln's Inn, wide space, is rail'd around,
> Cross not with vent'rous step; there oft is found
> The lurking thief, who while the daylight shone,
> Made the walls echo with the begging tone:
> That crutch which late compassion mov'd, shall wound
> Thy bleeding head, and fell thee to the ground.
> Though thou art tempted by the link-man's call,
> Yet trust him not along the lonely wall;
> In the midway he'll quench the flaming brand,
> And share the booty with the pilf'ring band.
> Still keep the public streets, where oily rays
> Shot from the crystal lamp, o'erspread the ways.

Eighteenth-Century Rhymes

A few minutes spent in looking at rhymes used by Gay, Pope, and their contemporaries can show students one way by which scholars can draw conclusions about pronunciations of the past. In Gay's lines above, for example, note that *wound* "injure" and *ground* are rhyming words.

Parallel Passages

To illustrate changes in the language between 1650 and 1800, show the class the parallel passages on pages 194–195 of this book, asking them to point out all the differences they note, and perhaps classifying them under such headings as spelling, punctuation, sentence structure, inflections, pronoun forms, and changes in vocabulary.

Questions and Negatives

When students are reading Bunyan, Swift, Addison, Defoe, or other prose writers of the period, spend a few minutes examining the forms of questions and of negative statements. The purpose will be to note the extent to which the *do*-transformations are used in these passages. Reading of earlier literature is made a little easier when students become familiar with questions and negatives that do not use the *do* that has become so familiar to us.

Changes in Second-Person Pronouns

As mentioned on page 200, *thou, thee, thy, thine,* and *ye* almost vanished during this period. Reading of a few passages ranging from 1650 to 1800 can illustrate the gradual take-over by *you, your, yours.*

Pros and Cons of an Academy

A student may report on the endeavors of the French and Italian academies to "fix" the language. Students may react to the question "Should the government establish an American Academy that would tell all of us how to spell and pronounce each word, tell us what grammatical principles to follow, and approve or disapprove every new word?"

History of Dictionaries

Students may report on the early history of dictionaries, on Dr. Johnson's dictionary, and on the methods used by modern lexicographers. Useful sources include James Sledd and Wilma R. Ebbitt's *Dictionaries and That Dictionary* (Chicago: Scott, Foresman, 1962) and Richard R. Lodwig and Eugene F. Barrett's *The Dictionary and the Language* (Rochelle Park, N.J.: Hayden Book Company, 1967).

8

The Nineteenth and Twentieth Centuries

CHANGES DURING THE PERIOD

Increase in Use of English

In 1800 there were only about 20 million native speakers of English in the world (the highest estimate is 40 million); by 1973 the total had grown to 350 million.[1] The numbers of speakers of other European languages had increased much less substantially: German from 30 million to 105 million; French from 27 to 80; Spanish from 26 to 220 (largely because of Latin America); Italian from 14 to 65; and Russian (exclusive of Azerbaijani, Tatar, Ukrainian, and Uzbek, which in 1973 totaled 66 million speakers) from 25 to 140.

During this period the British Empire reached its peak strength, justifying the boast that on it the sun never set. Exploration of Africa and the creation of colonies and business enterprises in that continent accompanied further exploration of the Asian subcontinent. British business was considerable also in Turkey, Persia, Siam, Korea, China, and elsewhere. Parts of the Commonwealth, notably Canada and Australia, flourished. But in the twentieth century the tide turned. Her riches and her manpower depleted by two costly world wars and by the unwillingness of the colonials to remain subservient, England step by step lost control of what for a number of decades had been the most extensive empire in history.

---

[1] The figures in this paragraph for the year 1800 are taken from Otto Jespersen's *Growth and Structure of the English Language,* New York: Free Press Paperback Edition, 1968, p. 233. Those for 1973 are taken from *Information Please Almanac* for 1973, p. 368, in a table compiled by Professor Mario Pei.

But as England declined, a former colony, the United States of America, rose. Its population passed 200 million in the 1960's, and although it was not imperialist in the old political sense, its industries invested heavily in scores of countries and thus influenced the economics and sometimes the politics and the very society of all those lands. Wherever Englishmen had gone, their language had gone with them and had often been learned by many of their new neighbors; wherever Americans went, much the same thing happened. So in places as far apart as interior Africa, Chile, and the islands of the Pacific, students by the hundreds or thousands studied English, and other people picked up a word here, a phrase there, a bit of pidgin English somewhere else.[2] The language that all these people encountered was not greatly different from English of 1800 or 1850, yet large and small differences did exist.

An Example of the English of 1800

When the second edition of the *Lyrical Ballads* by William Wordsworth and Samuel T. Coleridge was published in 1800, Wordsworth wrote for it a preface that has become a famous literary document. A modern reader encounters no serious problems in reading it, and if his reading is only casual, he might not guess that it is almost two centuries old. But if he reads with more attention to the language, he notes a number of ways in which Wordsworth's prose differs from most prose written today.

Wordsworth was a much less stuffy writer than many of his contemporaries and predecessors, yet the word *ponderous* does come to mind as one reads. The weight does not come from a highly Latinized vocabulary, for Wordsworth preferred "a selection of language really used by men." Rather, it comes from sentence length, which sometimes exceeds a hundred words and averages out above fifty—some two and a half times that to which twentieth-century prose has accustomed us.

The punctuation, too, is heavier than is now customary. The following sentence will serve to illustrate.

It was published, as an experiment, which, I hoped, might be of some use to ascertain, how far, by fitting to metrical arrangement a selection of the real

---

[2] The word *pidgin* is said to represent a Chinese attempt to pronounce *business*. A *pidgin* language is one used for communication between persons who have no other language in common and who settle upon a mixed language with simple grammar and vocabulary. One variety of pidgin may differ substantially from another—for instance, in syntax and in the number of words used. R.A. Hall's essay in the *Encyclopaedia Britannica* is a convenient brief introduction, which may be supplemented by Professor Hall's books on the subject.

language of men in a state of vivid sensation, that sort of pleasure and that quantity of pleasure may be imparted, which a Poet may rationally endeavour to impart.

The eighteenth and nineteenth were centuries addicted to much reading aloud, and authors frequently inserted commas merely to suggest that an oral reader should pause briefly; this may account for many of Wordsworth's commas. Today, unfortunately, oral reading is largely a lost art, so that commas are justifiably less frequent. Wordsworth's use of the colon also sometimes differs from ours, as in this sentence: "Aristotle, I have been told, has said, that Poetry is the most philosophic of all writing: it is so: its object is truth. . . ."

Wordsworth has not overcome the predilection for capitalizing nouns; although he is not always consistent, we find scattered instances of *Poems, Poets, Friends, Men, Authors, Historians, Sisters, Chemists, Tragedies,* and other nouns dignified by capitals.

Frequent use of the subjunctive is another indication of the time when Wordsworth wrote: "If this opinion *be* erroneous . . . ," "If it *be* affirmed . . . ," "though this *be* true," and some twenty similar expressions, as well as instances of inversion that are now comparatively rare: "*were* I convinced," "*had* I not a deep impression," "*were* there not added to this impression a belief. . . ."

Some of Wordsworth's words are now obsolescent or obsolete: *sensible* with the meaning "aware," *betwixt, thereto, whence, holden* "held," *nay, hath,* and *numbers* with the meaning "meter" (as Pope also used it: "I lisp'd in *numbers,* for the *numbers* came").

Wordsworth's use of *shall* and *will* is almost as unpredictable as that of generations of schoolboys: ". . . for this reason a few words *shall* be added," "I *will* not take upon me to determine . . . ," "we *shall* describe objects," and "A sense of false modesty *shall* not prevent me. . . ." *Should* and *would* are treated with no greater consistency.

Despite Wordsworth's preference for "real language," the eighteenth century's attitude toward "correctness" influences him. At one point he pauses to criticize Thomas Gray for the "defect" of using the adjective *fruitless* where the adverb *fruitlessly* would be standard. And he admits that in his own poetry, when he quotes from "humble and rustic" people, he has felt that their language had to be "purified indeed from what appear to be its real defects, from all lasting and rational causes of dislike or disgust." It is uncertain whether he is here referring to usage or to obscenity and profanity; perhaps both.

With the exception of sentence length, which has obvious implications for syntax, these differences between prose of 1800 and that of today are relatively small. But added together, they do provide evidence that though the rate of change in English grammar has slowed, the language does continue to move. We shall now look at some additional developments.

Other Changes in Usage and Grammar

In verbs, progressive tense forms like *was running, has been running,* and *may have been running* increased in frequency of use. Sometimes the progressive was in a passive form, such as *was being built,* a construction that for a few decades late in the nineteenth century aroused the ire of purists. Said George P. Marsh, a nineteenth-century philologist: "The phrase 'the house *is being built*' for 'the house *is building*' is an awkward neologism, which neither convenience, intelligibility, nor syntactical congruity demands, and the use of which ought therefore to be discountenanced, as an attempt at the artificial improvement of the language in a point which needed no amendment." Mr. Marsh does not say how he would distinguish "The girl was calling" from "The girl was being called" if he succeeded in outlawing the second form. Good sense prevailed, and today "The house was building" seems a very odd, inconvenient, or even unintelligible construction. Passives in general became more widely used than in previous centuries, and a rather new passive with *get* developed. As Baugh has pointed out, a passive like *he got hurt* serves a need, since *he was hurt* seems "too static" and *he became hurt* "too formal."

You were had largely disestablished *you was* by about 1820. *It is I* became "proper" at about the same time, but slipped in standing when Winston Churchill and other notables of the twentieth century normally used *"It's me"* and *"It's us." He don't,* still more frequent in popular speech than *he doesn't,* has been angrily frowned upon by purists for two hundred years; it actually represents one more attempt to get rid of an inflection.

Perhaps the largest growth has come in two-word or "merged" verbs, like *catch on* "understand," *care for* "like," and *keep on* "continue" or "continue wearing." Some of these are intransitive, as in "Teddy winked at me, but I didn't *catch on*" or "The plan *fell through.*" Others are transitive, like "He *made up for* his negligence" or "He *ran through* his money in a week." Most numerous are the transitive merged verbs that can take a direct object in either of two places: She *paid* him *off*" or "She *paid off* her helper." At least a thousand merged verbs are now in frequent use, and the total number in existence is much larger than that; some of them, like *take on* or *make out,* have several clearly distinguishable meanings.

The *there*-transformation, as in "There is a car coming into our driveway," which was a rather newly available option for Shakespeare, has become quite frequent. A different dummy subject appears in sentences like "It is true that she is religious"; this construction may also be gaining ground.

Simeon Potter in *Changing English* (1969) points out a number of changes that he believes to be at work in England in our own time; the following paragraphs, which apply to American as well as British English, are indebted to his comments.

Nouns appear to be gaining ascendancy over verbs; *Substantivseuche* "noun disease," the Germans call it. Potter illustrates with the modern preference for "London's growth is rapid" over "London is growing rapidly." American newspaper headlines—some of them almost unreadable—further illustrate the tendency. One of these, TEACHER PREPARATION LOAD DECREASE DEMAND, turns out to mean that teachers are demanding a decrease in the number of class preparations. Potter traces (pages 112–13) how a similar string can evolve "railway station waiting room murder inquiry verdict challenge"—a challenge made concerning the verdict of an inquiry into a murder that occurred in the waiting room of a railway station. Note that to understand such strings it is necessary to work backward—a burdensome process that suggests that this particular kind of development may not represent a desirable sort of change. Names of organizations often (and perhaps justifiably) consist of a series of nouns; a simple example is *Ohio State University Research Foundation.* Educational documents suffer from *Substantivseuche;* certainly not the worst example is the title "Inducing Conservation of Number, Weight, Volume, Area, and Mass in Disadvantaged Pre-School Children: A Mathematics Readiness Program."

Possessives of inanimates, such as "the house's roof," once condemned, are appearing more and more frequently in reputable publications.

In his discussion of verbs, Potter notes the increasing use of the progressive present to indicate future time, as in "We are moving shortly into a larger house." He comments also on the steady rise of *going to* and other signs of future tense; one may say that someone *is resigning, is to resign, is on the point of resigning, is about to resign,* and *is going to resign.* These forms are not new but are becoming increasingly popular, perhaps partly because people have worried so much about which is "correct"—*shall* or *will.* Potter is a bit unhappy about the ubiquitous *used to* to denote customary action, as in "Did you use to play rugby at school?" but apparently accepts it, although he chooses to remain openminded about whether *didn't use to* is "substandard." *Didn't ought* and *hadn't ought* distress him, as do "other strange [American] collocations" such as *might could* and *used to could*.

The gerund, says Potter, frequently appears now where the infinitive was formerly used, as in "When do you propose making (to make) a start?" Prepositions occasionally drop out, as in "All the arrangements have been agreed" (from *The Times*); a loss may be *compensated,* a wrong *protested,* and some nurses cannot *cope* (the words "with their problems" being omitted). Contractions (or "reduced forms" as Potter calls them) are gaining frequency both in writing and in formal speech. Articles are sometimes omitted; e.g., although *at college* has long been standard, *at university* is finally joining it. In adjectives, Potter believes, *more* and *most* are often replacing *-er* and *est: more common* and *more true* rather than *commoner* and *truer;* but *-est* is now sometimes added to participles: "the *swingingest* place." *Whom* survives mainly as an object of a preposition: e.g., *from whom*. What Potter calls "positive tags as afterthoughts" are increasing: "We all agree on this, or do we?"

Functional shifts are no novelties, but may be increasing. Potter points out that *audition, pinpoint, radio,* and *service,* normally nouns, are often used as verbs, and that conversely *mix, transplant, transform,* and other "verbs" may also appear in *a good mix, a heart transplant,* and *a transform* (as linguists use the term). The flurry of compounds with *-in* (*teach-in, sit-in, pray-in,* etc.) also attracts Potter's attention.

In all, Mr. Potter devotes about seventy-five pages to the changes summarized here. These pages should be read by anyone wishing more detailed information about the changes large or small that now seem to be afoot.

Vocabulary Increases

It is certainly not necessary to labor the point that English vocabulary has grown at an astonishing rate during the nineteenth and twentieth centuries. One difference from earlier periods, though, has been that most of the newer words have been scientific or technical and with some exceptions have not become known to many people. For example, although *penicillin* is widely familiar, other dictionary entries in the family, such as *penicilliosis* and *penicilloic acid* are not; still other spinoffs from the basic word *penicillin* are not found in unabridged dictionaries but are known only to specialists.

The automobile, the airplane, motion pictures, radio, and television have contributed many words to the popular vocabulary. In the 1920's, for example, *garage* was just becoming widely current. (It does not appear in the 1928 *OED*, but is included in the 1933 supplement.) At least three pronunciations of the word were common before it settled down to the one now generally followed. Words like *biplane, airport, hangar, jetprop,* and *jet age* mark the continued advance of aviation. Magazines like *Popular Photography* regularly employ terms that would have been completely unknown to our not-distant ancestors. Every invention with high social impact begets its own word-children.

Wars likewise beget words, alter words, or give wider currency to existing words. World War I made people familiar with *tanks, antiaircraft fire* (later shortened to *ack-ack*), *blimps, gas masks, periscopes,* and *doughboys* (who were *G.I.*'s in the next war). World War II found people talking about *Nazis* and the *Axis* (political coinages of the 1930's), and about *blackouts, dive-bombings, jeeps, beachheads, radar, commando raids;* unpatriotic citizens at home patronized the *black market* and *hoarded* sugar or gasoline, and everybody knew about *backlogs* of orders and about *bottlenecks* in production and about *ration books.* Denver Ewing Baughan has written this contrast between the language of the "Yank" in World War I and of "GI Joe" in World War II:

. . . the well-read Yank would find out what the newspapers had meant by trenches, dugouts, machine-gun nests, projectiles, whizz-bangs, gas, drives, and salients, just as the well-read GI Joe found out what they had meant by foxholes, pillboxes, booby traps, ack-ack guns, flame throwers, pushes, wedges, bulges, perimeters, infiltrations, pockets, beachheads, island hopping, withering on the vine, softening-up campaigns, and power-diving. If the Yank was unfortunate and had to be hauled off in an ambulance to do bunk fatigue in an evacuation hospital, he heard a lot of talk about shrapnel wounds, débridement, Carrel-Dakin solution, A. T. S. (antitetanic serum), trench fever, gas gangrene, and shell shock, just as the GI Joe who, under similar circumstances, had to be hauled off in a meat wagon to do horizontal parade rest heard a lot of talk about flak wounds, nerve shock, C. E. (combat exhaustion), jungle rot, jungle fever, malaria, Atabrine, blood plasma, sulfonamides, and penicillin.[3]

The Korean and Vietnam wars, though military personnel coined many words for use in local situations, resulted in fewer words becoming common to the States; *napalm* and *defoliants* are two of the unpleasant ones, and government officials and the press referred often to *Vietnamization.*

The theory can be supported that the faster the rate of social change, the more rapidly the vocabulary expands. Certainly that theory can be

---

[3] "Verbal Patterns in Two World Wars." *Word Study,* May, 1948, pp. 4–5.

exemplified by the nineteenth and twentieth centuries, which saw still largely rural peoples move at a fast pace toward urban sprawl; which saw more inventions in a single year than often in the past had been made in a century; which saw scientists and other scholars adding to human knowledge at a rate so fast that it doubled every decade; and which saw social, economic, political, and religious changes in institutions that were once considered almost immutable. Words by the thousands were needed to name and describe the changes, and words by the thousands consequently appeared.

A More Liberal Attitude

In language as in society, liberal and conservative elements constantly pull in opposing directions. In general, in the eighteenth century, conservative elements were in linguistic control. As one result, experimentation with language in poetry was rare; a thousand poetasters in the *Gentleman's Magazine* and other periodicals of the time sounded much alike, with verses written in couplets imitative of Pope's and filled with cliches like "the finny tribe" (which are fish), "balmy Sleep," and "Night, sable goddess." That which was exotic was largely disregarded by writers, and rugged mountains and stormy seas did not attract poets who preferred formal, planned landscapes, sylvan glades, and quiet pools.

But a few years later Thomas Moore wrote *Lalla Rookh,* the poetic narrative of a princess from India in an adventurous search for her betrothed; Byron used the high Alps as a setting for his *Manfred;* and the way was being prepared for Herman Melville's stories that took place on tempestuous oceans. Along with the literary interest in the exotic and the rugged came the need for unstereotyped language. The finny tribes disappeared. Words were borrowed or adapted from generally unfamiliar languages; obsolete English words were revived; the Scottish dialect poems of Robert Burns were acclaimed, although just a few decades earlier, right-thinking Englishmen would have considered them barbarous.

Since the Romantic era, the liberal and conservative forces have tugged back and forth. In literature, Pope's imitators have continued to have their own imitators, and so have the imitators of Wordsworth, Byron, and Shelley, but the true literary artists have insisted on speaking in their own voices for their own times. Browning, for instance, was a linguistic innovator, especially in syntax; so was Gerard Manley Hopkins; and across the water Emily Dickinson made her own linguistic rules.

The public attitudes toward language have been similarly ambivalent. Schools in the nineteenth and twentieth centuries have generally supported conservative positions, opposing language change, describing and prescribing "correct" language, and condemning "wrong" usages even when large numbers of educated persons followed them. "Like I said before," at least one teacher told her class, "never use *like* as a conjunction." Catering to all tastes, American publishers could bring out and sell—during the same short span of years—a book entitled *Watch Your Language* and another called *Leave Your Language Alone,* as well as guides to usage that, contradicting one another, supported any position from the most conservative to the most liberal.

A glance at reflexive or intensive pronouns like *himself* or *themselves* can be an instructive example. Most such pronouns are formed with a possessive plus *self* or *selves: myself, ourselves, yourself, yourselves.* But *himself* and *themselves* use the objective forms *him* and *them.* If the language were consistent, we would say *hisself* and *theirselves,* and both these words do exist in literature of the Middle Ages and the Renaissance alongside *himself* and *themselves.* The latter forms, though, have gained ascendancy, so that today *hisself* and *theirselves* are considered among the grossest of illiteracies. Also often condemned, though not so vigorously, is the use of a reflexive pronoun as subject or object: "My brother and myself went," "Dad sent my brother and myself." Shakespeare used such constructions, and so have other literary figures, but modern writers on usage are of mixed opinions about them. Bergen and Cornelia Evans say that "They invited my sister and myself" is "normal spoken English today" and that either that sentence or "They invited myself and my sister." is "literary English," though the latter has "an old-fashioned tone." But Margaret Nicholson says without qualification: "WRONG: *one of the party + myself.*" Margaret Bryant mentions that Franklin, Emerson, Hawthorne, E. B. White, and Eva LeGallienne used similar expressions in their writings. Roy H. Copperud, summarizing what "authorities" recommend, says "There is no consensus here but rather a 4–3 split" against the construction. Faced with such a division, a teacher is hardly justified in penalizing a student who writes "my brother and myself," but may well use the expression as an example of the fact that divided usages do exist and that some people don't happen to like *self*-words as subjects and objects. The teacher may also suggest that the user of the *self*-word in these ways often employs it because he simply is not sure whether *I* or *me, he* or *him,* etc., would be standard in the sentence he is composing.[4]

---

[4] The usage volumes referred to in this paragraph are Evans, *A Dictionary of*

In general, though, trends since the eighteenth century have been toward greater acceptance of deviation from a mythical norm. Linguistic strait-laces or strait-jackets have stretched, and some persons—professional writers and others—have refused to be laced or jacketed at all.

Dialects

In Great Britain, dialects have existed at least since the Angles, Saxons, and Jutes settled there. Today the dialectal differences seem considerably greater than they are in the United States. Northern, East Midland, Central Midland, West Midland, and Southern dialects are the broad classifications of dialect for England, but each of these can be subdivided shire by shire, and often further subdivided two or three times within the shire. Scotland has its own varieties, some of which do not differ greatly from the folk language that Robert Burns used, even though such dialectal forms are regarded with disdain by many educated Scotsmen, who themselves aim at their own versions of British Received Standard. Irish English reveals some Celtic influences and has some distinctive pronunciations sometimes represented in literature by such spellings as *moin* for *mine* and *thrue* for *true*.

Americanisms have had their effect on British English. Writing in *The Spectator,* February 5, 1943, British D. W. Brogan said,

"Even our newspapers, hitherto regarded as models of correct literary style, are many of them following in [Americans'] wake; and, both in matter and phraseology, are lending countenance to what at first sight appears a monstrously crude and imbecile jargon; while others, fearful of a direct plunge, modestly introduce the uncouth bantlings with a saving clause." So wrote John Farmer in 1899. So, with very slight modifications, could our contemporary viewers-with-alarm write today. In vain they belittle the merits of the importations from America ("belittle" is one of them). In vain they forbid Americanisms to darken our doors (and "darken our doors" is another). However talented as controversialists the defenders of the old tongue may be, they will find facts too much for them, such facts for example as the American origin of "talented."

H. L. Mencken mentions *reliable, lengthy, prairie, caucus,* and *bluff* as old Americanisms fully accepted in England, adds that newer importations like *highbrow, crook* "criminal," and *to feature* are widely used, and re-

---

Contemporary American English, p. 310; Nicholson, *American English Usage,* p. 356; Bryant, *Current American Usage,* p. 142; and Copperud, *American Usage: The Consensus,* p. 185.

marks that *hot-dogs* no longer need definition as "broiled sausages in split rolls," as the *London Observer* considered necessary in 1932. (Mencken lists scores of other examples).

Outside the Isles themselves, other varieties of English flourish. Australian English, like that in America, had to adapt to new things that settlers found in the land, and consequently borrowed or invented, for example, *billabong, swagman,* and other words familiarized to Americans by the song "Waltzing Matilda," as well as many more. Australian pronunciations often differ considerably from those generally heard in either America or in England (except among Cockneys): particularly noticeable is that the [e:] sound, as in *state,* is an [aI], so that *state* and *fate* rhyme with American *light.* Canadian English has been strongly influenced by that of the United States, although most Canadians seem to prefer British spellings like *honour,* and often insert an [ə] or [ʌ] sound before the diphthong in words like *out* and *about.* According to Canadian humorist Stephen Leacock, Canadians "use English for literature, Scotch for sermons, and American for conversation." South African English has been affected by Dutch settlers there, and to a smaller extent by Portuguese and by native languages. So *baas* "boss," *morgen* "about two acres," *veldt,* "open country," and other words not often heard elsewhere are in the vocabulary; a *camp* is a fenced field, and a *bioscope* is a motion picture theater.

The study of dialectal variations has become respectable in the twentieth century, because of scholarly work in England, on the continent, and in North America. No longer content merely to produce lists of lexical variants, modern linguistic geographers prepare detailed maps based on large numbers of interviews and showing variant pronunciations and morphological and syntactic variants as well as differences in word choice. Along with such study has come a new attitude toward dialects, which are now not considered quaint or inferior but instead are regarded as legitimate branches of language, all of which need to be considered if a description of the language is to be complete and accurate. Unfortunately, this attitude has not yet become universally accepted by the public, many of whom still tend to ridicule dialects different from their own—thus supposedly showing their superiority but actually revealing their provinciality. A twentieth-century British author, Simon Harvester, betrays his ignorance of dialectology when he writes in *Epitaph for Yankees,* "If Miss Whitcomb were an American, she would surely have an accent which would betray her. He shook his head. Many Americans have no accent at all, particularly New Englanders."

Through teaching units on dialects to show that speech variations are natural, are universal, and are interesting examples of language at work, the schools can combat such ignorance, narrowness, and prejudice.

Dictionaries

During the last part of the eighteenth century and much of the nineteenth, Samuel Johnson's dictionary, which underwent several revisions, was preeminent in England. Others were published, of which the best-known British books were Charles A. Richardson's *New Dictionary of the English Language* (1836–37) and J. Ogilvie's *Imperial Dictionary* (first edition 1850), which was the ancestor of a very good American dictionary, the *Century,* edited by Yale's William Dwight Whitney and published in 1891. (Noah Webster's dictionaries will be discussed in the next chapter.) The greatest of all dictionaries was still to come.

This was *A New English Dictionary on Historical Principles,* now usually called *The Oxford English Dictionary (OED,* often cited in this book). In 1842 a Philological Society was formed in England, dedicated to the study of language. Members first decided in the 1840's and 1850's to work toward the compilation of a list of "unregistered words," but a little later saw the need for a dictionary that would avoid weaknesses pointed out in 1857 by Dean Richard C. Trench: incomplete listings of obsolete words, omission of some words from their "families," lack of very early citations of use, omission of some important definitions, failure to distinguish adequately between synonyms, and inclusion of some materials not suited to dictionaries. The work, under a series of editors, required seventy years to complete, finally being published in full in 1928, with 15,487 pages (exclusive of a later supplement)—about 50 million words, and over 414,000 definitions enriched and illustrated by nearly two million quotations. Supported financially by the Oxford University Press, the dictionary during its development enlisted the aid of scores of contributor-readers in Great Britain and the United States. It represents by far the greatest scholarly linguistic achievement of any nation.

From 1889 to 1905, under the editorship of an Oxford professor, Joseph Wright, *The English Dialect Dictionary* was prepared as an attempt to include "all dialect words still in use, or known to have been in use during the last two hundred years." Such a dictionary serves not only as a linguistic repository but also as a reminder of folk customs and superstitions that may no longer exist. It is a valuable supplement to the *OED,* which did not attempt a thorough coverage of dialectal variations. Another excellent book is *The Oxford Dictionary of English Etymology* (1966).

Semantics

The word *semantics* goes back to Greek *semantikos* "significant" but was borrowed by English from French *la sémantique* of the late nineteenth century. Semantics deals with the "significance" of words in a broad sense. Whereas earlier writers, especially lexicographers, had been largely concerned with finding precise denotations of words, semanticists have been more interested in connotations—what words suggest beyond their dictionary definitions. Such connotations affect people emotionally, so semanticists became interested in these effects. They also realized that meanings vary with circumstances such as time and place. Thus *democracy* in the United States did not have quite the same meanings in say 1800 and 1900 and 1970, and in other nations it may never have had any of the precise denotations and connotations it has had in America.

The word *semantics* itself has different but overlapping meanings for the logician, the linguist, and the "general semanticist." It is the work of the general semanticist that has most importance for teachers. Based primarily on the thinking of Alfred Korzybski, a Polish scholar and engineer who made his home in the United States from 1917 to 1950, general semantics discusses, among other things, variant connotations, the differences between reality and the verbal symbols we use to represent reality, the need to avoid *either–or* distinctions (since other alternatives generally exist), and the unwisdom of reacting unthinkingly to verbal stimuli. Among the outgrowths of general semantics have been the establishment of an Institute of General Semantics, an International Society of General Semantics, and the publication of the magazine *Etc.* and of numerous books such as those of economist Stuart Chase, who has shown how social, economic, political, and military decisions tend to be influenced by choice of words. In the schools, units on semantics have been frequently taught, with particular attention to the uses that advertisers make of semantic principles as they attempt to influence prospective purchasers.[5]

The addition of semantics to the earlier kinds of word study may turn out to be as important a linguistic contribution as any other of the nine-

---

[5] For more details about uses of semantics in the classroom, see J.N. Hook, *The Teaching of High School English,* Fourth Edition, New York: The Ronald Press Co., 1973, pages 448–59 and 476–78.

teenth and twentieth centuries. Earlier studies had been devoted to words as things in themselves—things that could be classified, described, exemplified, defined, and etymologized. Semantics added a social dimension, showing how language influences the interactions of people. An especially striking example of such interaction occurred when Nikita Khruschchev ruled Russia. American newspapers reported that he had said to representatives of the United States, "We will bury you!" Some Americans were so angered that they urged immediate military action so that we would not be "buried." It happens, though, that the Russian verb also means "outlive," and "We will outlive you!" is certainly a much less threatening statement. There is no way of knowing which meaning Khruschchev intended, but the way his verb was translated was for several years harmful to American–Russian relations. Semantically responsible journalism would have pointed out the two possible interpretations—as a very few journalists indeed did.

The twentieth century has also become interested in nonverbal communications. For example, *The Silent Language,* written in 1959 by anthropologist Edward T. Hall, gave many examples of intercultural lack of understanding caused by differences in cultural outlooks and traditions. Being late for an appointment, for instance, may be expected and taken for granted in some societies, insulting in others. Conversationalists in some cultures are uncomfortable unless they are almost nose to nose, but in other cultures a distance of less than three feet causes speakers to back away a little. (The study of speakers' distances has a name of its own: *proxemics.*) In the late 1960's and 1970's the study of communication by touching (*haptics*) was popular, and a book by Julius Fast, *Body Language,* reached the best-seller lists, though probably not just for linguistic reasons.

VOCABULARY GROWTH AS A REFLECTION OF SOCIAL CHANGE

In this section we'll look at a specific recent period to note additional examples of ways in which new words or new meanings reflect changes occurring in society. The words discussed here are among those listed in two sources: *Britannica Book of the Year* for 1972, which in a section entitled "Words and Meanings, New" defines about a hundred words which had been invented or had attained prominence in 1971; and *The World Book Year Book* for 1972, which includes a "dictionary Supplement" consisting of some 150 selected words popularized sufficiently since 1963 to warrant inclusion in the 1972 *World Book Dictionary.*

Many of these words refer directly to social processes and concerns of the troubled early 70's. *Activism,* the use of direct methods, including force, to attain social goals, was favored by *activists,* but was usually opposed by the conservative *Silent Majority,* which included many *hardhats,* manual laborers who looked with distrust on anything disruptive. Fear was expressed that society was becoming *polarized.* Some of the activists represented the *counterculture,* usually young people who desired drastic changes in the *Establishment,* e.g., the *military-industrial complex.* Many of these young people were *Aquarians,* who felt that an *Age of Aquarius* was coming, in which previously unknown friendship and freedom would exist.

One of the problems that society was just becoming deeply concerned with was pollution. The term *ecology* tended to be restricted in the popular mind to the fight against *environmental pollution,* which came to include *noise pollution* as well as other varieties. Greatly concerned persons, who worried about possible *ecocide,* were called *environmentalists,* or, by their detractors, *ecofreaks.* These persons deplored the exploitation of man's natural resources, and advocated *imploitation* instead. One new tool of the environmentalists was *lidar,* a detector of atmospheric pollution.

Concern for others and for one's own mental health was reflected in *sensitivity training,* which sometimes took place in *T-groups* (short for *sensitivity-training groups*); *encounter groups* were similar in purpose. The *Women's Lib* movement claimed that women had long been second-class citizens because of the *sexism* practiced by *sexists.* (*Ageism* or *agism* arose as a protest against bad treatment of old people.) Asserting that the differences between sexes are much smaller than is generally believed, some people advocated *desexegration;* wearing of *unisex* clothing was in part occasioned by belief in the complete equality of the sexes. Concern for the welfare of future generations led to interest in *futurology.*

Consumerism was a movement to defend consumers against unscrupulous manufacturers and retailers. *Workfare,* formed by analogy with the much older *welfare,* was a program to provide work for the needy. As use of the metric system became more widespread, *metricate* and *metrication* were used as the verb and noun to signify a transition to that system. In matters of finance, there was much discussion of *negative income tax*; *no-fault insurance* for automobile owners was legally adopted by some states; and to raise money, some states encouraged *OTB* (*off-track betting*). *Headhunters* were people who recruited executives for business. And, some persons reasoned, if there were shortages in some materials or types of personnel, why might there not also be *longages*?

Technologists, as usual, were busy. A *cache* for a computer provided an auxiliary memory; it was related to the *databank*. The noun *peripheral* was used to designate computer equipment such as the keyboard and magnetic tape. *Thyristors* were transistors with characteristics of *thyratrons*. *Integrated circuits* appeared in computers and in television sets. *Microbooks* made it possible to record a thousand pages on a single card. *Cassettes* and *video cartridges* were becoming common. *Reprographic* was a useful adjective to describe any method of visual reproduction.

Glass could be salvaged, smashed, and put into a highway material called *glasphalt,* and automotive experts were experimenting with the *Wankel engine.* The increased popularity of snowmobiles led to the name *skidoo* (originally a trademark, *Ski-Doo*) for some of these; a sport called *snopolo* was played, with these vehicles being used instead of horses; and a *snowmobiler* was also called a *cold rodder.* A tunnel under a channel of water was a *chunnel.*

Still More New Words

Study of the human body led to new discoveries. *Calcitonin,* a hormone regulating calcium levels, *dopamine,* a hormone controlling nerve functions, and *prostaglandin,* any of six hormonelike substances, were discussed in technical journals, as was *methylphenidate,* a mild stimulant. Students of Zen Buddhism became interested in *macrobiotics,* a dietary system. *Lassa fever,* a virulent disease, was found in Lassa, Nigeria. *L-dopa* or *levodopa* was helpful in combatting symptoms of Parkinson's disease. Some doctors began specializing in treatment of adolescents; they were called *juvenicians.* There was discussion of the *body clock,* the body's natural cyclical rhythm that can be disturbed by long-distance flights and the like. To support the body, and perhaps to stimulate it sexually, *water beds* became fairly popular. Some girls wore *hot pants,* although conservative merchants preferred the less controversial older term *short shorts.* Some Aquarians wore *love beads,* which they could finger to relax themselves.

All branches of science continued to expand. Remains of a small Triassic reptile were found on three continents; this prehistoric creature was named the *Lystrosaurus. Genetic engineering* became the subject of controversy. The *green revolution* brought high-yielding grains to overpopulated countries. *Dioxin,* used in some weed-killers, was found to cause deformities in fetuses. The existence of a *monopole* was hypothesized by physicists, who said it was a particle with only one magnetic pole. *Plates* was the name given to the series of layers of the earth's crust; theories of their movements were known as *plate tectonics*. Chemical elements 104 and 105 were named *rutherfordium* and *hahnium*. *Polywater* has four times the molecular weight of water and fifteen times its viscosity. *Tribology* was the name given to the study of friction, wear, and lubrication. *Geobiology* and *neuropsychiatry* represented certain combinations of sciences. *Spin-off* was a term that rapidly became used in all walks of life, not just in science. Verbal spin-offs from lunar exploration included *lurain* "lunar terrain," *regolith* "moon rocks," and *mascon,* a term referring to certain material beneath the moon's surface believed to mark an increase in gravity; the word is a blend of *mass* and *concentration.*

The arts gave us *musicotechnocrats,* who produced or modified music electronically; *luminists,* who experimented with the uses of lights in various artistic patterns called *luminal art*; *earth artists,* whose *minimal art* used only basic shapes and colors. *Art Déco* (from French *Art Décoratif*) was the name for highly colored geometrical decoration. *Multimedia* presentations in schools combined recordings, motion pictures, poetry, and other art forms.

Slang flourished as always. Interest in and concern about addictive drugs resulted in scores of names for the drugs, as well as other slang terms like *head,* a user of drugs; *pothead,* a user of marijuana; *clean,* not addicted to or not possessing drugs; *tripsit* (analogous to the older *babysit*), to take care of someone who is on an LSD *trip*; and *narc,* a narcotics agent. *Pigs* were policemen; *grunts* were enlisted infantrymen; *Jesus Freaks* were young people, often in communes, who tried to follow Christian principles as they interpreted them; *teeny-boppers* were young girls who followed hippie ways; *creepy-boppers* were addicted to movies about monsters; *soul jockeys* were black disc jockeys who played soul music. *Bread* was money, a *bust* was an arrest, and a *trash* was an act of vandalism; *bust* and *trash* were also used as verbs. Many people stopped "talking"; they *rapped* instead. *"Right on,"* they would say to indicate approval. *Zilch* meant "zero," but could mean "anything worthless." When people parted company, those who went away were said to *split.*

These words are just a few among the thousands that came into the language in 1971 or a little earlier. A scholar of the distant future, armed only with a dictionary of the linguistic innovations of the period, could prepare a monograph that would pretty accurately portray the worries, conflicts, ideals, and scientific and artistic progress of the seventh and eighth decades of the twentieth century.

ACCOUNTING FOR SOME OF THE WORDS OF
MODERN ENGLISH

agnostic. Only occasionally can we name with reasonable confidence the coiner of a word. English biologist Thomas Huxley is given credit for *agnostic,* a word that he used in 1869 to signify "one who does not know whether God exists." He based it on Greek *agnostos* "unknowing" or "unknowable," from *a* "not" or "no" and *gnosis* "knowledge."

airedale, collie. The River *Aire* is in Yorkshire; the *Dale* of *Aire* is its valley. *Airedale* dogs take their name from this valley; reportedly they were specially bred by the poachers of that area. *Collie* dogs, from Scotland, were once predominantly black; the word is perhaps from *coaly* "black.' Robert Burns's "Twa Dogs" (1786) describes the dog thus: "The tither was a ploughman's collie, / His breast was white, his touzie back / Wee clad wi' coat o' glossy black; / His gawcie tail, wi' upward curl, / Hung owre his hurdies wi' a swirl." Like other breeds of domestic animals airedales and collies have changed considerably in appearance.

asteroid. Greek *asteroiedes* meant "like a star." (*Aster,* of course, the ancestor of *astronomy, asterisk, disaster,* and many other English words meant "star.") An eighteenth-century mathematician noted an oddity in the sizes of orbital diameters of the known planets: with one exception each such diameter was about half that of the next, with a progression of 4, 7, 10, 16, 52, and 100. To account for the jump from Mars's 16 to Jupiter's 52, the mathematician, Johann Bode, theorized that an unknown planet lay somewhere between. In 1801, a very small planet was found where he predicted, and later over two thousand more. Astronomer Sir William Herschel, remembering his Greek, called them *asteroids.* They are also called *planetoids* "like planets."

badminton. British military men stationed in India, when time was dragging, invented a game that they called *Poona,* perhaps adapting the game from the much older battledore and shuttlecock. When some army officers from India spent a leave at *Badminton,* the Gloucestershire estate of the Duke of Beaufort, they renamed the sport for that place. Within twenty years badminton was popular enough that the Badminton Association was formed.

bobby. London policemen are nicknamed *bobbies.* The name goes back to Sir *Robert* Peel, British secretary for home affairs after 1828, who fought a crime wave of his day by passing a Police Act and by importing large numbers of sturdy Irishmen as policemen. They were called *Bobby's men* later shortened to *bobbies.*

bowdlerize. Thomas *Bowdler,* a British physician, in 1818 published his edition of Shakespeare's works, in which "those words and expressions are omitted which cannot with propriety be read aloud in a family." The verb *bowdlerize* is still employed to refer to similar expurgating.

boycott. Captain Charles C. *Boycott,* a land agent for the estates of an Irish earl, drew the wrath of tenants whose rents he raised in 1880. They blocked his food and mail, shopkeepers refused to sell him anything, some of his property was destroyed, and he finally had to leave Ireland. The tactics of the tenants—especially that of refusal to conduct business—were emulated elsewhere and are still widely enough employed that *boycott* is familiar as both a verb and a noun.

chartreuse. Near Grenoble, France, since the eleventh century, has stood a famous monastery, La Grande *Chartreuse.* In comparatively recent times some of its monks developed an apple-green brandy that was named for the monastery. Then, late in the nineteenth century, a color similar to that of the brandy was also called *chartreuse.*

chauffeur, chafing dish. Latin *calere* "to be warm" and *facere* "to make" emerged in Old French as *chaufer* "to warm by rubbing," which in ME was *chaufen. Chafe,* which may mean either "to warm by rubbing" or "to irritate by rubbing," is a modern descendant, as is *chafing dish* "dish to keep food warm." In French a *chauffeur* was originally a stoker, someone who feeds the fire, as in a locomotive. With the invention of the steam-powered automobile, once more the person who stoked the fire was a *chauffeur,* and the term remained even when gasoline replaced wood or coal.

chauvinism, jingoism. Most loyal of Napoleon's followers was a soldier named Nicholas *Chauvin,* who even after his general's final defeat was loud and persistent in his praise. French dramatists ridiculed Chauvin and gave him wider publicity. *Chauvinisme* in the sense of "loud, unreasoning patriotism" thus entered French in about 1830, and was transferred to English as *chauvinism* by 1870. It antedates an equivalent English word, *jingoism,* based on *jingo,* the nickname for a supporter of military policies of Lord Beaconsfield (1878); today *jingoism* refers to belligerent patriotism.

cliché. In nineteenth-century printing when a stereotype plate was being made, the matrix was dropped into molten metal. The French coined the verb *clicher,* a variant of *cliquer* "to click," in imitation of the sound this act makes; *clicher* came to mean "to stereotype." The stereotype plate is used for repeated printings of the same item. By extension, an expression often repeated became known as a *cliché*; British author Andrew Lang was responsible for the first recorded use, in 1892.

first-rate. In the seventeenth century, British naval vessels were classified in six *rates* "categories" according to their size and armament. Both officers and seamen normally preferred to be on a *first-rate vessel,* which was usually not only larger but also faster and safer. By the nineteenth century *first-rate* was being employed to describe anything excellent.

hello. A variant of earlier *hallo, hollo, holloa,* or *hollow,* the greeting *hello* did not become generally used until the nineteenth century. Now for answering the telephone it is common in many parts of the world, including many countries in which English is not general. There are, however, interesting substitutes. A Britisher still often says *Are you there?* (which, to an American calling him, seems to have an obvious answer). A Frenchman may say *J'écoute* "I listen," a Spaniard *Dígame* "Speak to me," an Italian *Pronto* "Ready," a Finn *Huomio* "Attention," a Persian *Kujast* "Where is it?," an Irishman *Dia Dhuit* "God be with you," and a German *Hier ist Herr Schmidt* "Here is Mr. Smith."

iodine. Joseph L. Gay-Lussac (1778–1850), French chemist and physicist, experimented with a grayish-black solid resulting from the burning of seaweed. Heated, it gave off a blue-violet vapor. Gay-Lussac therefore named the new element, *iode,* from Greek *iodes* "violet-like." *Ione* was also suggested. Englishman Sir Humphrey Davy, though, in 1814 argued that *ione* could be confusing, and recommended *iodine,* the name that has become standard for Element 53.

mad as a hatter. Nitrate of mercury has long been used in preparing furs for men's hats. After long exposure to this chemical, hatters became shaky and were often afflicted with mental illness. As late as the nineteenth century, insanity was often the subject of jest, so Lewis Carroll's *"Mad Hatter"* was not regarded as a cruel caricature. Fortunately science has since come to the aid of the hatmaking industry so that today hatters are no more mad than other people are.

Melba toast. Dame Nellie *Melba* (1861–1931), a popular Australian soprano, ate little except toast when she was on a diet. On one occasion a chef's assistant at the London Savoy unintentionally gave her extra-dry toast, which she considered delicious. In her honor the chef (taking the credit) named it *Melba toast.* The word *toast* goes back to Latin *torrere* "to dry, parch," and is thus related to *torrid.*

nag. Norwegian and Swedish have a verb *nagga* "to gnaw, bite, nibble; to vex, irritate." The gnawing sound of mice and rats can obviously be irritating. In English *nag* (also spelled *knog, gnag,* and *nagnag*) was apparently first used in Northern dialects, in the early nineteenth century, with both the literal and the figurative Scandinavian meanings.

navy blue.   Until 1857, British sailors could dress about as they pleased, but in that year an act of Parliament required that seamen wear white trousers and blue jackets. The official shade of blue quickly became known as *navy blue* or *navy,* and also became popular with civilians. *Navy,* incidentally, is from Latin *navis* "ship," the source of *navigate* and many other words.

nocturne.   John Field, an Irish pianist–composer of the nineteenth century, composed short meditative pieces of music that he labeled *nocturnes,* going back to Latin *nocturnus* "of the night." A few years later Frederic Chopin made the word much better known with his own nocturnes.

ritzy.   César *Ritz* was a Swiss who built a reputation as a manager of excellent hotels. In the nineteenth century a group of Englishmen decided to build in London the world's best hotel. They secured Ritz as its manager and named the hotel for him. Because of the plushness and expensiveness of the Ritz, *Ritzy* (later *ritzy*) was used as an adjective to describe anything that had those qualities.

robot.   In 1920 Czech playwright Karel Capek in his play *R.U.R.* (*Rossum's Universal Robots*) adapted the Czeck *robotnik* "serf" to refer to a mechanical apparatus that could do the work of a man. Almost at once the word attained international acceptance.

sabotage.   The French *sabot* "wooden shoe" goes back to Arabic *sabbat* "sandal." An unconfirmed story has it that badly treated French peasants used to walk at night over their masters' crops in protest, and that they called this act *sabotage*. Another story is that they would throw their *sabots* into machinery to wreck it. In the twentieth century the word gained wide use because interference with production was advocated by The International Workers of the World, who were nicknamed the "Wobblies."

siren.   The *Sirens* who tried to lure Ulysses and his men were sea nymphs who could sing beautifully. In 1819 a French scientist, Baron Cagnard de la Tour, made a revolving plate to measure musical vibrations. He found that when partly in water it made a beautiful sound. Therefore he called it a *siren*. It was the ancestor of today's fire sirens, police sirens, and other makers of far-from-beautiful sounds.

spoonerism.   The Rev. William A. Spooner (1844–1930) of Oxford occasionally got his tongue twisted, with results like "The usher will sew you to a sheet," or "a well-boiled icycle" instead of "a well-oiled bicycle." His students began calling such slips *Spoonerisms* and started to concoct their own; today the noun, like the failing it names, is common. Actually, of course, Spooner was not the first person to mix his consonants amusingly. Back in 1622 Henry Peacham in *Compleat Gentleman* told of someone who "meaning to say, 'I must goe buy a dagger,' by transposition of the letters said: 'Sir, I must goe dye a begger.'"

sweater. Although *sweater* in the sense of "one who sweats" dates back to the sixteenth century, the garment of that name was a nineteenth-century invention—first used for a horse, later for a person.

tabloid. *Tabloid,* now generally used to mean "newspaper of small format," was originally a pharmaceutical term. In 1884 a British company registered the word as a trademark for its compressed medicinal tablets which became very popular. When the word began to be used to refer to other things that had been compressed, such as newspapers, the company took legal action to protect its sole right to *tabloid,* but a legal opinion in 1903 held that the word had acquired "a secondary sense" and might "be legitimately used so long as it does not interfere with their [the company's] trade rights."

tweed. *Twill,* a rugged kind of cloth, in nineteenth-century Scotland was called *tweel,* and Sir Walter Scott's *Guy Mannering* (1815) used that word. It was unfamiliar to his English readers, who confused it with the name of the River *Tweed.* Partly because of Scott's immense readership the cloth became popular in England and still remains so, under its mistaken name.

volt and other electrical terms. *Volt* gets its name from an Italian physicist, Alesandro *Volta* (1745–1827) ; *watt* from James *Watt* (1736–1819), the Scottish inventor of the steam engine; *ohm* from German physicist G. S. *Ohm* (1781–1854) ; and *ampere* from André Marie *Ampère* (1775–1836), a French student of electromagnetism. Seldom used today are several words honoring the discoverer of electricity: *Franklinic, Franklinism, Franklinist, Franklinize,* and *Franklinization.*

CLASSROOM ACTIVITIES

International Scientific Vocabulary

Russian, American, British, and increasingly the scientists of other nations use identical or nearly identical technical terms, and it is not always possible to determine the national origin of each term. Therefore one of the contributors to *W3,* Charles Sleeth of Princeton, coined the term International Scientific Vocabulary (ISV) to indicate many etymologies when "no positive evidence is at hand to show that it was coined in English." (See page 263.) If a copy of *W3* is available, interested students may find a few such words as examples, and may conduct a discussion of why an ISV seems highly desirable. (German scientists, oddly enough, were often slow in using ISV terms; as a result, a word like their *Fruchtkeimwissenschaft* has no discernible relationship to *embryology*.)

Names of Scientific Subjects

With some exceptions, older branches of science took their names from Latin, later ones from Greek. Have students make a list of all the branches of science they can think of and check the extent to which this statement is true. Examples: *horticulture* (Latin), *dendrology* (Greek), *botany* (G through L), *entomology* (G), *biology* (G), *chemistry* (L), *silviculture* (L), *ecology* (G), *phytogenesis* (G).

Words with Varied Technical Meanings

The word *pipe* has different meanings to musicians, plumbers, tobacconists, wine-makers, sailors, miners, geologists, and metallurgists, and to students who refer to "a pipe course." *Course* itself has different meanings to students, bricklayers, and sailors. It can be instructive for a class to think of a number of such words used with specialized meanings by various groups.

Names of Young Animals

A *kitten,* of course, is a young cat, but may also be a young beaver, fox, or puma. Students may list all the "young" names they can think of. Some that they may not know are *cygnet* (swan), *poult* (turkey), *leveret* (hare), *eyas* (hawk), *joey* (kangaroo), *owlet* (owl), *whelp* (wolf), *codling* (cod), *elver* (eel), *spike* or *tinker* or *blinker* (mackerel), *parr* or *grilse* (salmon), *stunt* (whale). Not only bears have *cubs;* so may tigers, foxes, lions, sharks, and whales. And calves may be the young of cows, elephants, hippopotamuses, moose, and whales. Young salmon are known by at least fifteen different names.

The *-ine* Families of Animals and Chemicals

It's handy to be able to say *canine* instead of "pertaining to dogs." Other *-ine* words sometimes useful to know are: *aquiline* (eagles), *asinine* (asses), *bovine* (cattle), *equine* (horses), *ovine* (sheep), *vulpine* (foxes). More rare: *accipitrine* (hawks), *anserine* (geese), *corvine* (crows), *hircine* (goats), *lacertine* (lizards), *passerine* (perching birds), *phocine* (seals), *psittacine* (parrots; a disease transmitted by parrots is psittacosis). The suffix *-ine* "pertaining to" entered English from Old French, from Latin *-inus,* Greek *-inos.* The *-ine* in names of halogens such as *chlorine* and *fluorine* comes from the feminine form of the same Latin suffix. Your science-minded students may look up some of these derivations.

An Exercise in Semantics

To show students how choice of words may affect our attitudes, tell them about the retired missionary who recalled his early years in Africa, when different cultures met head-on.

"Can you imagine," he said, "people so primitive that they love to eat the embryos of birds and slices from the belly of certain animals? Then they grind up grass seed, make it into a paste, burn it over a fire, and smear it with a greasy mess extracted from the mammary fluid of animals. Ugh!

"That's how some Africans reacted when they saw us eating eggs with bacon and buttered toast."

American Influence on Today's British English

Perhaps the best treatment of this topic is the chapter "The Impact of America" in Brian Foster's *The Changing English Language* (New York: St. Martin's Press, 1968) pp. 17–71. Among many examples of recently borrowed Americanisms mentioned by this British writer are *co-star, radio, disk-jockey, quiz, to get by, main street* (British high street), *by and large, that way* (as in "keep them that way"), *cash in on,* and *gimmick.*

Apostrophophiles and Apostrophophobes

Perhaps more in England than in America there is agitation to do away with apostrophes (and perhaps hyphens also). Harry Sharp, of the *World Book Encyclopedia* staff, in 1962 coined the words *apostrophophiles* for "apostrophe lovers" and *apostrophophobes* for "apostrophe haters." Students may discuss whether apostrophes are really needed, and classify themselves accordingly as . . . philes or . . . phobes. They should also consider hyphens and dashes. (And what should lovers or haters of these two be called?)

Changing Views of Usage

In 1881 Alfred Ayres in *The Verbalist* said that the following usages were objectionable. Your students may find it illuminating to discuss present attitudes toward the items.

> *anybody else's:* "It is better grammar and more euphonious" to
> say "anybody's else."

bad cold: "Inasmuch as colds are never *good,* why say a *bad* cold?"

dearest: "You call me your *'dearest* Maria': am I to understand that you have other Marias?"

denote: "an abomination."

dress: improper for *gown.*

ice-cream, ice-water: should be *iced-cream, iced-water.*

lunch: "an inelegant abbreviation for *luncheon.*"

specialty: should be *speciality.*

street: We should say that "we live *in,* not *on*" the street and that "houses are built *in,* not *on,* the street."

thanks: "in questionable taste to use *thanks* for *thank you.*"

widowhood: should be used for men, too, not just for women.

(Based on an article in *Word Study,* October, 1963.)

Figurative Language

Students may explore ways in which figures of speech extend or specialize meanings. E.g., *antenna* (of insects) extended to radio or television, and the small antennas on top of some TV sets are called *rabbit's ears. Crystallization* (symmetrical formation of crystals) extended to orderly arrangements of thoughts. *Escalator* led to *escalator clause* "contractual agreement to permit price adjustments."

De- and Other Affixes

Brian Foster's *The Changing English Language* remarks on the growing use of *de-* in words like *de-oathing, de-flying* "getting rid of tsetse flies," *de-internationalize, de-stinging* "removing stingers from wasps," *de-education.* What other unusual but probably legitimate *de-* words can your class recall or invent? Words with *dis-, ex-,* and *off-* (as in *off-white*) suggest other possibilities to explore. *-Dom* is considered a "dead" suffix (no longer active) but its use in words like *filmdom* and *gangsterdom* is relatively recent; any other examples? *-Ize* is a very active suffix today: *vitaminize, Vietnamize,* and *liquidize* come to mind as examples. Others?

Headline English

Lack of space makes headline writers do interesting things with language. Bring a newspaper to class (preferably a lively, uninhibited newspaper), and examine headline structure, noting what is done with verbs, how nouns sometimes are piled up, and what words are shortened, like *quake* for *earthquake.* Hard-to-read or ambiguous headlines may be analyzed. If you can get hold of a copy of *Variety,* you may find some especially colorful ones. (A famous old one is *Stix Nix Hix Pix,* which means that rural people don't like movies about rural people.)

Charactonyms

Thomas Elliott Berry (*Word Study,* December, 1949), suggested *charactonym* to designate the name of a fictitious character intended to suggest personal traits: Cooper's Aaron *Thousandacres* and Admiral *Bluewater,* Addison's Captain *Sentry* and Edward *Biscuit* (a butler), Franklin's Silence *Dogood,* Hardy's Damon *Wildeve* and Gabriel *Oak* (the shepherd whose constancy is so "deep-rooted"), *Hawthorne's Gathergold* and *Battleblast* (a loud-mouthed preacher), Jonson's Lady *Haughty* and *Cutbeard* (a barber), and Shakespeare's *Dull* (a slow-witted constable). Less obvious are Sidney's *Astrophel* and *Stella* (star-lover and star). In *Pilgrim's Progress* and the early morality plays, characters bear such names as Mr. *Badman* and *Good Deeds.* It may be added that writers like Dickens refine upon the art, using names that through their sounds more than their meanings suggest characteristics: *Scrooge, Pecksniff,* etc. Your students may recall charactonyms from their own reading.

The Ubiquity of *Up*

Up appears in hundreds of words and phrases, as the several columns in an unabridged dictionary can reveal: *cheer up, hurry up, buckle up, button up, make up, mix up* and *mix-up, blow up,* and so on and on. Students may build a list and note instances in which the *up* does or does not affect the meaning.

He and She

A few pleasant minutes can be spent discussing suffixes and other devices to indicate feminine gender. Even before Women's Lib, almost any woman writer preferred being called "author" or "poet" rather than "authoress" or "poetess." *Stewardesses* have apparently not objected strongly to that designation, nor have *waitresses* and *actresses.* Other indicators meriting mention are *-ette* (*usherette*), *woman* (*policewoman*), *lady* (*lady tailor*). Among lower animals, gender is regularly distinguished by different words: *horse, mare; fox, vixen; drake, duck;* etc. Your class can supply many more examples of gender-indicators, and can discuss when distinctions may be appropriate or necessary.

Have You Any Phobias?

Although English teachers are usually not qualified psychologists, it probably does no harm if sometimes they talk with students about things that some people fear. These are called *phobias,* from a Greek word for "fear." *Claustrophobia* "fear of enclosed places" is familiar. Others: *agora-* (open spaces), *ailuro-* (cats), *anthropo-* (people), *batho-* (deep places), *carcino-* (cancer), *cremno-* (overhanging cliffs), *cyno-* (dogs), *entomo-* (insects), *ergo-* (work), *geronto-* (old age), *hydro-* (water), *hypno-* (sleep), *hypo-* (low places), *mono-* (solitude), *necro-* (dead people), *pedo-* (children), *photo-* (light), *pyro-* (fire), *scopo-* (being seen), *scoto-* (darkness), *triskaideka-* (13), *xeno-* (foreigners).

Avoiding Provincialism in Language

An instructive discussion can be based on some of the rules followed by the editorial staff of the *United Nations World* magazine:

There is no place in the world "distant" or "far" (from where?).

No place, culture, custom or people is "strange" (to whom?), "exotic," "queer," or "bizarre."

People can be "illiterate" but never "ignorant"; they can be "simple" but never "backward."

There are no "heathen," no "pagan cultures," no "Christian ideals" (except in direct discussion), and no "chosen people."

Avoid the word "natives" as it has been shaped by imperial custom; use it only in the exact sense; e.g., as a "native of New York"—not "the natives of New Guinea."

"We" are *all the people.*

Give the FACTS. Be objective.

Newspeak

In *1984* (published in 1949) George Orwell describes "Newspeak," a form of language that would make it impossible for anyone to think "a heretical thought"— that is, any thought opposing principles espoused by the government. Words like *free* had "the undesirable meanings purged out of them," and many words such as *honor, justice, morality, internationalism, science,* and *religion* "simply ceased to exist." Students who read *1984* may conduct a lively discussion of Newspeak, giving illustrations and considering the possibility and the dangers of using language to manipulate people.

Doublespeak

The "Committee on Public Doublespeak" of the National Council of Teachers of English published in 1974 *Language and Public Policy,* a collection of articles intended to call attention to "dishonest and inhumane uses of language" by advertisers and public officials or candidates. Examples:

A White House spokesman, instead of saying that previous announcements were "false," said that they were "no longer operative."

In the Department of State, employees are not "fired" but may be "selected out."

Information at the Nixon White House was not "sought, compiled, filed, or revealed" but "developed." (Does *developed* mean "fabricated" or just "added to"?)

"Americans don't eat many beans anyway," said the Secretary of Agriculture after the price of beans skyrocketed. (Which Americans, and what does *many* mean?)

A profitable exercise for a class may be to gather and analyze numerous examples of doublespeak, from advertising and from the words of public figures. Any word, slogan, or sentence that appears to conceal or distort is eligible for the collection.

9

Developments in America

BRITISH VS. AMERICAN ENGLISH

Reasons for Differences

If the members of your family scattered to different parts of the world, almost immediately each of you would acquire a number of new words or new definitions to indicate phenomena you had not known when you were together: unfamiliar plants and animals and topographic features, local customs and sports and clothing and modes of shelter, features of weather and climate, etc. For example, a person who goes from "the lower forty-eight" to Alaska quickly learns *cheechako* "tenderfoot," *breakup* "time in spring when ice breaks up in rivers," *frost heave* "break in road caused by freezing," *permafrost* "permanently frozen ground," *williwaw* "violent gust of wind," *bush* "back country."

Among the people of your generation the changes would be confined mainly to vocabulary. But in the speech of your children, small differences in pronunciation would become noticeable, influenced by local sound patterns. A number of idioms not heard in your homeland would also appear in their speech; for example, they might occasionally use a different preposition or figurative phrase. Among your grandchildren the contrasts would perhaps be even more apparent, with a syntactic difference now and then, and perhaps slight modifications of spelling.

If your descendants were completely cut off from their cousins in your homeland or in other countries, the differences would eventually become so great that mutually incomprehensible languages could result. (That is what happened, you recall, when Indo-European developed into languages as unlike as Iranian and English; it is also what happened less completely when Latin became Italian, French, Spanish, Portuguese, and Rumanian.) But if contact with the homeland remained, the changes would be retarded; commerce, travel, the reading of the same books, and (today) radio and television would slow the rate of change.

Essentially this is what has happened to English in North America, Australia, and other parts of the world where English is spoken. In each area English has diverged from the language of England, and in each (e.g., Australia and Canada) the changes have not been identical, with the result that Australian and Canadian spoken English are readily distinguishable from each other. (Written language is more conservative and hence is harder to distinguish.) But since England and her colonies or former colonies have maintained constant contact with one another, the differences have remained rather superficial during the past two or three centuries. There is not really, for instance, despite the title used by H.L. Mencken, an *American Language,* nor is there a Canadian or an Australian language. There are merely a number of slightly different versions of the English language.

This section concerns some of the attitudes expressed toward the changes in English that occurred in North America; then examples follow of presently existing differences between British English and that of the United States. The final section will concern contributions made by the United States to English vocabulary.

Early British Criticisms of American English

Poking fun at American expressions has long been a source of enjoyment among the British. Some of the criticisms have been good natured; others have been savage. As early as 1744, Britisher Francis Moore wrote, ". . . the Bank of the River (which they in barbarous English call a *bluff*)." The charge of barbarity or at least of crudity was to be often repeated. In 1787 Thomas Jefferson's use of *belittle* was attacked: "What an expression! It may be an elegant one in Virginia, and even perfectly intelligible; but for our part, all we can do is *guess* at its meaning. . . . O spare, we beseech you, our mother-tongue!" The *Edinburgh Review* in 1808 complained that the excessively democratic Americans considered "one word as good as another," and in the same year the *Monthly Mirror* condemned "the corruptions and barbarities which are hourly obtaining in the speech of our transatlantic colonies" (ignoring the fact that the States were no longer colonies).

Such attacks, of which Mencken quotes dozens, were in part no doubt the result of striking back at the upstart colonies that had dared to defeat the supposedly invincible British military. In general, though, they arose from widespread contempt of the bumpkins so far from civilized London. Sydney Smith, in an oft-quoted passage, epitomized this contempt in 1820:

In the four quarters of the globe, who reads an American book? or goes to an American play? or looks at an American picture or statue? What does the world yet owe to American physicians or surgeons? What new substance have their chemists discovered? or what old ones have they analyzed? What new constellations have been discovered by the telescopes of Americans? What have they done in mathematics? Who drinks out of American glasses? or wears American coats or gowns? or sleeps in American blankets?

Said Captain Thomas Hamilton in 1833, "The amount of bad grammar [in America] is very great; that of barbarisms enormous," even in the "educated and respectable class." Among the sins of the Americans, according to Hamilton, were the use of *slick* and *boss,* the incorrect use of *expect, guess, reckon,* and *calculate,* the use of *suspicion* and *opinion* as verbs, and an accent on the penultimate syllable in words like *oratory, dilatory,* and *missionary* (a syllable which the British, then as now, tended to elide). Hamilton was offended "at finding the language of Shakespeare and Milton thus gratuitously degraded," and predicted that within a century "the dialect of the Americans will become completely unintelligible to an Englishman, and . . . the nation will be cut off from the advantages arising from their participation in British literature."

When another English captain, Basil Hall, visited Noah Webster in 1828, Webster argued that "his countrymen had not only a right to adopt new words, but were obliged to modify the language to suit the novelty of the circumstances, geographical and political, in which they were placed." Webster continued that "it is quite impossible to stop the progress of language—it is like the course of the Mississippi, the motion of which, at times, is scarcely perceptible; yet even then it possesses a momentum quite irresistible. Words and expressions will be forced into use, in spite of all the writers in the world." Why shouldn't a widely used Americanism become part of the language, he wanted to know. Hall had an immediate answer: "Because there are words enough already."

The Attitude of Dickens

Charles Dickens, who in his novels took obvious delight in portraying idiosyncratic or dialectal variation in British speech, was inexplicably hostile toward the variations that he found when he toured America in 1842. Except in Boston and New York, he reported, people spoke with "a nasal drawl," and almost everywhere he encountered "oddest vulgarisms" and "more than doubtful" grammar; white Southern women "speak more or less like Negroes"; forms of the verb *fix* were grossly overused.

Some years later, in "Mugsby Junction," Dickens has an American traveler addressing an English woman like this:

I tell Yew what 't is, ma'arm. I la'af. Theer! I la'af. I Dew. I oughter ha' seen most things, for I hail from the Onlimited side of the Atlantic Ocean. . . . And if I hain't found the eighth wonder of monarchical Creation, in finding Yew, and Yewer young ladies, and Yewer fixin's solid and liquid, all as aforesaid, established in a country where the people air not absolute Loonaticks, I am Extra Double Darned with a Nip and a Frizzle to the innermostest grit! Wheerfur—Theer!—I la'af! I Dew, ma'arm, I la'af!

Dickens' countryman, Edward Dicey, criticized passages like this as inaccurate representation, saying, "you might travel through the United States for years and never hear such a speech uttered out of a lunatic asylum." Dicey had been anticipated by Ralph Waldo Emerson, who had commented calmly:

No such conversations ever occur in this country in real life, as he [Dickens] relates. He has picked up and noted with eagerness each odd local phrase that he met with, and when he had a story to relate, has joined them together, so the result is the broadest caricature.

In defense of Dickens, it must be said that his attacks on American expressions and American customs were generally good natured rather than bitter. His rather apologetic dedication of *American Notes* (1842) reads: "I dedicate this book to those friends of mine in America, who, giving me a welcome I must ever gratefully and proudly remember, left my judgment free; and who, loving their country, can bear the truth, when it is told good humouredly, and in a kind spirit." And, rather ironically, Dickens has been given credit for establishing as standard in British English four previously reviled Americanisms, by his use of them in this book: *reliable, influential, talented, lengthy.* Mencken has shown that Dickens was not the first Englishman to use these words, but nevertheless his use of them probably strengthened their position. (Today, grounds for criticizing any of these words, as well as scores of others now standard but once considered vile, are hard to imagine.)

American Attitudes Toward Their Language

Not only the British were critical of American use of the language. Some Americans joined the chorus. John Witherspoon, president of the College of New Jersey (now Princeton University), wrote in 1781 an extended commentary. "I have heard in this country," he said with distress, "in the senate, at the bar [of law], and from the pulpit, and see daily in dissertations from the press, errors in grammar, improprieties and vulgarisms, which hardly any person of the same class in point of rank and literature would have fallen into in Great-Britain." (This was written while Bishop Lowth's followers were busily listing the blunders and improprieties of famous British authors!) Among the expressions that Witherspoon found objectionable were "to *notify* the publick"[1]; "a *certain* Thomas Benson"; "He is a very *clever* man" with reference to worth or integrity; "*this here*" and "*that there*"; the pronunciations *drownded, gownd,* and *attacted;* "equally *as* well, and equally *as* good"; "said *as how*"; "walk *in* the house, for *into* the house"; "*once in a while*"; confusions such as *eminent* for *imminent* or *ingenious* for *ingenuous;* and *fell* for *fallen, rose* for *risen, spoke* for *spoken.* It is instructive to note that some of these expressions are now accepted without question and that others are still, after two centuries, classroom targets; others, such as "*partly all* gone" and "*every* of these states," have apparently disappeared, although we can't say with assurance that Witherspoon deserves the credit.

Like Witherspoon, other Americans felt that it was their duty to enlighten and correct their "fellow countrymen" (another term that Witherspoon disliked). Lindley Murray's grammar was mentioned in Chapter 7. John Pickering, praised after his death in 1846 as the "most distinguished philologist" of America, prepared in 1816 *A Vocabulary or Collection of Words and Phrases which have been supposed to be peculiar to the United States of America*—the first of many such lists, culminating in the scholarly 1946-page *Dictionary of Americanisms,* edited by M. M. Mathews in 1951. In the essay prefacing the five hundred or so words, Pickering lamented that the English language "has in so many instances departed from the English standard, that our scholars should lose no time in endeavouring to

---

[1] "In English," Witherspoon asserted, "we do not notify the person of the thing, but notify the thing to the person."

restore it to its purity, and to prevent future corruption." Pickering granted that Americans, like anyone else, had the right to coin new words, but felt that only "the learned and polite" should determine which coinages ought to be kept. Among the words he discussed are a number that were seldom used even then and that have become obsolete: *citess* "female citizen"; *docity*, described as "a low word, used in some parts of the United States to signify quick comprehension"; *to happify; clitchy* "clammy, sticky, glutinous." Of Pickering's other "Americanisms" (not all of which were actually of American birth, as he supposed) many have survived, although some have been heavily lambasted by Pickering and others: *accountability, backwoodsman, appreciate* "increase in value," *appellate, balance* "remainder," *bookstore, to demoralize, to energize, to evoke, fall* "autumn," *governmental, presidential, to progress, to solemnize, squatter, stockholder,* and *to systematize.*

Some writers, though, did not choose to improve American speech or to apologize for it. Timothy Dwight used a *tu quoque* argument against British critics, saying that they were hardly qualified to condemn American pronunciations when some Englishmen said "hisn," "chimly" (for *chimney*), "nowheres," and "kiver" (for *cover*). A few asserted, quite correctly, that a number of American expressions that the British called "barbarisms" were actually dialectal words used in parts of England, and that some of them could be found in Chaucer, Spenser, or Shakespeare. Edward Everett declared in 1821 that "on the whole, the English language is better spoken here than in England," and that "there is no part of America in which the corruption of the language has gone so far as in the heart of the English counties." James Fenimore Cooper was somewhat ambivalent, arguing against *boss* and *help* (for *servant*), but also, as Mencken has said, "Cooper argued stoutly against the artificial English standards, mainly out of the Eighteenth Century, that the contemporary grammarians were trying to impose upon American, and contended that it should be left to its own devices, with due regard, of course, for reason, analogy, and any plausible indigenous authority that might develop."

James Russell Lowell, in the preface to his dialectal *Biglow Papers* (1848), had this to say:

The English have complained of us for coining new words. Many of those so stigmatized were old ones by them forgotten. . . . Undoubtedly, we have a right to make new words as they are needed by the fresh aspects under which life presents itself here in the New World; and, indeed, wherever a language is alive, it grows. . . . Here, past all question, is to be its great home and center.

And not only is it already spoken here in greater numbers, but with a far higher average of correctness than in Britain.

In 1855 Charles Astor Bristed, a grandson of John Jacob Astor, examined "the course of a great living language, transplanted from its primitive seat, brought into contact and rivalry with other civilized tongues, and exposed to various influence, all having a *prima facie* tendency to modify it." He found that in America new meanings were often—and legitimately— attached to English words; e.g., in England *creek* means "a small arm of the sea" but in America it means "a small river." American usage, such as *sick* for *ill,* was not reprehensible. Some words tended to be overused on both sides of the water: "In English conversation, the panegyrical adjective of all-work is *nice,* in America it is *fine.* Both people often use their pet adjective inappropriately; perhaps the Americans do so in fewer cases than the English."

Walt Whitman and Mark Twain both applauded the character and the vigor of common American speech, which interested them more than that of the lecture hall. Whitman said that his *Leaves of Grass* was "only a language experiment—an attempt to give the spirit, the body, the man, new words, new potentialities of speech—an American—range of self-expression. The new world, the new times, the new peoples, the new vistas need a tongue according—yes, what is more, will have such a tongue—will not be satisfied until it is evolved." On another occasion he wrote, "Ten thousand native idiomatic words are growing, or are today already grown, out of which vast numbers could be used by American writers, with meaning and effect—words that would be welcomed by the nation, being of the national blood—words that would give that taste of identity and locality which is so dear in literature." Whitman argued that Americans needed a "Real Dictionary" and a "Real Grammar," for "Nobody ever talks as books and plays talk." Included should be "slang words among fighting men, gamblers, thieves," and words of "coarseness, directness, live epithets, words of opprobrium, resistance . . . limber, lasting, fierce words"—not just "delicate lady-words" or "gloved gentleman-words."

"A nation's language," said Mark Twain, "is a very large matter. It is not simply a manner of speech obtaining among the educated handful; the manner obtaining among the vast uneducated multitude must be considered also." And he summarized and defended what many others in his century were saying: "The [English and American] languages were identical several generations ago, but our changed conditions and the spread of our people far to the South and far to the West have made many alterations in our pronunciation, and have introduced new words among us and changed the meaning of many old ones."

Noah Webster

Special attention needs to be paid to Noah Webster (1758–1843), who probably did more than anyone else to influence Americans' attitudes toward their language. Schoolmaster, ardent patriot, laborer on behalf of the Convention responsible for the Constitution,[2] publisher, author of schoolbooks that included the most widely used speller of all time (70,000,000 copies!), and the nation's premier lexicographer, he is best known for his dictionary— the book that made "Webster says" a commonplace phrase. His pronouncements concerning language, and particularly his practices, contributed to the formation of attitudes like those summarized above, and they are at least partly responsible for twentieth-century opinions and practices good or bad.

No sooner was the Constitution ratified than Webster published what might be called a Declaration of Linguistic Independence. In his "Dissertation on the English Language" (1789) he said:

As an independent nation, our honor requires us to have a system of our own in language as well as government. Great Britain, whose children we are, and whose language we speak, should no longer be *our* standard. . . . Numerous local causes, such as a new country, new associations with people, new combinations of ideas in arts and sciences, and some intercourse with tribes wholly unknown in Europe, will introduce new words into the American tongue. . . . We have therefore the fairest opportunity of establishing a national language and of giving it uniformity and perspicuity, in North America, that ever presented itself to mankind.

According to Mencken, Webster was "far too shrewd to believe, like Johnson and the other English lexicographers and grammarians, that language could really be brought under the yoke." But he was often torn, as many men and women after him have been torn, between love of order and love of freedom, and he was often tempted to say, in effect, "Your language will be best if you use it as I dictate." At times, like Johnson and Lowth, he told his readers that a word was "low," thus attempting to impose his

---

[2] His *Sketches of American Policy*, written when he was 27, has been called by James Kent, an authority on constitutional history, the first written proposal for a form of government approximating that actually framed by the Constitutional Convention. Washington and other dignitaries visited the thoughtful but argumentative young man in his Philadelphia lodgings during the Convention in 1787—a sign of how highly they regarded his little book.

own feelings. His recommended or "correct" pronunciations were ordinarily those of educated New Englanders, even though he claimed that "general custom" was his guide in all things: "Common practise, even among the unlearned, is generally defensible on the principles of analogy and the structure of the language. . . . The most difficult task now to be performed by the advocates of *pure English* is to restrain the influence of men learned in Greek and Latin but ignorant of their own tongue." He could write ". . . my principal aim has been to check *innovations*," yet he wanted to reform spelling and to a small extent succeeded. "Grammar," he said, "is formed on language, and not language on grammar," thus recognizing the truth of what Joseph Priestley had said earlier in England; and he did indeed in his *Grammatical Institute* try to make his own grammar more a reflection of reality than did the Lowthians, but he was not averse to an occasional inclusion of Websterian prescriptivism. He favored a "standard" and he favored "uniformity," but the standard and the uniformity should be what Noah Webster happened to like.

His *Compendious Dictionary,* 1806, was followed by school abridgments in 1807 and 1817, and by his most definitive work, *An American Dictionary of the English Language,* in 1828, with a "corrected and enlarged" edition in 1841. These books differed from the dictionaries of Johnson and others in several ways: they attempted to reform spelling; they advocated largely unvarying American pronunciations which sometimes were different from British lexicographers' preferences; since Webster could read twenty languages, his dictionaries corrected many false etymologies (but kept or added many no less false); they contained the most accurate and clear definitions yet written;[3] and for the first time many of the new words of science and industry were included—words that the bookish Johnson had not thought worthy of definition. The *American Dictionary* had 70,000 entries—larger in number and more far-ranging in content than any of its predecessors.

The early sales of Webster's dictionaries were relatively modest; his income derived mainly from his spellers. Through much of the nineteenth century, from 1830 on, a series of dictionaries by a former aide to Webster, Joseph E. Worcester, outsold Webster's. The compactness of some of the Worcester books was a recommendation, and their price—as low as thirty cents in 1888—was another. They were indeed respectable competitors,

---

[3] A perhaps apocryphal anecdote illustrates Webster's precision in use of words. According to the story, Noah's wife saw him kissing their maid. "Noah!" she said. "I am surprised!" "No, my dear," he answered. "*We* have been surprised. *You* are astonished."

acclaimed by Harvard's President Charles Eliot as "by far the best authority as to the present use of the English language,"[4] and they forced Webster's publishers, G. and C. Merriam, into several revisions. Webster's sales were good enough, though, that in a quarter of a century they brought his heirs a quarter of a million dollars in royalties—much more than the author himself had ever received.

Webster can be praised for increasing the linguistic consciousness of his countrymen and for showing them that it was not necessary to toady to British preferences or to be ashamed of American departures from the language of the London publishing houses. He led in nose-thumbing the critics—English and American—who considered American English vulgar or barbarous. But at the same time he was building the idea of a single standard of correctness in spelling, usage, and word-choice. The tremendous success of his spelling book—studied in almost every school, and the final authority in thousands of spelling bees—attached more importance to spelling than the subject rightly deserves. The success of his dictionaries (and those of his competitors) further reinforced linguistic authoritarianism and discouraged linguistic experimentation: if a child or a professional writer used a word imaginatively, colorfully, or forcefully but could not validate its use in the pages of a dictionary, then the child or the professional writer must be wrong.

A Gradual Rapprochement

It is significant that in 1789 Webster approvingly predicted that English and American would become as different from each other "as the modern Dutch, Danish, and Swedish are from the German," but that thirty-nine years later he had decided that such a separation was neither likely nor desirable. Just after the Revolutionary War, men even more chauvinistic than Webster had proposed that, to make the break with England absolute, Americans should adopt Hebrew or Greek as their language; at least one person, in fact, argued that since we had won the war, we should take over English as our own and force the British to adopt Greek! But tempers cooled, more English settlers came to America, commerce with England increased, and Americans continued to read British books and Englishmen began to read American writings. It is true that for many years to come

---

[4] Even as late as 1890, Harvard students had to follow Worcester's spellings when they differed from Webster's. A president of Princeton praised Worcester in a dictionary cover blurb. But supporters of Webster no doubt merely shrugged, for Webster was a Yale man and could expect no accolades from Harvard and Princeton.

mutual linguistic criticisms sailed back and forth across the Atlantic, and it is also true that for a long time some Americans felt rather ashamed of their language, considering it a poor relation. It is true that for decades stage Englishmen in American plays were characterized by their "Blimy" and their treatment of *h*'s in expressions like "Hopen yer heyes, 'enry," while stage Americans in British plays aroused laughter with their "I guess" and "reckon" and "calculate." In general, though, the criticisms became increasingly good natured—sometimes mere banter as between friends.

The rapprochement became particularly evident during the twentieth century. Americans, now secure in their strength, felt less need to be defensive about anything. They fought side by side with the British in the trenches of World War I, and the two nations were the staunchest of all allies in World War II. Many Americans traveled in England, and some Englishmen in the United States. Radio and television and exchange of motion pictures provided other links. Americans admired Winston Churchill and developed a fondness for the royal family; the British reciprocated with friendly feelings for some American Presidents, and for astronauts and other cultural or scientific figures. Although Anglophobia still existed in some Americans, Anglophilia or at least a tolerance for things English was more usual. The realization grew that British and American English are merely two varieties of the same language, just as two varieties of apples may differ superficially but both share the characteristics implied by *apple*.

BRITISH AND AMERICAN PREFERENCES IN WORD CHOICE, PRONUNCIATION, SPELLING, AND SYNTAX

In this section the main concern will be with existing differences (and the much greater similarities) in British and American word choice, pronunciation, and spelling, and with the very few differences in syntax. A little book on this subject that both teachers and students may enjoy is *A Common Language,* a series of conversations between British Professor Randolph Quirk and American Professor Albert H. Marckwardt, recorded and published for the BBC and the Voice of America in 1964. This book stresses the similarity of the two varieties of the language. Its foreword says, for instance, "If only to illustrate how slight are the differences between us, British spelling is adopted in the contributions of the British professor, and American spelling in those of the American professor." Very seldom, though, can one tell from the language alone whether the Britisher or the American is speaking.

Word Choice

Probably everybody knows that American *elevator* is British *lift* (although the British often use *hoist* for the American *freight elevator*). Also well-known are differences in terms relating to automobiles: *gasoline—petrol, hood—bonnet, top—hood, trunk—boot, windshield—windscreen, spark plug—sparking-plug, truck—lorry*. And any American who has traveled in England or has read much recent British literature has also become aware of differences like the ones in this list:

barber—hairdresser	bathrobe—dressing gown
billboard—hoarding	billion—milliard
canned fruit—tinned fruit	check—bill (in a restaurant)
cracker—biscuit	deck of cards—pack of cards
drugstore—chemist's shop	first floor—ground floor
garbage collector—dustman	ice cream or sherbet—ice
line (to stand in)—queue	mail—post
pants—trousers	period (punctuation)—full stop
punctuating—pointing	quotation marks—inverted commas
roast (*n.*)—joint	round trip—return trip
run (in a stocking)—ladder	shoes—boots
soft drinks—minerals	subway—underground, tube
ticket office—booking office	toilet—WC, water closet, lavatory
undershirt—vest	vacation—holiday
z—zed	

Seldom, though, do the differences result in more than momentary confusion. One exception may be *billion,* which in America is 1,000,000,000 but in England is 1,000,000,000,000 (American *trillion*). Another may be *homely;* in America it means "unattractive," but in England it means "domestic, pleasant to have about the house." It is reported, too, that an American girl was shocked when a British young man told her, "I'll knock you up at eight o'clock"; he was not threatening to make her pregnant, but was only telling the time when he would knock on her door. An American looking at a British *bill-of-fare (menu)* may encounter some moments of puzzlement until he learns that *crisps* are potato chips; that *chips* (as in fish 'n' chips) are French fries; that Yorkshire pudding is not a pudding in the American sense; that a *tart* is a fruit pie (British *pies* are ordinarily made with meat); that a *sweet* is a dessert; and that a *trifle* is a piece of elaborately garbed sponge cake. But such differences are not much greater than in different parts of America, where, for instance, what is a *soft drink* in one place may be *pop, soda pop, soda, tonic,* or even a *dope* somewhere else, or where one person's *corn bread* may be another's *corn pone, pone,* or *johnny cake.*

Usually, in fact, when different names for things exist on the two sides of the Atlantic, both names are recognized and perhaps used. Thus, although many Americans think that the British always refer to *cinema* rather than *movies* or *motion pictures,* actually all three words are used in both countries. A Britisher may say *goods train* but he understands *freight train. Radio* is now more general in England than is *wireless.* The Englishman still thinks of a *bug* as a nasty little thing that may bite you in bed, but he understands that to most Americans any insect may be a bug. A *store* in England still generally refers to a storehouse, but the Englishman does sometimes use *store* for his more usual *shop,* especially for a large establishment like Selfridge's in London. (Incidentally, it is interesting that even Americans go *shopping,* not *storing.*) *Blizzard* for *snowstorm* is comprehensible to the Englishman, but because snow seldom blows with great ferocity in England, he has little use for the term. American coinages like *disc-jockey, double talk, commuter,* and *blurb* often catch on in England, and Randolph Quirk says, "I wonder which of us [an Englishman or an American] was the first to think of having 'baby-sitters' to look after our children."

Even though differences in vocabulary do exist between the two countries, it is impossible to overemphasize the fact that the similarities are much greater. For example, I have just read a randomly selected twenty pages of recent British fiction and nonfiction, looking for words that an American would not be likely to use in the given contexts. I found a total of only fourteen—less than a word per page. A different selection, of course, might give a smaller or larger number.

In science it is especially important that terminology be as nearly identical, at least in its referents, as possible. Many terms—some originating in England, some in the United States, and some elsewhere—are now used internationally. *Webster's Third New International Dictionary* marks hundreds of such words *ISV* (for International Scientific Vocabulary; see also page 244). For example, among the ISV *sulf-* words are *sulfamic acid, sulfamide, sulfanilic acid, sulfochloride,* and more than twenty others. In such words the national barriers have broken down not just between England and the United States but throughout the world.

Pronunciation

Consonant sounds are pronounced almost the same on both sides of the water. An exception is [r], which in much of England is not pronounced in words like *heard* and *author.* The late poet laureate, Robert Bridges, complained that he often could not tell whether his countrymen were saying *flaw* or *floor, laud* or *lord, alms* or *arms, sauce* or *source, ah* or *are*. However, in the western part of England and in Lancashire as well as in Scotland and Ireland, the *r*'s are pronounced. Conversely, in much of the Northeastern United States, such *r*'s are not heard. So, in this instance as well as others in pronunciation, "Some do and some don't" is the best generalization.

Similarly, some British and some Americans use the vowel sound [a:] in *glass,* but others use [æ] and some have a sound somewhere between the two. According to Mencken, there are about 150 such words in which both the British and the New Englanders are likely to use a sound approximating [a:]. Usually these are words in which the next sounds are those of *f (laugh), ft (draft), m (calm), nch (branch), nd (command), nt (chant), sk (ask), sp (clasp), ss (grass), st (last),* or *th (path),* but there are exceptions such as *and, stamp, elastic, gas,* and others.

Some other vowel sounds tend to differ also, but again it is not accurate to name one pronunciation "American" and another "British."

AMERICANS TEND TO SAY:	BRITISH TEND TO SAY:
[gat] *got*	[gɔt] (also in *not, stop, clock,* etc.)
[šo:n] *shone*	[šɔn] (also sometimes in *home,* etc.)
[e:t] *ate*	[ɛt]
[bIn] *been*	[bi:n]
[ɛvəlu:šən] *evolution*	[i:vəlu:šən] but [rɛvəlu:šən]
[zi:nəθ] *zenith*	[zɛnəθ]
[tu:b] *tube*	[tIu:b] (also in *news, due, nude,* etc.)

A few other individual words may also vary between the countries. Thomas Pyles mentions *fragile,* British [fræ jaĺl] *nephew* [nέvju] ; *trait,* which loses the final *t; figure* [fĺgə(r)] ; *squirrel* [skwĺrəl] ; *vase* [va:z] ; *lieutenant* [lɛftέnənt] ; and others. British [šέdju:l] and [kla:rk] are very familiar examples.

In some words British and American speakers accent different syllables. For instance, I have heard a Britisher argue that the usual British emphasis on the second syllable of *concentrate* is logical because when one concentrates he *centers* his attention ; he was reluctant to admit that logic has little to do with pronunciation. The British usually stress the second syllable of *corollary* and the first syllable of *frontier.* In words ending in *-ary, -ery, -ory,* and *-oly* the British tendency is to elide the vowel sound before the *r* or the *l,* resulting in the loss of a syllable and of a secondary accent in such words as *secret'ry, cemet'ry, laborat'ry* (which the British stress on the second syllable rather than the first and the fourth), and *melanch'ly.*

This tendency toward elision shows up in other British words also. The two-syllable pronunciations of *Gloucester* [glɔstə(r)] and *Leicester* [lɛstə(r)] are old and familiar, and [čʌmlI] for *Cholmondeley* only a little less so. According to a character in Angela Thirkell's *Wild Strawberries* (who may be exaggerating a bit), *Westhampton Pollingford* should be pronounced "Wumpton Pifford." Shopkeepers often shorten *thank you* to [kIu]. In words like *registrar* and *bursar* the American [a:] is reduced by the British to [ə]. British actor George Arliss once commented, "The chief fault in speech in America is sloppiness and the outstanding defect in England is snippiness."

A century ago Thomas Carlyle said that "All speech, even the commonest speech, has something of a song in it." Perhaps the biggest difference between British and American speech is a difference in the tunes. The British ordinarily use a somewhat larger range of tone (sometimes over two octaves), and their patterns of intonation within sentences often differ from those of Americans. In questions, for example, the British tend to start at a relatively high pitch, drop to normal, and drop further at the end, but Americans tend to start at normal pitch and then rise and fall at the end.

Travel, movies, radio, and television have familiarized so many Americans with British speech, and vice versa, that today there is seldom any real difficulty in understanding. The only frequent exception to this statement is in connection with nonstandard dialects. An American, for instance, may have problems in understanding a Cockney, a Yorkshireman, or some speakers of Scottish, such as many residents of Glasgow. And a Britisher may encounter comparable problems in understanding some black or Puerto Rican English or that of certain Appalachians.

Spelling

The person most responsible for American divergence from British spellings is Noah Webster. He set out very ambitiously to simplify spelling, although he later retreated to less far-reaching recommendations. Among his intended reforms that never caught on were *giv, imagin* (and other words with a useless final *e,* but not in words like *pine* where *e* is needed for differentiation from *pin,* etc.), *crum, meen, masheen, wo, soe* for *sew, fether, farewel, grotesk, porpess, tung, ake, skreen, spunge, soop, iland, insted, leperd, thret, bilt, relm,* and *wimmen.* He was more successful in a number of other words. He argued, for instance, that *u* is unneeded in words like *colour, armour, honour,* and *flavour,* and in consequence Americans dropped it but the British still keep it. Similarly, he said that *c* alone can do the work of *ck* in *musick, fabrick,* etc.; the *k* has been lost in both countries, partly because some Britishers were already dispensing with it. At the end of words like *centre,* said Webster, we pronounce the vowel sound before that of the consonant, so why not write *center, caliber, theater,* and so on? The British still cling to *-re,* and although Americans write *-er* in most such words, they are still ambivalent about a few, such as *theater—theatre.*

Webster got rid of the useless letters in words like *gramme, programme,* and *quartette,* but many Britishers still like them. In words like *traveller* he said that one consonant before the suffix is enough, and most Americans have believed him. He made *defense* and *offense* standard in America instead of British *defence* and *offence. Axe* became *ax, waggon* changed to *wagon, mould* is now usually *mold, gaol* became *jail* (now usual in England too), and his preference for *catalog, dialog,* etc., has been fairly widely accepted in the United States but is still rarely followed in England. Other miscellaneous changes successfully urged by Webster include *plow* (British *plough*), *milk* cow (British *milch* cow), *draft* (British *draught*), and *sentinel* (now standard on both sides; the spelling *centinel* was once used).

Many other Americans (as well as British) have urged spelling reform, but the results have been small. Benjamin Franklin wanted a new alphabet, with a different symbol for each important sound (or phoneme, as we would call it); he turned his scheme over to Webster, along with specially cast type, but Webster preferred his own less sweeping reforms. Members of the American Philological Society came out in favor of *ar, catalog, definit, gard, giv, hav, infinit, liv, tho, thru,* and *wisht.* The National Education Association late in the nineteenth century began using in its publications *altho, catalog, decalog, pedagog, program, prolog, tho, thorofare, thoroly, thru,* and *thruout.* Andrew Carnegie gave up to $25,000 a year to a Simplified Spelling Board, whose recommendations appealed to Theodore Roosevelt, but Congress threatened to withhold White House funds if he persisted in using *thru* and the like.

Recommendations of the Simplified Spelling Board were interestingly similar to those made with equal lack of success by Webster. For example, drop silent *b* in words like *debt* and *doubt,* giving *det* and *dout;* use a single rather than a double consonant at the end of a word: *ad, bil, bluf, buz, clas, eg,* etc.; drop the *e* from *oe: fo, ho, to, wo* (but *foes, hoed*); drop an unneeded *h* in *gh: gastly, goul, agast;* substitute *f* for *ph: alfabet, emfasis, fonograf.* Sensible though many such changes might be, the money of a millionaire, the support of a group of esteemed scholars, and the enthusiasm of a President were not enough to bring them about.

Throughout the twentieth century various groups and individuals have continued to urge spelling reform. The *Chicago Tribune* and some other newspapers used their own system for a while, with, for example, *frater* for *freighter*. Upton Sinclair in his old age tried to get President Kennedy's backing for any system that would be simpler than the existing one. A group of businessmen, centered in Chicago, urged that more systematic spelling could save business and industry countless dollars, would help to bring machine translation to reality, and might result in a "voice typewriter" which would automatically type whatever was dictated to it. Educators have repeatedly argued that more consistent spellings would make it easier for children to learn to read; children in Russia, Spain, and Finland, it has been asserted, have fewer difficulties with reading than American or English children because the languages of those countries have fewer idiosyncrasies of spelling. The editor of *Parents' Magazine* has repeatedly pleaded for simplified spelling. For a time the Modern Language Association of America used selected simplifications in *PMLA* and other of its publications.

Across the water, too, there was continued interest in spelling reform. Shortly after World War II, Parliament almost passed a bill that would have required a consistent new spelling in official government publications. Each [aɪ], for instance, would be spelled *ai*, so that *kind* would be *kaind* and *height* would be *hait;* when *f* is pronounced [v], it would be spelled *v: ov*, for instance; similarly, a "soft g" would be spelled *j: jem*. Silent letters would be dropped: *hav. One* would be *wun. Th* would be retained in words like *thin*, but the voiced *th* as in *these* would be spelled *dh*, resulting in *dheez*. A shift of two votes would have brought such changes about, at least in publications emanating from Parliament and other governmental bodies.

Such changes would be easier to learn and apply, and much more economical, than would be a system requiring a new alphabet, like Benjamin Franklin's or that of the winner of a contest that resulted when George Bernard Shaw left much of his estate to further the cause of spelling reform. A different alphabet would require everyone to relearn how to read and write, and all typewriters and typesetting machines would have to be scrapped and the operators of the new machines retrained.

Some of the existing differences between British and American spellings have been mentioned in the discussion of Noah Webster. Here are a few other miscellaneous ones:

CUSTOMARY AMERICAN SPELLING	CUSTOMARY BRITISH SPELLING
baritone, cider, tire	barytone, cyder, tyre
catsup or catchup or ketchup	ketchup
check (bank)	cheque
civilize, civilization, realize, realization	civilise, civilisation, realise, realisation
connection	connexion˙
curb (of a street)	kerb (now often *curb*)
esthetic, anesthetic	æsthetic, anæsthetic
gray	grey
jewelry	jewellery
pajamas	pyjamas
pygmy	pigmy
story (of a building)	storey
vial	phial

It must be added, though, that some Britishers use the American forms, and vice versa. It would be unwise and unrealistic for an American teacher to label "wrong" such spellings as *pigmy, grey,* and *jewellery.*

Syntax

Differences between British and American syntax are trivial. The same sentence patterns are used, and in approximately as great frequency. Virtually the same phrase structure and transformational rules are applicable.

Perhaps the most noticeable difference appears in a sentence like "The government are considering the matter" or, in an account of a cricket match, "Australia are favoured over Wales." In British thinking, a government consists of a number of persons, and in the second illustration *Australia* refers to a number of players. In American thinking, *government* is a singular abstract noun, and *Australia* is here the name of a team.

In *A Common Language* Quirk and Marckwardt make the point that inverted order in sentences, as in "Ignored has been the simple truth that . . . ," though infrequent in both countries, is more frequent in America, particularly in some journalistic prose. Marckwardt hazards the guess that *Time* magazine, which has employed inversion as a characteristic of its style, may be responsible for the difference.

Standard on both sides is a sentence like "Give it to me," but British usage sometimes (though infrequently) omits the *to:* "Give it me." "Has he brought them you?"

Quirk and Marckwardt revive an old joke about an American who asked an Englishwoman, "Do you have many children?" and was answered, "Oh, no, only one every couple of years." The point of an otherwise pointless joke is that some puristic Britishers believe that *do have* questions should be used only with reference to habitual actions. Most Britishers, though, including nonpurists, would phrase the question "Have you many children?" or "Have you got many children?" (*Gotten,* incidentally, as in the American "I've gotten several replies," was once used in England but now rarely appears.)

Americans in their turn—at least most of those who write textbooks and grade children's compositions—are more puristic about the placement of words like *only* and *scarcely* than are the British. Gallons of red ink have been used in margins to criticize sentences like "We only had ten minutes left"; most Englishmen, though, would find "We had only ten minutes left" a bit odd.

Subjunctive forms such as "Were this true . . ." and "If we be in danger . . ." seem more common in England than in America, but less so in both countries than they once were.

Dialectal Differences in America

Since the subject of American dialects is large enough that many books and articles have been devoted to it, we can do no more than touch on it here. Regional dialects exist mainly because those who settled in the various regions came from different areas of England and other countries. Thus the early British settlers of New England and the South came largely from Southern England, and left the imprint of their speech in those places to this day. Later many of the English immigrants came from Central and Northern England; they tended to move farther inland and carried their dialects with them. In addition, immigrants from many other countries tended to settle fairly close together: the Germans of Pennsylvania who are responsible for the "Pennsylvania Dutch" of that state, the Scandinavians of Wisconsin and Minnesota, the Mexican-Americans of the Southwest, and so on. Speech "islands" sometimes resulted, and most of the foreign languages also had at least some general linguistic impact.

Several useful textbooks on American dialects are now available for secondary school classes.

AMERICAN CONTRIBUTIONS TO THE VOCABULARY

Mitford M. Mathews' *A Dictionary of Americanisms* has fifty thousand entries, most of them with illustrative citations, in its 1,946 two-column 8½ × 11" pages. Mathews defines *Americanism* like this:

As used in the title of this work, "Americanism" means a word or expression that originated in the United States. The term includes: outright coinages, as *appendicitis, hydrant, tularemia;* such words as *adobe, campus, gorilla,* which first became English in the United States; and terms such as *faculty, fraternity, refrigerator,* when used in senses first given them in American usage.[5]

Since Mathews' book was first published many more Americanisms have entered the language. *Webster's Third New International Dictionary (W3),* (1961), contained a hundred thousand words that were not in *W2,* 1934. So during that twenty-seven year period new words entered the language and attained dictionary recognition at the rate of almost four thousand a year or about ten a day. (Countless others were coined but were not used widely enough to get into the dictionary.) Not all these new words, of course, were Americanisms, but many of them were.

In this section we'll glance at a tiny fraction of American contributions to the vocabulary, paying most attention to our borrowings and our new applications.

Words Borrowed by Americans

When the early settlers came to North America, they encountered many phenomena that they had not known in the Old World; naturally they would sometimes ask a friendly Indian, "What do you call that?" Then, if they bothered to write the name down, as in a letter or a diary, they had to figure out how to spell the sounds that they thought the Indian made. There were sometimes no corresponding sounds in English words. So it is not surprising that the name of the animal we call *raccoon* was spelled in the seventeenth century *rahaugcum, raugroughcum, aracoune,* and *rarowcun.* Which of these spellings represents most closely what Indians (usually Algonquians) actually said is doubtful.

In general the borrowings from the Indian languages were nouns identifying animals, plants, foods, or features of Indian life. Besides the ones listed in a class exercise on page 286 they included:

[5] Mitford Mathews, *A Dictionary of Americanisms,* Chicago: University of Chicago Press, 1951. Preface.

Trees: catalpa, hickory, pecan, tamarack

Animals: carcajou, caribou, quahog, terrapin

Food: hominy, pemmican, succotash

Features of Indian life: mackinaw, manitou, sachem, squaw, tepee, toboggan, wampum, wigwam

Some borrowings, including some from Western Indians, came later than others. *Tepee* is in this group, as well as *cayuse, chautauqua, chinook, hogan, hooch, potlatch* (a time for giving gifts), and *sequoia* (named for the brilliant Cherokee inventor of a syllabary).

Special mention should be made of place-names from Indian tongues. Every state has some, and about half of the names of states themselves are of Indian origin. Chicago and many other cities bear Indian names, as well as thousands of towns and hamlets, streams, and mountains, and all the Great Lakes except Superior.

Sometimes the settlers used English names to describe Indian customs that they observed. In this way we got *bury the hatchet, medicine man, paleface, pipe of peace, to scalp, war paint,* and *warpath,* as well as *Indian file, Indian giver,* and *Indian summer.*

Some Indian words reached English at second hand. The French first borrowed *carcajou* and *bayou,* and the Spanish (especially in the West Indies or Mexico) borrowed native words that the English later found useful: *barbecue, canoe, chigger, chocolate, hammock, mesquite, tamale, tapioca, tobacco, tomato.*

According to Mencken, Spanish was destined to contribute more words to the American vocabulary than any other continental European language, although most of these words came in after the Louisiana Purchase (1803). In the Southwest, Spanish place-names abound; instances are most of the hundreds of names beginning with *La, Las, Los, San, Santa,* or *Santo.* Other borrowings include:

Geographical: arroyo, canyon, mesa, sierra, tornado

Rural: alfalfa, bronco, burro, chaparral, cinch "saddle girth," corral, lasso, mustang, ranch, stampede

Household: adobe, frijole, patio, plaza, poncho, siesta, sombrero, tequila, tortilla

Miscellaneous: bonanza, placer (mining)

Early borrowings by English-Americans from French reflected the prowess of the French as explorers: *portage, voyageur, cache,* and *prairie,* for example. Later came *brassiere* (in our own century), *butte, coulee, chute, crevasse, depot, lagniappe, levee, picayune,* and perhaps *shanty.*

German gave us *sauerkraut* (temporarily renamed *liberty cabbage* during a burst of patriotic zeal in World War I) and *noodle,* both in Colonial days, and later *beer-garden, dachshund, delicatessen, frankfurter* and *hamburger* and *wiener* (named for *Frankfurt, Hamburg,* and *Vienna*), *kindergarten, ouch* (probably), *pretzel, pumpernickel, sauerbraten, schnitzel,* and *zwieback.* Perhaps also the pejorative terms *loafer* and *bum* are of German origin, and it has been hypothesized that the *ker-* in words like *kersplash* or *kerplop* is derived from the German verbal prefix *ge-.* Wars gave us words like *howitzer* (first Czech, then German, then Dutch, then English) and *blitzkrieg* "lightning war."

The Dutch contributed place-names like *Brooklyn, Flushing, Harlem, Hell-Gate* (Dutch *Helle-Gat*), *Staten, Yonkers,* and the *Bowery,* as well as others with *hook* "point of land" (e.g., *Kinderhook*) or *kill* "channel" (*Peekskill, Catskill,* and *Schuylkill*). A moment's thought about history will recall why these are mainly New York (formerly New Amsterdam) names. *Cruller, cole-slaw* (often *cold slaw* by folk etymology) *cooky, smearcase,* and *waffle* illustrate how the Dutch enriched our tables. Miscellaneous contributions include *boss,* perhaps *bush* in the sense "back country," *dope, pit* "seed," *Santa Claus* (from *Sant Klaas,* Dutch for *St. Nicholas*), *scow, sleigh, snoop, spook, stoop* "porch," and probably *Yankee* (from a Dutch pirate, Jan Kees).

Some Yiddish words have become fairly familiar: *bar mitzvah, blintz, kibitzer, kosher, matzoth, mazuma,* and *Yom Kippur,* for example.

Explanations of *O.K.* (the Americanism most widely known around the world) have been many and fanciful: that Andrew Jackson, our least literate President, approved documents by marking them O.K. for "oll korrect"; that an "O.K. Club" was formed to support Martin Van Buren, who was called "Old Kinderhook" in honor of his birthplace; that Orrins-Kendall, a Civil War baking company, stamped its boxes of biscuits O.K.; that (as Woodrow Wilson believed) it was based on a Choctaw word for "It is so"; or that it stood for Old Keokuk, a Sac chief. But in the New York *Times* (January 8, 1971), David Dalby traced the expression back to 1815, when it was used by blacks in South Carolina and Jamaica. According to Dalby, it probably derives from African languages, Mandingo *o ke* "that is it" or "certainly" and Wolof *waw kay* "yes indeed."

Other words from African tongues include *banjo, buckra* "white man," *cooter* "turtle," *goober, gumbo, hoodoo, jazz* (?), *juke* box, *poor Joe* "blue heron," *pickaninny* (from Portuguese), *voodoo,* and *zombie.*

The following are some American borrowings from other languages.

Italian: cacciatore, macaroni, pizza, pizzeria, policy "a type of lottery," salami, spaghetti

Chinese: chop suey, chow-chow "relish," chow mein, fan-tan, foo yong, joss, tong "clan"

Japanese: hara-kiri, ju-jitsu, karate (Japanese for "empty hand"), tycoon

Czech: kolach, rohlik

Swedish: lingon "berry," lutfisk "a fish delicacy"

It should be remembered that words listed here are believed to have been borrowed in America before they became known in England; thus words like *tea,* from Chinese, and *geisha,* from Japanese, are not listed because they first appeared in England. A few of the words, though, such as *sauerkraut* and *noodle,* although first borrowed in England, were apparently largely forgotten there and were reborrowed in the United States.

Very few of the American borrowings referred to abstractions, intangibles—perhaps because most such words as seemed needed already existed in the language, or perhaps because people developing a new country are too busy doing physical things to devote much time to abstract thought. In contrast, the number of culinary words is noteworthy; because America attracted people from all parts of the world, American cooking is today extraordinarily varied, and literally thousands of our terms relating to food have been imported.

New Applications of Old Words

Sometimes instead of borrowing a name for a previously unfamiliar phenomenon the English settlers would simply apply in a new way words that they already knew. When they heard a bird that meowed, it was natural to name it *catbird,* and a fish with "whiskers" suggesting those of a cat was of course named *catfish. Lightning bug* and *razorback* (hog) were named in similar ways. *Foot* combined with other words to create a number of meanings: *foot box, foot cavalry, foot evil, foot gin, foothills, footlog, foot muff, foot scraper, foot screw, foot trail, foot washing, foot-washing Baptist, footwear, foot wheel*—none of which are recorded in the *OED.* A peach from which the pit could not be readily removed was called a *clingstone.* Land from which trees were cut was a *clearing.*

Some of the names were more imaginative than others—even poetic. One flower that grew wild has an erect spadix over which a spathe arches; it reminded early settlers of a minister in an oldfashioned canopied pulpit, so they named it *jack-in-the-pulpit.* The settlers noticed that another flower

(technically *Viola tricolor,* and known in England as *heartsease*) grew
with extreme rapidity in rich North American soil; they called it *Johnny-
jump-up.*

They used onomatopoeia to name the *katydid,* whose three "notes"
sounded something like the name they gave it. The *rattlesnake* rattles,
June bugs are most numerous in June, *potato bugs* eat potato leaves, *butter-
nuts* have a buttery taste, and a *muskrat* looks like a rat but has a musky
odor.

Sometimes the settlers tended to use one English word rather than another, so that the second eventually became relatively unfamiliar. Thus
brook was used less than *creek, branch,* or *run.* The old words *chase* "a
place for game," *bog, dell, down* or *fell* "wasteland," *heath, lea, moor,
tarn,* and *weald* or *wold* "an unwooded flat area" have never enjoyed much
popularity in America although most of them are still known here.

Conversely, some English words remained popular in America but declined in use in England: *andiron, bay window, beef* (for the live animal,
as "a beef"), *cesspool, clodhopper, cordwood, flapjack, greenhorn, home-
spun, to hustle, loophole, molasses, ragamuffin, shoat, stock* "cattle," *trash,
to whittle, to wilt.* Some British dialect words, such as these from Essex,
became rather general in use in the United States: *kilter* (as in "out of
kilter"), *pesky, to scrimp, to snicker.* Some pronunciations once (and perhaps still) fairly frequent among American common folk came from the
same source: [ɛləm] for *elm,* [hɔs] for *horse,* [kɪvɚr] for *cover,* [ja:rb]
for *herb.*

Some words were given different meanings west of the Atlantic, often
simply because of faulty identification. For instance, a *robin* in England is
a warbler with an orange breast, but in America the name is that of a
thrush with a reddish breast. Other examples:

MEANING COMMON IN ENGLAND		MEANING COMMON IN THE U.S.
barn	place for storing grain, etc.	place to keep livestock, hay, etc.
beech	*Fagus sylvatica*	*Fagus grandifolia*
biscuit	American "cracker"	small cake of shortened bread
blackbird	songbird, black with yellow bill	any of several black birds
clerk	office worker	salesperson
corn	wheat, rye, oats, barley	maize
dry goods	grain or other non-liquids	textiles
freshet	fresh stream entering salt water	sudden overflow of a stream
hemlock	a poisonous plant	a type of evergreen tree
lark	the skylark	the meadowlark

MEANING COMMON IN ENGLAND		MEANING COMMON IN THE U.S.
lumber	miscellaneous stored articles	boards, planks, etc.
oriole	a bird of the family Oriolidae	a bird of the family Icteridae
partridge	a plump-bodied bird, genus *Perdix* or *Alectoris*	any of several game birds, e.g., grouse, quail
rabbit	a short-tailed, burrowing mammal	a hare
rock	a large stone, e.g., "Plymouth Rock"	a stone of any size
walnut	a straw-colored nut	a black nut

American houses were often different from English houses, largely because trees abounded. So there were *log cabins, log houses,* and *frame houses* with wooden *shingles* and *clapboards,* and *smokehouses.* In New England wooden *lean-tos* were added to barns to shelter livestock. Where there were few trees, houses might be *sod shanties* or *sod houses.* The song "My Little Old Sod Shanty on the Claim" uses *claim* in the sense of "land obtained free or cheaply by claiming it from the government." Someone who lived on land not his own was a *squatter,* to whom the law gave specified *squatter's rights.*

Purchases might be made at a *general store,* a *hardware store,* a *shoe store,* or a *dry goods store;* the English *shop* tended to be used in America to name a place where a certain kind of labor was performed: *blacksmith shop* (or *smithy*), *barber shop, carpenter shop.*

Groups of Americans often got together to perform tasks that would be difficult for one or two to do alone. Some unknown poet of the language, perhaps recalling the social instincts of bees, began calling such purposeful gatherings *bees.* (The etymology is uncertain, though.) Bees proliferated. There were *raising bees* (where men got together to raise the heavy timbers for a new house), *quilting bees, apple bees* or *paring bees* (preparatory to making apple butter or dried apples), *sewing bees, husking bees, threshing* (popularly "thrashing") *bees, cellar-digging bees.* Sometimes the gatherings were for pleasure rather than work, as the once immensely popular *spelling bees* attested. In the days before automobiles, movies, and television, such gatherings were eagerly anticipated social occasions; many a marriage resulted from a *bee.* The words in vogue at any given time are among the best pieces of evidence concerning the life of that time and the characteristics of the people then living.

Most of our examples have come from rural language, because the urbanization of America is a relatively recent occurrence. And most have come from the speech of relatively uneducated persons, for before the twentieth century a college or even a high school education was rare. There were, of course, some coinages more bookish than most we have noted: *to antagonize, to deputize, to eventuate, to immigrate,* and *to legislate,* plus others like *congressional, gubernatorial,* and *presidential.* The usual pattern here involved the attachment of an affix to an already existing word; thus *deputy* goes back to ME, but *deputize* is first reported from 1730.

ACCOUNTING FOR SOME OF THE WORDS OF MODERN ENGLISH

also-ran. Reporters on horse races often name the first-, second-, and third-place finishers and then list other horses, not necessarily in order of finish, that "also ran." Other reporters transferred the term to other applications, so that, for instance, political candidates who secure few votes may be *also-rans.*

apartment house. Although John Evelyn referred in his seventeenth century diary to living in an *apartment,* the first recorded use of *apartment house* was in an American newspaper in 1876. (The British are still inclined to use *block of flats,* and what an American calls an *apartment* is customarily a *flat* to the Englishman. Charles II and his court are responsible for introducing *apartment* into English; they generally used it in the sense of "room." Returning from French exile in 1660, they revealed their occupational interests by popularizing a number of other French words: *caprice, caress, burlesque, ballet, blonde,* and *brunette.*) In an American railroad journal of 1834, *apartment* had been used for a *compartment* accommodating eight to twelve persons in a passenger car. H.B. Fuller's novel *The Cliff-Dwellers* (1893) gave some popularity to that designation for people living in tall apartment houses.

apple-pie order. Meticulous cooks in the old days did not just dump sliced apples into a crust but arranged the slices carefully in rows. By transference, anything so neatly arranged is said to be in *apple-pie order.*

ballyhoo. The ultimate origin of *ballyhoo* is uncertain. *Ballyhooly,* in Ireland, and *ballahou,* a fast-sailing ship, have been suggested. The South Side Club of Long Island had elaborate initiation rites. Said *Harper's Magazine* in 1880, "Another green South-Sider was sent in pursuit of birds as remarkable as anything in the mythology of the ancients: they were provided with four wings and two heads, and possessed the wonderful power of whistling through one bill while they sang through the other. Subsequent references to the '*ballyhoo* bird' were never relished by the victim of the practical joke." When singing and whistling, as well as dancing, etc., became parts of circus sideshow come-ons, the term *ballyhoo* was (apparently) transferred to this noisy advertising, and later it came to refer to any sort of sensational publicity.

bark up the wrong tree. Sometimes a raccoon, pursued by dogs at night, climbs a tree and then climbs across branches to other trees, leaving the dogs *barking up the wrong tree*. By a transfer of meaning, a person who is misdirecting his efforts is also said to be barking in this manner.

basketball. In the early 1890's James Naismith, a Canadian teaching at the YMCA in Springfield, Massachusetts, nailed two peach baskets ten feet above the floor and made rules for a competitive game with nine players on a side; Cornell in 1892 even had fifty players on each team. Almost immediately the game became internationally popular. It has given rise to many specialized terms, such as *backboard* or *bankboard, center line, dribble, double-dribble, foul line, free-throw circle, three-second violation;* the terms still change somewhat as the rules change.

blurb, bromide. In 1907 American humorist Gelett Burgess (author of "The Purple Cow") ridiculed publishers' practice of putting sensationally commendatory statements on book jackets. For his *Are You a Bromide?* he drew a jacket with a saccharine young woman, whom he named Miss Belinda *Blurb,* who was "blurbing a blurb to end all blurbs." Burgess and Miss Blurb did not succeed in ending blurbs, but a useful new word did enter the language. In addition, *bromide* in the sense "boring person" or "platitude" derived from the book's title; in chemistry, potassium bromide is known to be a sedative.

buccaneer. Tupi or Carib Indians used to smoke the meat of a wild ox over a frame called *mocaen* in Tupi. French sailors of the seventeenth and eighteenth centuries found this meat delicious, prepared it often when they were ashore, adopted the word for the frame as *boucan,* and used *boucaner* as a verb. Many of the sailors were pirates, and the name *boucanier* "one who cures meat on a barbecue frame" was applied to them because of their food preference. Thus our *buccaneer* comes ultimately from an Indian culinary term. As early as 1661 an English book about Jamaica referred to *Buckaneers,* although the author defined them as "Hunting French-men."

bunk. For the meaning "nonsense," *bunk* is a shortened form of *bunkum,* from *Buncombe,* a county in North Carolina. The Congressman from that district in 1820, Felix White, "arose to address the House, without any extraordinary powers, in manner or matter, to interest the audience. Many members left the hall. Very naively he told those who remained that they might go too; he should speak for some time, but 'he was talking only for

Buncombe.' " *Debunk* and *bunco* come from the same source, and *hokum* is apparently a blend of *hocus-pocus* and *bunkum.*

caboose. On the decks of their merchant ships, the Dutch used to have a small box-like kitchen called a *kabuis.* The name entered English in the eighteenth century as *caboose* (or *canboose* or *camboose*). In the nineteenth century, Americans attached a small car at the end of a freight train, for their workmen to ride and eat in, and adopted the name for this appendage. (In England it's called the *brake van.*)

canoe. Columbus reported that the Indians used as a boat a hollowed-out log that they called a *kanoa.* The word quickly entered Spanish as *canoa,* and *canoa* is recorded in sixteenth-century English. John Smith, 1608, referred to *canowes.* The present spelling has been used in English since the eighteenth century.

carpetbagger. George Rose, in *The Great Country* (1868), wrote, "Many of them are what the Southerners call 'carpet-baggers,' men travelling with little luggage and less character, making political capital out of the present state of affairs." The "little luggage" was often a *carpetbag,* a suitcase made of ordinary carpeting. Early carpetbaggers were also called *carpetbag adventurers, carpetbag gentry,* and *carpetbag scrubs.*

casket. In 1863 Nathaniel Hawthorne wrote, " 'Caskets'!—a vile modern phrase which compels a person . . . to shrink . . . from the idea of being buried at all." *Casket* was used in English as early as 1467, generally to mean a box for holding valuables, like Portia's "caskets" in *Merchant of Venice,* but its employment as a euphemism for *coffin* is apparently an Americanism originated in Civil War days. (See also *mortician.*)

coeducation, coed. In 1852 the *Pennsylvania School Journal* commented thus on *co-education:* "The instruction of males and females in the same room and in the same class, is supposed by many to be an evil; and, as such, it is avoided in large towns, by the separation of the sexes into different schools." By 1902 a new fear was being voiced, as a Chicago newspaper implied: ". . . it is probable that the coeducational system may be continued at the Northwestern without any danger of the institution being converted into a female seminary." *Co-ed* was first reported in 1889, and by 1900 *Dialect Notes* said it was "used generally."

crawfish. *Crayfish,* from Old French *crevice,* existed in ME as *crevice* or *crevisse,* but because the creature lives in water the ending was early confused with *vish* "fish." In the United States this crustacean became commonly known as *crawfish,* although purists still write and say *crayfish.* When in difficulty, the crawfish rapidly moves backward. Americans began using the word as a verb describing this movement, and soon were applying it to human activities. A quotation dated 1842: "I crawfished out of that place monstrous quick, you may depend." In 1850 "craw-fishing" was used in a reference to withdrawing a set of resolutions.

date. A farm boy, with little free time, often had to make an engagement with his girl several weeks ahead of time, on a particular *date*. The engagement itself became known as a *date* during the nineteenth century; e.g., George Ade's *Fables in Slang* (1899) has a reference to "her Date Book." The noun gradually extended to verb use, although the Kansas City *Star* as late as 1934 felt it desirable to use apologetic quotation marks in "An Emporia girl who 'dates' a wrestler . . . ."

Dixie. Back in the days when banks were authorized to issue their own currency, a New Orleans bank issued ten-dollar bills with a large DIX (French for "ten") printed on each side. *Dixie* became a nickname for New Orleans, and then, reinforced by chance through association with the *Dixon* of *Mason-Dixon line,* became a nickname for the entire South.

eggs Benedict. Why should eggs topped with hollandaise and lying on broiled ham above toasted halves of English muffin be called *eggs Benedict?* W3 says cautiously, "prob. fr. the name *Benedict.*" The *American Heritage Dictionary* says with assurance, "Invented by Commodore E.C. Benedict (1834–1920), American banker and yachtsman." With equal assurance Wilfred Funk gives the credit to a New York "man-about-town and member of New York's café society," Samuel Benedict, who in 1894 had the chef at the Waldorf-Astoria prepare the dish (but with bacon instead of ham) as a cure for a hangover. Take your choice.

gangster. *Gangster* was a late nineteenth-century coinage for members of political *gangs* who sometimes used physical violence on election days. The word became most widely used, though, during the Prohibition Era of the 1920's, when *gangsters* trafficked in illegal liquor and then branched out into *hijacking* (a word of unknown origin that also became widely used in the 1920's), prostitution, and other activities.

gat. The Union forces in the Civil War made some use of a machine gun, the *gatling gun,* invented by Richard J. Gatling of Indianapolis. Twentieth-century writers began using *gatling,* then *gat,* as slang for a pistol or a revolver. Whether gangsters made frequent use of the term is dubious.

gerrymander. Elbridge Gerry, an early governor of Massachusetts, was partly responsible for dividing his state into districts so that his political party would benefit. On the map, one of these districts happened to have the shape of a salamander. Painter Gilbert Stuart noted the resemblance, decorated the map with head, wings, and claws, and called the result a *gerrymander.* The name for the shameful procedure, like the procedure itself, still exists; after each census, politicians use the excuse of population shifts to attempt a little more gerrymandering.

go haywire. After 1828 hay was compressed by machine, and the bales were fastened together with *haywire,* also called *baling wire.* But the wire sometimes became badly tangled, even winding itself around parts of the machinery, the workmen, or the horses' legs. In broadened use, anything that does not function or turn out properly may be said to *go haywire.*

hickory. The different guises assumed by Indian words before they settled down to present forms are well illustrated by *hickory.* Here are early spellings recorded in America:

1608—pawcohiccora	1618—pockerchicory	1634—pokickery
1653—pohickery	1671—hickery	1705—hiccory
1792—hickory		

high-muck-a-muck. Although seldom used today, this term was once popular slang for "a pompous person," "a person of importance." (Another slang name for such a person was *big bug.*) In the Indian language called Chinook Jargon, *hiu* meant "plenty" and *muckamuck* meant "meat and drink." A person with plenty to eat and drink, or the act of eating and drinking heartily, could be called *hiu muckamuck.* An Oregon newspaper in 1856 advertised "*Hiou Muckamuck* of all kinds, but *Halo Lum* [no rum]."

hobo. Although the origin of *hobo* is unknown, one theory is that migratory farm workers were called *hoe boys* and that the term was altered in pronunciation to *hoboes.* Some such workmen were less fond of work than they were of wandering. Quite early they were called *tramps,* but a newspaper dated 1889 said, "The tramp has changed his name, or rather had it changed for him, and now he is a '*Hobo.*'"

hoodoo, voodoo. *Voodoo* is a New Orleans variant of *hoodoo,* which is an African word referring to a person or thing that supposedly would cause bad luck. In the West Indies, voodoo worship proved troublesome to slave owners—so much so that in 1782 the governor of Louisiana forebade bringing in any more Negroes from Martinique (and later Santo Domingo), saying that such slaves were "too much given to voudouism and make the lives of the citizens unsafe." Nevertheless "voodoo doctors" flourished in Louisiana through much of the nineteenth century, as did various voodoo practices.

hotel, etc. *Hotel* and *hostel* are from the same source: Old French *hostel* became later *hôtel.* The English first used *hotel* in the seventeenth century to refer to a large French residence, but by the eighteenth century it meant "an elegant inn." Tobias Smollett in 1765 complained about "The expence of living at an hotel." With the coming of automobiles to the United States, it proved desirable to have lodgings where one could drive to the door; *cabins, tourist cabins, tourist lodges,* and *tourist homes* came into being. The blend *motel* "motor hotel" came in a little later, and now near some airports are *airtels.* Other variants include *motor lodge, motor inn, autotel,* and commercial names like *Travelodge.* A tour sponsor advertises a trip down the Amazon on a *boatel.*

julep. In medieval times the English borrowed *iulep* or *iuleb* from the French, but the word has been traced back to Persian *gul-ab* "rose-water." In England a julep was only a sweet syrupy drink, often used to hide the taste of bitter medicine. When Americans, probably in the eighteenth century, began mixing whiskey or brandy with sugar, ice, and mint, the celebrated *mint julep* was born.

jumbo. P. T. Barnum, the great showman of the nineteenth century, exhibited a 13,000-pound elephant called *Jumbo.* The name is African in origin. It may be part of *mumbo-jumbo,* signifying an evil spirit that frightened quarrelsome women, but more likely it is akin to Gullah *jamba* "elephant." Broadened in application, it now occurs in expressions like "jumbo peanuts" or "jumbo tube of toothpaste."

Kodak. One of the few made-from-scratch words in English. George Eastman, inventor of a small camera ("You press the button, we do the rest") in 1888 wanted a unique name for it. Considering *K* a strong letter (it was also the first letter of his mother's family name), he tried various combinations beginning and ending with *K,* and finally settled on *Kodak.*

Kriss Kringle, Belsnickel. Another name for Santa Claus (from the Dutch) is *Kriss Kringle,* from the German *Christkindlein* "Christ child." In parts of Pennsylvania Dutch country the same generous person is known as *Belsnickel* or *Belschnickel;* its source is *Pelz* "fur" and *Nickel* "Nicholas."

land-office business. From the Maryland Archives, 1681, the *Dictionary of Americanisms* quotes, "An Act relating to the *Land Office* also passed in these words." Land offices were usually run by government agents who transacted business concerning public lands. In boom times they were extremely busy. By extension any thriving concern was later said to be doing a *land-office business.*

lobby. Old High German *Laube* meant "arbor." By extension this became "a covered walk," then "anteroom." People wanting to influence legislation in America began waiting in anterooms or lobbies until the legislators emerged and could be buttonholed. Since they were in a lobby, they began to be called *lobbyists,* and their job obviously was *to lobby.*

lot. OE *hlot* referred to an object, such as a piece of wood, drawn from a container to settle a dispute. Each disputant would cast in his *hlot,* and someone would draw blindly to determine the winner (or loser). The word *lottery* refers to this practice, which was common among Teutonic people. When other methods were used to make decisions by luck, the term *lot* was extended to them. "Man's *lot* in life" reflects the idea that chance determines what happens to us. In the American colonies, when land was assigned by a drawing, each parcel of land was called a *lot;* today we may buy a city *lot,* a cemetery *lot,* etc. The sense of "many," as in *lots of* and *a lot of,* may be derived from the fact that one who owns a number of *lots* (either "chances" or "pieces of land") is considered well off: "He has lots of money."

maverick, gobbledygook. Samuel A. Maverick (1803–1870) was a Texas cattleman who did not brand his calves; he lost many of them because unscrupulous neighbors put their brands on his calves, derisively calling them *Mavericks.* Since that time any person, like Maverick, who does not conform to the custom of his group has come to be called a *maverick.* Another Maverick, Congressman Maury Maverick, coined *gobbledygook,* a word that he applied in 1944 to inflated language like that in many speeches and government publications. "It must have come in a vision. Perhaps I was thinking of the old bearded turkey gobbler back in Texas who was always gobbledygobbling and strutting with ludicrous pomposity. At the end of this gobble there was a sort of gook." As Chairman of the Smaller War Plants Corporation he prohibited his subordinates from using such language. "Anyone using the words *activation* or *implementation* will be shot."

mortician, etc. Modeled on *physician, mortician* was coined c. 1895. Morticians, like the general public, are reluctant to refer directly to death; therefore euphemisms like *pass away, go to his reward,* etc., have long been common. Undertakers have of late liked to be called *funeral directors.* Other euphemisms associated with their craft include *patient, casket (q.v.), case, slumber-robe* "shroud," *funeral car, reposing room, funeral home, funeral parlor, mortuary, funeral chapel, mortuary consultant, memorial park, burial abbey, mortarium,* and *crematorium.* The suffix *-ician* has also appeared in *beautician, cosmetician, fizzician* "soda jerk," *lubritician* (who works in a *lubritorium*), *radiotrician, shoetrician,* and even *whooptician* "college cheerleader." (Mencken's *American Language,* Supplement I, pages 565–639, offers hundreds of examples of American euphemisms and their opposites, dysphemisms.)

Ms. Apparently *Ms.* as a title for a woman dates back to 1950. A note in *Word Study* (October, 1950) says: "An old problem, with a suggested solution, is discussed by Roy F. Bailey, of the Bailey-Krehbiel Newspaper Service in Norton, Kansas. Mr. Bailey believes that we should have a word with which to address a woman whether she is married or single. Many women sign their names without indicating their marital condition. Many firms, when they are unable to discover what that condition is, write 'Miss.' Mr. Bailey suggests 'Ms.,' to stand for either *Miss* or *Mistress* and as an equivalent of 'Mr.' "

new deal. Franklin D. Roosevelt named his economic policy the *New Deal,* but he did not coin the phrase. Mark Twain, in *A Connecticut Yankee* (1889), where the Yankee was urging political reform in King Arthur's court, wrote, "It seemed to me that what the nine hundred and ninety-four dupes needed was a new deal." No doubt card players had used the term more literally long before that.

poinsettia. A South Carolina politician, J. R. *Poinsett,* Secretary of War under President Van Buren, was later a special minister to Mexico. There he found, and brought back to the United States, the showy red and yellow flowers that now bear his name. We pay him homage each Christmas.

potato, tomato. Both *potato* and *tomato* entered English from Spanish. The Spaniards had adapted their *patata* from *batata* of the Tainos, a West Indian people now extinct, and had taken *tomate* from Mexican *tamatl.* The Irish were the first Europeans to cultivate potatoes extensively, Irish Presbyterians introduced potatoes to New Hampshire in 1719, and the 1845 "potato famine" in Ireland drove many Irish families to America; for these reasons the white potato is often called *Irish potato.* An entirely different plant, the *sweet potato,* was originally a tropical vine; Americans gave it its name because it is sweet and because the tubers grow underground like potatoes. The tomato was often considered poisonous, but it was also believed to be an aphrodisiac; hence its French name *pomme d'amour* "apple of love." (The Italian is *pomi d'oro* "apple of gold.") In French, potatoes are *pommes de terre* "apples of the earth."

Pyrex. An interesting combination of English and Latin. In 1915 the Corning Glass Works perfected a pie pan of heat-resistant glass. They considered naming it *Pie King,* but then thought that a little Latin would add elegance: *Pie Rex,* which was changed to *Pyrex.* Now much cookware other than pie pans bears the same name.

sidehill dodger. Mid-nineteenth century Americans enjoyed tall tales, especially about fictitious animals. One of these was the *sidehill dodger* or *guyascutus,* whose legs were longer on one side so that he could easily walk around hills (if he always went in the same direction). The female was *guyascuta;* the male and female names were sometimes shortened to *cute cuss* and *cuter cuss.* Other names for the creature were *gyanosa, lunkus, prock, ricaboo racker,* and *sidehill gouger.* The prock, a Western creature, even had a mock-scientific name, *perockius Oregoniensis.* (See Supplement I of Mencken's *American Language,* pages 250–51, for information about other marvelous creatures.)

spellbinder. The verb *to spellbind* "to hold as in a spell" has been in English at least since the early nineteenth century. However, in the United States of the 1880's, political oratory reached a flowery climax, and especially persuasive speakers became known as *spellbinders.* Thus the New York *Tribune* in 1888 describes a dinner given at Delmonico's by "the Republican Orators—'Spellbinders'—who worked during the recent campaign."

stool pigeon. An 1871 book about Americanisms defines *stool pigeon* as a decoy pigeon "with its eyes stitched up, fastened on a stool, which can be moved up and down by the hidden fowler." (*Stool crows* were mentioned as early as 1811.) Figuratively a human decoy might also be called a stool pigeon; thus Washington Irving in 1836 wrote, "One man . . . was used like a 'stool pigeon,' to decoy the others." One method of decoying, or betraying, one's fellows is to "squeal" on them, and a 1901 publication uses *Stool-pigeon* and *Squealer* as synonyms.

stump. When settlers were clearing land, the removal of stumps was the most difficult part of the job; sometimes an extra large stump would have to remain until it rotted. Gradually anything else very baffling or difficult was said to *stump* a person.

teddy bear. Named for Theodore Roosevelt, who was once shown in a cartoon with his back turned to a bear cub that he refused to shoot. Since small toy bears were popular with children at that time (1902), the toys took their name from this incident.

telephone. Americans, like the British, have tended to go back to Latin and Greek roots for the names of many inventions and scientific discoveries. Alexander Graham Bell's invention takes its name from Greek *tele* "far" and *phone* "sound, voice." *Telephone* occurs in many combined forms, such as *telephone booth, call, directory, exchange, girl, message, operator, pole, receiver,* and *stand,* as well as in such words as *telephoner, telephonic, telephonically,* and *telephony.*

turkey. Centuries ago an African guinea-fowl became widespread in *Turkey.* Early American settlers saw large wild birds that they confused with such guinea-fowls and hence called them *turkeys,* even though there is no relationship. Even Linnaeus, the eighteenth-century founder of Linnaean nomenclature, was confused, assigning the scientific name *Meleagris* to the native American bird, although the African-Turkish fowl is the only one entitled to it. So the mainstay of our Thanksgiving dinners exists under two misnomers.

washout. At first a literal term for the washing away of part of a road or railroad track, *washout* gradually acquired the figurative meaning "failure." Obviously a washout could cause failure to reach one's destination. Miners used the term to refer to sluice boxes that contained no gold after the washing process was complete.

CLASSROOM ACTIVITIES

Noah Webster

A panel discussion of Webster's life and his influence on the language can be rewarding. The G. and C. Merriam Publishing Company of Springfield, Massachusetts, long the publishers of the official Webster dictionaries, can supply useful materials or suggest sources of materials.

British Attitudes Toward American English

Several students may read in Mencken for details about what Englishmen have said about American English, and report to the class, giving examples. See Chapter I in *The American Language* and Chapter I in Supplement I. For a briefer account, see Chapter 2 in J. N. Hook's *The Story of American English.*

The Indian Name Game

Give your students one or more early spellings of the Indian names for familiar animals, plants, etc., and ask them to guess what the word is today. If necessary, provide clues such as "It gives off a bad odor," "It is a tree," etc. The following is a possible list.

aoutem (totem)

appossoun (opossum)

isquonteraquash (squash)

maskinouge (muskellunge)

moggizons (moccasins)

moosu (moose)

munnawhattecug (menhaden)

otchock (woodchuck)

papaios (pawpaw)

pappouse (papoose)

ponap, appones (pone)

powah, powwas (powwow)

putchamin (persimmon)

rahaugcum, aracoune (raccoon)

segankw, squunck (skunk)

tacca hacan, tamahaac (tomahawk)

It Makes Sense To Call It a _____

Early settlers tended to attach simple, rather descriptive names to what they found in America. Ask a small group of students to use the following list and prepare a set of questions like "What would you have called an insect that eats potato leaves?" (*potato bug*) The group then asks the questions of their classmates, who attempt to think of the names actually used. (This exercise is especially interesting to urban children, to whom some of the names may be unfamiliar.)

bluejay	bullfrog	bullhead	butternut	canvasback
catfish	copperhead	eggplant	foot muff	garter snake
groundhog	ground squirrel	June bug	katydid	lightning bug
mockingbird	muskrat	peanut	popcorn	(firefly)
razorback	roasting ear	slippery elm	sweet potato	rattlesnake
				underbrush

Georgianisms of 1827

In 1827 a Baptist minister from New York compiled a list of expressions he heard in Georgia, including *tote* "carry," *monstrous* "very," *whole heap of* "many," *et* "ate," *crittur* "horse," *scrouge* "crowd" (*v.*), *wrench* "rinse," *raised* "brought up," *proud* "glad," *holp* "helped," *truck* "medicine," *get shut of* "get rid of," *bar* "bear" (*n.*), *Alabam* "Alabama," *Kaintuc* "Kentucky." Ask your students whether now, 150 years later, they ever hear any of these expressions. If so, are they confined to one geographical area? Do your students themselves use any of the expressions? (A similar list, followed by similar questions, could be prepared for New England on the basis of Lowell's *Biglow Papers,* and one for the far West on the basis of Mark Twain's *Roughing It.*)

George Washington's Spelling and Pronunciation

Washington's spelling (at least when he was a boy or young man and was keeping diaries) provides clues to Virginia pronunciations of the eighteenth century. Thus his *ams* suggests the *r*-less pronunciation of *arms;* he wrote *plaister* for *plaster, pumpion* for *pumpkin, quishion* for *cushion, ploorees* for *pleurisy.* If your library contains any unmodernized excerpts from his diaries, one or two students may try to draw some conclusions about what his spellings seem to reflect concerning his pronunciations.

American Place-Names

A student may report on George R. Stewart's delightful book *Names on the Land.* Still more information is in Stewart's later book, *American Place-Names,* which is in dictionary format; its introduction provides a useful and thorough classification of the "mechanism of origin" of place names. More elementary is the chapter "Names Over America" in J. N. Hook's *The Story of American English,* which classifies names as mainly historical (*Pennsylvania*), descriptive (*Oak Grove*), reflective of ideals (*Independence,* religious names), and humorous (*Rabbit Hash*). Incidentally, the study of the origin of names is called *onomastics.*

Patterns of Immigration

Let a class pool its knowledge concerning who settled where in the United States—e.g., Dutch in early New York, Mexicans in California, etc. Use of pins on a map may help to clarify the extent and nature of the influence of foreign settlements on American English.

Place-Names from the Ancients

What names of places in your state come from mythology, ancient history, or the Bible? As an example, here are a few from Illinois: *Antioch, Argo, Athens* and *New Athens, Bethany, Carthage, Cicero, Crete, Eureka, Flora, Hebron, Lebanon, Mount Carmel, Mount Olive, Nebo, Orion, Palatine, Palestine, Paris, Sparta, Thebes, Troy, Zion.*

If You Drive in England

Some British road signs baffle American motorists. Your students may try to decode these:

BENDS (sharp curves)
DEAD SLOW (reduce speed)
DIVERSION 100 YARDS (detour 100 yards ahead)
END OF PROHIBITION (end speed zone)
LAY-BY 100 YARDS (emergency parking 100 yards ahead)
NO STOPPING ON VERGE (no parking on shoulder)

ROAD LIABLE TO SUBSIDENCE (road with holes, dips, or bumps)
ROUNDABOUT (traffic circle)

(I was puzzled by RUNNING IN, in the back windows of some British motor cars, usually new ones. I decided that it must mean that the car was being "broken in," and hence could be expected to travel slowly.)

Mark Twain as Wordmaker

When your students are reading Mark Twain, ask them to be alert for interesting linguistic twists. Among other of his characteristics was a willingness to coin words: *barbed wire, billiard parlor, cussword, dust-storm, ex-convict, forty-niner, hay-ride, press notice, race-prejudice,* and *wild west* are attributed to him by C. Merton Babcock, as well as others less known today: *disenthuse, humanbeingship, jumbulacious, mental telegraphy, perhapser, psychologizer, Shakesperiod, soda-squirter, type girl, uncledom,* and *vinegarishly.* (*Word Study,* October, 1966, p. 2)

The Moment of Truth

Aficionados of Hemingway, especially if they know any Spanish, may note bullfighting terms borrowed or translated from that language. *Matador* and *picador* are two obvious examples. Less obvious is *the moment of truth,* a direct translation of *el momento de la verdad.*

Words from Sports

Students may think of the technical names used in any sport with which they are familiar, and discuss the probable origin of the names. Most often they will find that the names are simple, direct, and descriptive; e.g., *two-base hit, end run.* But sometimes the terms are metaphorical and somewhat poetic: *grand slam, picking foul, red-dogging, hashmarks,* etc.

Where Do You Stay Overnight, and Where Do You Eat?

Students may enjoy thinking of the various names given to places that accommodate travelers. (See *hotel,* page 280.)

Signs representing places to eat may also be interesting. A place advertising EATS (subjective judgment based on experience suggests) is likely to serve poorer food than one with the sign RESTAURANT. Well-traveled students may attempt to arrange in probable order of excellence places whose signs say *dining room, coffee shop, eat, café, cafeteria, grill, chuckwagon, buffet, diner,* etc. For further exercise in semantics, students may consider more or less pejorative names for places to eat: *beanery, eatery, hashhouse, greasy spoon,* etc.

Slang of World War II

Let your students try to figure out the meanings of these slang terms used by American soldiers or sailors in World War II. (They'll be re-creating an era.)

alligator (landing barge)
armored cow (canned milk; *sea cow* in the Navy)
Army banjo (shovel)
barrel (floating mine)
battery acid (coffee)
beep (small jeep; a *peep* was a still smaller jeep)
bird-dogging (dancing with another soldier's girl)
bloomers (gun covers)
bubble-dancing (washing dishes in KP)
collision mats (pancakes)
costume jewelry (officer's insignia)
dog show (foot inspection)
dog tags (identification tags)
flat top (aircraft carrier)
general's car (wheelbarrow)
grass (salad)
greasepot (Navy cook)
gremlins (mythical little troublemakers)
gruesome twosome (Army shoes)
hashburner (a cook)
homing device (furlough; technically, a device for guiding a missile)
jamoke (coffee)
mosquito boats (Patrol-Torpedo boats; also called *P-T's*)
mud on a shingle (hash on toast)
ninety-day wonders (officers with only three months of training)
red lead (ketchup)
ride the beam ("Eyes front")
second Louise (a WAC second lieutenant)
serum (strong drink)
sugar report (a letter from one's girl)
superman suit (long underwear)
tin can (destroyer)
tin fish (torpedo)

umbrella (protective screen of fighter planes)

warphans (children of parents killed in the war)

A Project for Future Cooks

Girls (and possibly some of the boys) may be interested in tracing the origins of food names. One way to proceed is to have volunteers examine various cookbooks and note names like *coq au vin* or *spaghetti* that do not appear natively English. Then they may look up derivations in a dictionary. They will find, for instance, that the Italian source of *spaghetti* means "string."

Modern Shortenings

Spend a few minutes exploring with a class the ways that some modern people, especially in service occupations, tend to shorten expressions that they use frequently. Thus an elevator starter may say "Oppkar. Goynop." "Donkar. Goyndon." The barker outside a popular movie house may promise "Plennyseatsnabalkny." The policeman may exhort "Keymoovun." The waitress shouts to the cook "Scramltoowisydafrench." "Lemawf," the subway guard orders. (And "Wadjasay?" is the sentence most often spoken by Americans.)

The Do-It-Yourself Blender

It's fun to blend some of your own words, following a pattern similar to that of *brunch: brupper* (breakfast and supper), *linner* (lunch and dinner), *misnack* or *mack* (midnight snack), *garan* or *garcan* (garbage can), *doiler* (double boiler), *kink* (kitchen sink), *blamp* (bed lamp), *broolippers* (bedroom slippers), *toosh* (toothbrush). Your students can quickly coin another dozen.

The *in* Thing

At the time of this writing, *in* is in in *sit-in, teach-in, kiss-in, love-in,* and countless other compounds. Maybe the fad will have died before you read this, but if not, let your class compile an *in*-list, define the terms informally, and perhaps invent a few new ones. Otherwise, do something similar for some newly popular in-word.

In Defense of Slang

A member of the G. and C. Merriam editorial staff once wrote, "No more vivid descriptive word was ever coined than *rubberneck*." He may have been right, for the word creates an instant picture of a person whose head turns every which way as if it were mounted on a rubber neck. Other picturesque words, once slang if not now, include *bellhop* and *lame duck*. What modern slang words are also picturesque? What others, in contrast, are blah? Which are more likely to survive?

The Language of Advertising

Study of a few current magazine ads may have linguistic value. Students note the choice of words, brevity, alliteration, etc. Some TV commercials (which often cost more to produce than a full-length program) have been called truly artistic creations. How can such a statement be justified?

Research in Dialects

Roger Shuy, in *Discovering American Dialects* (NCTE, 1967) provides materials useful for students who interview members of their community to explore variants in pronunciation and lexicon. Other suggestions and materials are in J. N. Hook, *People Say Things Different Ways* (Chicago: Scott, Foresman, 1974).

Among the New Words

In the latest yearbooks of the *World Book Encyclopedia* and the *Encyclopaedia Britannica,* explore with your classes the sections devoted to new words. (See pages 236–239 of this book.) Among other possible questions: To what general fields do most of these words belong? Why? Does borrowing, compounding, or something else appear to be the most frequent source? Was each word needed? Are any of the words old ones to which new meanings have been attached? What recent words can you think of that have not been included?

10

What Happens to Words

In previous chapters we have noticed, in passing, the ways in which many words have entered the language and what has happened to them after they got in. In this chapter we'll classify the processes more systematically, using additional examples as well as some previously mentioned.

Your students can profit from awareness of some of the ups and downs of word life: Words are conceived and born; some die in infancy but others flourish; many undergo physical changes; some "go bad" and others become sedate citizens; some reach out and encompass wider territories, but others are restricted to a narrow niche; many have offspring of their own. The vicissitudes of words, which are human creations, can be as great as those of their creators. If your students come to think of words as living, changing things, they can use them more perceptively and can read literature with greater sensitivity.

HOW WORDS ENTER THE LANGUAGE

Borrowings from Other Tongues

Suppose that the Anglo-Saxons had been completely isolated from other peoples, and remained so through the centuries. What would today's English vocabulary be like? It would unquestionably be much smaller than it is, although no doubt it would be considerably larger than it was in King Alfred's day. Some Anglo-Saxon words would have taken on additional meanings; some would have been put together as compounds; kennings— figurative expressions like *wave-traveler* "boat" and *whale-path* "sea"—

would probably have become more numerous; affixes would have been attached to existing words to form other parts of speech. But without borrowings, the language would probably lack names for some now familiar concepts and things (partly because the concepts and things would themselves not have reached the Isles), and it would certainly lack the rich variations and· shadings that it now has.

Of the 20,000 most-used words in Modern English, less than a fifth are traceable to Anglo-Saxon. (In a running count, though, the proportion is much higher because of the frequent repetition of Anglo-Saxon words like *the, and,* and *he.*) Beyond the 20,000, the fraction from Anglo-Saxon shrinks steadily, so that of 100,000 most-used words less than a tenth are of native stock. Well over three-fifths of our words come from Greek, Latin, or Latin-derived languages, especially French. The remaining fraction consists of miscellaneous borrowings from languages around the world.

In this book we have traced much of the borrowing and have noted how historical events have resulted in growth rings of varied thickness. The contributions of Celtic, early Latin, and Scandinavian, though important, were numerically very small. Norman French provided a much thicker growth ring, and Greek and Latin during the Renaissance the thickest of all. Since that time each ring has been a mélange, with Latin and its descendants occupying most of the space, but with Greek, American Indian, Asiatic tongues, and others speckled through the mixture.

Words from Scratch

"Speaking generally, we may say that no word is ever created *de novo,*" says Ernest Weekley in *The Romance of Words.* He mentions *gas* as a possible exception, but comments that its namer was influenced by Greek *chaos.* (See page 171 of this book.) *Kodak* (page 281) is one word that we can say with assurance was a wholly new creation. When anyone attempts to name something, it seems that he tends to adopt or adapt words that he already knows or can find, whether in English or some other language.

Onomatopoeia

Onomatopoeia, also called *echoism,* has resulted in a few hundred English words imitative of sounds. Many of these are animal sounds, such as *bowwow, meow, cackle,* and *tweet.* Interestingly enough, the imitations as rendered in different languages are seldom identical and often not even similar. Thus a French dog barks *gnaf-gnaf,* a Spanish dog *guau,* an Irish

dog *amh-amh,* and a Japanese dog *wung-wung;* a Hebrew cat goes *yimyum*;
a French rooster crows *cocorico* but one in Sweden says *kuckeliku*; a Hungarian pig says *röff-röff,* which is certainly not much like an American pig's
oink.

Other echoic sounds, not generally related to animals, include *bang, burp,
fizz, gurgle, hiccup, hiss, honk, jingle, ping, sizzle, splash, tinkle,* and *zoom.*
It has been argued, though not very convincingly, that some combinations
of sounds tend to suggest certain ideas—that *gl,* for instance, suggests
"light," since it appears in *glare, glaze, glimmer, glint, glisten, glitter, gloss,*
and *glow.* Unfortunately for the theory, *gl* also appears in hundreds of other
words in which there is no hint of light: *gladiator, gland, glean, glide, globe,
gloom,* and *glucose,* for example.

A small number of words are attempts to spell involuntary utterances
like *haha* to designate the sound of laughter. Words for such utterances
tend to rise and fall in popularity. Older literature rather than that of recent
times is most likely to turn up examples of *tehee, pish, tush, pshaw, er* (to
denote hesitation), *fie,* and *pugh* or *phew. Yect* or *yetch* (spellings vary)
may be the leading exclamatory sound of the present younger generation.

Compounding

The joining of two words as one is a productive source of new words,
although less widely employed in English than in German, which has many
compounds consisting of more than three words and twenty or thirty letters.
The practice is an old one: OE has many words like *lygeword* "lying word,"
londwela "land wealth, earthly possessions," *brēostcearu* "breast-care, anxiety." *Barn* goes back to two OE words meaning "barley" and "place," an
example that shows that some compounds are now difficult to recognize.

It is possible to take almost any parts of speech and combine them.
Usually two nouns result in another noun, such as *inkblot,* but not necessarily: the nouns *ship* and *shape* give the adjective *shipshape.* An adjective–
noun combination (perhaps the most common) tends to give a noun:
hothouse, blueberry; a noun–adjective pairing, though, usually gives an
adjective: *footsore, watertight.* Adverbs and nouns most frequently result
in nouns: *downfall, overhead,* or, in reverse order, *kickback, holdup.* An
adverb plus an adjective usually becomes an adjective: *evergreen, downright.* There are many other possible combinations not illustrated here.

In writing or in print, compounds often go through two or three stages.
In the first stage the words are separate: *basket ball.* As the term becomes
better known, it may be hyphenated: *basket-ball.* When it is very familiar,

it often becomes solid: *basketball.* Sometimes, though, one or even two of the stages are omitted, and sometimes systematization is a long time coming. *High school* has been familiar for a century, but only a few publications print it as *high-school* or *highschool;* as a modifier, it is hyphenated by some publishers, as in *high-school courses,* but others prefer *high school courses.*

A special kind of compound is a *blend,* also called a *blend-word,* a *telescopic word,* or a *portmanteau word.* This last term is from the name of a suitcase consisting of two compartments. Of a word like his *slithy*—from *lithe* and *slimy*—Lewis Carroll said, "You see, it's like a *portmanteau* . . . there are two meanings packed up in one word." Carroll was also responsible for *chortle,* from *chuckle* and *snort,* and *galumph,* from *gallop* and *triumph. Brunch* and *motel* are two of the most familiar of the later blends. Others include *electrocute, infanticipate, insinuendo, nucleonics,* and *slanguage,* as well as Clare Boothe Luce's *globaloney—global* plus *baloney* —a word that Mrs. Luce used to poke fun at the "one world" concept. In any successful blend, obviously, the major parts of the parent word must be kept: *motel,* for instance, keeps *mot-* from *motor* and *-otel* from *hotel;* Walter Winchell, in coining *infanticipate,* managed to hold on to all of *infant* and all of *anticipate.*

Affixes and Combining Forms

Another prolific source of new words involves the addition of prefixes or suffixes to existing words, with the result usually being a different part of speech. Let's choose *rare* "scarce" from the thousands of possible examples. The word entered ME from Latin, probably in the fourteenth century. Among its progeny in the next few centuries were these words: *rarefy* (1398), *rarely* (1523), *rarity* (1560), *rareness* (1588), *rarefiable* (1656), as well as *rarefaction* (1603), *rarefication* (1616), and *rarefactive* (1656), in all three of which the Latin verb *facere* "to make" also played a part.

The affixes may be native English or borrowed. Among those from OE are *be-, -ful, -less, mis-, -ness, -dom, -hood, -ish, -ly, un-,* and *-y.* Greek has given us, among others, *-ac, amphi-, anti-, di-, dys-, -ic, -ics, -ism, -ize, peri-, poly-,* and *syn-.* Among the very large number of our affixes from Latin are *ab-, -able* or *-ible, -ance* or *-ence, de-, dis-, -ent, -er, -ess, extra-, inter-, intra-, -ion, -ment, post-, pre-, pro-, sub-, super-,* and *-ure.* (See also pages 187–188.)

Like other features of language, some affixes are popular for a while and then fade. For example, the OE suffixes *-dom* and *-hood* are today seldom attached to form new words, nor are Latin *-culum* and *-bulum*, both of which meant "a place that."

Affixes sometimes occur in disguised forms. Thus the prefix *in-* "not" is *im-* in *impossible*, *ir-* in *irresponsible*, and *il-* in *illiterate*, and the affix *-er* "one who" is *-eer* in *engineer*, *-ier* in *bombardier*. Often ease of pronunciation is the reason for such changes; e.g., *inpossible* would be harder to say than *impossible* is.

The fact that different prefixes may have the same form may cause a little confusion. For instance, *in-* may mean either "not" or "in," the latter being illustrated by *income* and *inweave*. The word *inflammable* (based on *inflame* "to set on fire," where *in-* is merely a verb-formative) now appears as *flammable* on most gasoline trucks and storage tanks because some people believe mistakenly that *inflammable* means "not flammable." *Invaluable*, another confusing word, does contain *in-* "not," but its meaning, instead of "not valuable," is "not capable of being valued or appraised; priceless."

Not the same as affixes are *combining forms*, which are word elements derived from full words rather than from prefixes or suffixes. Examples are *electro-* in *electromagnet*, *micro-* in *microbiology*, and *-logy* in the same word. Such combining forms have a share in many thousands of English words.

Functional Shift

Dictionaries define many words as more than a single part of speech. For example, *chalk* is a noun in *a piece of chalk*, a verb in *to chalk the cue*, and a modifier in *a chalk mark*. *Like* occurs as six different parts of speech in *He looks like her, Do it like she does, I like it, . . . in like manner, . . . a small-like car*, and *I never saw the like*. The process of changing a word to a different part of speech, without adding an affix, is called *functional shift*. Occasionally a purist becomes upset when such a change occurs, arguing for instance that *like* just isn't a conjunction and shouldn't be used as one, or that *contact* is a noun and that its use as a verb is "wrong." Since there are countless precedents for such shifts, and since the language has not been damaged by them, the purist's arguments are largely emotional— he just happens not to like *like* used like conjunctions are.

Functional shift, in contrast to the other methods of word-formation we are looking at, results in new meanings rather than new words. In effect, though, whoever first used *chalk* as a verb was being about as innovative as he would have been had he said *chalken* or something else, for he was naming an action that had not previously been named. For reasons like that, functional shift is generally considered a type of word-formation, although it also illustrates what may happen to a word once it gets into the language.

Words from Proper Nouns

In other chapters we have looked at numerous examples of common nouns based on proper nouns; e.g., *badminton, bedlam,* and *begonia.* There are also examples of proper nouns becoming verbs, such as *bowdlerize* or *boycott,* which can be either noun or verb; *chartreuse* is a noun or an adjective; *chauvinistically* (see *chauvinism,* page 241) is an adverb. One of the surest paths to immortality is through getting a form of one's name into the dictionaries; probably few people today would remember the fourth Earl of Sandwich had this not happened to him.

Fictional characters, too, may be immortalized, though some tend not to lose their capital letters easily; *malapropism, Gargantuan, Lothario, Pollyanna, Don Juan,* and *man Friday* are examples. Mythological figures, especially gods and goddesses, presumably don't need dictionary recognition to attain immortality, but we nevertheless find them in *jovial, martial,* and *terpsichorean.* (See page 182 for a much longer list.)

Common words are often based on names of places. A few examples are *babel, bourbon, bunk, china, hamburger,* and *utopia.*

In their origins, most trade names are formed as other words are, although sometimes spelling gimmicks are used to attract attention. *Kleenex,* for example, is basically a respelling of *clean,* and *Arco, Conoco,* and *Sunoco* are acronyms for names of oil companies. *Vaseline* is a hybrid borrowing of German and Greek words for "water" and "oil." When a trade name becomes well known, there is a tendency to apply it to other similar products; so *Kleenex* is often used for any facial tissue, and *nylon,* a name invented by the du Pont Company, lost its original capital when the privilege of manufacture was sold to other companies. Lawyers for some firms spend much time protecting against infringements, but often in vain, since users often insist on applying words like *Celluloid* and *Coke* to products other than the original.

In all, approximately 3,000 dictionary-recognized common words owe their present existence to proper names.

Two-word Verbs

He ran across a friend is grammatically different from *He ran across a lawn.* The second example uses as its verb *ran,* which is followed by a prepositional phrase, and *lawn* is the object of the preposition *across*. But in the first, the words *ran across* constitute a unit, approximately equivalent to *met* or *encountered*, and *friend* is the direct object of the verb *ran across*. Such two-word verbs (there are also three-word verbs) are sometimes called *merged verbs* or *verb–adverb combinations*. They are becoming much more numerous in Mod E than they ever were before. (See page 226.) Other examples include *cut down on, egg on, lead off, rub off on*, and *set up*. Foreigners learning English have considerable difficulty in mastering the merged verbs, since the combination takes on a meaning not implicit in the words themselves. Thus when you *run across* a friend, you probably aren't running and you don't cross him, and when you *cut down on* something you don't use a knife.[1]

Miscellaneous Word Origins

In the twentieth century acronyms have proliferated. *Acronym* is a recent coinage from Greek *akros* "topmost" (which also appears in *Acropolis*) and *onoma* "name." Acronyms are formed by combining the initial ("topmost") letter or letters of several words, preferably in a pronounceable combination: NOW (National Organization of Women), NASA (National Aeronautics and Space Administration), *radar* (radio detecting and ranging), and *laser* (light amplification by stimulated emission of radiation). One of the earliest was *Dora,* for the British Defence of the Realm Act, in World War I.

In OE and ME, *pease* was both singular and plural; one could say "a pease" or "some pease." But by about 1600 *pease* seemed plural, so a new singular, *pea,* was formed. *Pea* illustrates a linguistic process called *back formation:* creation of a new word by deleting what is erroneously believed to be an affix from an existing word. *Cherry* thus came from OE *ciris* as *pea* came from *pease*. Other examples are *laze* from *lazy, sherry* from *sherris, grovel* from *groveling, sidle* from *sideling, burgle* and *buttle* from *burglar* and *butler,* and *typewrite* from *typewriter*. (Incidentally, in the nineteenth century *typewriter* could designate either the machine or its user; in those days a girl might aspire to become a female typewriter.)

Slang terms are ordinarily created in the same ways that other words are. *Kook* "oddball" is shortened from *cuckoo*. *Oddball* itself is simply a compound to which a new meaning has been attached. Many slang terms

---

[1] An attempt to help Japanese users of English with this facet of language is Ryoji Inoue and J. N. Hook's *Two-Word Verbs,* published in Tokyo by Kaitakusha in 1970. The book lists, classifies, and defines about 800 of these verbs.

are only generalized and constantly changing expressions of approval or disapproval: *swell, great, real George, the cat's pajamas, cool, tough,* and *lousy, square, from Squaresville,* and *applesauce. Split* "leave" is only a figurative extension of *split* "divide sharply or cleanly." A few slang words may possibly have been coined from scratch; at least no one can with assurance explain the origins of *hep* or *hip, heebie-jeebies,* and the once unbelievably popular *twenty-three skidoo* (which may be a variant of *skedaddle,* whose origin is also unknown).

Literary coinages, too, are like other coinages. Because authors are often rather well educated, they frequently tend to turn to Latin or Greek for their new words, as Milton did for his *pandemonium* and *impassive,* Chaucer for *attention,* Spenser for *blatant,* and H.L. Mencken for *ecdysiast* "strip-teaser" (from *ecdysis,* the scientific name for "molting" or "shedding feathers," from Greek *ekdyien* "to take off"). Many such coinages were the "inkhorn terms," mentioned in Chapter 5, that have never become widely used. Some authors create useful compounds, like Will Irwin's *highbrow* and the much older *lovingkindness* and *noonday* of Miles Coverdale, or *peacemaker* and *broken-hearted* of William Tyndale. Tennyson is given credit for *moonlit* and *fairy tale.* Sir Walter Scott popularized in English some Scottish words such as *glamour, gruesome,* and *raid,* and reintroduced such old words as *fitful* and *thews.* James Joyce coined numberless words (usually distortions of existing words), but apparently none of these coinages have come into general use; nor have humorous coinages like Christopher Morley's *infracaninophile* "lover of the underdog" and Mencken's *booboisie* "bourgeois boobs, middle-class fools."

Getting a Word Accepted

Only a small portion of words coined ever find their way into a dictionary. An "unabridged" dictionary is actually very much abridged. The Third Edition of *Webster's New International Dictionary* (*W3*) contained only 450,000 entries, in comparison with the 600,000 of *W2,* although it had 100,000 new entries; this means that the editors had deleted 250,000 entries between 1934 and 1961. Not all the new words got in; in the twenty-seven year span, chemists alone had developed a quarter million new terms, but only 17,000 of them are in *W3.* (A chemical dictionary devoted exclusively to terms related to carbon could be as fat as an "unabridged" dictionary.)

There are practical reasons, of course, why dictionary editors do not try to include every word. First of all, it would simply be impossible to

find every new word, since many coinages are merely oral. Second, if all
words could be included, the result would be many volumes the size of
the 2,662-page *W3;* few people would buy such a monster, for it would
be both very expensive and difficult to use. Third, not all words deserve
to be included. Some have become obsolete. Some are so highly technical
that perhaps no more than a dozen people would ever need them. Others
are *nonce words,* used only once or a very few times. For instance, a boy
found the misprint *satsified* for *satisfied,* and remarked humorously that it
is the past tense of *sitsified.* The story is "cute," but *sitsified,* a nonce word,
obviously does not belong in a dictionary.

Who decides whether a word is sufficiently useful to be included? The
procedure of Merriam-Webster (and of other dictionary publishers with
large staffs) is to accumulate citations, called "cits" [saIts] for short—
6,200,000 for *W3.* These "cits" are cards that record sentences using the
words, along with the sources and other pertinent information. A word
cited infrequently is likely to be excluded unless it might obviously be important for a considerable number of people to know. The staff gets advice
from outside consultants who, *Time* magazine remarks, "cover every field,
from Knots and Logic, Mosses and Liverworts, to Cocktails and Girl
Guiding." The consultants advise whether a word is worth including, and
help in preparing accurate definitions and customary pronunciations.

Moderately extensive use is the chief criterion for inclusion.[2] Sometimes,
as in space exploration, words become widely known very quickly; Russia
launched its first *sputnik* on October 4, 1957, and on October 5, millions
of Americans were saying and writing the word. *Boondoggle* "to waste
time on pointless work" was coined in 1925 by a scoutmaster, R. H. Link,
with reference to the rather useless plaited leather cord worn around the
neck by Boy Scouts, but the word gained wide currency only in 1936 when
President Roosevelt used the term in contemptuous reference to unproduc-
tive labor. Sometimes a century or more may pass before a word gains
dictionary acceptance, and most words never do. Obviously a coinage has
the best change to live if it fills a need and if it seems to be a clear and
natural way to refer to the thing being named or described.

---

[2] A coinage of mine, *syntacticon,* may serve as an example of words not used often
enough by enough people to be included. It is parallel to *lexicon,* but refers to the
syntactic structures that a person or a language has available; some people have
larger syntacticons that others, and syntacticons vary from language to language,
just as lexicons do. But the word will never find its way into a dictionary unless
other people interested in language start employing it. In other fields, no doubt, many
fairly useful words like *syntacticon* are floating about.

Some words have to beat out competition before becoming accepted. A good example is *automobile.* The first automobile race, between Chicago and Evanston on Thanksgiving Day, 1895, was called a "motorcycle contest" because the word *automobile* was not yet current in America and *motorcycle* was not specialized as it was to be a little later. *Automobile* was attacked by purists, since it smacks of miscegenation (Greek and Latin). A Bostonian thought that *trundle,* an eighteenth century name for a cart or carriage with small wheels, was more appropriate; the driver would be a *trundler,* certainly less clumsy than *automobiler* (neither word ever really caught on). Other suggested names for the new invention were *autogen, autogo* (which led to an obvious joke), *autopher, autovic, autokinet, electromobil, ipsometer, molectros,* and *self-motor.* By about 1910, *automobile* was becoming rather widely accepted in the United States, but it was still not included in the 1928 *OED;* a later supplement labeled it "Chiefly U.S."

If a word does not find its way into an ordinary dictionary, it may still get into a specialized one. The catalog of the multilingual dictionaries published by the American Elsevier Publishing Company lists over 75 such books, some of them consisting of several volumes. Its *Dictionary of Forestry* has 10,000 entries, its *Telecommunication Dictionary* 9,928. Imagine 6,000 words pertaining to *Packaging,* or three volumes of nautical terms! It is perhaps not surprising that the *Medical Dictionary* lists over 35,000 entries, but 1,500 entries in the *Sugar-Beet Glossary* seems astonishingly high to the uninitiated, and the 5,426 entries in the *Dictionary of Rolling-Mill Terminology* may make one wonder about the narrowness of his own linguistic horizons.

Louis Muinzer (*Illinois English Bulletin,* November, 1960) makes the interesting point that a word that stops its spread before attaining dictionary status is often a dialect word within its circle of use. To illustrate, he tells of a mythical Mrs. O'Brien, who creates a delicious chocolate cookie that she whimsically calls *chookie.* Soon her family are talking about chookies, then her neighbors, then others in town. A local woman's editor uses the headline "The Whole Family Will Adore Chookies!" and thus the word spreads through the county. On it goes, and "Thirty years hence, it is a respectable entry in the dictionaries of the world." But, says Muinzer,

. . . [this] fanciful (but not at all unusual) progression . . . might have been halted at any of the numerous dialect frontiers. *Chookie* might have been avoided by the British as an Americanism. Miss Prim might never have used the word in her cookery column, dooming it to local use in Mrs. O'Brien's community. Or perhaps she might have used the word without its attracting notice.

Moreover, Mrs. O'Brien might not have mentioned her confections to the lady next door, or that lady might have found *chookies* an irritating term. For that matter, Mr. O'Brien might have exclaimed, "For God's sake, Margaret, quit using those silly words." In that case the invaluable *chookies* would have vanished into the mists of lost verbiage. The odds against a given word going so far in the world would, in fact, be great. Yet, how did *brownie* (American) come into being if not by this process? Or the internationally known *lady finger* (General English)?

Most new words are nouns, adjectives, verbs, and adverbs—probably in that order. English pronouns, prepositions, and conjunctions very rarely gain new members, although over a period of centuries their forms and to some extent their meanings may change.

WHAT MAY HAPPEN TO A WORD THAT IS IN

Although most words die in infancy or are never known to more than a small group, others grow up to enjoy wide and lasting popularity. But just as people change through the years, so do words. Here we'll look at the major types of change undergone by English words.

Changes in Physical Form

Jeopardy entered English in medieval times, but it has not always been spelled in that way. It came from an Old French chess term, *iu parti,* referring to an "even game" and hence an uncertain chance of winning. Among some twenty early spellings we find *iupartie, ieperte, iuberte,* and *iopardie,* with fewer instances of *jupertie, jeupartie,* and others. Francis Bacon spelled it *ieopardy* in 1597, and when *i* and *j* finally straightened out their differences, the modern spelling *jeopardy* became standard.

Old English *spearua* or *spearwa* finally became our *sparrow,* but at one time or another was also written and printed as *sperwa, spearewa, sparewe, spearuwa, speruwe, sparuwe, sperow, sperrowe, sparou, sparu, sparw, sparoo,* and a few other ways. The invention of printing helped to eliminate orthographic anarchy, and *sparrow* has been the usual form since the seventeenth century.

Since morphemes and the graphemes (letters) that represent them have never corresponded completely in English, there is not an absolutely "right" spelling for a word. Rather, after a time one spelling happens to become the conventionally accepted one. This does not always occur, though; you may still choose *ax* or *axe, brunet* or *brunette, carat* or *karat,* and *cozy* or *cosy* or *cosey* or *cozey* or *cosie* or *cozie,* and find one or more modern dictionaries to uphold your choice. In general, however, each word has acquired a single conventional spelling that teachers and spelling books insist is the only "right" one.

If a word entered the language after the invention of printing, its variations were normally much less numerous than we saw for *jeopardy* and *sparrow*. In 1605, for instance, Shakespeare coined the word *multitudinous* (based on the earlier borrowing *multitude*), and its spelling has never changed. Words coined today are ordinarily given spellings that conform to the most widely accepted conventions, and so are unlikely to exist in more than one form. (The slang *hep—hip* is one exception.)

A special kind of spelling change, called *metathesis*, reflects a change of pronunciation in which two sounds exchange places. Examples include *grass*, once *gærs*, *wasp*, once *wæps;* and *bird* and *third*, in which the sounds of *r* and *i* were switched.

Some words become shorter. Today nobody talks of *periwigs*, but many people wear *wigs*. *Phone* and *photo* are familiar clipped forms, as are *taxi* and *cab* from *taximeter cabriolet*. *Curio* is a shortened and specialized variant of *curiosity*. *Cute, mend, tend,* and *sport* were originally short ways to say *acute, amend, attend,* and *disport*. A *fan* used to be a *fanatic*. A *piano* was originally called in Italian *piano e forte* "soft and loud" (referring to the fact that the pedals may soften or sustain the musical sounds). Nobody today rides an *omnibus* to the *zoological* gardens. *Goodbye* long age was derived from a whole sentence, *God be with ye*. *Propaganda* is not a shortened word, but is one part of *congregatio de propaganda fide* "congregation for propagating the [Catholic] faith."

Seldom is a word lengthened, although *thunder* was *þunor* in OE and *sound* was *soun* in ME. Duplication is illustrated in *bonbon* and *goody-goody*.

Folk etymology also results in alteration of word forms. *Asparagus* doesn't sound very English and is sometimes confused with *grass* so that some folks call it *spare-grass* or *sparrow-grass*. *Belfry* in ME was *berfrey* "tower," but since some towers have bells, people "corrected" *berfrey*, which they thought must be a mistake. *Humble pie* has nothing to do with humility; it was a pie made of *umbles* "scrappy pieces of venison." *Pickax* comes from French *picois*, ME *pikois* or *pikeis*, but the first element was confused with *pick* and the last with *ax*. A creek in Arkansas called by the French *L'Eau Froide* "cold water" became converted by speakers of English to *Low Freight*, but it is now officially *L'Eau Frais*, questionable French for "fresh water." *Smackover*, a town in Arkansas, used to be *chemin-couvert* "covered road," perhaps referring to a covered bridge or to overarching branches; if you say "chemin couvert" rapidly a few times, you can understand how it changed to "Smackover." An English inn, *Goat and Compasses,* got its name from *God encompass us.* Margaret Bryant delightfully illustrates the process of folk etymology by telling of a little girl who didn't like anyone to be *sourcastic* and who was interested in *c-gulls* and *e-gulls.*

The other changes we shall note deal with meanings rather than forms.

Expansion

Words refuse to be narrowly restricted in meaning. That is another way of saying that people keep adding new shades of meaning to existing words. Often they see new, figurative applications of a word, and soon those applications are parts of the complete definition. In 1900, Greenough and Kittredge illustrated the process with the word *power,* from Old French *pouer,* Modern French *pouvoir* "to be able." From this central meaning, they pointed out, eleven distinct meanings of *power* radiated, including, for instance, "physical strength," "moral or intellectual force," the *power* of a number in mathematics, and "an effective quality of style in writing or oratory." The *OED* devotes four of its tightly packed columns to the word, and *W3* offers almost thirty definitions. The original meaning is illustrated in an *OED* quotation dated 1325: "fre power to chese," a phrase meaning that man "is able to" choose freely. But the Bible of 1611 said "By his power and wisdome he built a Temple"; here the ideas' of strength, riches, and leadership appear to have been added. "Ballance of Power" appeared in 1701, with reference to nations rather than individuals. Benjamin Franklin in 1747 referred casually to "a power of attorney"—a specific kind of legal document. The other definitions developed at various earlier and later times.

What has happened to *power* has happened repeatedly to other words. *Run* fills forty-one columns in the *OED.* It is easy to see how some of its figurative meanings developed. A *run* in a stocking is a rapid unraveling. To score a *run* in baseball the *runner* must move fast. In a *run* on a bank the people are in a hurry to get their money out. When an engine *runs,* or a creek *runs* between its banks, or a whisper *runs* through a crowd, there is still the central idea of fast movement. A little more difficult to explain are a *run* in some games of cards, *running* for office, *running* into trouble, and *running* a risk. Compounds like *rum-running,* though, are easily related to the basic sense.

The role of metaphor in expansion of meaning is considerable. Parts and functions of a living body, for example, are often associated with inanimate or even abstract things, so that we may refer to the *hands* of a clock, the *legs* of a table, the *foot* of a hill, the *eye* of a hurricane, an *arm* of the sea, the *heart* of the problem, a *breath* of spring, etc. Words like *short* and *long* describe physical distances but are often transferred to time. We switch words from one physical sense to another ; thus *soft,* a word of feeling, refers to sight in *soft colors* and to sound in *soft music. Warm, cold, sharp, clear, ugly, pretty, sweet, bitter, loud,* and *gloomy* are among the many other words no longer confined to a single physical sense.

Even without such obviously metaphorical extensions, a word can expand its meanings by becoming associated with slightly different things. So *horse* is no longer just a large, animate quadruped, but also a toy (*rocking horse*), a piece of gymnastic equipment vaguely resembling a horse, a colloquial name for the knight in chess, and cavalry (a hundred *horse*). And by functional shift to a verb, one may *horse* someone (give him a horse to ride, or put him on a horse, or flog him like a horse), and in slang one may *horse around* (cavort like a young horse). Among countless other examples of expansion are *joint, jump, kill, knot, light, lodge, loop,* and *loss* (a few quick choices from one part of the alphabet).

Generalization and Specialization

Some words start out with rather specific meanings and gradually attain more general meanings ; others reverse the process. In OE and other Old Germanic languages a *þing* was primarily a judicial assembly, a kind of court or council. But by extension any matter brought before the þing was also called a *þing*. Outside the court it became possible to refer to any matter of concern as the *þing*. By the fourteenth century the word was approximately equivalent to *something, anything,* as in Wycliffe's ". . . we shulen shewe you a thing." From there it was an easy step to the modern definition of *thing* as "whatever can be perceived, known, or thought to exist, whether real of imaginary." Obviously *thing* now has a much more general meaning than it had in OE.

Here are some other examples of generalization. *Go* (OE *gān*) often was restricted to "walk," but today one may also *go* on horseback, on a ship, in a car, in a plane, etc. One may *sail* on a ship powered by diesels, and what one *drives* no longer need be animate. A *quarantine* is no longer for forty days, the early meaning. *Rum* was and is an alcoholic beverage distilled from molasses or sugar cane, but in the prohibitionists' warnings "Demon Rum" was generalized to mean any alcoholic drink. Once a *mill* was a place where grain was ground into meal, but now there need be neither grain nor grinding, in a textile or steel mill, for instance; a mill is only a place where something is manufactured. *Manufacture* itself illustrates generalization; its root meaning is "make by hand," but now a variety of processes may be used. *Nice* comes from Latin *nescius* "ignorant," passed into French as *nice* "foolish," came into English as *nice* "foolishly fastidious," lost the idea of foolishness, changed the idea of "fastidious" to that of "precise" (as in "a *nice* distinction"), and then made a leap to the meaning of "praiseworthy, pleasant," which is its popular sense today.

Generalization clearly overlaps and may be part of expansion, which has already been discussed. It differs, though, in that the central meaning changes, becomes wider, in generalization, and an older meaning is often lost: the central meaning of today's *thing* is not at all that of OE *þing*.

When a word moves in the opposite direction, it shows specialization. *Girl* long ago meant "young person"; today it means "female young person." *Knave,* like the cognate *Knabe* in Modern German, once meant "boy," then "boy employed as a servant," then "naughty servant," and finally "wicked person, usually male." *Ghost* once referred to any kind of spirit, but today is popularly restricted to "a foggy wraith that haunts houses." In Chaucer's line "And smale foules maken melodye," *foules* meant "birds"; now we limit *fowls* to domesticated birds like chickens and geese. When Shakespeare referred to *deer,* he meant "animals," but today the word covers only animals of the family Cervidae; similarly a *hound* was once any dog, but now is only a hunting dog with certain characteristics; the German cognates *Tier* and *Hund* have not specialized, but retain meanings like those of OE. Other well known examples include *liquor,* formerly "liquid of any sort"; *meat* "any kind of solid food"; *starve* "to die (from any cause)"; *coast,* formerly "side" or "frontier" but now "seacoast";[3] *token,* formerly "sign of any sort" but now often something physical, such as a small payment or a metal slug used for subway fare; and *disease* "discomfort, lack of ease."

Abstraction and concretization may be considered special forms of generalization and specialization, respectively. Louis A. Muinzer mentions *heart* in the sense of "courage, fortitude" and *false alarm* in the sense of "disappointment" as examples of abstraction. Concretization is exemplified by *fastness,* which once had the abstract meaning of "state of being firmly fixed" but then changed to "fortress, stronghold." *Honor* in "your Honor" (addressed to a judge) also shows concretization.

---

[3] Shakespeare has been accused of geographic ignorance because he referred to "the coast of Bohemia," a country with no seashore. But he was no doubt using *coast* as "frontier" or "edge."

Elevation and Degradation

The word *melioration* is sometimes used for *elevation,* and *pejoration* or *deterioration* for *degradation.* All these terms refer to social attitudes toward words. Often, for instance, a word begins in an attempt to ridicule or condemn, but rises in reputability as the thing that it names gains respect: *Tory* and *Whig* were at first pejorative names but later were no more so than American *Democrat* or *Republican.* Alternatively, a word may start out as neutral or favorable and then take on connotations of distaste: *lust* was once an innocent word for "pleasure" but came to mean "excessive or unrestrained sexual craving."

In the nineteenth century and much of the twentieth, words considered profane and those referring to reproductive and excretory acts seldom appeared in print (although occasionally they were suggested by *d——n* or a prurient blank); even Hemingway, in *For Whom the Bell Tolls,* used the word *obscenity* for the "obscenity" itself. But today magazines on coffee tables and in school libraries print the four-letter words unabashed, and *hell* and *damn,* at least, are not infrequent on television. Such words, then, though they have hardly attained high status, are relatively more elevated than they were not long ago.

Back to earlier times. A *knight,* before he became a chivalric figure, was a "servant," and any "warrior" could be called an *earl. Chivalry* itself, in its origins, simply referred to riding on horseback. A *marshall* once held horses, a *chamberlain* was a male chamber-attendant, a *steward* took care of the pigsty, a *minister* was a servant, *bards* and *minstrels* were wandering buffoons, and an *angel* was a messenger. *Enthusiasm* was once associated with madness or at least fanaticism, and was often condemned in the Age of Reason. Later the attitudes toward the referents of all these words became comparatively elevated. So did attitudes toward *Puritans, Quakers, Shakers,* and *Yankees.*

Perhaps more attitudes have moved in the opposite direction; at least degradation can be even more readily illustrated than can elevation. It is well known that a *boor* was once any "peasant" and that a *villain* was a farm laborer (earlier, anyone who lived or worked at a villa). A *lewd* statement was once simply a statement by a layman. A *crafty* person knew his craft, a *cunning* person was "knowing," and a *sly* one was clever and resourceful. *Criticism,* although it can still refer to unslanted evaluation, tends more and more to be considered negative or even hostile, and *censure,* which Shakespeare could use to mean "opinion," has deteriorated to "blame." Anything pertaining to the common people was once labeled *vulgar,* but now the sense of "indecent" has largely taken over for that word. *Suggestive,* formerly equivalent to "suggesting," now often has sexual connotations. *Stink* or *stench* was once no worse than *smell* or *odor* is today. In World War II *collaborator* took on the meaning of "one who helps the enemy." *Fair,* once a term of praise, now most often means "average, passable, not very good." A *demure* maiden was once "modest," but now if a girl is called demure, it is frequently assumed that her modesty is not genuine. The human tendency to procrastinate is revealed in *by and by* and *presently,* which earlier meant "without any delay at all."

Intensifiers, which are words like *very,* lose their strength from over-exposure, and replacements keep filtering in. OE *swipe,* equivalent to our *very,* dropped from the language. Chaucer and his contemporaries used *full*; Chaucer's pilgrims traveled "with ful devout corage," and in *Troylus* we find "Ful unavysed of his wo cominge," which means "Completely unaware of his approaching misfortune"; the usage survives in "You know full well." *Right* and *exceeding(ly)* were other early favorites; Chaucer's Clerk was not "right fat," and Longfellow was echoing an old usage when he said that the mills of the gods "grind exceeding small." *Sore,* as in "sore afraid," is a cognate of *sehr,* German for "very," but is now archaic. The eighteenth century liked *vastly*: something could be "vastly good," "vastly tasty," even "vastly small." *Prodigiously* was tried for a while. *Quite* still survives, but has been weakened from "thoroughly, completely" to a meaning not much stronger than that of *somewhat.* Profanity has been used frequently for intensifying purposes, but *damn(ed) hot* no longer seems much hotter than plain *hot.* Among the favorites of our own century are *real(ly), sure(ly), awful(ly),* and *terrible* (or *terribly*), none of which add much strength. *Very* itself, especially when it occurs frequently, hardly intensifies at all; it is a favorite target for editors' blue pencils.

Euphemisms and Dysphemisms

Stephen Foster entitled one of his songs "Old Folks at Home"; today the wide spread of a euphemism might have resulted in "Senior Citizens at Home." In modern war we send in *reinforcements* instead of *replacements,* which suggests empty spots that the Pentagon prefers to be quiet about. In Nazi Germany millions of Jews might be gassed in an innocently named *Konzentrations-lager* "concentration camp"; prisoners were not "killed" but might be *liquidated.* There are no longer any "poor" or "stupid" children in our schools, but some are *from low-income families, disadvantaged, culturally disadvantaged, culturally deprived, psycho-socially deprived, lacking in cultural opportunities, from depressed areas, minimally prepared, relatively low in accomplishment, intellectually disadvantaged, in need of remediation,* or *mentally handicapped*; no one can count the number of hours spent in U.S. Office of Education projects in trying to find completely inoffensive terminology.

Behind all euphemisms lie such attempts not to offend, or attempts to "make the worse seem the better cause." Kindness is often the motive: if people don't like to be called "old," let's use the supposedly less offensive *senior*; if they don't want to be reminded that everyone "dies," let's substitute *pass away* or *go to one's reward.* Squeamishness about direct reference to reproductive and other bodily needs has also been a factor.

So Victorian ladies not only hid their own legs and discreetly covered the legs of tables and pianos, but also, in eating chicken, ate *drumsticks, dark meat,* and *white meat* so that they would not have to say "leg" or "breast." Their "underwear" was *unmentionables,* and regions south from the navel (I can use euphemisms too) were *private parts.* No one "went to the toilet" but perhaps *excused himself* or *went to wash his hands.* There were no "bulls" in the pastures, but *he* or *the creature* or possibly even a *gentleman-ox* might be there. West of the Atlantic, Noah Webster in 1833 had wanted to bowdlerize the Bible, substituting *peculiar members* for "testicles" (*stones* in the King James Version, which has its own euphemisms), *nourish* for "give suck," *lewd woman* for "whore," *go astray* for "go a-whoring." Americans largely abandoned the venerable word *cock,* substituting *rooster,* and *cockroach* was shortened to *roach.* As late as 1928 a botany teacher in the Ozarks did not dare refer in class to a "maidenhair fern."

We know, from books like Ronald Pearsall's *The Worm in the Bud: The World of Victorian Sexuality* that the Victorians weren't any "better" than other generations, that there were over 50,000 prostitutes in London, and that sexual interests and escapades matched any of today. But in the custom of the time "nice people," especially "ladies," avoided talk about anything even remotely sexual, and if references were unavoidable, indirect terms replaced the direct ones.

But customs and attitudes change. The sex-euphemisms of the Victorians have almost disappeared as a result. Nobody says *with child* or *in a family way* or *in a delicate condition* any more. Subjects like premarital intercourse, abortion, venereal disease, and the menopause are treated openly in prime-time, family TV entertainment. Ours is a much less euphemistic age than that of even a generation ago, but we do have our *senior citizens,* our *custodians* or *supervisors of building maintenance,* our reluctance to say "die," our probably praiseworthy unwillingness to offend with our language.

Maybe it is a plus mark for human beings that we have never had as many dysphemisms as euphemisms. The motive for a dysphemism is to offend, to shock, to anger, to ridicule. Oldtime politicians were expert name-callers. (Read in history books what Lincoln was called: *ape* was one of the kinder terms.) Modern politicians, with a few publicized exceptions, are more genteel, often preferring to avoid direct mention of an opponent. Outside of politics, nicknames for members of ethnic or racial groups are the most frequent dysphemisms: *cheskey, chink, coon, dago, dinge, greaseball, greaser, gringo, harp, hebe, honky, kike, kraut, mick, nigger, polack, roundhead, spook, squarehead,* and *wop* (some of them occasionally capitalized) are only part of a possibly much longer list, all revealing the tendency to separate people into "them" and "us"—with "them" of course deserving derogation because they aren't just like "us." In *All in the Family,* most widely watched TV program in the early 1970's, Archie Bunker, our century's leading dysphemist, used most of these terms, and also constantly called his wife a *dingbat* and his son-in-law a *meathead.* To Archie, the principle of guilt by association applied even to words: "If they live in a *commune,* they must be *communists!*" Earlier Archies had referred sneeringly to Franklin D. Roosevelt's advisers as *eggheads* and members of a *Brain Trust.* In England, to insult a Scot an Englishman calls him a *Scotchman*—an appellation that may lead to a fight.

Obsolescence

Some words outlive their usefulness or are gradually replaced by other words. A word apparently on its way out is called *obsolescent;* if it is still occasionally used but has an oldfashioned flavor, it is *archaic.* (The two adjectives are sometimes used interchangeably, and *archaic* also sometimes is equivalent to *obsolete.*) If the word is not used at all by modern writers, it is most often called *obsolete.* The whole movement toward verbal death is *obsolescence.*

Obsolescence results from any of several causes. One is technical change. When, for instance, modern weaponry replaced *muskets* and *muzzle-loaders,* the terminology associated with those guns disappeared except in the lexicon of antiquarian gun-lovers. More recently the invention of the transistor is causing obsolescence in the names of the more bulky items that the transistor replaces.

Another cause is change in concepts. When Ptolemaic astronomy was superseded by Copernican, some of the words associated with the earlier theory went out. Or when one reads Locke, Hume, Bentham, or other philosophers of a couple of centuries ago, some of their language seems strange because modern philosophical concepts are different.

Historical events like the Norman Conquest result in synonyms from two languages living side by side for a while, but then one of the synonyms frequently drops out. So OE *āwierdan* gave way to *destroy,* from French, and *brōdettan* lost to *tremble.*

Some words die simply because they are not needed. This is why most of the Latinized "inkhorn words" of the Renaissance did not survive: better ways of expressing the same ideas already existed.

The words that do not die—at least while any speakers of the language remain—are for the most part the everyday words that appear in sentence after sentence: especially pronouns, prepositions, and conjunctions, but also those nouns, verbs, adjectives, and adverbs that people use regularly— words like *man, woman, child, eat, drink, run, good, well.* Even these may change in pronunciation, inflection, and spelling, but they tend to remain alive and active in their altered forms.

Why Words Won't Stay Put

Suppose that a language could be invented in which there was a word for everything known to man, and that each word had a single meaning, and that all these words, meanings, pronunciations, and spellings were meticulously presented in a necessarily huge dictionary. Then, in theory, language wouldn't change, because it would be perfect and there would be an infallible final authority to appeal to in case any questions arose.

But, in practice, this wouldn't work, and changes would occur. For one reason, every day there are new discoveries, inventions, ideas, and insights, and new words or new meanings for old words are necessary to name them. For another, few people would master the total contents of our huge, imaginary dictionary, and most people would use words in the ways that seemed "right" to them without bothering to look them up; they wouldn't all use words in quite the same way, and shades of meaning (from expansion, generalization, specialization, elevation, and the like) would inevitably develop. In addition, there are always linguistic rebels who are irked by constraint; they feel, rightly, that language should be a tool but not a vise. "When I use a word," Lewis Carroll's Humpty-Dumpty said, "It means just what I choose it to mean—neither more nor less."

So even in such a situation words wouldn't stay put. No more will they in a world where languages have just "growed" to what they are today. New words will continue to be born, and some old words will die. And every day someone, somewhere (really many someones in many somewheres) will use an existing word in a way not quite like the ways in which it has been used before, and the language will change by that amount.

There is no more point in fighting language change than there is in trying to sweep back the sea. Some teachers may resent the changes and try to eradicate those that they especially dislike, and among the general population there will always be purists who fight on their little battlegrounds about the conjunction *like* and the verb *contact*. Teachers and purists would both be better advised to devote their strength not to such trivia but to constantly insisting upon clarity of thought, expression, and understanding, and to building awareness of the new connotations that words steadily acquire.

CLASSROOM ACTIVITIES

Authors as Wordmakers

Margaret Bryant ascribes a number of words to authors, and asks students to determine the sources used by the authors. (*Modern English and Its Heritage,* Second ed., p. 228)

Jeremy Bentham: international
Gamaliel Bradford: psychography
Thomas Browne: hallucination, retrogression, incontrovertible, insecurity, electricity, literary, medical
Robert Browning: artistry
Edmund Burke: colonization, diplomacy, electioneering
Lewis Carroll: galumphing
Samuel T. Coleridge: pessimism
Thomas Huxley: agnostic, agnosticism
Samuel Johnson: irascibility
Thomas B. Macaulay: constituency
John Milton: pandemonium, Satanic, liturgical
Isaac Newton: centrifugal
William Shakespeare: multitudinous
G. B. Shaw: superman
William Whewell: scientist

Among the fictional characters whose names are sometimes used almost as common nouns are Chaucer's *Pandarus* (who gave us *panderer*), *Legree* (from Harriet Beecher Stowe's *Uncle Tom's Cabin*), Sinclair Lewis's *Babbitt,* and Shakespeare's *Benedict.* Others?

More Words from Proper Nouns

Students may enjoy noting the connection between the common words listed below and the proper nouns from which they came.

(Many more examples are included in the "Accounting for Some of the Words" sections of this book.)

calico	champagne	china	epicurean	fez
jersey	mecca	mesmerism	pasteurize	pheasant
platonic	polonaise	quixotic	spaniel	surrey

Compound Words Today

Students may list compound words found in newspaper or magazine articles, noting their approximate frequency and observing which parts of speech seem to have been put together. (Caution students not to overlook very common words like *overlook* and *income*.)

Creating Words by Affixation

Suppose that the following words existed only in the forms given. By the use of affixes, create variations so that each word may be used as a noun, a verb, an adjective, and an adverb. (Either "real" words or students' coinages may be accepted.)

| ample | auction | civil | claim | code | compare |
| machine | modern | object | person | satire | tragedy |

Example: comparation, compare, comparable, comparably.

Borrowings from Russian

Because of current interest in Russia, students may be interested in looking up the origins and current English meanings of *balalaika, bolshevik, borscht, Pravda, samovar, steppe, troika, tundra, vodka*.

Borrowings from French

In current maganizes about ladies' fashions girls may find a number of borrowings from French, including recent ones. *Boutique* is one example—a word related etymologically to *apothecary, bibliotheca,* and *discotheque,* since all go back to a Greek word for "case."

A Word Safari

Students may choose any word with an interesting etymology and write its story in some such fashion as this: "When speakers of Arabic made a *safari* (which then was any sort of journey) into parts of Africa where Swahili was spoken, the natives borrowed the word and added another, *msafara,* for a group of people who journey together. The English heard *safari* in East Africa, and took it *on safari* to

England. Englishmen began talking about *hunting safaris* and *big-game safaris,* and *on safari* became a familiar expression. *Safari* then *safaried* across the Atlantic, but Americans tended to use it in just one of its meanings, a journey after big game. A movie, *Safari,* made in the 1920's, familiarized millions of Americans with *safari* in this sense."

Different Origins for the "Same" Word

Sometimes words spelled just alike are actually different words and come from different sources. Thus *bit* "part of a bridle," *bit* "a tool for drilling," and *bit* "part of a key" all come from OE *bite* "action of biting; sting; bite"; but *bit* "small piece or quantity" comes from OE *bita* "morsel." Students can locate other examples in a dictionary.

Back Formations

Here are some back formations to add to those on page 298. Students may attempt to guess the earlier form.

automate (automation)	cobble (cobbler)
diagnose (diagnosis)	eavesdrop (eavesdropper)
frivol (frivolous)	hawk "sell" (hawker)
housekeep (housekeeper)	intuit (intuition)
loaf "be idle" (loafer)	locate (location)
orate (oration)	partake (part taker)
peeve (peevish)	process (procession)
sightsee (sightseeing)	televise (television)

Clipped Words

Students may collect words clipped from longer ones: *ad, hood* (*hoodlum*), *mike, phone, sax,* etc. Which of these have largely replaced the longer forms?

Shortenings That Endured

Students will find that these words, besides those mentioned on page 303, are shortened forms: *brandy, cad, chap, gin, hack* (n.), *Miss* (title), *nincompoop, per cent, pert, pros and cons, sweets, van, wag,* "joker."

Professional Writers' Use of Functional Shift

Margaret Bryant (*Modern English and Its Heritage,* Second ed., p. 257) asks students to find the functional shifts in these (and other) phrases: Shakespeare's "sicklied o'er with the pale cast of thought";

"Lord Angelo dukes it well"; Tennyson's "diamond me no diamonds"; Keats's "Lethewards had sunk"; Joyce's "hitherandthithering waters"; Cummings's "the feline she"; Pound's "the lights . . . are pearled"; Lindsay's "bronze-brown wing." Students may be alerted to note others in literature.

More Examples of Functional Shift

Checking a dictionary will reveal that functional shift is by no means new. The noun *crown* was used as a verb in the twelfth century, and so, not much later, were *worship, pride* (oneself), *rust, stream, cripple, hook, spur, dust, pen,* and *gleam.* Early examples of verbs becoming nouns include *a chew, a fall, a look, a miss, a quake, a shove, a show, a weep, a wish.* Why then, asks Donald W. Lee (*Word Study,* May, 1950), should some people now object to the similar *to contact, to loan, to price, to process, to sculpture, to taxi,* and *an assist, a combine, a defy, a raise, a steal?*

Students may provide many examples of names of parts of the body as verbs. E.g., *to beard, to chin, to elbow, to finger, to mouth, to muscle, to skin, to stomach, to thumb, to toe, to tongue.* Or names of occupations: *to barber, to butcher, to cook, to tailor,* etc. Or names of household articles: *to bed, to carpet, to chair, to picture,* etc.

Specialization

By looking in a dictionary at earlier meanings of a word (including the meaning of the word in the source language), students can find many examples of specialization. Besides words mentioned in this chapter, these are good examples: *adventure, ambition, apparition, ballad, fate, goods, lesson, mansion, moral* (n.), *myth, planet, pocket, tyrant, undertaker.*

Generalization

Other examples besides those on pages 305–306: *allergic, assassin, case, forum, injury, layman, philippic, religion.*

Antonomasia

Use of a person's name as a generic word is fairly common: a *Romeo,* a *Scrooge,* etc. Other examples?

Synecdoche and Metonymy

"*Cocktail* lounge" and "a hundred *head* of sheep" are examples of synecdoche, in which a part represents the whole or vice versa. *Glasses* for *spectacles* and *ball and chain* for *wife* illustrate metonymy, which involves reference to something by the substitution of a word that suggests it. Students may spend a pleasant five minutes finding other examples. (Don't worry if they aren't sure which, synecdoche or metonymy, is the proper classification for an example; the basic principles are the same.)

On the Misuse of Hyperbole

First Movie Producer: How's your new picture doing?
Second M.P.: Excellent.
First M.P.: Only excellent? That's too bad!
The anecdote suggests how, as Leo Rosten says, "superlatives drive sobriety out of circulation"—a variation of Gresham's Law. *Terrible, horrible, perfect, terrific, sensational, amazing,* and *astounding* have been used so much that now it is difficult to find words to say what they originally expressed. Perhaps your students can supply some examples of rash hyperbole.

Euphemisms

A few minutes may be spent on recalling euphemisms for *die* or *death, drunk, falsehood,* names of occupations, *pregnant,* and various terms relating to drugs or drug abuse. Also, many expressions like *gosh* or *geewhiz* are euphemisms for profanity.

Figures of Speech in Sports

Sports terms in newspapers afford many examples of how important figurative language is in our lives. Think, for example, of words that sportswriters use as synonyms for the verb *defeat: beat, down, nip, clip, rip, trip, slip past, clobber, maul, stun, stagger, whale, sock, rock, bash, bop, thump, murder, ruin, tip, top, outlast, crush, flog, jolt, drub, dump, belt, rap, slap, drop, lick, tame, halt, batter, punch, slug, sink, torpedo, rout, outgun, shave, edge,* and many more. Students who feel that figurative language is something loved only by poets and English teachers may change their minds when they consider such an array.

What Does It Really Mean?

Many expressions are metaphorical; some of them endure but others don't. Gladys Hasse (*Word Study,* May, 1945) wrote about such expressions that had puzzled her as a child. Find out which of these your students understand; inquire about what the literal meanings would be.

Pete Jensen gave up the ghost today.

He worked only halfheartedly.

His eyes are bigger than his stomach.

He has bats in his belfry.

I was on needles and pins all the time.

She's always up in the air about something.

I'm up against it.

I've barked up the wrong tree.

Handy Words

Various uses of *hand* offer excellent illustrations of how a common word may extend its meaning. Consider these: *farm hands,* writes a clear *hand, hand* of tobacco, twelve *hands* high, on the other *hand, hand* it over, out of my *hands,* be on *hand,* arguments that get out of *hand,* have a *hand* in, a *hand* of bridge, give me a *hand,* the audience gave her a *hand,* near at *hand,* and delivered by *hand,* as well as *handicraft, handiwork, handkerchief, handicap, hand-me-down, handcart, handily,* etc. *Head* and *foot* are among many other words useful for the same purpose.

Terms of Radio, Television, Etc.

Every large new industry adds words to the language, or new meanings for old words. Thus nineteenth-century railroading familiarized people with words like *cowcatcher, brakeman, express office, flying switch, semaphore,* and the names of various types of railway cars. The automobile and its tangential industries have now contributed hundreds more, and radio and television have been responsible for large numbers of technical terms as well as familiar terms like *picture tube, quiz show, soap opera.* Students may list as many such terms as they know in a few fields, and try to figure out why these names, rather than others, were chosen.

For Mountain-Climbers

At a time when mountain-climbing is becoming increasingly popular, some of your students may want to find out what these words mean to the mountaineer: *aiguille, arête, belay, bergschrund, cairn, col, cornice, couloir, courte-échelle, crampons, crevasse, cwm, dent, firn, fohn, glissade, hitch, ice-fall, joch, massif, mouraine, moulin, névé, piton, rappel, rib, screes, sérac, snow-bridge, traverse, verglas.* Students not interested in mountain-climbing may list and define technical terms from some other sport or occupation. Skiing and water-skiing offer rich possibilities, including many picturesque terms that are still regarded as slang.

Unusual *uns*

Generally *un-* means simply "not." Yet *unbooks* are really books (they are decorative volumes for giving and displaying rather than reading). The usual meaning of *uncanny* is not the opposite of the meaning of *canny*. *Unloosen* means the same as *loosen*. Someone may be *uncouth* or *unkempt,* but except humorously no one is called *couth* or *kempt*. One student used "dulating," thinking that it was a positive form of *undulating*. Students may think of other unusual uses of *un-*; a large dictionary may remind them of still more.

Similar are words with a few other prefixes. We refer to *infamy* but not to *famy;* someone may be *disgruntled* or *distraught* but not *gruntled* or *traught*.

A Wallop of Words

A New York haberdasher, interested in terms like "covey of quail," "gaggle of geese," and "pride of lions," invited men to suggest similar nouns of assembly that may be applied to men's clothing. Among the responses: "resplendency of robes," "tintinnabulation of ties," "spectrum of scarves," "easement of slippers," "freshet of furnishings." Your students may coin others for men's clothing, women's clothing, groups of specific kinds of trees or flowers, signs along highways, etc.

Poke Your Finger

"There's *something* of interest in every word." To prove the truth of this statement, ask your students to close their eyes, open a good desk dictionary at random, and touch any entry. They open their eyes, find something interesting in the etymology, meaning, or some other feature of the word, and share (sometimes with mild hilarity) the information with the class.

11

A Summary of Trends

LOOKING BACK AND LOOKING AHEAD

The purpose of this chapter is to present a brief summary of some of the major trends in the development of the English language over the past ten or twelve hundred years, and on the basis of what has happened earlier, to venture a few timid guesses about the future. Necessarily these can be no more than guesses, which could be largely or entirely negated by war or natural disaster or even by large economic shifts or changing balances in such intangibles as human initiative.

Worldwide Spread

From the language spoken by a relatively few thousand Anglo-Saxon invaders in the fifth century, the language of England has spread throughout the world. On the continent of Europe it is studied more extensively than any other second language. In Asia it is widely required in the schools of Japan and India, less so in other countries, although many Chinese can speak or at least read it. It is the national language of Australia. In the Pacific islands, if "real" English is often unknown, the form called pidgin frequently provides the communicative link between people who otherwise could not converse at all. English is the leading second language of Africa. It is an elective or required course in thousands of South American schools. In North America, it is the official language of the United States; in Canada nine of the ten provinces are called "English-speaking," although 31 per cent of Canada's population is French. English is one of the official languages of the United Nations. In all, over 350 million persons speak

English as their primary language, and as a second language it is known to at least as many more. ("Known to" is here a weasel expression. The total figure can vary enormously, depending on the degree of fluency postulated.) In all, about a fourth of the world's population have some familiarity with English. Chinese in its varieties is known to at least as many, but most of the speakers of the Chinese languages are concentrated in one large area.[1]

Other languages continue to borrow extensively from English, sometimes against the opposition of national leaders. For instance, Premier Jacques Chaban-Delmas in 1970 was alarmed by 15,000 "barbarous" borrowings by the French, and appointed commissions to stem the tide. In 1973 the commissions proscribed, at least for official use, a long list of words. Thus *one-man show* would henceforth be *spectacle solo, flashback* would be *rétrospectif, bulldozer* would be *boul-dozeur,* and *pipeline* would be pronounced [pi:p-li:n]. According to one report, a Frenchman-in-the-street shrugged and said, "So what?"

Whether English will continue to spread will depend on social, economic, and political developments. If, for example, the United States becomes a second- or third-rate economic power—as is entirely possible—there will be fewer reasons for other countries to learn English, and stronger reasons for them to learn the language of their new economic leader.

There has been some agitation at times—for instance, in the United Nations—to make English the official second language of the world. This could imply that almost every child the world over would study it in school, and that it would be the established language for international dealings of any sort. Given present national rivalries, though, such a development is unlikely. English or some other language, for economic reasons mainly, may happen to become an almost worldwide second language, but it is doubtful that official pronouncements by the United Nations or anyone else could bring it about.

An artificial language, such as Esperanto or Interlingua, has often been urged for adoption as a second language, on the ground that nationalistic jealousies about the choice could then be avoided. So far, though, no such language has been learned by more than a few million people, largely, as Mario Pei has said, because of "the general indifference of the world's masses." If a few major nations from different linguistic families began

---

[1] The 1973 *Information Please Almanac* estimates the numbers of speakers of Mandarin at 555 million; Cantonese, 80 million; Min, 55 million; Wu, 55 million; Hakka-Miao, 25 million. In varying degrees these are mutually unintelligible or nearly so.

using a mutually agreed-upon artificial language in conduct of business among themselves, others would no doubt follow, but there is no present indication that such a step will be taken. (For one example of Esperanto, see page 332.)

Growth of Vocabulary

The English vocabulary has grown and still continues to grow with enormous rapidity. A modern dictionary of Old English lists about 35,000 headwords. By 1700, according to Fries's estimate, there were about 125,000 words in the language. The Merriam-Webster unabridged dictionary of 1934 included 600,000 entries, but as we noted in Chapter 9, even an unabridged dictionary does not list nearly all words actually used in a language. Depending on how and what one counts, an estimate of a million words in present English seems very conservative.

Almost assuredly the growth will continue, but whether the pace changes will again be determined by nonlinguistic factors. If, for instance, English-speaking countries remain in the forefront of scientific and industrial achievement, there is no reason to believe that the pace will slow down. But if some other country takes the lead in science and industry, words from the language of that country will probably gain priority, although even then English will no doubt borrow and adapt the names it finds useful, and so keep on growing.

Syntactic and Morphological Changes

Over the centuries the most important syntactic change in English has come about because of changes in morphology—the loss of inflections. In a highly inflected language, word endings show the relationships between parts of sentences, and word order, though it may become conventionalized, is relatively unimportant. But in a largely uninflected language like Mod E or Chinese, a certain word order is essential to meaning. One can't say "The bird chased the cat" if the meaning is "The cat chased the bird."

The only living inflections of English (inflections that we still apply to newly formed words) are the -ed, -ing, and -s of verbs, the -s or -es and the 's or s' for plurals and possessives of nouns (the forms with the apostrophe being mere graphemic conventions), and the -er and -est of adjectives and a few adverbs. Will any of these few survivors be lost? Not likely, but possible. In the dialects of a fairly large number of persons, particularly some blacks, some of these inflectional endings are missing or appear in some contexts but not in others. Such an almost completely uninflected language is not inferior and not grammarless, and it can be highly systematized, as studies by William Labov and other scholars of black dialects have demonstrated.

Another trend noticed earlier has been that toward shorter sentences, at least in printed materials. Within the past century writers appear to have learned a great deal about how much the ordinary human mind can easily grasp in one sentence, and for this or other reasons have reduced average sentence length to about twenty words. Whether sentences will become even shorter remains to be seen. Since very short sentences seem jerky and primerish, and since they make it difficult to show relationships of ideas, it seems probable that the present average length will not be much reduced. It may indeed become greater again, although monsters of one hundred or two hundred words will probably remain rare.

Another of the syntactic movements we have observed is that from parataxis to hypotaxis—a decrease of compounding and a consequent increase of subordination. Subordination in OE was not nearly so frequent as it is today. However, the very long sentences of the seventeenth century were rich in subordination, so that there has been a backward movement since that time. (Research by Kellogg Hunt has shown that subordination within written sentences increases as today's children move through school, and that professional writers subordinate more than do twelfth-graders. Subordination, then, appears to be a concomitant of linguistic maturity, but, like other good things, it can become excessive.)

Mod E has natural gender, not the grammatical gender of OE, German, and the Romance languages. For a foreigner learning a language, natural gender is a great asset, since he is not faced with the added vexation of having to remember whether each noun is masculine, feminine, or neuter. This simplification of English is certainly one that shows no signs of reversal.

Changes in Pronunciation

In discussion of pronunciation, we have noted the conservatism of English consonants and the substantial alterations in vowel sounds. Such a pattern is not followed by all languages. For instance, the changes that are described by Grimm's Law, and that occurred long before there was an English language, were major shifts in consonants.

Of the consonant sounds of Mod E, all but one, [ž], which came in because of French influence, existed in OE. However, [ŋ], [ð], and [v], and [z] did not occur except between voiced sounds. OE diphthongs were replaced with others by ME times. The major change, though, was the Great Vowel Shift that took place approximately between 1400 and 1700 and that was caused by the raising of the place in the mouth where the tense vowels were formed. A smaller change, but still important, was the loss (in sound but not in spelling) of the final *e* in words like *take,* which Chaucer pronounced [ta:kə]. Lost earlier were the two rounded sounds of the OE blade vowel in words like *brȳd* "bride" and *cyssan,* "kiss," which became unrounded to modern "long *i*" and "short *i*." Also lost were the velar sounds in words like *niht* "night" and *āgan* "own."

According to Margaret Bryant, there is a "general tendency in all language for the area of sound production to become ever more restricted and for superfluous sounds to fall away." People tend to seek, unconsciously, the easiest possible pronunciations. Bryant believes that because the sound of *wh* [hw] in words like *white* is moderately difficult, it may drop out completely, and that the "unstable sounds . . . at the fringes of the vowel area" may also depart, "since English could be made more compact by their loss." But she cautions that "such changes take place very slowly and might be delayed for centuries or even millenniums."[2]

Spelling

In the absence of printing and of dictionaries, writers of both OE and ME spelled about as they pleased. Usually their spellings seem to have approximated their pronunciations, but often the same writer spelled the same word in several different ways. Writers of the fifteenth century were perhaps the most imaginative spellers of all, using many spellings just barely credible. Then, after the invention of printing, spelling became more and more standardized, so that today there is a single "correct" spelling for almost every word. Most English spellings are reasonably in accord with the phonemes represented, but since the alphabet has fewer symbols than there are sounds in English, various compromises, often inconsistent with one another, have had to be reached. The fact that English has borrowed many of its words and sometimes has retained approximately the original spellings has added further complexity.

Attempts at spelling reform date back to the Middle Ages. Because of the newness of the printing press, the Renaissance had the best opportunity to systematize spelling (and not just standardize it), but the chance was incompletely grasped. Later spelling reformers worked under the handicap

---

[2] Margaret Bryant, *Modern English and Its Heritage,* New York: The Macmillan Co., Second edition, 1962, p. 199.

of trying to change spellings that by their time had the sanction of age, so that Noah Webster's recommendations of spellings like *ake* and *wimmen* were laughed out of existence. Spelling reformers are still busy and hopeful, but there is no indication that their efforts will succeed.

English spellings are not only difficult in themselves to master, but they also slow down the gaining of reading skill, for children constantly encounter words like *bough, cough,* and *through* to which no generalized principles can be applied. In addition, unsystematized spellings impede the efforts of foreigners trying to read and write the language. The use of English as a truly international language might be closer than it is if its spellings were more consistent.

The Role of "Error" in Language Change

When OE inflectional endings first started to disappear, every person who dropped an ending was guilty of error, if unorthodoxy is equated with error. When someone said "bird" and "wasp" instead of "brid" and "waps," he committed an error. Whoever began pronouncing his tense vowels a little higher than other people did was in error, but he was starting the Great Vowel Shift. Whoever shortened "mobile vulgus" to "mob" and "taximeter catriolet" to "taxicab" was in error; today we might bless him if we knew his name.

Such examples could be multiplied. What some parts of society have considered "errors" have often become standard English. Since language can't be entered in a profit-and-loss statement, no one can say for sure whether more gains or losses have resulted from the present acceptance of erstwhile errors like those mentioned. In so far as errors have led to simplification, they should ordinarily be considered on the plus side.

Obviously many language changes result from borrowing, innovations by a leader, or some other force; not all are attributable to error. But the role of yesterday's "error" as the creator of today's "correct English" is not trivial. And many of today's "errors" will no doubt be "correct English" tomorrow.

Changing Attitudes Toward "Correctness"

Not until the late Renaissance did many people worry much about whether or not their language was "correct." If the hearer or reader could understand, that was enough. Gradually, though, the feeling developed that some English usages and structures were better than others, and in the eighteenth century, self-appointed arbiters began to prescribe and proscribe, thus building the still widely held belief that there is always a single "right" or "preferred" way to express any idea. In the nineteenth and twentieth centuries a disproportionately large amount of school time has been spent in a usually futile attempt to eradicate whatever the textbook authors considered "wrong." These authors were for the most part merely echoing and elaborating upon the precepts of eighteenth-century Bishop Robert Lowth, even though there is no strong evidence to suggest that the bishop had obtained his information directly from God.

However, in our own century, especially in the sixties and seventies, permissiveness has begun to extend to usage. British schools tend to stress content, interest, clarity, fluency, and effectiveness rather than *shall* vs. *will,* and American schools are moving, though more slowly, in the same direction. There is concurrently much interest in dialects and dialect study, and an increasing willingness to accept dialectal usages without condemnation.

If there are no linguistic constraints at all, if "anything goes," clarity of communication may suffer, although the linguistic anarchy feared by some people is unlikely to develop. On the other hand, if there are many constraints, and especially if some of them deal with trivia such as split infinitives and terminal prepositions, most people will not bother to learn and apply them. Our society appears to be searching or groping for only a limited number of constraints, chosen largely on the ground that they are especially needed for clearness and effectiveness. Teachers can aid the search by selecting for instructional purposes only those constraints that they honestly believe contribute to intelligibility and effect.

Professor Louis A. Muinzer has made this wise observation:

. . . Historically speaking, language is a tension between the old and the new, the linguistically conservative and the linguistically radical. Stated in human terms, the tension exists between society as the champion of conservatism and the individual as innovator and rebel. We may represent the conflict graphically as a tug of war between the two opposing forces:

inertia	*change*
traditional language ⎱	⎰contemporary language
society ⎰	⎱the individual[3]

Modern Experiments with Language

Many users of English have always been willing to try new things: the forces of conservatism have never been fully in charge. Many of the changes

[3] Louis A. Muinzer, "Historical Linguistics in the Classroom." *Illinois English Bulletin,* November, 1960, p. 26.

described in this book (e.g., the reduction in inflections, the loss of grammatical gender, the Great Vowel Shift, the growth of vocabulary) reflect such willingness. So do the puns and other language play of the Elizabethans. And so do the language experiments that abound in modern English.

In the advertising in *The New Yorker,* for instance, one encounters playfulness like this:

> "Did you ever think Pink Mink? . . . Or you can play Opossum." (from an ad for furs)
>
> "It makes great things happen in the dark." (slide projector)
>
> "Can the man who has everything have more?" (neckties)
>
> "What has blond hair and blue water?" (Norwegian Caribbean Cruises)
>
> "Is the old ticker running out on you?" (a watch)
>
> "In 1482 the fair city of Perth lost out as capital of Scotland. But there's nae doubt that it's still the Scotch capital!" (Scotch whisky)

e e cummings eschewed capitals, played with punctuation, and split or spread out words or let them drift like leaves down a page. Many other poets explore and extend the connotations of words. James Joyce was endlessly inventive. Russian-born Vladimir Nabokov delights in multilingual puns and elaborate metaphors. Some TV commercials are cameo art blending pictures, music, and words. English written in emerging nations of Africa has a flavor never apparent in England or the United States.

Such experimentation shows that the language is not becoming fossilized. Encouraging your students to be alert to it and to try it themselves can increase their joy in language.

Systematic Study of the Language

Before 1800, most of the few writings about language were impressionistic and opinionated rather than based upon hard data. In the nineteenth century a number of scholars studied languages comparatively and were able to detail relationships previously only guessed at; a few beginnings were made in the description of oral (in contrast to written) language; and study of dialects began to arouse interest and attain respectability.

Only in the twentieth century, though, did language study come of age. Linguistic atlases of Europe and America began to appear. Anthropologists systematically studied the languages of American Indians and other groups. Historians of language examined minutely the earlier versions of English and traced the developments that seemed most significant; after 1960 they began to apply generative-transformational theory to early as well as modern forms. The great *Oxford English Dictionary* finally appeared after many decades of labor, and was supplemented by the *Dictionary of American English,* the *Dictionary of Americanisms,* and numerous specialized dictionaries of Old English, Middle English, and slang. Linguistic courses in universities proliferated after mid-century, and specialties developed in such fields as sociolinguistics and psycholinguistics; doctoral dissertations were written on such esoteric subjects as "Pro-sententialization and the *do it* construction in English" and "Theoretical implications of Yawelmani phonology." Traditional Latin-based descriptions of grammar were increasingly considered unsatisfactory, and first structural grammar and then generative-transformational grammar were developed as possibly more accurate replacements; the search for the most scientifically accurate statement still goes on. Semantics grew in stature as people realized more clearly how much words can influence them. The study of how children learn their basic language and how they develop it is occupying the attention of increasing numbers of scholarly observers and theoreticians.

Out of all this research, confused and confusing and scattered as it is, and trivial as some of it may be, there is inevitably emerging a clearer understanding of what language was and is, how it works, and what its roles are in personal and social development.

Changing Emphases in the Schools

Another outgrowth of the scientific study of language has been changes in school programs. Although educational practices are notoriously laggard, a gradual shift is noticeable here, away from simplistic sentence analysis and right–wrong polarization, and toward broad, balanced, scientifically accurate but highly interesting study that shows language as a varied, ever-changing tool essential to man in nearly all his undertakings.

A language curriculum developed in Minnesota in the 1960's, for use in grades 7–12, exemplifies well the potential richness that schools should strive to encompass. Among its twenty-eight units are some on the origin of language, words as symbols, transformational grammar, our system of spelling, semantics, lexicography, historical study of the English lexicon, historical study of other linguistic developments, dialects, the languages of persuasion and of evocation, and the social and psychological implications of language. Such a curriculum, obviously, is potentially far more useful and attractive than that of, say, 1940, when close to fifty per cent of English class time was devoted to labeling sentence parts and to the correction of errors in fabricated sentences. The Minnesota curriculum, and others similar to it, reflect awareness of the ways in which language study, intelligently conceived, can help students to understand and use most clearly and effectively the most valuable tool in their possession.

CLASSROOM ACTIVITIES

Why Does a Language Change?

Students may name and discuss as many causes of language change as they can think of. They are likely to come up with a list that will include wars and military conquest, exploration, emigration and immigration, new discoveries and inventions, intermarriage, literary experimentation, the influence of leaders, social developments, laziness (which may result in "easier" pronunciations), increase in literacy, acquaintance with another language, and others.

Comparisons of Biblical Versions

If students look at two or more versions of the Bible, from different centuries, they can observe a number of significant changes. Examples in this book are on pages 72 and 108, one of the many twentieth-century translations, including a partial one in a black dialect, can provide further enlightenment.

Distinguishing Similar Words

The following words in each group have the same sources but differ in suffixes and usually in meaning. Students, using a dictionary as needed, may try to differentiate between them and use them in sentence examples.

arbiter, arbitrator	emergence, emergency
categorial, categorical	informant, informer
continual, continuous	instinctive, instinctual
continuance, continuation	normality, normalcy
council, counsel	racialism, racism
elemental, elementary	respectfully, respectively

This exercise may be supplemented by a look at some frequently confused words that come from different sources, like *statue, stature, statute.*

Belief in Word Magic

People have long believed that some words have magic powers. Primitive people may believe that harm will come to them if they utter certain words. To the ancient Greeks the Furies were terrible, vengeful goddesses; to propitiate them, Greeks called them *Eumenides* "the well-minded ones." For the same reason the Greeks called the stormswept Black Sea *Euxine* "hospitable." Today people say "I haven't had a cold all winter" and then knock on wood to avert the consequences of their boast. Some hotels have no floors or rooms numbered *thirteen*. What other examples of supposed word magic can your students give?

Where Does the Accent Go?

Two contrary tendencies in pronunciation may be illustrated by *disputable*. One is the tendency for accent to fall on what appears to be the most important syllable: *disPUTable*. The other is the tendency for accent to move toward the beginning of the word: *DISputable*. Students may consider the variations in *research, police, lamentable, despicable, interesting, illustrative, sonorous, decorous, abdomen*, and other words.

Dictionary Study

Publishers of major school and college dictionaries usually have available various aids to dictionary use, which they will often provide free or at low cost. Write to the publishers for information.

Pun-fun

As suggested earlier, puns can help to arouse interest in words. Sometimes several may be combined in a little story. For instance, some University of Colorado students, snowbound in Lincoln, Nebraska, while returning from Christmas vacation, wired President Robert L. Stearns: "Dear Uncle Bob: Transfer credits to University of Nebraska. S'now use coming back. Get the drift?" The president wired back. "Don't let disgust of snow upset you. Lincoln your skis and we'll give you the warmest welcome you ever thaw. Uncle Bob and Anti-Freeze."

Ain'tno, Mo.

Fun for the last three minutes of class: Think of the abbreviation of a state name (not necessarily the two-letter abbreviations now recommended by the post office), and name a town to fit with it. Examples: Seriously, Ill.; Dr. Brown, Md.; Hittor, Miss.; Poor, Me.; Oola, La.; Raidy, O.; and Off, Ky.

Alliterative Phrases

What familiar alliterative expressions can your students think of that are similar to *spic and span, rough and ready, tit for tat?*

A Debate on Spelling Reform

In an informal debate, two groups of students may advance all the arguments they can think of, favoring or opposing substantial spelling reform.

Miniwordwise

Have students choose an affix that seems very active at present, and think of or search for as many recent examples as possible. *Mini-,* for instance, appears in *miniskirt, minicourse, miniburger,* and countless others. Russian *-nik* was attached hilariously to many words after *sputnik* became famous, although the affix was already active in Yiddish: *alrightnik* "prosperous person," *beatnik* "hippy," *nudnik* "one who pesters," *nudenik* "nudist," *peacenik* "one who works for peace," *sicknik* "one who likes sick humor." *-Wise* continues to grow astonishingly: *transportationwise, athleticwise, football strategywise,* etc. (Students may support or oppose this statement by British Simeon Potter: "On the whole these fashionable derivatives in *-wise* are too vague and imprecise to merit survival." Is *-wise* really less precise than the corresponding *-ly* added to adjectives? Does it serve a need?)

Rip Van Winkle Today

Ask your students to imagine that they went to sleep twenty years ago and awoke today. What changes would they find, e.g., in schools, supermarkets, science, transportation? What changes in language, especially in vocabulary, reflect some of these developments? (A book related to such a discussion is Monica Baldwin's *I Leap Over the Wall,* London: Hamish Hamilton, 1949. Miss Baldwin lived a very secluded convent life from 1914 to 1941. In her book she described the astonishing changes she found when she emerged. She did not understand, for instance, references to *jazz, lend-lease, unknown soldier,* and *Hollywood,* and slang of the 1940's baffled her.)

Social Changes

Students may enjoy a discussion of vocabulary developments related to social change. E.g., dating customs change frequently; how does this affect the language? Or, today's America is largely urban; how is that fact reflected in our speech habits?

A Class Investigation of Usage

Each student selects an item of usage that interests him—an item that he is likely to encounter often in listening and reading. For instance, he may try to find out whether *he* (*his*) or *they* (*their*) is more common after a word like *somebody* or *everybody,* as in "Everybody brought his (their) lunch." Over a period of several days he counts the number of times he encounters each form in print, and the number of times in spoken English, and writes down any especially interesting examples. At the end he may prepare a brief oral or written report. (Many locutions, such as *everybody . . . their,* students will find, are quite frequent in speech, rare in printed material.)

Dictionary of Current Slang

Many English classes prepare dictionaries of current slang, recording their citations first and then preparing entries that show spelling (and possibly variant spellings), pronunciation(s), part(s) of speech, and definition(s). (Unfortunately, the origin of slang expressions can seldom be found.) This exercise illustrates clearly how lexicographers work, and often increases use of and interest in dictionaries.

What Words Do We Need?

Many phenomena exist that have not been named in English. For example, although *twilight* can mean either the dim pre-dawn light or the dim post-sunset light, it might be useful to have a different word for each. What nameless phenomena (or phenomena in need of descriptive words) can your students think of? The fields of sound, smell, and taste may be especially rewarding. Students may try to coin words to fill the gaps they find.

Language Tomorrow

Joseph E. Milosh (*Teaching the History of the English Language,* pp. 33–34) suggests that students may discuss the kinds of words that might be needed in case of an important future invention, such as travel by means of mental concentration plus electrical charges. Also, "Letting students speculate about future social, economic, scientific, and cultural changes and the language changes that might accompany them could be an effective way to teach the cultural determination of language." How, Milosh asks, may language change if pollution becomes so bad that people have to wear filters over their noses and mouths?

Effects of the Media

Discuss: "Is it likely that television, the movies, and other media, combined with the great mobility of Americans, will lead to the near-elimination of dialects in this country?" (Dialectologist Henry Lee Smith, who on the basis of a few pronunciations was able to spot the precise county where an informant grew up, felt that such a stunt is becoming increasingly difficult.)

What Will "Modern English" Be Called in 3000 A.D.?

The terms "Old English," "Middle English," and "Modern English" are not really satisfactory, because they are relative terms. What we call "Modern English" will no doubt be very different a thousand years from now. Discuss: What may our distant descendants call our "Modern English"?

English for Everyone?

Discuss: How likely do you think it is that English will become a second language for most people in the world? Is any language likely to become the sole language of the world?

Esperanto

Best-known of the artificial languages that have been considered for world use is Esperanto. A student, after consulting a good encyclopedia, may report on examples of its chief characteristics: grammatical regularity, use of roots most common in European languages, and a systematic pattern of affixes (e.g., the endings -o, -a, -e, and -i are respectively the markers for nouns, adjectives, adverbs, and the infinitives for verbs; -j always signifies a plural; mal- makes any word into its opposite, as bona "good," malbona "bad.") Here is a piece of propaganda put out by an Esperanto society:

La inteligenta persono lernas la interlingvon Esperanto rapide kaj facile. Esperanto estas la moderna, kultura lingvo por la internacia mondo. Simpla, fleksebla, praktika solvo de la problemo de universala interkompreno, Esperanto meritas vian seriozan konsideron. Lernu la interlingvon Esperanto.

(*Question:* Would Esperanto be as easy for a Japanese or a Chinese to learn as for an Englishman or a Frenchman?)

Appendix

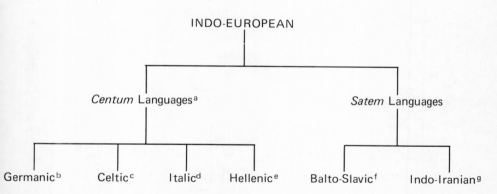

a. Hittite and Tocharian, two long-extinct languages of the Middle East and Central Asia, are also generally considered to be branches of the *centum* languages. b. A chart of the Germanic languages follows. c. Chief living descendants of Celtic are Irish Gaelic, Scots Gaelic, and Welsh. d. The major ancient Italic language was Latin. Modern descendants are French, Italian, Portuguese, Rumanian, and Spanish. e. Modern Greek (Koirne) is a Hellenic language. f. Russian is the major modern Balto-Slavic language. Others are Bulgarian, Czecho-Slovak, Lettish, Lithuanian, Polish, Serbo-Croatian, and Slovenian. g. Sanskrit was an Indo-Iranian language. Modern descendants include Iranian (Persian) and Benagli, Hindi, and Romany.

Major Branches of Indo-European Languages.

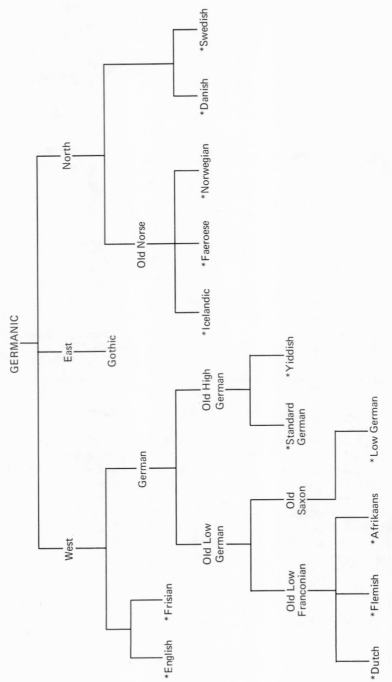

Germanic Languages.

* Asterisks indicate modern languages.

A Pictorial Message.

Four Dialects of Old English.

Selected Bibliography, Annotated

A much longer bibliography would be possible, but only those books especially useful to teachers are included. Some are also likely to be of interest to students of high school age.

HISTORY OF BRITISH ENGLISH

BAUGH, ALBERT C. *A History of the English Language.* New York: Appleton-Century-Crofts, Second ed., 1957. Richly detailed.

BLOOMFIELD, MORTON W. AND LEONARD NEWMARK. *A Linguistic Introduction to the History of English.* New York: Alfred A. Knopf, 1963. Applies linguistic principles to history.

BOLTON, W. F., ed. *The English Language: Essays by English & American Men of Letters, 1490–1839.* Cambridge: Cambridge University Press, 1966. Paperbound. Caxton, Dryden, Swift, Webster, and Emerson are among the twenty men of letters discussed.

BRYANT, MARGARET M. *Modern English and Its Heritage.* New York: The Macmillan Co., Second ed., 1962. Especially strong in basic phonology.

COOK, ALBERT B., III. *Introduction to the English Language: Structure and History.* New York: The Ronald Press Co., 1969. Treats history in reverse order, E Mod E to OE.

FARNHAM, ANTHONY E., ed. *A Sourcebook in the History of English.* New York: Holt, Rinehart and Winston, Inc., 1969. Paperbound. Carefully edited selections from OE to twentieth century, with translations of the older pieces.

FOSTER, BRIAN. *The Changing English Language.* London: Macmillan and Co., Ltd., 1969 ed. Changing language in twentieth-century England, with a long chapter on "The Impact of America."

FRANCIS, NELSON. *The English Language: An Introduction.* New York: W. W. Norton & Co., Inc., 1965. General introduction, historically oriented.

337

HOOK, J. N. *The Story of British English*. Glenview, Ill.: Scott, Foresman and Co., 1974. Paperbound. For students.

JESPERSEN, OTTO, *Growth and Structure of the English Language*. New York: The Free Press, 1968 ed. (1938). Paperbound. By the great Danish philologist. Useful information about words.

MARCKWARDT, ALBERT H. *Introduction to the English Language*. New York: Oxford University Press, 1942. Brief historical treatment, still readable though outdated in spots.

McLAUGHLIN, JOHN C. *Aspects of the History of English*. New York: Holt, Rinehart and Winston, Inc., 1970. A largely transformational treatment.

MILOSH, JOSEPH E., JR. *Teaching the History of English in the Secondary Classroom*. Urbana, Ill.: NCTE, 1972. Paperbound. Rationale for teaching, with suggestions on content and technique.

MYERS, L. M. *The Roots of Modern English*. Boston: Little, Brown and Co., 1966. Brief and readable. A companion book of textual readings was published in 1972.

PEI, MARIO. *The Story of English*. Philadelphia: J. B. Lippincott Co., 1952. Popularized account, informative but sometimes inaccurate or outdated. By the same author: *The Story of Language*.

PETERS, ROBERT A. *A Linguistic History of English*. Boston: Houghton Mifflin Co., 1968. Transformational descriptions.

POTTER, SIMEON. *Changing English*. London: Andre Deutsch, 1969. Many examples of modern changes.

————. *Our Language*. London: Penguin Books, Rev. ed., 1967. Paperbound. Chatty, brief.

PYLES, THOMAS. *The Origins and Development of the English Language*. New York: Harcourt Brace Jovanovich, Second ed., 1971. Emphasizes internal history; generally readable. Companion workbook by Pyles and John Algeo.

RIGG, A.G., ed. *The English Language: A Historical Reader*. New York: Appleton-Century-Crofts, 1968. Paperbound. Sourcebook of old textual material, including parallel passages from various Bible translations.

ROBERTSON, STUART, rev. by Frederic G. Cassidy. *The Development of Modern English*. Englewood Cliffs, N.J.: Prentice-Hall, Inc., 1954. Revised edition of Robertson's excellent 1934 book.

SCOTT, CHARLES T. AND JON L. ERICKSON, eds. *Readings for the History of the English Language*. Boston: Allyn and Bacon, Inc., 1968. Articles by recent scholars; somewhat technical.

STEVICK, ROBERT D. *English and Its History: The Evolution of a Language*. Boston: Allyn and Bacon, Inc., 1968. Emphasis on phonology and morphology.

AMERICAN ENGLISH

BABCOCK, C. MERTON. *The Ordeal of American English*. Boston: Houghton Mifflin Co., 1961. Paperbound. Scores of very short reactions, old and fairly new, to American English.

DILLARD, J. L. *Black English: Its History and Usage in the United States*. New York: Random House, 1972. An analysis of the characteristics of English spoken and written by black Americans, and its contributions to Southern and other American English. Good section on evolution of Negro proper names.

FRANCIS, W. NELSON. *The Structure of American English.* New York: The Ronald Press Co., 1958. Examination of written and spoken American English.

HOOK, J. N. *People Say Things Different Ways.* Glenview, Ill.: Scott, Foresman and Co., 1974. Paperbound. American dialects; written primarily for students.

———. *The Story of American English.* New York: Harcourt Brace Jovanovich, 1972. Paperbound. For students.

MATHEWS, M. M., ed. *The Beginnings of American English.* Chicago: University of Chicago Press, 1963. Paperbound. Eighteenth- and nineteenth-century comments on the English language in America.

MENCKEN, H.L. *The American Language.* New York: Alfred A. Knopf, 1965 ed. With Supplement I and Supplement II. The most nearly definitive work on the subject. An abridgement of the three volumes has been prepared by Raven I. McDavid, Jr.

PYLES, THOMAS. *Words & Ways of American English.* New York: Random House, 1952. Paperbound. Pleasant account of how the American version of the language has developed.

REED, CARROLL E. *Dialects of American English.* Cleveland: World Publishing Co., 1967. Paperbound. Suitable for student use. 32 maps.

SHUY, ROGER W. *Discovering American Dialects.* Champaign, Ill.: NCTE, 1967. Paperbound. Suitable for student use.

STEWART, GEORGE R. *American Place-Names.* New York: Oxford University Press, 1970. Dictionary format; about 12,000 entries. Suitable for student reference.

DICTIONARIES, LEXICOGRAPHY, USAGE, AND WORD STUDY

BRYANT, MARGARET M., ed. *Current American Usage.* New York: Funk & Wagnalls Co., Inc., n.d. Based on scores of smaller studies.

COPPERUD, ROY H. *American Usage: The Consensus.* New York: Van Nostrand-Reinhold Co., 1970. Comparison of treatments of items in seven dictionaries of usage.

CRAIGIE, WILLIAM A. AND JAMES R. HULBERT, eds. *A Dictionary of American English on Historical Principles.* Chicago: University of Chicago Press, 4 vols., 1944. Companion to the *OED.*

EVANS, BERGEN AND CORNELIA. *A Dictionary of Contemporary American Usage.* New York: Random House, 1957. The most readable of usage studies. Suitable for student reference.

FOLLETT, WILSON AND OTHERS. *Modern American Usage.* New York: Hill and Wang, 1966. Conservatively inclined. Suitable for student reference.

FOWLER, H.W. *A Dictionary of Modern English Usage.* Oxford: Oxford University Press, 1944. A favorite British reference for several decades.

FUNK, WILFRED. *Word Origins and Their Romantic Stories.* New York: Grosset and Dunlap, 1950. Popularized etymology. Suitable for student reference.

GARRISON, WEBB B. *Why You Say It.* New York: Abingdon Press, n.d. Paperbound. Lively but sometimes too imaginative accounts of the origins of "700 everyday words and phrases." Suitable for student reference.

GRAY, JACK C. *Words, Words, and Words about Dictionaries.* San Francisco: Chandler Publishing Co., 1963. Paperbound. About twenty articles, Samuel Johnson to the present, concerning lexicography. Exercises for student use.

GREENOUGH, J.B. AND G.L. KITTREDGE. *Words and Their Ways in English Speech.* New York: The Macmillan Co., 1961 ed. Paperbound. First published in 1900, but still useful for information on word development.

LAIRD, HELENE AND CHARLTON. *The Tree of Language.* Cleveland: World Publishing Co., 1957. Simple introduction to etymology, with many word stories. Suitable for junior high school age.

LODWIG, RICHARD R. AND EUGENE F. BARRETT. *The Dictionary and the Language.* New York: Hayden Book Co., Inc., 1967. Paperbound. History and methods of lexicography. For students.

MATHEWS, MITFORD M., ed. *A Dictionary of Americanisms on Historical Principles.* Chicago: University of Chicago Press, one-vol. ed., 1956. Fifty thousand entries.

MOORE, JOHN. *You English Words.* New York: Dell Publishing Co., 1961. Paperbound. Specializes in "odd" words like *yawp, pilligrub, nuncle, inspissate.*

MORRIS, WILLIAM, ed. *The American Heritage Dictionary of the English Language.* New York and Boston: The American Heritage Publishing Co., Inc., and Houghton Mifflin Co., 1969. The appendix on I-E roots is especially valuable to the linguist.

NICHOLSON, MARGARET. *A Dictionary of American-English Usage.* New York: Oxford University Press, 1957. Based on Fowler's *Modern English Usage.*

Oxford English Dictionary. London: Oxford University Press, 1928, 1933. 13 vols. The great authority on etymology. A micrographically reduced edition, to be read with a magnifier, appeared in 1971 in two vols. The first of several projected updating vols. appeared in 1972.

POOLEY, ROBERT C. *Teaching English Usage.* New York: Appleton-Century-Crofts, 1946. Historical background, facts about usage, and suggestions for teaching. Long an influential book. Revised ed., 1974, published by NCTE.

REANEY, P.H. *The Origin of English Place Names.* London: Routledge and Kegan Paul, 1961. Celtic, Anglo-Saxon, Scandinavian, French, and Latin influences on place-names.

SHIPLEY, JOSEPH T. *Dictionary of Word Origins.* New York: The Philosophical Library, Second ed., 1945. Interestingly written etymologies, suitable for high school reference.

SLEDD, JAMES AND WILMA R. EBBITT. *Dictionaries and That Dictionary.* Glenview, Ill.: Scott, Foresman and Co., 1962. Paperbound. Mainly articles on the controversy following publication of *W3.*

WAGNER, GEOFFREY. *On the Wisdom of Words.* New York: Van Nostrand-Reinhold, 1968. Lively writing on semantics.

Webster's Third New International Dictionary. Springfield, Mass., 1961. The third edition of the best-known American "unabridged" dictionary.

WEEKLEY, ERNEST. *An Etymological Dictionary of Modern English.* New York: Dover Publications, Inc., 1961. 2 vols. Paperbound. Originally published in London, 1921. Etymologies only.

———. *The Romance of Words.* New York: Dover Publications, Inc., 1961. Paperbound. Reprint of the 1911 classic treatment.

BOOKS OF READINGS ON ENGLISH

BAILEY, DUDLEY, ed. *Introductory Language Essays.* New York: W. W. Norton & Co., Inc., 1965. Paperbound. Modern essays on language, with some by nineteenth-century writers.

CLARK, VIRGINIA P., PAUL A. ESCHHOLZ, AND ALFRED F. ROSA, eds. *Language: Introductory Readings.* New York: St. Martin's Press, 1972. Paperbound. Articles on language, grammar, lexicography, American English, and non-verbal communication.

DEAN, LEONARD F. AND KENNETH G. WILSON. *Essays on Language and Usage.* New York: Oxford University Press, Second ed., 1963. Paperbound. Sections on lexicography, history, structure, usage, and style.

GERBER, PHILIP L., ed. *Lessons in Language.* Belmont, Calif.: Wadsworth Publishing Co., Inc., 1968. Paperbound. Numerous rather popularized articles on slang, dialect, usage, simplified spelling, etc. Intended for student use.

HOGAN, ROBERT F., ed. *The English Language in the School Program.* Champaign, Ill.: NCTE, 1966. Readings, mainly from educational journals, on language theory, usage, and curriculum.

KERR, ELIZABETH M. AND RALPH M. ADERMAN, eds. *Aspects of American English.* New York: Harcourt Brace Jovanovich, Second ed., 1971. Paperbound. Thirty-seven articles on historical, regional, social, and other aspects of American English. Suggestions for student reports.

KOTTLER, BARNET AND MARTIN LIGHT. *The World of Words.* Boston: Houghton Mifflin Co., 1967. Paperbound. About fifty readable modern articles on various aspects of language. Suitable for students.

LAIRD, CHARLTON AND ROBERT M. GORRELL. *English as Language: Backgrounds, Developments, Usage.* New York: Harcourt, Brace Jovanovich, 1961. Paperbound. Sixty articles on "Language As It Works," "The Language As It Was," etc. Suitable for students.

LEE, DONALD W. *English Language Reader.* New York: Dodd, Mead & Co., 1963. Paperbound. Articles on definition of language, history, lexicography, and grammar. Suitable for student reference.

RYCENGA, JOHN A. AND JOSEPH SCHWARTZ. *Perspectives on Language: An Anthology.* New York: The Ronald Press Co., 1963. Readings in language history, linguistic structure, usage, and metalinguistics.

GENERAL

BODMER, FREDERICK. *The Loom of Language.* New York: Grosset and Dunlap, 1944. Paperbound. Historical treatment of language, with emphasis on Romance and Teutonic languages. Excellent comparative tables of words in Teutonic languages.

BROWN, ROGER. *Words and Things.* New York: The Free Press, 1958. Thoughtful analysis of the nature and uses of language, with emphasis on semantic principles.

DINNEEN, FRANCIS P., S.J. *An Introduction to General Linguistics.* New York: Holt, Rinehart and Winston, Inc., 1967. Concepts of linguistic form from the Greeks to Chomsky. Historical treatment.

FRIEND, JOSEPH H. *An Introduction to English Linguistics*. Cleveland: World Publishing Co., 1967. Paperbound. Very brief treatment, with glossary of linguistic terms.

GELB, I. J. *A Study of Writing*. Chicago: University of Chicago Press, rev. ed., 1965. Paperbound. Scholarly summary of many early systems of writing.

GLEASON H. A., JR. *Linguistics and English Grammar*. New York: Holt, Rinehart and Winston, Inc., 1965. Comprehensive treatment of various grammars; good history of the study of grammar.

GLORFELD, LOUIS E., ed. *A Short Unit on General Semantics*. Beverly Hills, Calif.: Glencoe Press, 1969. Paperbound. Five basic articles on semantics. Suitable for student use.

HALL, EDWARD T. *The Silent Language*. Greenwich, Conn.: Fawcett Publications, Inc., 1968 ed. Paperbound. The languages of time, space, etc., in various cultures. Suitable for students.

HOOK, J. N. AND MICHAEL CROWELL. *Modern English Grammar for Teachers*. New York: The Ronald Press Co., 1970. Basic concepts of transformational and other grammars, and suggestions for teaching.

HUGHES, JOHN P. *The Science of Language: An Introduction to Linguistics*. New York: Random House, 1963. Treatment of broad fundamentals. Good chapters on history of language study.

JENNINGS, GARY. *Personalities of Language*. New York: Thomas Y. Crowell Co., 1965. Paperbound. Delightful discussions of oddities of English. Suitable for students, though sometimes risqué.

LAIRD, CHARLTON. *The Miracle of Language*. Cleveland: World Publishing Co., 1953. Also available paperbound. Spritely writing by a learned man.

MALMSTROM, JEAN. *Language in Society*. New York: Hayden Book Co., Inc., 1965. Paperbound. Simple introduction to language study, including the world spread of English. For students.

RÉVÉSZ, G. *The Origins and Prehistory of Language*. New York: Philosophical Library, 1956. By a Dutch professor of psychology.

WILSON, RICHARD A. *The Miraculous Birth of Language*. London: J. M. Dent and Sons, Ltd., 1941. Foreword by G. B. Shaw.

Index of Words

(Words in italic are treated in the sections entitled Accounting for Some of the Words of Modern English.)

General Index